FORT JESUS

A Portuguese Fortress on the East African Coast

FORT JESUS

A Portuguese Fortress on the East African Coast

JAMES KIRKMAN
O.B.E., M.A., PH.D., F.S.A.

OXFORD
AT THE CLARENDON PRESS
1974

Oxford University Press, Ely House, London W. 1

GLASGOW NEW YORK TORONTO MELBOURNE WELLINGTON
CAPE TOWN IBADAN NAIROBI DAR ES SALAAM LUSAKA ADDIS ABABA
DELHI BOMBAY CALCUTTA MADRAS KARACHI LAHORE DACCA
KUALA LUMPUR SINGAPORE HONG KONG TOKYO

ISBN 0 19 920035 1

This book is Memoir Number Four of the British Institute in Eastern Africa

Printed in Great Britain
at the University Press, Oxford
by Vivian Ridler
Printer to the University

Foreword

FORT JESUS was built by the Portuguese in the years 1593–6. Since its first occupation, unlike many castles and fortresses, it has only once been abandoned, for a brief period, between May and August 1632. The original use as a barracks and fortress was continued by the Omani Arabs after they had captured it at the end of 1698, and was only terminated when the British Protectorate was proclaimed in 1895. It was then used as a prison for over sixty years, until 1958. In that year it was declared a historical monument, and the work of excavation and reconstruction, made possible by a generous grant from the Gulbenkian Foundation, was begun.

The history of Fort Jesus is well documented and was marked by dramatic incidents. It included the murder of a Portuguese Captain, together with his wife and daughter, in the gatehouse; the great siege which lasted for two years and nine months, in which for six weeks the garrison consisted largely of African women; and, in the Omani period, the murder of two of the Arab governors in 1746 and 1828. The story has been told by Justus Strandes (1899), C. R. Boxer and Carlos de Azevedo (1960), and Eric Axelson (1960). Here only a brief résumé is given, based on their work, and, for the revolt of 1631, on the Vatican Processus material found by G. S. P. Freeman-Grenville. The incidents of the Omani period can be found in the *Kitab al Zenuj*, in the anonymous history of Mombasa, and in Al Amin's history of the Mazrui.

The material for the history of the structural development of the Fort consists of the actual buildings; records in the Portuguese archives and other documents, mainly Portuguese; three inscriptions; and the archaeological evidence from the finds in the excavations.

In Part I, Chapter 1, the Fort is described as a unity, and in Chapters 2–10 in its component parts. Building materials and the literary sources are discussed in Chapters 11 and 12. Lists of Captains, Viceroys of Goa, and Sultans of Oman, Mombasa, and Zanzibar are given in an appendix at the end of the book.

In Part II, the finds are discussed in five chapters: Chapter 13, the Ceramics, with eight sub-headings; Chapter 14, Glass; Chapter 15, Beads; Chapter 16, Cannon and Cannon-balls; and Chapter 17, Minor Objects, as a contribution to the study of the individual subjects to which they belong. All levels in the Fort were dump levels, so the circumstances in which any object was found is of limited significance.

Acknowledgements

I HAVE much pleasure in acknowledging the help I have received from many colleagues and friends, who have answered my queries and queried my conclusions. I am most grateful to all of them for the trouble they have taken, as a result of which the text is greatly improved. Besides the ladies and gentlemen mentioned in the footnotes, I would like to pay my tribute to Mr. H. N. Chittick, Mrs. M. Sharman, and Mr. R. Soper of the British Institute in Eastern Africa; Professor C. R. Boxer; Mr. J. Dalkin and Major R. C. Bartelot of the Royal Artillery Institution, Woolwich; Miss L. Cole, who re-drew most of my plans; and above all to my wife, whose suggestions in clarifying obscurities in my text and whose typing and re-typing of my manuscript have added a new dimension to the term *ad nauseam*; and finally to the Clarendon Press for the care they have taken with a difficult text.

Above all, I must thank the British Institute in Eastern Africa and the Calouste Gulbenkian Foundation for their generosity in underwriting the cost of publication.

Mombasa, 1972.

Contents

List of Figures

PLANS AND SECTIONS

CERAMICS AND OTHER OBJECTS

List of Plates

THE FINDS

Part I. The Buildings

1. *History and General Description of the Fort*

(Figs. 1–6)

THE construction of a fortress at Mombasa was undertaken only after the Portuguese had been masters of the East African coast for nearly a hundred years. During this period the headquarters of the 'Captain of the Coast' was an unfortified factory at Malindi. The benefit to the Portuguese from their presence on the Swahili coast (the present Kenya and Tanzania) became increasingly obscure as the sixteenth century progressed. The revenue, at least what reached the crown, was negligible, and the hopes of finding a southern route to Ethiopia equally illusory. Apart from the element of honour—what we have held, we hold—the main object seemed to be to provide a strong point to protect the route to India or, perhaps more precisely, to prevent a hostile force, namely the Turks, from making a base in East Africa to prey on the routes between Africa and India.

The Portuguese were well aware of their weakness on the East African coast, but views on how to rectify it varied, as they would have done today, between conciliation and intimidation of the local inhabitants.[1] The former had the advantage that it was cheaper both in capital investment and current expenses, for in the Portuguese east there was a chronic shortage of men, ships, and money. However, whether it was relevant was a matter of opinion. They had little to fear from the unaided enmity of the inhabitants of the Swahili towns, and little to expect from their goodwill, which was unlikely to be more than negative in the event of foreign attack. Actually, the defence of the Fort during the first year and nine months of the siege of 1696–8 was largely, and for six weeks exclusively, due to the loyal Swahili. This loyalty could not have been foreseen at the time the Fort was built, and without the Fort could not have been shown. The Turkish raids of 1585 and 1588 decided the issue. If the coast was to be free of Turkish attack, it was necessary to build a fortress to protect it. Instructions were given to the Captain of the Coast, Mateus Mendes de Vasconcelos, to take his fleet to Mombasa and build a fortress to be called Jesus of Mombasa. He left Malindi on 10 January 1593,[2] and on 11 April the fortress was dedicated, probably soon after the plan had been traced on the ground.[3] The fact that it fell a little more than a hundred years after it was built is no proof that it was mistaken policy to build it. The Turkish threat faded away, but the Dutch, who were

[1] *Archivo Portuguez Oriental*, iii, pp. 46, 141, 146; see Boxer and Azevedo (1960), pp. 25, 95.

[2] Brit. Mus. Add. MS. 28432, f. 126.

[3] Inscription on the wall above the inner gate.

tearing the Portuguese empire to pieces, would have made short work of the unfortified settlement at Malindi. They never attacked Mombasa. It took the Omani Arabs two years and nine months to take the Fort, and it fell even then only because of the death by disease of nine-tenths of the garrison. If the garrison had numbered twenty-five and not nine on 13 December 1698, the Arabs would never have attacked and the Portuguese fleet that arrived the following week would have relieved it.

Relations between the Portuguese Captain and the Sultan of Mombasa began to deteriorate after the departure of the first Captain, Mateus Mendes de Vasconcelos. There were disputes over the Sultan's share of the customs, the Sultan's claim to Pemba, and subsequently over the tribute to be paid for Pemba, and whether the Sultan's trading privileges were a royal perquisite or a personal favour. The continual demands of the junior partner destroyed the goodwill, little enough in any case, of the Portuguese Captains trying to carry out the duties of their office and at the same time to recover the money they had paid or owed for it.

In 1614 the Sultan, Hasan bin Yusif, was murdered by the Musungulos, the African tribe of the mainland, at the instigation of the Portuguese Captain, Manuel de Melo Pereira. In 1626 the son, Muhammad Yusif, who had received a Portuguese education in Goa and who had been baptized with the name of Dom Jeronimo Chingulia, was made Sultan. The former confrontation between Captain and Sultan was repeated, with the added personal complications resulting from the Sultan's education and religion, but the *dénouement* was different. On 16 August 1631 the Sultan burst into the Fort and killed the Captain, Pedro Leitão de Gamboa. During the next two weeks the whole Portuguese population of Mombasa, consisting of forty-five men, thirty-five women, and seventy children, was massacred. The Portuguese had been taken by surprise and there was no fighting inside or outside the Fort. An expedition was sent from Goa to retake it, but after two months' fighting (10 January to 19 March 1632) the attackers were beaten off without great difficulty. However, the Sultan by then had discovered that he disliked his compatriots as much as he disliked the Portuguese, and he abandoned Mombasa on 16 May and became a pirate. He died six years later at Jedda, after a fight with some fellow Arabs in the Red Sea. A small Portuguese force had remained at Zanzibar under the Captain-elect, Pedro Rodrigues Botelho, who reoccupied the Fort on 5 August 1632.

During the next twenty-nine years life at Mombasa seems to have been uneventful, marked only by the peaceful succession of the Captains. However, the power that was to drive the Portuguese from Mombasa was coming into existence. In 1650 the Yaarubi Imam of Oman, Sultan bin Saif I, took Muscat and the other Portuguese forts on the coast of the Persian Gulf,[4] and in February 1661 he sent an expedition to Mombasa which sacked the Portuguese town but did not attack the Fort. It was not until 1696 that a larger expedition was organized by his son, Saif bin Sultan I, to

[4] For the history of Oman see Badger, and Miles. There are also valuable references in Guillain and in the history of Africa by Fadhil bin Sheikh bin 'Umar al Buri, translated by J. M. Ritchie

take the Fort. After collecting reinforcements at Pate, a town in the Lamu archipelago, the centre of opposition to the Portuguese in the seventeenth century,[5] it reached Mombasa on 13 March, and established a base at Kilindini, the harbour on the opposite side of the island of Mombasa. The Portuguese, with their allies, retired into the Fort, which was blockaded by outposts in the town and in the open country around. Later a battery was set up on the mainland and the Fort was bombarded at a range of about 500 metres. The original garrison comprised between fifty and seventy Portuguese, but they are stated to have been aided by 1,700 loyal coast Arabs, although this number is questionable, in view of the size of the Fort. It was relieved at the end of the year, when the defence was on the point of collapse, but the reinforcements brought plague with them, and by 16 June 1697 all the Portuguese were dead. The Fort was then held by a Sheikh Daud of Faza with seventeen of his family, eight African men, and fifty African women. They were reinforced on 15 September by the crew of the relief ship on its way back to Goa from Mozambique, and were relieved at the end of December by a ship from Goa. By the following December, 1698, the new garrison was down to the Captain, nine men, and probably a priest,[6] and the Fort fell on the morning of 13 December; seven days later the third relief fleet arrived and sailed on to Mozambique.[7] The siege cost the Portuguese at least 950 men, a frigate, four galliots, and an unknown number of Arab subjects.

With Fort Jesus the whole coast of Kenya and Tanzania, and the islands of Zanzibar and Pemba, fell into the hands of the ruler of Oman. In 1728 the African soldiers in the Fort mutinied against the Arab officer, Nasir bin ʻAbdulla al Mazrui, who had been left in charge during the absence of the governor. Failing to gain recognition from the Mombasans they offered the Fort to the Sultan of Pate. The Sultan, Bwana Tamu Mkuu, who was becoming increasingly embarrassed by the presence of the Portuguese fleet which he had invited as a protection against the Omanis, handed the Fort over to the Portuguese. They reoccupied it on 16 March 1728, but in April 1729 the Mombasans revolted and blockaded them. With insufficient supplies to sustain a siege, they were in a serious position and, anticipating the arrival of an Omani fleet, they capitulated on 26 November. They were given two small vessels to take them to Mozambique. The rule of the Omani governors was then resumed.

In 1741, when the ruling house of Oman changed from the Ya'arubi to the Busaid, the Governor of Mombasa, Muhammad bin ʻUthman al Mazrui, declared his autonomy. Six years later he was murdered in the Fort by assassins sent from Oman, but his brother escaped and, with the help of the neighbouring Africans and an English merchant captain, recovered the Fort, killed the assassins, and made himself

[5] For the history of Pate see Stigand or Freeman-Grenville (1962); a critical examination by Chittick (1967 and 1969), and Kirkman (1964).

[6] Obituary of Fr. Manoes de Jesus, 'and he died when the Fort was taken by the Arabs on 13th December, 1698', Rego, da Silva (1955), p. 276.

[7] *Arquivo Português Oriental* (new ed.), iv (ii), Part II, p. 331.

governor. His successors held Mombasa and the Fort until 1837. From 1822 they were under intermittent attack from the Sultan of Oman. In 1824 they obtained British protection, which was withdrawn in 1826. At the beginning of 1828 they were obliged to hand over the Fort, but at the end of the year the Sultan's garrison was starved into surrender. In 1833 the Fort was bombarded without success, but in 1837 the last governor was forced by internal dissensions to submit and the Fort was occupied by Omani soldiers.

From 1837 to 1895 the Fort was used as a barracks for the soldiers of the Sultan of Oman and later of Zanzibar. After the death of Saiyid Said in 1856, Zanzibar had become an independent Sultanate. In 1875 the Commander, Muhammad bin ʻAbdulla al Bakshuwain, revolted, and fired on the town of Mombasa. At the request of the Sultan, two British men-of-war bombarded the Fort until it surrendered.

After the proclamation of the British Protectorate and Colony of Kenya in 1895, the Fort was used as a prison. In 1958 the prisoners were removed and the work of conversion from a gaol to a historical monument was begun.

Fort Jesus was built during the period when Portugal was a possession of the Spanish crown (1580–1640). It was designed by an Italian, Giovanni Battista Cairati (João Baptista Cairato), who was a leading military architect of the day and a protégé of King Philip II of Spain. He had also worked at Manar in Ceylon, Malacca, Muscat, and Ormuz, but his principal achievements were at Damão and Bassein, in Portuguese India. He selected the site and laid out the plan of Fort Jesus with Vasconcelos, but probably never saw the completed building. He died in Goa in 1596, anxious to return to his home in Milan, waiting for a replacement from Europe who never arrived.[8]

The Arab town of Mombasa lay about a mile from the entrance to the creek between the island of Mombasa and the north mainland, at a place where a shelving beach provided an ideal anchorage for the shipping of the Indian Ocean. Fort Jesus was built about half a mile away on the seaward side, thus barring the approach to the town. The preferred channel runs along the island side, so that any ship entering the harbour would come within point-blank range of the Fort guns. Almost the whole perimeter of the island of Mombasa consists of coral cliffs, broken by gullies, and between the old town and Ras Serani at the entrance of the harbour there are several possible sites for a fortress. The position was decided by the existence of a sandy bay, where small boats could land supplies in an emergency and be protected from the town by the Fort. This bay, 100 yards south from the Fort, was in fact used by the relief ships during the great siege.

The direction of the harbour is roughly south to north, and the coral ridge on which the Fort is built runs into it at right angles. On the north was a natural slope which was cut back to a vertical face. On the east, where the ridge sloped down to the sea,

[8] Boxer and de Azevedo (1960), pp. 91–5.

retaining walls filled with rubble were built to support a rectangular projection. On the south and west there was no natural separation between the site of the Fort and the surrounding country and it had to be isolated by a ditch. The ditch was on average 4·60 m below the level of the counterscarp and followed the line of the Fort, with a width varying from 3 m on the south and south-east sides to 9·14 m on the north.

The Fort had many of the features of an Italian fortress of the late sixteenth century (Fig. 1). The plan was quadrilateral, with a wide bastion at each corner and a rectangular projection between the two seaward bastions. The flanks of the landward bastions, S. Filipe (north) and S. Alberto (south), were made with deep re-entrant angles where they faced each other, to provide screened gun positions. The other flanks and the landward flanks of the seaward bastions, S. Matias (north) and S. Mateus (south), were square, without re-entrant angles. There were two blind spots at the corners of S. Filipe and S. Alberto which were not visible from S. Matias and S. Mateus; otherwise the bastions covered each other and the lengths of wall between them on the landward sides.

On the seaward front, where the danger from storming parties was considered to be least, the faces of the bastions S. Matias and S. Mateus were swept back to provide the widest possible field of fire. The north and south faces of the rectangular projection were covered by the seaward bastions, but the main face, the east wall, was protected only by the guns of the outwork in front of it.

The main gate was in the lee of S. Matias, covered by the east flank of S. Filipe, and was reached by a wooden gangway across the ditch. Above it was the gatehouse, consisting of an upper and a lower room. There were two subsidiary gates in the east wall of the projection, reached from the central court by a sloping passage (the Passage of the Arches) and by a flight of steps (the Passage of the Steps), and a third in the east wall of S. Mateus. The purpose of the subsidiary gates was to provide access to the Fort for supplies landed by sea, as during the great siege, and also to communicate with the outwork below the front of the projection. It is not known why it was considered necessary to have so many gates, which were all potential points of weakness. It is possible that in some fortresses gates were made and immediately blocked, so that they could be opened in emergency without damage to the fabric of the building and perhaps without being observed by the enemy.

The original defences on the landward sides consisted of a 4·27 m thick wall, comprising a parapet nearly 2·75 m wide and 1 m high, backed by a parapet walk and firing-step. On these sides of the Fort there were no merlons or embrasures, but gaps were left in the re-entrant angles between the west curtain and the bastions, which were apparently only filled in when the Fort was reconstructed between 1634 and 1639 (Fig. 2). At this time the ditch was only partially excavated, so that on the landward sides the parapet could not have been more than 4·60 m above the surrounding country. In fact, the defence relied on an adequate number of trained soldiers and an irresolute enemy. The first factor did not always exist.

The establishment consisted of the Captain, 100 men, a Master Gunner, and four gunners. However, they were not always available for duties in the Fort. Twenty-five soldiers and one gunner were posted to the forts covering the ford at Makupa, which connected the island with the mainland, and an unspecified number to the two coastal patrol ships.[9] In addition, there were the Keeper of the Gate, four masons, one carpenter, two blacksmiths, and, in the *Livro de Fazenda* (1606), six watchmen.[10] The watchmen were dropped later; they were probably no more reliable than they would be today. The Surgeon, who does not appear in the earlier list, and the *Vigario Forane* should also be included. The Surgeon may have lived outside the Fort with the other officials, such as the *Ouvidor* (Judge) and the Factor, in the street called *La Raposeira* (the Foxhole); the *Vigario Forane* had a house in the Fort. In fact, numbers were seldom up to strength. According to a *processus* in the Vatican Archives,[11] only three men, specified as soldiers, were killed during the massacre of 1631. No doubt a proportion of the thirty-five unclassified males in the casualty list were soldiers, but even then the total is not impressive. At the beginning of the great siege of 1696 there were probably no more than fifty professional soldiers in the Fort.[12]

On the seaward side successive rebuildings have destroyed the original defences. The defences of S. Matias may have consisted of a low, plastered kerb, over which a wall was later built with three arched gun-ports with double splays. In S. Mateus the later gun-platform obscured the whole length of the wall, and the only feature of the original defences found in the excavations was the gate.

The walls of the rectangular projection, actually retaining walls, have survived on the south side beside, and at the end of, the Passage of the Steps; on the east at the end of the Passage of the Arches; and on the north below later walls. The north and south walls, but not the east, were covered on the inside with a thick brown plaster, similar to the retaining wall below the outwork. The wall extended all along the south side of the Passage of the Steps, then turned south under the later angle tower. This would suggest that the steps were intended to be outside the Fort, and that the original wall of the Fort ran west along the north side of the steps, turning south along the east wall of the prison 'lamp room' to join S. Mateus. In this case, it might have resembled the Portuguese fort at Muscat, known as the Jalala.[13] It is possible that the plastered foundation walls and the Passage of the Steps are part of an earlier fortress, which Father Monclaro mentions in the account of his voyage of 1569 as having been begun during the Viceroyalty of Dom Pedro Mascarenhas (1554–5), but never completed.[14] So far as I am aware there is no other reference to such a project in Portuguese records.

9 Bocarro/Rezende (1635) in *Arquivo Português Oriental* (new ed.), pp. 47–9.
10 Gray (1947), p. 20.
11 Unpublished section of translation by Freeman-Grenville (1967).
12 Axelson (1960), p. 158; Boxer and de Azevedo (1960), p. 59; Strandes (translation Wallwork), p. 215.
13 *Arquivo Português Oriental* (new ed.), iv (ii) II, p. 368.
14 Freeman-Grenville (1962), p. 140.

The buildings within the walls consisted of barrack rooms, a church, a large cistern, storerooms, and the Captain's House. All these, except the cistern and the L-shaped building in S. Matias, disappeared in the course of the eighteenth century. However, the stumps of the walls of the barracks along the north and south curtains served as foundations for the later prison buildings.

The construction of Fort Jesus, begun by Mateus Mendes de Vasconcelos in 1593, was said to have been completed by 1596. However, there were continual complaints that it was not in fact completed and that there were no vouchers to support the expenditure of 30,000 *xerafins*[15] which had been voted for the works. In the time of Captain Jorge Barreto (*c.* 1609), it was specifically stated that the ditch was unfinished and that the walls were exceedingly low, but that work was in progress to heighten them.[16] What exactly is meant by this is uncertain. The original parapet, except perhaps along the east face of S. Matias, is clearly of one period and the curtain walls are hardly a heightening of an existing wall, but a new project which is more reasonably ascribed to the reconstruction following the revolt of 1631.

Work was continued during the years 1618 to 1626 under Captain Francisco de Sousa Pereira and Captain João Pereira Semedo. The latter actually spent on the Fort the one per cent of the customs duties which was levied for this purpose, and the Viceroy reported that to his amazement no criticisms had reached Goa about him. It should be recorded that the Captaincy came to João Pereira Semedo through his wife, who showed her worthiness for the grant by the selection of an admirable husband to perform its duties.[17] His successors, appointed in a less bizarre way, were by no means so honest, and it was their inadequacy and tyranny which led to the tragedy of 1631. It has been impossible to assign any works or changes in the Fort to the period of the rebel Sultan, except possibly the filling of the bastions of S. Alberto and S. Filipe to the level of the parapet walk. No evidence has been found to substantiate the statement that he destroyed the Fort before he fled, unless the whole east wall of the rectangular projection, which had no brown plaster on the inside, is to be regarded as a rebuilding.

After the Portuguese recovered the Fort on 5 August 1632, they carried out a major reconstruction which, by reducing its aggressively modern features, brought it more into line with the role it was to play as a secure base against an unsophisticated attack by land from the Swahili and Africans, or a sophisticated attack by sea from the Dutch. The recommendations for the new works were made in Goa in April 1633,[18] so it is unlikely that they were started before 1634. Curtain walls were made on the landward side without gun-ports, except in the north wall facing the town. The gaps between S. Alberto and S. Filipe and the west curtain wall were filled with a heavy roll-moulding made to screen the junction of wall and coral face. The floors of the

[15] *Xerafin*, a silver coin valued at 300–400 *reis*, also called *pardão*. The double *pardão* later became the rupee. (Strandes, tr. Wallwork, pp. 145, 286.)

[16] Axelson (1960), p. 79.

[17] Axelson (1960), p. 84.

[18] Marinho (1634).

three bastions of S. Alberto, S. Filipe, and S. Matias were raised with a filling of coral chips and red earth to the level of the old parapets, and new walls with 1·22 m wide gun-ports were built on top of them in S. Alberto and S. Matias. The west face of S. Matias was extended in the form of an elliptical bastion, and an outer gate, which led to the old inner gate by a covered passage, was made between the extension and the north curtain wall. The approach to the gate was commanded by two gun-ports in the east face of S. Filipe. The effect of these works was to protect the gate from bombardment by land as well as by sea. The fourth bastion, S. Mateus, which was the most vulnerable to attack from the sea, was protected on the seaward side by a 3·96 m wide gun-platform. Another platform was built on the landward side with two gun-ports covering the east face of S. Alberto and the south curtain wall. Between the two platforms was a sunken court which led to the gate by a vaulted passage under the seaward platform. Angle towers were built at the junction of the rectangular projection and the seaward bastions.

Subsequent Portuguese works between 1634 and 1696 consisted of the construction of two cavaliers in the landward bastions to cover the approaches from Kilindini, the old harbour of Tuaqua or Chwaka,[19] and from Makupa, the ford of the Zimba; a second raising of some of the walls which were pierced with vertical musket-slits; guardrooms against the cavaliers and in S. Mateus; perhaps the lower part of the watchtower on the north curtain, besides repairs and minor modifications to existing buildings. The hospital mentioned in the inscription on the cavalier of S. António has not been located.

During the great siege the Captain's House was badly damaged. When the Fort was restored by the Arabs in the early eighteenth century (Fig. 3) the area occupied by the outer rooms was filled with rubble to the level of the top of the Portuguese walls to make a broad platform, which was protected by a crenellated wall with musket-slits and gun-ports. It was probably at this time that the court in S. Mateus began to be filled in, and the door leading through a guardroom to the main court was blocked. In the main court a square well with a small open cistern and a washing place were made behind the great cistern. During the second half of the eighteenth century the portico in front of the Captain's House was converted into a *baraza*, or audience hall, and houses were erected on top of the cavaliers and at the south end of the west curtain wall. The barracks continued to be used in an increasing state of dilapidation, while much of the central court was occupied by huts for the soldiers and their dependants. In the early nineteenth century a small mosque was built against the south wall of the guardroom in S. Mateus.

In the early Arab period, that is until the time of the Mazrui, the Arab governors did not all live in the Fort. A Portuguese intelligence report of 1710 mentioned that the Arab governor lived in the town.[20] However, there is no evidence to suggest that

[19] Monteiro (1593), in Gray (1947), p. 21.
[20] MS. *Liss. Cons. Ultr.* No. 854, Moçambique (Strandes, tr. Wallwork, p. 240).

Muhammad bin 'Uthman al Mazrui and his successors did not have accommodation in the Fort which they occupied from time to time. Suleiman bin 'Ali is specifically stated by Captain Owen in 1825 to have resided there. The most likely areas would have been behind the filled-in Captain's House and in the bastion of S. Matias. The nineteenth-century Arab captains (Akidas) probably lived in the same areas, though the L-shaped building in S. Matias was described by Guillain as store-rooms.

In the nineteenth century six round watchtowers were erected: one at each end of the rectangular projection; at the corners of S. Matias and S. Mateus on the seaward sides; at the west end of the south curtain and at the inner projection of S. Alberto on the landward side. The idea was derived from the Portuguese turrets on the cavaliers, but the reason for their construction at any particular time is unknown. Their purpose was to keep an inconspicuous watch on the surrounding countryside. They differed in detail, which suggests that they were built at different times. Four had entrances with square lintels, but the two oldest had rounded lintels, like the seventeenth-century pillar at Mbaraki, overlooking Kilindini.[21] There were two types of roof: one a shallow cupola, the other a tall conical cap. In both cases a 12·7 cm ledge was left visible on the outside between the base of the roof and the wall of the turret. The earliest appear to be the turret in S. Mateus, a cupola, and the turret at the south end of the rectangular projection, a cone. The finials of the turrets in the rectangular projection were similar to the finials of contemporary pillar tombs. They are supposed to be phallic, but this explanation is perhaps more subjective than scientific. They are more likely to represent a spearhead, the symbol of majesty and power. The conical finial on the two-storeyed turret on the north wall, the 'tarboosh' in S. Matias, and the 'golf tees' on the south wall and in S. Alberto are not in the old coast tradition, or indeed any tradition, and seem to be personal idiosyncrasies.

After the expulsion of the Mazrui in 1837 there seems to have been little change in the Fort until the middle of the century, when large houses, running the length of the bastions, were built in S. Alberto and S. Matias, a room above the Audience Room of the Mazrui, and a number of small houses or huts in S. Filipe and against the north curtain. The bombardment of 1875 caused great damage to the buildings behind the platform in the projection and the L-shaped building in S. Matias. It is possible that these buildings were not repaired before the proclamation of the Protectorate and the establishment of the prison in the Fort in 1895. The plan of 1899 shows the layout at the end of the Arab period, with the addition of a few new constructions, some built on old foundations. (Fig. 6)

The original prison comprised only the east end of the court, including the bastions of S. Matias and S. Mateus and the Audience Room of the Mazrui. The other parts of the Fort were used as barracks for the security forces and temporary accommodation for various officials, such as the Provincial Medical Officer. However, owing to the new opportunities for individual betterment provided by the construction of the

[21] Kirkman (1964), Pl. 15.

Uganda Railway, it soon became necessary to extend the prison over the whole area of the building. The extended prison is shown on a plan of 1954.[22] The long room on the south side of the court became a line of cells for Asian prisoners; the Arab house in S. Alberto was used as warders' quarters and finally as the carpentry workshop, and a line of cells was built on the gun-platform of the projection. The house on the top of the cavalier in S. Alberto, marked as a magazine in the 1899 plan, became a store, and nearby a 'hangman's drop' was made against the re-entrant angle. The house on the cavalier of S. Filipe became the quarters of the chief warder and the prison office, while the two houses in the projection were converted into the tailor's workshop.

In the main court the church and the west line of barracks had disappeared in the course of the eighteenth century. In the 1899 plan an open veranda is shown along the west curtain. This was replaced by cells with a wash-place and lavatory at the north end, later used as stores. The houses in S. Filipe, and against the north curtain wall shown on the 1899 plan, were cleared away, and three cells constructed against the curtain. The rooms over the gate became a warder's quarters. In S. Matias the L-shaped house was used as the night-warders' quarters and then as the juvenile prison. A flight of steps was built from the lower to the upper level of the bastion, where a hospital, dispensary, and latrine were constructed.

The work of excavation and investigation was begun in 1958 and completed in 1969. In 1960 a museum was built, and the Fort was opened to the public as a historic monument.

[22] Plan in Fort Jesus.

2. *The Main Court*

MOST of the buildings of the Fort were situated in the central court at all periods of its history. On the north, south, and west it was bounded by the original ramparts, which were later crowned by curtain walls. On the east was the rectangular projection with the Captain's House.

THE WALLS (Figs. 7 and 8)

The original ramparts were 4·44 m thick, of rubble and red earth faced with coral blocks 33 cm by 23 cm, coursed and with a plastered face rising to a parapet walk and firing-step at varying heights above the surface of the court, 96 cm on the north, 1·10 m on the west, and 1·20 m on the south. The actual parapet was 2·66 m thick, with a level top, 52·8 cm wide and an outer face sloping downwards at an angle of 75°. There was a flight of steps in the middle of the west and north parapet walks, but not in the south walk.

When the Fort was reconstructed in 1634–9, a wall was built along the outer edge of the old parapet, 93·6 cm wide on the north, 98·4 cm on the west, and 1·27 m on the south. The wall was also at varying heights above the top of the old parapet, 1·36 m on the north, 1·27 m on the west, and 2·04 m on the south. The new walk along the top of the old parapet was 1·72 m wide on the north, 1·68 m on the west, and 1·32 m on the south. On the north there were two gun-ports (Fig. 27 C, D) and musket-slits (Fig. 29 E, F), facing the town and commanding the Portuguese street, *La Raposeira*, represented by the present Ndia Kuu. The north parapet walk was raised to the level of the old parapet and subsequently covered by the prison warders' kitchen and other buildings shown on the 1899 plan. The west parapet walk was filled in with coral chips among which were found British India coins of 1835 and 1862. The south walk appears never to have been disturbed.

Later the walls were raised about a metre. The heightening of the west wall with its well-cut musket-slits (Fig. 29 C, D), was probably Portuguese. The slits were made so high up that a temporary wooden scaffolding must have been erected whenever they were to be used. The fact that the slits were slanted, the south group to the north and the north group to the south, shows that they had a defensive purpose and were not merely air vents, such as were often made high up in the walls of Arab houses on the coast. Along the top of the wall was a gable-coping and in the middle a small gun-port, both Arab of uncertain date. In the 1899 plan an open veranda is shown running along the length of the wall, using the lower part of the back wall of the barracks, restored where necessary as at the north end, as the retaining wall. There was a latrine in the wall at the north end, and in front of it a wash-place with diagonal drains leading to a central sump. Later a line of store-rooms was built, extending over the veranda and supported by a new revetment wall.

The top course of the north curtain was built after 1846, since it is not shown on the Guillain sketch. The top course of the south wall is shown on the Guillain sketch and is clearly an addition to the turret. The additions were considerably thinner than the old walls, which served as a narrow sentry walk behind them. These works, and the upper storey of the north turret, were probably carried out by the Akida Muhammad bin ʻAbdulla (*c.* 1865–75), whose relations with the Mombasans were generally bad.[1]

Turrets were built as watchtowers at the corner of the south curtain where it met S. Alberto and in the middle of the north curtain. The turret on the south curtain was attached to the Portuguese wall and was entered by steps or a ladder, which would have rested on the old parapet. The entrance was square-headed and the jambs slightly convex. A single round-headed aperture overlooked the high ground to the south of the Fort and a narrow slit, probably of much later date, looked down into the court. Above the low dome is a finial on a short stem, like an inverted golf-tee. The 'tee' is made of cement, but the form is similar to the finial on the S. Alberto turret, which is of cut coral. Oddly enough the turret was shown by Guillain but omitted by von der Decken.

The turret on the north curtain (Fig. 26 L) was double-storeyed. The lower storey would have been reached by two steps, and had two openings looking down the two main streets which converged in front of the Fort. This section, in view of the similarity of the moulding round the top to the moulding of the outer gate, may be Portuguese. The Guillain sketch shows the turret with a disk on top, like the turrets in the cavaliers. The upper storey was reached from the later sentry walk by a door on the west side. At the junction of the two storeys was a half keyhole moulding, a typical Zanzibar decorative feature.[2] The dome is conical with a conical finial on a short stem.

THE GATE (Figs. 9 A and 20 B; Pls. 7 B, 9 B)

The present inner gate (Fig. 24 G, H) was the original entrance of the Fort, although it may have been rebuilt. Like the outer gate and unlike the gates to the Passage of the Steps and the bastion of S. Mateus, it had no voussoirs and was built of plastered rubble. It was situated in the angle of the north curtain wall where it met the west flank of S. Matias. Above it an inscription records the dedication of the Fort in the name of Jesus of Mombasa, as follows:

REINANDO EM PORTUGAL PHELLIPE DE AUSTRIA
O PRIMEIRO . . . POR SEU MANDADO [foi fundada esta?]
FORTALEZA DE NOME IESUS DE MOMBACA
AOMZE DABRIL DE 1593 [sendo?] VISSO REI DA
INDIA MATHIAS DALBOQUERQUE [e capitao mor?] MATHEUS

[1] Hinawy, Mbarak bin ʻAli (1950). [2] Garlake (1966), pp. 43, 72, Fig. 2 D.

MENDES DE VASCONCELLOS QUE PASOU COM ARMADA
E ESTE PORTO [e sendo?] ARQUITECTO MOR DA INDIA
JOAO BAUTISTA CAIRATO SERVINDO DE
MESTRE DAS OBRAS GASPAR RODRIGUES.

This can be translated:

When Philip of Austria was reigning as Philip I of Portugal this fortress was founded at his command with the name of Jesus of Mombasa on the eleventh of April, 1593. At this time Matias d'Albuquerque was Viceroy of India, and the Captain Major Mateus Mendes de Vasconcelos had arrived with his fleet at this harbour with the Chief Architect of India, João Batista Cairato, with Gaspar Rodriguez serving as Master of the Works.

It was carved on a black stone which must have been imported. The Teixeira plan (Fig. 4 B) shows above it the standard group of the shield of Portugal flanked by the shield with the cross of the Order of Christ and the armillary globe. Today only part of the crown above the shield of Portugal and part of the 'spindle' border have survived, cut in fine-grained coral (*mutambawi*), on the wall of the gatehouse above the outer passage.

The gatehouse is described in the Boccaro/Rezende account of 1635, as follows: 'Along the wall above the gate there is a quadrangular building with a flat roof, in which are two store-rooms where powder is kept.' These rooms were one above the other, and it is believed that the upper room was the solarium above the gate[3] in which the Captain, Pedro Leitão de Gamboa, was murdered on 16 August 1631. It was probably here also that his wife, Domina Joanna, his eleven-year-old daughter, Barbara de Acosta, the chaplain, Father Andrea Veloso, and a Portuguese named Manuel de Souto Mayor, who was in the Fort on the day of the revolt, suffered the same fate. This room has been entirely rebuilt, possibly more than once. The round-headed window openings with an ogival nick at the apex (Fig. 24 J), once three, now only one on each side, and two at the east end, are Arab, although in Portuguese times there would have been windows facing outwards and towards the court, as at S. Sebastião, Mozambique.[4] A tall fragment of wall at the west end of the east face seems to be original, and indicates that the top of the first wall was about 91 cm below the present crenellations.

The lower room, the powder-magazine, has retained much of its original character. The only openings were the door and a square 36 cm aperture in the wall facing the court. The present low ceiling is probably no lower than it had ever been, but is comparatively recent. The lower part of the walls is 1·32 m thick, compared with 53 cm in the upper room, but most of the latter wall has been restored. This may have been in consequence of the blowing-up of the powder-magazine by a Portuguese soldier, António de Barbosa, after the fall of the Fort on 13 December 1698.[5,6] The room is

[3] Freeman-Grenville (1967), pp. 356, 359. [4] Lobato (1945).
[5] *Arquivo Português Oriental* (new ed.), iv (ii) II, pp. 332–3.
[6] Cienfuegos plan (discussion by E. Vasconcelos).

divided in two by a 30 cm thick partition wall which was added later, probably in the Arab period. The smaller section has a ceiling of boards tied together with coconut fibre, which were once part of the hull of a *mtepe*, the sewn boat of the coast.[7]

The gatehouse was approached on the west side of the entrance to the Fort by a flight of steps (Pl. 9 B) which passed under a round arch of Arab type (Fig. 24 I) in line with the south wall of the gatehouse. Beyond the arch was a right-angled turn, down two steps into the lower room. The flight of steps continued to the level of the floor of the upper room, which was at one time entered directly from them. Later a wall was built on the inside of the steps, leaving a lobby at the top. A door in the old west wall of the upper room opened on to a second flight of steps which led down to a kitchen and lavatory behind the north curtain.

The crenellations above the gatehouse are smaller and more irregular than those on the façade of the rectangular projection. The average size is 33 cm wide and 49 cm high, but at the west end of the south line there are some which are 51 cm wide, while the whole east line is only 36 cm high. Below them are splayed slits, shorter and wider than those on the projection and resembling those in the outwork. From their height above the roof they could have had no practical use. Both crenellations and slits may be a restoration after the bombardment of 1875.

The use of the gatehouse in the eighteenth and nineteenth centuries is unknown. The blocking of the six windows in the upper room, and the partition wall resting on the floor in the lower, are probably connected with the conversion of the room from public to private use. No windows are shown on the Guillain sketch, but the angle of sight was probably too low, and no reference to the gatehouse is made by Owen, Guillain, or Thornton. All the modifications may be as late as the prison period, when the gatehouse was the senior Asian warder's quarters.

Against the inner face of the main gate is an extension consisting of a passage with two small rooms at the inner end. The room, or lock-up, on the west is entered from the passage. The room on the east was entered from S. Matias on the 1899 plan (Fig. 6) and was marked 'guardroom', but it is now approached from the main court. On the Héredia plan (Fig. 4 A) a wide guardroom is shown, occupying the area of the inner passage and the rooms on each side of it. It was connected with a series of rooms extending into the court, which have disappeared. On the Cienfuegos plan (Fig. 5 B) the guardroom is shown, and on the Lopes de Sá plan (Fig. 5 C) the passage is clearly marked, with apparently two rooms each side of it. The two extra rooms are probably the result of trying to show the room above and the passage below the gatehouse on the same plan.

The walls of the inner passage and rooms were composed of red earth, lime, and small stones. When the whitewash was removed from the east face of the passage, the wall was like a piece of seedcake and it was almost possible to put a finger through it. The west wall of the lock-up was little better. On each side were benches with

7 Hornell (1941); Grottanelli (1955); Prins (1959).

curved ends in Arab style, which are eighteenth- or nineteenth-century. The façade on the court consisted of two attached half-columns with moulded capitals (Figs. 25 C, 26 D) rising from cross walls which were lengthened after the seats were added. The roof was made of roughly squared stones and lime carried on beams, and had been frequently renewed.

The outer passage was formed by the construction of an elliptical bastion against the west face of S. Matias, which was joined to the north curtain by a wall with a gate. Over the passage was a flat roof of coral blocks carried on beams, probably similar to the present roof but with the beams running lengthwise, supported by an arch across the middle of the passage. Subsequently, when the beams had to be renewed, bearer walls were built on each side to carry them. The platform and seats on either side in their present state are modern. At the far end of the passage, high up in the wall, is a niche with a red trellis background for a statue, perhaps of St. Anthony, in honour of whom the harbour of Mombasa was renamed Barra de S. António.

The construction of the outer gate (Figs. 24 E, F, 26 F) was one of the recommendations of Marinho and was carried out by Cabreira, though the elliptical bastion which must have preceded it, may have been due to Botelho. Marinho wrote as follows: 'For the service of Your Majesty and the defence of the Fort a wall should be built from the curtain of the gate of the Fort [i.e. the north curtain] at a place which I have marked, and a strong door with a good lock be made for the gate. A guardroom should be made for use during the day with a flat roof over it as a protection from rain and sun, and seats below where the soldiers of the guard can sit.' This description could apply to the inner passage, but is more likely to refer to the outer passage. The gate consisted of a rounded arch carried on two square pillars with moulded capitals. Above was an inscription in fine-grained coral, recording the construction of the gate and the military achievements and honours of Francisco de Seixas Cabreira, Captain of the Coast from 1635 to 1639 (Pl. 7 B). The text reads:

EM 1635 O CAPITAO MOR FRANCISCO DE SEXAS DE CABREIRA O FOI DESTA
FORTALEZA POR 4 ANOS SENDO DA IDADE DE 27 E A REEDIFICOU
DE NOVO E FEZ ESTE CORPO DE GUARDA E REDUZIU A SUA MAGESTADE A CO
STA DE MELINDE ACHANDO A ALAVANTADA PELO REI TIRANO
E FEZ LHE TRIBUTARIOS OS REIS DE OTONDO MANDRA LUZIVA
E JACA E DEU PESSOALMENTE A PATE E SIO HUM CASTIGO NAO
ESPERADO NA INDIA ATE ARRAZAR LHE OS MUROS APENOU
OS MOZUNGULOS CASTIGOU PEMBA E OS POVOS REBELDES
MATANDO A SUA CUSTA OS REGEDORES ALEVANTADOS E TODOS OS MAIS
DE FAMA E FEZ PAGAR AS PAREAS QUEM AVIAO NEGADAS A SUA MAGESTADE QUE POR TA

IS SERVICOS O FEZ FIDALGO DA SUA CASA TENDO JA DESPACHADO POR
OUTROS TAIS COMO O HABITO DE CHRISTO E 50 MIL REIS DE TENÇA E 6 ANOS DE
GOVERNADOR DE JFANAPATAO E 4 DE BILIGAO DOM FACULDADE DE PODER NOMEAR
TUDO EM SUA VIDA E MORTE SENDO VICE REI PEDRO DA SILVA ERA DE 1639 A.

This can be translated as follows:

In 1635 Francisco de Seixas de Cabreira, aged twenty-seven years, was made for four years Captain of this Fort which he had reconstructed and to which he added this guard-room. He subjected to His Majesty the people of this coast who, under their tyrant king, had been in a state of rebellion. He made the kings of Otondo, Mandra, Luziwa, and Jaca[8] tributary to His Majesty. He inflicted in person punishment on Pate and Sio[8] which was unexpected in India, extending to the destruction of their town walls. He punished the Musungulos and chastised Pemba[8] where on his own responsibility he had the rebel governors and all leading citizens executed. He made all pay tribute to His Majesty who had neglected to pay it. For these services he was made a Knight of the Royal Household[9] after he had already for other services been given the habit of the Order of Christ[10] and a yearly grant of fifty milreis and the governorship of Jafnapatan for six years and of Belgão[11] for four years, with the right to make all appointments during his life and in the event of his death.

During the Viceroyalty of Pedro da Silva in the year of our Lord 1639.

Above the inscription there is now a bare rectangle, which in Owen's sketch is shown with one shield in the middle and another shield on the left. These two shields formed part of the standard group: the arms of Portugal, flanked by the Cross of the Order of Christ on the left and the armillary globe on the right. In the pediment were

[8] Otondo, the present Utondwe near Saadani north of Bagamoyo in Tanzania.

Mandra, the ruined town of Manda on the island of that name opposite Lamu, 217 miles north of Mombasa.

Luziwa, the ruined town known as Uziwa, about 5 miles from Mkunumbi, 196 miles north of Mombasa on the road to Lamu.

Jaca, the ruined town of Shaka about 5 miles east of Kipini on the shore of Formosa Bay, about 188 miles north of Mombasa.

Pate, once a large town on the island of the same name, beyond Manda.

Sio, the town of Siyu on the island of Pate.

Musungulos were the African tribe on the mainland behind Mombasa during the seventeenth century. The name has survived as Mushunguli, a small Bantu tribe living between Jamame and Gilib in southern Somalia (private communication from Mr. P. Toulmim-Roche). It may originally have been the name of the whole group of north-east Bantu, which were later called the Nyika or Mijikenda (Nine People).

Pemba, an island opposite Tanga, now united with Zanzibar.

[9] This was an honorary position without insignia, duties, or pension.

[10] The Order of Christ was created by King Denis after the dissolution of the Portuguese branch of the Templars in 1312. Prince Henry the Navigator was Grand Master of the Order and used its revenues to finance the exploration of the sea route to the East. In 1487, the Grand Mastership of the Order was vested in the crown. Fifty milreis was not a great sum. Its value if paid in silver would have been about 250 coins of the weight of a half-rupee each.

[11] Jafnapatan is the present town of Jafna in Ceylon. Belgão was a small fort south of Colombo.

the letters I H S with a cross rising from the horizontal bar of the H, all within a radiant sun. I H S was a monogram for the name of Jesus formed by the first three letters of the Greek word. It was a motive favoured in architectural ornament by the Dominicans, and later by the Jesuits. Over the pediment was a wide dripstone to protect the inscription.

In the Owen and von der Decken sketches the door was shown as coffered with a wicket gate in the middle. A photograph[12] taken in 1905 depicts a door with two leaves and a postern, but with a centre post fixed to one leaf and decorated with rosettes, in Arab style. The brass spikes in the present door may be original.

The gate was commanded by two gun-ports in the east flank of the bastion of S. Filipe, which would have made any attempt to storm it extremely costly, and indeed it was never attempted.

Set on a plinth over the entrance were five small pinnacles, perhaps once surmounted by crosses (Fig. 27 A). Originally they were free-standing, but are now partially embedded in a wall. Behind them was an open court, the floor of which formed the roof of the entrance passage. This court may not have been intended to be used. However, the pleasant elevated situation, protected from the sun for most of the day, would sooner or later have appealed to some Captain, and it is possible that the wall behind the pinnacles was built for security at that time. The court was approached from the south between the end of the north curtain wall and the gatehouse, where there was a gap of 1·22 m, which at later times was provided with a gate. It was blocked when the kitchen for the chief Asian warder of the prison was made along the north curtain wall.

THE BARRACK BLOCKS (Fig. 10 A, B; Pl. 8 A, B)

Against the parapet walks were barrack rooms built of coral blocks with pent-roofs, which are shown along the north and south walls on all plans of the Fort. The west range is not shown on the earlier plans and first appears on the Cienfuegos plan.

The north block ran behind the north parapet walk between the north-west bastion and the gatehouse. It consisted of eight rooms, divided in the middle by a flight of three steps leading to the parapet walk. In the late seventeenth century the steps were covered and replaced by a ramp. The Lopes de Sá plan (1728) shows seven rooms with a passage between the third and fourth rooms, counting from the west.

On the east side of the central steps the first/second and the third/fourth rooms were intercommunicating. In the east wall of the fourth room was an arch, 1·22 m high, supporting the steps that led up to the gatehouse, and in the alcove below the arch was a bench with a hollow in the centre for a water jar. In the middle of this room was a low rectangular platform which was probably a hearth, such as occurs in Arab houses even today. A similar platform was found in the room across the gorge

[12] In Fort Jesus Museum.

of S. Mateus. The floors of these rooms were relaid at the end of the seventeenth century, 30 cm above the original surface, but were not disturbed again until the bombardment of 1875, when the room immediately to the east of the steps was destroyed. The end of a Hale rocket was found in the debris, with nineteenth-century china and porcelain. An eccentrically positioned room, perhaps a thatched shelter, is shown on the site in the 1899 plan, but of this there was no trace. The other three rooms were undamaged and appear in this plan.

In the early twentieth century a block of five prison cells was built, using the rear wall of the three Portuguese rooms, but with a new front wall, 45 cm inside the line of the old wall. The thatched shelter was pulled down and a long work room, the joiner's, was built, covering the room beneath it, the steps, and the first two rooms to the west of the steps. Between the five cells and the workroom a passage to the parapet was left.

The first room to the west of the steps was disturbed by four shallow pits and one deep pit, in which were found necks of glass bottles of the period 1750–70, similar to Fig. 77. 8 and 10. It did not appear to have been rebuilt before the eighteenth century. The east wall of the second room and the whole of the third room had been disturbed, and nineteenth-century china was found on the original floors. The passage of the Lopes de Sá plan passed between these two rooms. The fourth and last room had three floor levels: the original; an interim floor about 30 cm above it, with a plastered depression 46 cm in diameter and 15 cm deep in the middle; and a third floor 16 cm above that. Both later floors were eighteenth-century.

On the 1899 plan (Fig. 6) two houses, divided by a passage, are shown in the area. The house to the east consisted of four rooms, and was carried over the first two original rooms and the parapet walk behind them and forward into the main court. The second house consisted of five rooms, built over the parapet walk and the old room and was carried round the corner into the bastion of S. Filipe, and also into the court, in line with the south wall of the other house. A large square window was made in the north wall, and in the east wall of S. Filipe a small window, looking straight on to the gate, with an arched opening in a square recess, similar to the window in the house in the re-entrant angle of the bastion. To the right of this window was a spy-hole, like those in the outwork, directed towards the blank wall of the north curtain. In the filling of the outer room was found a $3\frac{1}{2}$-inch iron shell from the 1875 bombardment. A flight of steps between the house and the cistern led to the bastion.

In the early twentieth century these two buildings were demolished and the area they had covered was converted into a place for washing sisal, with two long troughs extending from the west end of the block to the east wall of the first old room on the east side of the steps. Later three prison cells for debtors were built over the site of the three back rooms of the house on the west, and a platform or terrace over the two front rooms.

The south line of barracks was a single block. The external plan remained unchanged, but partitions and doorways were altered during the Portuguese and Arab periods, and again when the prison cells were built on top of the old outer walls. In the original arrangement there were only four rooms and seven doors. In the middle of the three smaller rooms at the west end there were pillars, of which the lower 45 cm remained, which were not present in the rooms at the east end. The block was modified by the conversion of the four rooms into six, with six doors, as it appears on the Lopes de Sá plan.

The original floors were 45 cm above the coral, which at the east was 1·52 m and at the west and centre 91 cm to 1·06 m below the cement floor of the prison cells. At the east end there was early-nineteenth-century china lying on the original floor, but in the centre and west end, floors with nineteenth-century china overlay an eighteenth-century deposit on the original floor. Between the original floor and the coral there were sherds of late-seventeenth-century porcelain. The first surviving floor, therefore, must be late-seventeenth-century, though the outer walls, I believe, belonged to the time of the first building of the Fort. The late-seventeenth-century floors at the west end were broken by a large number of pits containing nineteenth-century ceramic, which suggests that at some period the area was derelict. In one of the few early pits a fine polished red vase (Fig. 75. 5) was found. Outside the block, below the Museum veranda, the lowest levels contained Ming porcelain and had not been disturbed until the nineteenth century.

The reconstruction of the walls in rubble and red earth is dated to the nineteenth century by an East India Company coin of 1835, by sepia printed china, and a cartridge case with a mark $18^{II}_{R}73$. The east end is called 'tailor's workshop' and the west end 'stores' on the plan of 1899.

The west line of barracks consisted of two blocks which were separated by a flight of steps, 1·83 m wide, going up to the parapet walk (Pl. 8 A, B). At the south end were three rooms, described on the Lopes de Sá plan as the *casa do Vigario da Vasa*, or house of the *Vigario Forane*. The title meant 'external vicar', in this case perhaps the vicar who came from outside, not who went outside. In the account of the massacre of 1631, the Augustinian Prior of Mombasa is described as 'also *Vigario Forane* in the said fortress'.[13]

The first two rooms at the south end were filled with black earth and gravel, with sherds of K'ang Hsi porcelain and a single sherd with a rosette border, which I consider eighteenth-century. Outside was an open enclosure covered by a similar deposit to that found below the floor of the room, but with a few more eighteenth-century sherds. In the third room (the room of the stands), next to the steps, was a group of small platforms or stands, the purpose of which may have been to provide supports for boards on which rolls of cloth could be stacked. Cloth was the chief article of

[13] Freeman-Grenville (1967), p. 356.

trade and the major unit of currency on the coast. Unless it was raised from the floor it would have rotted with the damp. The loss by deterioration incurred in the cloth trade is constantly mentioned in the early-sixteenth-century factors' accounts of Sofala.[14] Alternatively, the room may have been the sacristry, where the chests to hold the church vestments were kept, which would have rested on the masonry stands.[15] The north and east walls of this room were rebuilt in the last quarter of the seventeenth century, in connection with the remodelling of the chapel and the construction of the enclosures behind it, and a new floor was laid over the old floor of the stands. The finds consisted largely of late-seventeenth-century porcelain, similar to the deposit over the steps to the north of it. In the eighteenth century, a house, also of three rooms, was built over the old house of the *Vigario Forane* with a floor 1·22 m above the original floor. At the back of the second room was a hearth and lavatory pit. This house remained in use until the construction of the veranda over the old parapet and parapet walk early in the nineteenth century.

The steps consisted of a flight of four, and this was reduced to two when the enclosures behind the chapel were built and the level raised. Several shallow square pits were found, cut either in the parapet itself or in the coral filling over the parapet walk. In one was a stone, probably a tombstone, carved with seriffed letters reading '. . . ENDO . . . KEFIC . . .' in two lines.

The barrack block at the north end of the west wall, beyond the steps, was demolished at the time of the construction of the enclosures behind the chapel. The stones were removed and the rubble left behind in a mound containing K'ang Hsi sherds which extended to the bastion of S. Filipe. This deposit was disturbed when the well was dug between the parapet and the cistern in the early eighteenth century.

THE WELL (Fig. 10 B)

The well is described on the Lopes de Sá plan as the 'well made by the Arabs', presumably between 1698 and 1728, which is confirmed by the finds. The ground around on the west and south, up to the level of the parapet walk, consisted of oily black earth and gravel, containing eighteenth-century sherds from the cleaning of the well. Only in the lowest level were there no eighteenth-century sherds. The well is 3·05 m square, with a tank on the west side, opening on to one of two narrow enclosures, which afforded privacy, between the well and the parapet walk. It was buttressed at the four corners and the original parapet would have stood about 1·37 m above ground level. There is normally about 45 cm of water standing in the bottom.

THE CHURCH (Figs. 9 B, 10 A; Pl. 9 A)

The church was built at the west end of the main court opposite the steps leading to the west parapet walk. This building served as the chapel of the Fort, although it is

[14] Lobato (1960). [15] Suggestion by R. Lewcock, A.R.I.B.A.

always referred to as a church. On the Cienfuegos plan it is called *ygreja parochial*, and in the Lopes de Sá plan the *madre sé*. The only other places of worship mentioned in Mombasa are the Augustinian Convent of S. António founded in 1617,[16] and the Church of the Misericordia. There may never have been a parish church, in which case the chapel would have been regarded canonically as the parish church, though the church in the convent was probably more generally used.

It was entered at the east end from the middle of the main court, and the altar was at the west end. The nave was 13·87 m long and 7·16 m wide, and was covered by a flat roof supported by pilasters at intervals of 3·89 m, 4·5 m, and 3·58 m down the long sides. The sanctuary was 4 m long and 5·3 m wide, entered by a 1·67 m opening. On the south side of the sanctuary, and projecting from the line of the south wall, was the baptistery shown on the 1636 plan. The bases of the pilasters, the floor of the sanctuary, and probably the whole inside of the building were painted with red ochre. In the nave were four low platforms 1·52 m long and 11 cm high, sited between the pilasters. Their purpose is unknown; if they were the foundations of side chapels, there would have been a space only 4 m wide for the regular services of the church.

The church may be the structure shown in the same position on the Herédia plan, but this was on a north-to south, instead of an east-to-west axis. It is not mentioned in the Bocarro/Rezende account, although it is shown on the plan—but with a tower at the south-east corner.

In the late seventeenth century the west end of the church, including the wall between the nave and sanctuary, was rebuilt and a step or platform made at the end of the nave, 22·9 cm above the old floor (Fig. 10 A). At the end of the sanctuary two large pillars with moulded bases (Fig. 27 B) were built to carry an arch over the altar, which backed on to the rear wall. There were two square-lined pits, 80 cm deep, in the floor of the later sanctuary, one in the entrance (early period), the other on the north side (later period). Both were empty and both were too small for burials.

Blocks of tufa, some with a rolled edge or a square margin, were found used as steps in front of the entrance, in the sanctuary, and in the enclosure to the north of the church. They may have come from the Comoro Islands and be fragments of seats or doorways. Traces of burials were found below the floor of the nave, damaged by later post-holes. There were no distinguishing features and they have not been further disturbed. According to the *Historia da Mombaça*,[17] on 24 August 1697 the Captain, António Mogo de Mello, knowing his end was near, handed over the Fort and two Portuguese children to the care of the young Arab Sheikh of Faza, and ordered his grave to be dug in the church, where he was buried four days later.

In an account of the fall of the Fort in 1698, given to the Viceroy a year afterwards by an Indian cook, Bras Fialho, he said that the church, which was being used as

[16] Rego, A. da Silva (1955).

[17] MS. in Biblioteca Nacionale de Lisboa, No. 584, in Strandes,/Wallwork, p. 226.

a powder-magazine, was blown up by a Portuguese soldier when the Arabs broke in.[18] This cannot be true, however, because when the Portuguese recovered the Fort in 1728, they were delighted to find it untouched, even to the chest containing vestments. It had been used as a store, and presumably continued to be used in this way after the return of the Arabs. Subsequently, a new floor was laid and a line of pillars set down the middle of the building to support the sagging roof. One of these was aligned with one pair of pilasters; the other three were merely on the axial line. The furthest to the east was larger, and was unrelated to the others. It may have been the base of a Portuguese monument. In the earth over it were found the remains of a furnace and a Maria Theresa dollar converted into a ring. At some period in the eighteenth century the altar at the west end was removed and a new entrance made between the pillars of the arch in front of it. A diagonal wall was built from the south pillar to the south jamb of the entrance to the sanctuary, blocking the way to the baptistery, which was demolished.

The church is not mentioned by Owen (1824), Guillain (1846), or von der Decken (1861) and it probably collapsed at the end of the eighteenth century. The walls at the west end survived to a height of 91 cm, as opposed to 15·2 cm at the east end, and it is possible that the west end continued to be used after the east end had disappeared. It may have been the powder-magazine mentioned in the dispatch of Captain W. F. Prideaux, dated 23 June 1875, after the bombardment of the Fort by the Royal Navy: 'The magazine is badly situated, being merely a square stone building near the centre of the Fort, and was struck by a couple of round shot . . .'[19]

At the time of the rebuilding of the church in the late seventeenth century, two enclosures were made between it and the barrack rooms, which may have had pent roofs supported on posts along the sides. No pattern could, however, be drawn from the post-holes, most of which seem to be of later date. The outer, or south, enclosure was immediately in front of the room of the stands, and in the south-west corner was a curious construction of two parallel walls with a gap between them. It was possibly a bucket latrine which would have had a wooden screen round it. The enclosure was entered by a wide door in its east wall next to the baptistery. The inner, the north enclosure, lay between the back of the church and the steps going up to the parapet walk, and was entered from a doorway in the west wall opposite these steps and from the south enclosure.

The site of both the church and the enclosures, and in fact the whole west end of the main court, was covered by a surface 61 cm above the floor of the sanctuary, sloping upwards to the parapet walk, which was about 1·65 m above the level of the sanctuary and the north enclosure. This was the final prison surface, laid over an earlier gravel surface which was an average 12·7 cm below it. Beneath this was

[18] *Arquivo Português Oriental* (new ed.), iv (ii) II, (1938), pp. 332–3.

[19] Letter from Ag. Consul-General Euan Smith to Earl of Derby, 25 July 1875—by courtesy of Sir John Gray.

a mixed deposit of red earth and rubble from the collapsed walls, with many sherds of eighteenth- and early-nineteenth-century porcelain, showing that it was not until the nineteenth century that the court was levelled over the debris of the Portuguese buildings. Below the floor of the enclosures was Ming porcelain lying on the natural coral of the hill. There were many pits, some lined, probably latrines, others unlined rubbish pits, which would have belonged to the huts mentioned by Owen and von der Decken as filling the main court. In the north enclosure were two skeletons, which had been buried in the eighteenth or early nineteenth century, apparently on top of each other in opposite directions in the east–west position—an extremely unusual form of burial, to say the least.

THE CISTERN (Fig. 10 A and B)

The cistern was a rectangular structure 4·3 by 6 m and 12·20 m deep, cut in the coral ridge on which the Fort is built, with a barrel-vault. It was begun between 1601 and 1603,[20] and was frequently repaired. When the church was rebuilt, the opportunity was taken to improve the supply of water to the cistern. The north end of the west wall of the sanctuary was doubled, presumably to carry a tank, from which water was led down a vertical drain in the north wall of the north enclosure into a horizontal drain running into the cistern (Fig. 10 A). A small open tank, with steps at each end in Arab style, was built against the north wall of the church from which a drain led, most unhygienically, into the cistern. The open tank would have contributed to the casualties during the siege, most of which were due to disease rather than enemy action. The cistern was apparently in good order during the siege because there were no complaints of lack of water. It went out of use in the later eighteenth century, and Owen mentions finding it with great difficulty among the huts surrounding it.

The sanctuary drain was used during the early prison period, when the cistern end was broken to receive a cement drain leading from the twentieth-century level above it. Later, cement channels carried water from the roofs of buildings in S. Filipe. The wall round the top of the cistern was raised to create a washing enclosure for prisoners, and an iron girder was laid along the top of the barrel-vault to hold a pulley. Early in 1940, when it appeared likely that Mombasa would be bombed, the cistern was filled with water by the Fire Brigade, in case the mains were destroyed and there was a shortage. Some months later the medical authorities realized that this reserve water supply was a fine breeding ground for mosquitoes. Fortunately, fears of bombs and mosquitoes were equally groundless: there were no hostile attacks, and when inspected the cistern was found to be empty; the water had disappeared through a leak in the bottom.

The third independent Mazrui governor, Masud bin Nasir (1762–87) was buried near the flagstaff in the middle of the main court,[21] but no trace of the tomb has survived.

[20] Axelson (1960), p. 79.

[21] al ʿAmin bin ʿAli al Mazrui, tr. Ritchie (unpublished).

At the east end of the main court the modern ticket office has been built on a group of prison cells, which themselves were built over an earlier construction. In the grey earth below the floor of the cells were found K'ang Hsi sherds, and fragments of a case bottle, resting on an earth surface. The walls may have belonged to the buildings shown on the Herédia plan, south of the gate. No trace has yet been found of the two blocks with central courts between the gate and the south barrack block in the Rezende plan, and they do not appear on the Cienfuegos or Lopes de Sá plans.

Between the ticket office and the gatehouse is an interesting door, 91 cm wide (Pl. 14 A) with two panelled leaves. Each sunken panel is decorated with a palm-leaf motif in relief and has short iron spikes at the corners. The workmanship is clearly local, and the door is not in its original position. It could be eighteenth- or even seventeenth-century, but no parallels are known to me. In the tympanum is an inscription, commemorating the proclamation of the Protectorate:

BRITISH EAST AFRICAN PROTECTORATE,
Proclaimed 1st July 1895
A. H. HARDINGE Esq. C.B.
Commissioner

Arthur Hardinge, later Sir Arthur Hardinge, was Consul-General in Zanzibar and the first Governor (called Her Majesty's Commissioner) of the Protectorate and Colony of Kenya (1895–1900).[22, 23]

[22] Hardinge (1928). [23] Mungeam (1966).

3. *The Passages to the Outwork*

THE PASSAGE OF THE ARCHES (Figs. 12, 15 A and B, 16 A; Pl. 10 A)

THE Passage of the Arches began at a point in the main court opposite the gate, and descended to the outwork facing the harbour, a fall of about 12·20 m in 42·67 m. The passage was 4·27 m wide at the court end, but was narrowed to 2·13 m by natural buttresses of coral 6·10 m from the outlet. Beyond, it widened again to an average of 2·74 m before passing through a narrow tunnel 2·44 m long, to emerge at the back of the outwork. Between buttresses and tunnel, ledges 76 cm wide were left on each side to carry the walls of a barrel-vault. The depth of the cutting varied from about 46 cm in the court to 7·31 m at the tunnel end.

The sides of the passage were reasonably smooth at the upper end, but were very irregular in the middle section, particularly on the north side. At places where the wall of the passage met the floor, projections were left, hard pieces of coral to be removed by somebody other than the digger at the time. At the end, beyond the buttresses, there was a return to regularity.

The entrance to the tunnel was rounded but asymmetrical—the spirit of 'good enough' was obviously present in the Fort at the time of the construction of the passage. The width of the tunnel was 1·67 m on the inside and 2·74 m on the outside. In the coral face at the end were sockets for the frame of a door and a socket with a diagonal slot on the opposite side for the beam which barred it. At the inner entrance was a sill with a drain below it, and outside two steps led down to the outwork. The tunnel was continued as a cutting in the outwork outside the Fort for a distance of two metres.

At the end of the passage the coral face was vertical, 5·49 m high, approximately the same height as the coral buttresses and 2·44–3·05 m above the ledges on each side. It is strange that, though there are several references to the excavation of the ditch, there is no mention of the excavation of the passage, which would appear to have been as formidable a task and more interesting to report.

On the seaward face the wall of coral blocks above natural coral was strongly battered and rose 11 m above the outwork to the floor of the Captain's House. The end wall, above the tunnel, had been rebuilt at the level of this floor in coral-block masonry, and would appear to be Portuguese. In the middle was an oculus or round air vent (Fig. 14). This is a familiar feature of the west façade of Portuguese churches in India in the seventeenth century,[1] but in East Africa the only examples known to me are in nineteenth-century Arab houses at Kilwa Kivinje.

[1] Mitterwallner, (1964).

The passage (Fig. 12) was spanned by three arches dividing it into sections, 4·27 m, 7·31 m, and 5·18 m long from west to east, to carry the walls of the rooms above it. All three were semicircular, and were built with untapered voussoirs with a 15 cm face, unlike the arch at the base of the Passage of the Steps or the arch of the passage in S. Mateus. The two inner arches sprang from the coral face on each side, but the third rose from pillars standing on projecting coral buttresses. The first two had centres 61 cm below the springing line. At a later period the floor over this section collapsed, and when it was rebuilt the arches were strengthened by a second row of voussoirs on the inside, 33 cm thick.

The arch on the pillars was slightly elevated with the centre 15 cm above the springing line, and rose from the back, not the face, of the pillars. The pillars were considerably smaller than the coral buttresses, and no attempt had been made to screen the junction. A possible explanation of these anomalies is that it was a relieving arch, not an arch of communication. The original arch with the wall above it would have been removed when the level of the passage rose to the level of the pillars, and the room in the outer section could be reached from the new level of the passage.[2] If this view is correct, the transformation would have been carried out in the second quarter of the nineteenth century, on the evidence of the china found below the level of the pillars. Any other explanation would involve the separation of this arch from the others, which I believe is inadmissible. Above the arch is a doorway without rebates with a wooden lintel, opening into the room over the outer section. It is nineteenth-century, and belongs to the period when the passage had been filled up to this level.

The middle section of the passage was the longest and, I believe, was open to the sky. On the north side foundations were found below the present room wall, which do not belong to it and perhaps were part of a parapet. Rooms were built on the north, west, and south sides, but the area above the passage remained open until late in the nineteenth century. The lower parts of the wall on the south side and the wall above the arch on the west belong to these rooms, which had square-headed casements opening on to the passage.

On the south side of the middle section was an ammunition store, approached by three steps up from the passage (Fig. 13 A). It consisted of two rectangular chambers, one 5 m by 3·6 m, the other 5·18 m by 3·0 m, and both 9·4 m high, and extended 7·31 m from the passage to the wall on the north side of the Passage of the Steps. The sides were nearly vertical, and the roof, which was about 1·83 m below the surface level above it, was concave. On the east side of the outer chamber were two depressions in the ground for rotary quern mats. This is the magazine mentioned by Bocarro/Rezende: 'Further within the walls is a magazine, cut in the rock itself, to keep provisions and munitions. This is a very damp place because it is deep below the ground, and for this reason it is seldom that anything is kept in it.' The criticism

[2] I owe this suggestion to T. W. Mackenzie, A.R.I.B.A.

is just. The cannon-balls found in the magazine were in far worse condition than most of those found in other levels in the excavations.

The section of the passage before the tunnel is interesting on account of the rock ledges on each side, on which rested coral-block walls which would have supported a barrel-vault. The vault would have been approximately at the level of the base of the buttresses, so a space large enough for a room would have existed below the floor of the Captain's House. This room, with or without an opening on the middle section of the passage, was probably used as a store and could only have been entered by a trapdoor from the room above. It is not known when the vault collapsed, but some large stones were found with late-seventeenth-century ceramics in the mud at the bottom of the passage, so it may have fallen early in the eighteenth century.

The passage is shown on the Herédia and Teixeira plans as a flight of steps, but there is no sign of steps today, except in the last section. It is described by Bocarro/Rezende, but not shown on the plan: 'This fortress has, as can be seen from the plan, an outwork which goes down to the harbour and which can be defended by soldiers who go out of the Fort by a postern gate [*puerta falsa*] which emerges in the middle of the outwork.' It was up this passage that Dom Jeronimo and his followers came to murder the Captain on 16 August 1631, and later Marinho recommended that it should be properly defended: 'As for the gate which is below the Fort in the outwork, by which the enemy entered who made themselves masters of the Fort, this gate also should be secured against incursion by means of a cannon set in the mouth of the passage.'[3]

The passage is mentioned during the siege in connection with the landing of supplies from the relief ships in January 1697: 'The entrance was so narrow that the boxes had to be broken up outside, which was the cause of great loss.'[4] It was probably also used in the sorties carried out by Joseph Pereira de Brito, but it may have been blocked before the end of the siege. A gate has to be guarded, and with the diminishing garrison a blocking of the gate would have been an obvious way of economizing in manpower. Whether it was subsequently reopened, either by the Arabs, or by the Portuguese during their reoccupation of 1728–9, is uncertain. It is, however, marked on the Lopes de Sá plan in the middle of the back wall of the outwork as 'Postern gate for bringing in supplies from the shore' (*puerta falsa para a introducão das socorros da marinha*). The gate is last mentioned, curiously enough, by Guillain, but by this time it must have been blocked: 'At the base of this (curtain wall) there is a gate protected by a sort of crenellated tambour, or outwork.'

At the gate-end of the passage was a deep deposit of mud from the drainage of the court after the gate had been blocked. In the mud was found a typical collection of late-seventeenth-century ceramics: K'ang Hsi porcelain, Portuguese blue-and-white maiolica, Persian blue-and-white, the corresponding local earthenware, a few sherds of Ming porcelain, and the contemporary polished black and red wares. The Portuguese

[3] Marinho. [4] Strandes (tr. Wallwork), p. 222.

blue-and-white included the base of a plate with the arms of a Portuguese bishop, Cardoso, quartering Teixeira and perhaps del Matos (Pl. 42. 1). Without change of stratum, the sherd pattern changed to eighteenth-century with the appearance of sherds of porcelain in rose-pink and blue-and-white with rosette borders, or comb and chrysanthemum pattern; also pale yellow and green glazed earthenware and bowls with a rough brown glazed surface. Then, with the mud from the court still accumulating, appeared the characteristic sherds of the early nineteenth century: porcelain with trellised medallions in iron red, green and yellow, blue-and-white with sprays in a trellis, and the 'shou' character pattern.

The ammunition store was filled to within 46 cm of the roof with the same deposit. On a cushion of mud, 12·7 cm above the plastered floor, 2,258 cast-iron balls were found, of which 1,124 were for a four-inch cannon; and a few eighteenth-century sherds. The only other find was a large rotary quern (Fig. 86. 26). The upper stone was on the floor and the lower stone on top of the mud. They fit perfectly and are a pair, but they are separated by about 100 years of mud. The mud could only have flowed into the store with the filling of the passage outside, but when the passage was excavated it was found that the mud level did not reach the sill of the store. Evidently, at some later date, the mud in the passage had been removed, exposing the lower stone which was placed on top of the mud together with a broken jar base and a truncated late-seventeenth-century culverin, as a barrier against children or animals.

Lying over the mud in the passage were large stones and brown earth, and in the first section slabs of broken plaster from the floor of the room above it. In this deposit were many sherds of English china: plain cream dishes, blue- or green-bordered plates, willow-pattern and other print wares; pink-and-blue lustre, banded mugs and bowls, and gold on white. The porcelain and glazed earthenware were similar to that found in the mud beneath them. Across the mouth of the ammunition store, in the passage, was a 4½-inch late-eighteenth-century cannon, 1·98 m long, with the mouth blown off (Fig. 81. 5). The touch-hole had been mended with a brass inset. It could have been one of the Mazrui guns used in the battles with Saiyid Said. The building debris may be the result of the bombardment of Saiyid Said in 1827, but the quantity of china would indicate a later date for the closing of the deposit. English and European china are mentioned by Guillain in 1846, as beginning to replace Chinese porcelain.[5] I doubt if much would have reached Mombasa before its incorporation in Saiyid Said's dominions.

The deposit was covered by a rough and undulating earth surface sloping downwards and then slightly upwards at a level about 46 cm above the top of the coral buttresses. Over this was another deposit of mud, red, or grey with streaks of yellow, containing similar sherds and also sherds of flowered china, including sherds with the mark of the Utzschneider factory opened in 1858, so this stratum cannot be earlier than the third quarter of the nineteenth century. By this time the passage had a relatively

[5] Guillain, Part III, p. 347.

level surface 3·05 m below the soffit of the arches. About 1·50 m above this surface there were slots for a beam in the coral wall of the passage on the inner side of the middle arch. The passage at this time may have been used as a cattle byre; it is difficult to think of any other use, in view of the roughness of the surface. 'An old arch choked with rubbish' is mentioned by Richard Thornton (p. 77) when he visited the Fort with von der Decken, so in 1861 the passage was still visible.[6]

Subsequently, the openings below the arches on both sides of the middle section were blocked, perhaps with the intention of laying a floor when the level had risen to the sill of the casement above the middle arch. However, only 30 cm of grey earth had accumulated before the bombardment of 1875. When the Fort was taken over in 1895, the debris caused by the bombardment, including fragments of the painted dado of the dais outside the audience room, was thrown on top of the grey earth, and a new floor laid a little above the sills of the casements.

The remains of the floor of the room above the east section, which had collapsed early in the nineteenth century, were found covered with the same grey earth as was found in the middle of the passage. Over them was lying a 3·66 m deposit of fallen masonry, consisting of the roof of the room and other debris from the 1875 bombardment. In the rubble were found East India Company coins of 1835 and 1853. The Guillain and Krapf sketches show a palm-frond roof over the middle of the platform in the position of the passage. This roof was later removed and a lime-concrete floor built to join the two ends of the platform.

At the west end of the passage, the debris of the floor over the first section was found to contain late-nineteenth-century china, covered with the grey earth which had been thrown in to fill the cavity. The passage did not appear in the 1899 plan, but the wall over the westernmost arch (the old west wall of the room over the passage) is shown as the perimeter wall of the prison enclosure. Later the perimeter wall was moved out to the north-west corner of the audience room of the Mazrui, and the level raised another 61 cm.

West of the first section, and leading up to the main court, the same succession of deposits was found. In the grey earth there were two late-nineteenth- or early-twentieth-century burials with heads to the east.

THE PASSAGE OF THE STEPS (Figs. 15 A, 24 D; Pl. 10 B)

The Passage of the Steps was made at the south end of the rectangular projection. It consisted of more than twenty-two steps, 3·96 m wide, cut in the coral and descending to an arched doorway, 1·45 m high and 1·75 m wide, with tapered voussoirs, 25 by 20 cm, which was situated 91 cm from the south-east corner of the projection. It was bounded on the south by the south wall of the projection and on the north by a plastered retaining wall with a rounded top. Soon after it was built, the retaining

[6] Diary of Richard Thornton, unpublished. By courtesy of H. A. Fosbrooke.

wall had to be strengthened by a buttress which partially obscured the left jamb of the doorway. The buttress wall had the same red-brown plaster as the original south wall and cannot be much later.

The original south wall of the projection by the doorway was 6·40 m high, but at the top of the steps it became a mere kerb or plinth and then turned south towards S. Mateus, in the same way that the north wall of the projection became the kerb along the east face of S. Matias. On the north side of the steps, high up in the wall over the buttress was an arched recess, which I believe was a niche for a statue.

The only mention of the Passage of the Steps is on the Cienfuegos plan, although it is one of the earliest structures in the Fort. The fact that it emerged 3·05 m above the outwork suggests that it was made before the outwork was levelled. The quality of the arch at the bottom is comparable to that of the arch in S. Mateus, and is infinitely superior to the arches of the other passage (Fig. 24 D; Pl. 10 B). The passage must have been open to the sky when it was in use, since there were no signs of supports for a roof on the walls on either side. The Cienfuegos plan shows a black square at approximately the position where the steps began, with the legend '*puerta sourança quebra a la couraça*', which may be translated 'blocked door overlooking the outwork'. The Cienfuegos plan I have considered to be earlier than 1648 because of the absence of cavaliers.

The passage was filled in when the Captain's House was extended to the south wall of the projection (Fig. 15 B). In the filling was found late Ming porcelain but no K'ang Hsi. There was no difference between the sherds from this filling and the sherds from the filling of the bastions. Its later history is included in the account of the Captain's House and the Gun-platform (Chapter 4).

4. *The Captain's House, Gun-Platform, and Audience Room of the Mazrui*

(Figs. 13 B and 14–16 A; Pls. 11 A and B, 12 A)

THE Captain's House was built along the front of the rectangular platform, overlooking the outwork. There was no protecting parapet and the building was exposed to the fire of enemy ships in the harbour or a hostile battery on the other side of the creek, a distance of about a quarter of a mile. This is in fact what did occur during the great siege, in the course of which the east wall on the north side of the Passage of the Arches was destroyed and the house so badly damaged that the Arabs did not think it worth while to repair it when they captured the Fort. The stump of this wall, 1·52 m thick, was found by burrowing into the mass of lime and rubble backing the foundation wall of the later gun-platform. The only part of the north end of the house to survive was the lower section of the north wall with a window similar to a gun-port, but with sockets for shutters (Fig. 29 A, B). The walls were 3·35 m high and carried a roof of semicircular 'spanish' tiles, of which thousands of pieces were found in the excavations. The northern and southern ranges, divided by the Passage of the Arches, were not homogeneous in construction. The inner walls of the northern section were built of coursed coral blocks, like the barrack rooms, while the southern section, apart from the wall above the Passage of the Steps, was of plastered rubble like the church. In addition, the inner walls of the two sections were not in the same line, which one would have expected if they had been built at the same time.

The north range was approached by a door in the south wall of the room (A) over the inner section of the passage (Fig. 15 B). The original floor at the south end of the room would have been carried on beams laid across the passage and resting on the coral face of the cutting. When this floor collapsed, holes were made in the spandrels of the arches for the beams of the new floor, to avoid disturbing the south wall. The new floor survived until the latter half of the nineteenth century, and when it collapsed the cavity was filled with grey earth up to the level of the old floor. The floor at the north end of the room rested on solid coral. Here the plaster of the second floor was scorched, probably by the rockets used in the bombardment of 1875. In the filling above it were found rows of 18-pounder cannon-balls.

The east and west walls of the room were curiously out of line with the arches, and the room was 30·5 cm wider at the north compared with the south end. This kind of informality is not uncommon in the Arab buildings of the coast, but rarely to this degree of error, and may be due to rebuilding. In the east wall there was an opening or casement looking down into the central section of the passage. Further north there was a door leading into a long room running west to east (Room B), with another door at the east end. Across the room ran a square covered drain which emptied into the passage.

Beyond this room was an L-shaped ante-room (C), which was equipped with a row of niches, Swahili *kidaka*, along the east wall at a height of 1·75 m from the floor. Near the north-east corner was a masonry pedestal, 91 cm high, which may have served as a place for washing utensils. There would have been a drain through the outer wall, which was destroyed with the upper part of the wall in the 1875 bombardment. The room was approached by two other doorways in the west wall, both leading from what was an open enclosure on the north side of the long room. Shortly after the house was built, on the evidence of the Ming sherds in the filling, the northern of these doors was blocked, the end of the room shut off by a wall parallel to the north wall, and the space between it and the wall filled in. On the top of this wall was a groove for a drain, showing that the roof terminated at this point, leaving a 1·22 m wide platform. Near the west end of the north wall was a chamfered edge, which would appear to be the jamb of a wide gun-port. The purpose of these works was apparently to provide a solid base for cannon used to bombard ships which had succeeded in getting past the guns on the seaward side and were entering the harbour. At the back of the wall between the L-shaped room (C) and the outer room was a rough revetment wall of large stones enclosing a filling of black earth and rubbish. This might have been a temporary firing-step made during the siege when the outer wall had collapsed.

The outer room (D), embraced by the L-shaped room, was entered by a doorway near the corner of the L. It would have been lit by a row of windows similar to the window in the north wall (Fig. 29 A, B). From it a door led by a step up to a room carried on wooden beams over the outer section of the Passage of the Arches. This room (E) was also entered by a narrow doorway from the L-shaped room.

The south range consisted of a room immediately to the south of the Passage of the Arches (F), and later a room above the Passage of the Steps (G). The only features of the first room were two arched recesses, 43 cm from the floor, which were intended for jars. They were set on each side of a door in the west wall. The north wall above the Passage of the Arches demanded continuous attention. There were two doors in it, with sills of different heights, which are unlikely to have been in use at the same time. The original floor had sunk and the second was worn down to it. The older of the two doorways, that is, the one with the lower sill, had a sloping architrave with traces of a plastered volute moulding. The south wall of the room was built of blocks, like the north range, and stood on the reinforced wall of the Passage of the Steps. In the middle was a blocked doorway leading into this room over the passage. The blocking of the doorway indicated that the end room was at some time separated from the rest of the house. Its south wall, which was the south wall of the projection, was rebuilt after the bombardment of 1875; the west wall had disappeared, but the tufa sill of a doorway near the south end of it had survived.

The Captain's House is shown on the Herédia, Teixeira, and Bocarro/Rezende plans. On the Cienfuegos plan a building is shown at the north end of the projection, in the position of the room over the inner section of the passage and extending some way to the south of it. Evidence of this may be the room over the first section of the passage.

The house was badly damaged in the siege, and when the Arabs took the Fort they filled the outer rooms with lime-concrete and rubble to the height of the inner wall, making a high gun-platform (Fig. 16 A). The north range of rooms had suffered most and the rebuilt outer wall was backed by a 2·74 m thick mass of lime-concrete. On the north side of the Passage of the Arches a plain retaining wall was built, without an inner face.

Below the floors of the rooms in the north and south ranges were sherds of late Ming porcelain, but no K'ang Hsi. On the floors and in the filling of the rooms were quantities of K'ang Hsi porcelain, Portuguese blue-and-white maiolica, and roof tiles. In the south chamber were a few sherds of the white bowls with the so-called 'secret' pattern under the glaze and blue diamond border, which I think are early-eighteenth- rather than late-seventeenth-century. On the plaster on the south wall of this room was a red-and-black diamond decoration, which is more Arab than Portuguese, and it is possible that the room was not filled in immediately, as the outer wall here was intact. The reconstruction was, however, completed and the Captain's House a thing of the past by the time of the Lopes de Sá plan (1728).

The platform was continued above the Passage of the Arches, presumably on rounded timbers. The room below may have remained, entered from the room on the south side so long as it existed, and subsequently by a trapdoor from the platform. The platform was 6·4 m wide at the north end and 4·42 m at the south. The wall, 2·13 m high, was crowned by a line of crenellations, 46 cm wide, with gable tops, irregular and sometimes lopsided. There were two pairs of gun-ports, on each side of the Passage of the Arches, and a line of musket-slits (Fig. 29 I, J). At the south-east corner, outside the later turret, the earlier raised corner can be seen with its hollowed slopes, similar to the corners of an Arab tomb, such as the pillar tomb beside the Palace at Gedi.[1]

Some time in the eighteenth century, or as late as the early nineteenth century, as a result of the bombardment of Saiyid Said, the outer wall of the southern section, from the Passage of the Arches to the south-east corner, began to collapse. Before repairs could be carried out, it was necessary to excavate part of the filling. The inner face was cleared of earth and a new wall built, increasing the thickness of the old wall by 38 to 46 cm but not reaching the original floor. This also involved cutting off the ends of the two short walls. In the excavated and redeposited earth were found sherds

[1] Kirkman (1963), Pl. VII.

of porcelain with decoration in rose-pink and blue-and-white chrysanthemum designs. These are typical late-eighteenth-century types.

Subsequently, turrets or small watchtowers were built at each corner. The south-east turret had vertical slits and was entered by three steps under a rounded arch. It was surmounted by a small cupola with a four-sided dart-shaped finial, such as is often seen in Muslim cemeteries. On the inside walls were pictures of dhows, incised or in carbon black. The original north-east turret was destroyed in the 1875 bombardment. The turrets were an addition to the wall of the crenellations and were not shown on the Owen sketch (1824). They appear on the Krapf and Guillain sketches (1846) with the existing finials, and were probably built in the last years of the Mazrui between 1824 and 1837.

In the nineteenth century a room was built on the platform, which may have been Tanggai's *baraza*, referred to by Thornton in 1861 as 'a good large room with a fine view of the sea'.[2] On the 1899 plan this is described as a 'tailor's workshop'. The construction of the room involved raising the wall along the northern two-thirds of the platform and adding another row of crenellations above the old, 5 cm wider and taller (Fig. 14). Small slits were made in the new crenellations in the centre of the wall above the Passage of the Arches, similar to those in the north wall of the gate-house. A photograph of 1894[3] shows the incomplete row of crenellations. (Pl. 5 B)

The bombardment of 1875 made large holes in the two flanks of the platform but, by the caprice of war, left the main face unscathed apart from the north-east turret. Fragments of unexploded fuses from early Armstrong shells were found embedded in the plastered foundation wall of the south flank. One had entered the wall from the outside, the other from the inside over the east wall at a plunging angle of 45°. Almost the whole of the middle of the south face was destroyed. It was rebuilt without an inside face and backed with earth up to the wall on the north side of the Passage of the Steps. On the north side, where damage was not so extensive, a wide pit was made in the platform and filled with rubble and lime as a foundation for a new wall. A similar rough 'patch' was found below the wall in the re-entrant angle of S. Filipe and the east wall of S. Mateus. The north-east corner turret was rebuilt with the original finial, which had apparently fallen off but was undamaged.

During the early prison period a small room, the first European cell, was built against the north wall with a window which, appropriately, overlooked the Mombasa Club, one of the oldest colonial buildings in Kenya. In those days, it was considered extravagant to make provision for more than one criminal European at any one time. Later the estimate was raised to four and accommodation was built in S. Alberto. The cell and Tanggai's *baraza* were eventually pulled down and a line of cells built all along the platform. The raised wall and crenellations were then extended over the remaining third of the seaward face. Considerably later a room was built against the

[2] Diary of Richard Thornton, unpublished. By courtesy of H. A. Fosbrooke.

[3] In the National Maritime Museum, Greenwich.

south wall as an addition to the prison warder's quarters, which had been built over the south-east corner tower and are shown on the 1899 plan.

The area west of these rooms may have survived the Omani attacks of 1828 and 1834, but it was badly damaged in the British bombardment of 1875, and was not rebuilt until the prison period. The long room (B) on the north side of the middle section of the Passage of the Arches was rebuilt, with a door in the west wall above the old door. The casements which had opened on to the passage from the room over the first section and from the room or open area on the south side, were blocked, and a new room, or rather cell, was made over the passage, with a door in the west wall.

To the south of the passage is an area extending to the wall on the north side of the Passage of the Steps, which is shown as occupied by a prison cell in the 1899 plan. Below it were the remains of a plaster floor. In the middle were found the stumps of two square pillars which would have supported the roof, but there was no evidence of any relation between the pillars and the surrounding walls, and no sign was found of a west wall, other than the later prison wall. It is possible that in the late Portuguese period there was a room in this area, represented today only by the stumps of the pillars, which was demolished when the Captain's House was filled in. There is no indication of it in the Cienfuegos or Lopes de Sá plans.

The wall on the inner side of the Passage of the Steps was composite. At the east end was a buttress attached to the west wall of the Captain's House, with a plaster cornice high up in the wall above the steps. Running half-way along the line of the passage were three courses of blocks, an extension of the buttress of the cornice, but beyond and above the blocks was rubble masonry. The blocks may be the remains of the Portuguese building of the pillars, or of a supposed earlier outer wall (see p. 8).

This area was bounded on the west by a wall and a portico which fronted the main court. In the wall were two doorways, which were subsequently blocked. One of them was the entrance to the area, the other was the door leading to the Passage of the Steps. When the passage was filled in, the doors in the perimeter wall were blocked, and a new portico was built with an elaborate doorway, attached pillars, and seats along the wall (Pl. 11 B). The first portico had a sloping roof supported on pillars, of which two remained and were incorporated in the later building (Figs. 25 B and 26 A). These two pillars were spaced on either side of the blocked door and must therefore be associated with it, rather than with the later door. At the north end of the portico are the remains of an early structure which I do not understand. It consists of a kerb with a rounded back above the Passage of the Arches and what appear to be two steps at its east end.

The doorway of the new portico had a rounded arch standing on two pillars projecting from the wall, and was surmounted by a horizontal moulding with a slight cavetto (Fig. 26 B and E). In each spandrel was a coral boss carved with a marigold or sunflower. Against the wall were three attached pillars with capitals and bases, similar to those of the doorway (Figs. 25 A and 26 C, G, H, I), one in each corner and one between the doorway and the south-east corner. In front of the pillars was a masonry bench with a rounded edge, a refinement otherwise unknown in East Africa. North of the doorway and round the north wall there was the normal bench with a straight edge, but this was a repair. Above the bench on the south and west walls was a painted dado of lotus tendrils in red and green (Pl. 12 A). The remains of moulding at the level of the capitals of the attached columns is visible on the north wall, broken by the insertion of a later window. In the Arab period the pillars were strengthened and a bench with a square edge made between the north pillar and the south end of the room. The space between the north-west corner and the pillar next to it was left open as the entrance from the main court, when the portico became the audience room.

The lime-concrete roof was supported on squared timbers on four of which were carved Arabic texts. Around the east and south walls was a wall plate carved with another Arabic text and a decoration of tendril scroll with broad leaves on the under side. The texts consisted of poetical thoughts and verses from the Koran, in five groups, which have been translated by the Revd. J. M. Ritchie. The inscription begins at the west end of the wall plate at the south end of the room and continues along the wall plate on the east wall. The first words at the end of the beam are lost in the wall, but are the opening of the Kalima or creed, followed by dedicatory verses which read:

> To its owner happiness and safety
> and length of life so long as there coos a dove.
>
> And perpetual glory without
> Any humiliation in it,
>
> And prosperity until the
> Day of Resurrection.

This is followed by Koran *sura* xlviii. 1–4.

There are four carved beams in the roof, one at each end and two resting on the pillars in the west wall. The beam at the south end is carved with *sura* iii. 25, 26; the next beam on the south pillar, with *sura* cviii, *Surat al Kawthar*, and *sura* cxvi, *Surat al Ikhlas*; and the beam at the north end with *sura* ii. 256, the well-known Throne verse. On the beam resting on the north pillar is a poem, which in translation reads:

> I wearied myself with the building of my house and made it my home.
> Then I passed one day by a graveyard and my heart said to me,
> You will be moved from there to here. In this there is a moral.
> Be patient in the face of all the perplexity of misfortunes.
> It may be when the affairs of life become twisted and tied in knots,
> The decree descends from heaven and they are unloosed.

All the inscriptions are partially buried in the west wall, where they begin, and no room has been left for the end of the beam. This does not mean that the beams were made for another roof, but merely that the direction or workmanship was incompetent. The inscription usually starts well but becomes crowded and slovenly as it proceeds; the carver was evidently worried about his ability to fit the text on to the beam. Mr. Ritchie informed me that a South Arabian claimed that it was a desideratum of good writing to crowd the words at the end of the lines, as if the paper was not big enough for what you wanted to say.

There is another carved wooden beam in Fort Jesus, the original position of which is unknown. It is 6·27 m long and 20 cm square with a scroll of rosettes on two adjacent sides, an inscription on the third, and one side blank. About 20 cm from the end of the beam there is a hole, 12 cm in diameter, perhaps so that it could be moved on a pivot, like a barrier. The inscription consists of the pious invocation, the *bismillah* followed by *sura* xlviii. 1, 2; ix. 18; xxxiii. 56; iii. 163, 164; lxi. 13; xiii. 12; and ends with the final statement of the creed. Mr. Ritchie pointed out that there are minor variations from the Koranic text, showing that the carver was working from memory. The most significant is the use of the fifth form instead of the passive of the first form of the root *ruzag*. This is a common variation from the classical in the speech of South Arabia generally. In smaller letters is written the date, Wednesday, fifteenth Ramadhan 1248. The inscription was made, therefore, in 1833, during the last years of the Mazrui, but the scrolls are by another hand and may be older.

Later, when an upper storey was added in the nineteenth century, the spaces between the pillars were filled in to support the added weight. Square windows with shutters were made in the west and north, and at the south end of the east wall. The present floor is of hydraulic lime, which is unlikely to be earlier than the prison period. The original lime floor is 15 cm below it.

On the walls, incised haphazardly in the plaster, were pictures of dhows, perhaps recording the successful performance of the Pilgrimage. These are illustrated and discussed, with similar sketches which have been found on walls and mosques in East Africa, by Garlake.[4] They occur in other places in the Muslim world—rather unexpectedly at the Khan al Harir in Damascus, built in 1572.[5] No satisfactory explanation for these drawings has yet been produced, if indeed an explanation is required. Ships were, of course, as much part of the mental background of the Mombasans of the seventeenth and eighteenth centuries, as are horses of girls educated at private schools in the England of the twentieth century. However, I feel that dhows, unlike the quadrupeds, have some special significance in popular belief whereby, on certain occasions or in some circumstances, it was merit-worthy to make a picture of a dhow on a wall. If this is so, it seems strange that it has never been recorded in writing in any part of the Islamic world.

[4] Garlake, and Garlake, (1964).
[5] Sauvaget (1932), p. 83.

South of the door, high up on the wall, was painted an inscription recording the pilgrimage to Mecca of the fifth Mazrui governor, Ahmad bin Muhammad, in the year 1793. The inscription reads:

> 1208 A.H.
> Ahmad bin Muhammad bin 'Uthman al Mazrui
> performed the Pilgrimage
> and visited the grave of the Prophet.
> He departed the 11th day Saturday of Rama-
> dhan 1208 A.H. None of the governors before
> him had made this journey. The Governor
> arrived on a day (or in the month of) Rabia al
> Akhar after a journey of 68 nights.
> (Trans. Revd. J. M. Ritchie)

This structure is an exotic among the buildings of the coast, and the decorative features indicate that the builder was an Indian. The date of its construction is uncertain. The fact that it is Indian in style has little relevance to the question of whether it was built by a Portuguese Captain or an Arab Governor, since either could have employed an Indian mason. In favour of the Portuguese is its monumental character at the entrance to an important residence and its position opposite the door at the south range of the Captain's House. In favour of the Arabs is its absence from the Lopes de Sá plan, and an acceptable simplification of the history of the building. The evidence of the sherds below the area between it and the Captain's House, and from the main court outside the west wall, would suggest a date in the eighteenth century. In these levels were sherds of local earthenware with a red ochre finish, and mixed seventeenth- and eighteenth-century porcelain. The excavation below the floor of the room produced only the inconclusive evidence of a few sherds of jars, which also were more likely to be eighteenth- than seventeenth-century, but the floor could have been relaid. On balance I prefer to regard it as Portuguese.

The negotiations which led up to the British Protectorate of Mombasa from 1824 to 1826 took place in this room, which is described by Owen as follows:

> After passing the large vaulted entry in which some Arab soldiers were stationed, I was conducted to a building which appeared to have been originally occupied by the main guard, though now reduced in height and covered by an ornamental roof. This served as a council chamber. The Arabs sat on huge stone benches projecting from the walls while, as a mark of attention, two old-fashioned three-cornered chairs were brought in for the accommodation of myself and companions.

This is the only building in the Fort with stone benches and a decorated roof, though why it should be called the main guardroom I do not know. The three-cornered chairs were of a carved and pierced black wood in north Indian style. There are some fine examples in the Governor's Palace at Mozambique and in the Red Fort at Lourenço Marques. I saw two in Mombasa at the 1960 installation of the Timam or Head of the Twelve Tribes of Mombasa—possibly these chairs themselves.[6]

Outside the east wall of the audience room were two structures, one on each side of the monumental doorway. One was a round pit or sink at the north and draining into the Passage of the Arches. It stood on a small platform edged with blocks of tufa, similar to those found beside the church. Against the wall of the audience room was a low wall ending in a broken pillar, and at the south-east corner of the platform the stump of a pillar. The pillars are similar to those in the portico, and they may be sections of one that is missing.

On the other side of the doorway was a dais, 76 cm high, approached by four steps at its south-east corner. At its back was the old entrance, which had been converted into an alcove, perhaps as a background for a chair of state. The north and east faces of the platform were painted with bands of diamonds and semicircles in red and black. When the dais was excavated a piece of mid-nineteenth-century china was found among the sherds at the base of the blocking of the door. There was no hard surface to the dais and it is possible that these sherds got in when the alcove was filled flush with the wall. The dais would be most appropriate in the period of the Mazrui, but it is possible that it was built by the Akida Muhammad bin ʽAbdulla as part of his ill-fated policy of overawing the population of Mombasa.

The floor of the enclosure outside the entrance remained in use until the twentieth century, since the platform with the pillar and the dais are shown on the 1899 plan. Later, the floor was raised to the level of the dais. In the fill were found ironwork from broken gun-carriages, cannon-balls, flints, and English and European china of the late nineteenth century. Among the pieces were two bowls, one in brown and silver, the other in yellow and silver lustre, with the mark F. B. & Co. surmounted by a crown and surrounded by the name Peera Dewjee Zanzibar. F. B. & Co. was the Staffordshire firm of Frank Beardmore & Co., Fenton, 1902–14. Peera Dewjee was a Customs Master of Zanzibar, who retired about 1895 and subsequently opened a store.

The audience room abutted on a room (H) which had been built in the angle of the south end of the old perimeter wall and the platform in S. Mateus. It is marked 'lamp room' on the 1899 plan, and was entered from the main court. In the wall opposite the door was a square niche, 30 by 35 cm, with wide irregular margins, 25 by 18 cm, at a height of 1·17 m from the original floor. Later a door was made in the east wall to the left of the niche, and the old doorway was replaced by a window. Nothing was found below the original floor, but above it were three later floors which all contained nineteenth-century china. The purpose of this room, other than its later

[6] The Twelve Tribes of Mombasa, which played a leading part in the history of Mombasa in the eighteenth and nineteenth centuries are discussed in Guillain (1856), Lambert (1958), Kirkman (1964), Prins (1968), Berg (1968), and Berg and Walter (1968).

use as the 'lamp room', is unknown. It appears to have been in existence in the later Portuguese period, with a single door into the main court.

Above the audience room and the 'lamp room' were two rooms entered from the S. Mateus bastion. The one over the audience room was 1·06 m lower than the other and was reached from it by a flight of cement steps. A door in the east wall was approached by steps on the south side of the dais, as shown on the 1899 plan. Later, the steps were removed and the lower half of the door blocked by an iron railing. Similar railings were found in the warder's house above the cavalier of S. António. A new door was made in the north wall with a flight of steps leading to the ground above the filled-in Passage of the Arches, as shown on the 1954 plan. These rooms were part of the warders' quarters in the south-east angle tower, shown in the 1899 plan.

All this area was the heart of the early prison. Subsequently, when the prison was extended over the whole Fort, it was relegated to the status of a women's gaol, while the cells on the gun-platform were used for lunatics.

5. The Angle Towers

(Figs. 15 B and 16 A)

OUTSIDE the north angle of the platform, where it meets S. Matias, a tall pillar with the arms of Portugal is shown on the Herédia and Teixeira plans. During excavations in the angle tower the pedestal of a pillar was found, with cannon-balls sticking into the side of it. This must have been the pillar of the plans, and the cannon-balls would have been fired in the course of the unsuccessful attack on the Fort by Francisco de Moura in 1632. After the recovery of the Fort a tower was built covering the angle and burying the stump of the pillar. In the north face of the tower were the remains of a gun-port covering the face of S. Matias. At a later date the tower may have been filled in to the height of the gun-platform.

This is probably the tower which was destroyed in the bombardment of 1875, referred to in the dispatch of Captain W. F. Prideaux to the Earl of Derby, dated 23 January 1875, as follows: 'One very successful shot from the Rifleman's six-ton gun completely brought down the right turret on the harbour face of the Fort, together with the matchlock men inside it.' It was roughly rebuilt, but the ground was again disturbed by the construction of a septic tank for the prison latrines.

The southern angle tower was polygonal, which may have been the original form of the northern tower. A paved surface, similar to the surfaces found in the cavaliers, was found below the narrow cell which now occupies part of it, so probably there was a gun-port covering the east flank of S. Mateus. In the early eighteenth century, the east section of the tower was filled in solid to the level of the gun-platform in S. Mateus, and a gun-port was made in the east face above the filling. On von der Decken's sketch a house is shown in the western section. This house was double-storied and would have communicated with the gun-platform in S. Mateus and perhaps also, by a bridge, with the gun-platform in the projection. During the prison period most of the lower storey was filled in solid and the kitchen and store of the warders' quarters built on top of it. These buildings are shown on the 1899 prison plan (Fig. 6). In Owen's sketch and possibly in von der Decken's, which is far from clear, a door is indicated on the outside, at the base of the south face of the tower. There is no sign of this door today and it is doubtful if it ever existed.

6. *The Bastion of S. Alberto*

(Figs. 7 D; 17 A, B; 18 A)

THE bastion of S. Alberto was named after the Archduke Albert of Habsburg, Archbishop of Toledo and Viceroy of Portugal from 1594 to 1596. His arms, the double eagle of Austria surmounted by a mitre, were carved on a plaque on the west face of the bastion (Pl. 14 B). On the Cienfuegos plan it is named the bastion of S. António, but this is probably an error, since the cavalier of S. António, identified by an inscription, is in the corresponding bastion of S. Filipe.

The ramparts, 4·6 m thick, were faced with coral blocks, on an average 30 by 23 cm, coursed and with a plaster face, rising to a parapet walk and firing-step, 1·46 m above the floor of the bastion. The actual parapet was 2·73 m thick, with a level top 45·6 cm wide, and an outer face sloping downwards at an angle of 75°. At two places rounded and pierced bosses were set on the edge of the parapet for stays for flag poles. This description applies to the south and east sections of the bastion (Fig. 7 D).

The south-west corner and the west section were hidden by later buildings: a cavalier bastion of the seventeenth century, and prison cells for Europeans built in the twentieth century. The re-entrant angle on the north flank of the bastion had no parapet walk, and the wall was butted against the west parapet. The masonry of this wall was inferior to that of the parapet, and it had no plaster face on the inside. On the outside, the base of the wall, where it rested on the coral, was marked with a roll moulding. It would appear that there was originally a gap in the wall between the parapet walk and the projection of the bastion, which was only closed when the level of the bastion was raised. In the Teixeira plan (Fig. 4 B) (before 1634) cannon are shown in the re-entrant angle. The statements and denials in Portuguese documents about the completion of the Fort[1] could be explained by peculiarities of this kind. Later a small gun-port, 53 cm wide by 99 cm high, was made in the wall at the level of the raised bastion.

The area of the bastion was used as an open working floor with an uneven red-earth and coral surface. At the west end was a circular lime-kiln with walls of rubble and red earth, which had been buttressed at three points on its circumference. The walls sloped outwards and were unlikely to have been more than 2·13 m high. In the middle of the bastion were the foundation courses of a similar structure, and a small shallow red-earth pit, 46 cm deep, for puddling earth.

In the early seventeenth century a wall was built across the opening of the bastion, from an extension of the west parapet walk to the corner of the south parapet walk.

[1] Strandes, tr. Wallwork (1968), pp. 145–6.

It was a revetment wall, plastered on the outside, rising about 72 cm or a little more above the main court. The space in the bastion enclosed by the wall was filled with red earth and coral chips to form a platform for cannon. The platform would have been reached by a ramp, as at the Fort of S. Sebastião at Mozambique, probably on the east side, against the south barrack block. The difference between the level of the bastions and the central court is shown for the first time on the Lopes de Sá plan of 1728, but the raising of the bastions must have been very much earlier.

A parapet, 1·37 m wide, with the typical sloping outer face was built on the edge of the old parapet, leaving a new 1·3 m wide parapet walk behind it. Three 1·22 m wide embrasures for cannon were made in the south wall, and one in the east flank covering the face of the south curtain wall and the opposite face of S. Mateus. Behind two of them coral-block platforms have survived. The filling of the bastion and the raising of the parapet during the reconstruction of 1634, were confirmed by the late Ming porcelain found in the filling.

At the south-west corner a cavalier was constructed (Figs. 17 A and B). This consisted of a solid platform, resting on the coral fill of the bastion and rising 1·06 m above the parapet, with a paved floor as in the cavalier of S. Filipe. On the west was a low wall, 61 cm high and 1·07 m thick, but on the south only a low kerb, similar to the kerb in S. Matias. The original parapet and parapet walk ran under the cavalier, so it must have been an addition, perhaps the improvement to a landward bastion carried out by Francisco de Sousa Pereira in 1618.[2] At a later date the cavalier was extended 2·13 m to the east and the floor raised 53 cm. In the corner was built a turret with three vertical slits and a conical top (Fig. 26 J; Pl. 12 B). The south wall was 99 cm thick with a gun-port near the east end, 45 cm wide inside, with a splay of 84 cm, a row of musket-slits and a gable-coping. On the west was a wall of the same thickness with a flat top, 2·44 m high. At the south end near the turret was a curious gun-port with a double splay, 81 cm on the inside and 1·22 m on the outside (Fig. 28 G, H, I). The jamb of the inner splay on the north side was concave, so that a marksman standing in the embrasure could fire southwards almost parallel with the wall. The rest of the wall and the north and east walls were altered by the construction of an Arab house, shown on the von der Decken plan, and the magazine of the 1899 plan. The line of square openings along the west wall, similar to those in the north wall of the cavalier S. António, may be Portuguese. No datable sherds were found in the vital filling between the old and new walls of the cavalier, but it is clear from the coral-block masonry that the enlarged cavalier and turret are Portuguese.

In the late seventeenth century the parapet of the bastion was raised again by the construction of a flat-topped wall on top of the old sloping parapet. The wall was 1·15 m wide, with rectangular musket-slits and a shelf, 19 cm wide, on which to rest the elbow when firing through the slits. To make easier access to the slits, the parapet walk was raised 45 cm, with lime and rubble, held in position by a low retaining

[2] Axelson (1960), p. 84.

wall on the edge of the parapet walk. The embrasure in the east wall was widened and another added. Further along the wall an arched gun-port with wide splay, 66 cm inside and 1·06 m outside, was made. The flat top of the wall, the rectangular musket-slits, and the wide splay of the gun-ports are Portuguese features, but the use of small stones in the construction is in Arab style.

The cavalier shown on the Lopes de Sá plan is approximately the same size as the cavalier in S. Filipe, so it is clearly the enlarged cavalier. It may be the bastion of S. Angelo, referred to in the lost inscription mentioned by von der Decken and Thornton in 1861. They did not actually see the inscription but were given a copy, which read:

DO CAPITAO MOR JOSEPH [RE]
NOVO ESTE BALUARTE SANTO ANGELO
IA TODA EM RO[N]DA DE PERAPEITOS E CE
OS [?] COA RO BALUARTES FES OMESMO
DO E ABRIO HUM POCO DENTRO
MUITAS OBRAS DE O[?Q]UE ESTA
[NECE]SSITAVA POR ESTAR DES[A]BARS[3]

—which can be translated: 'Captain-Major Joseph . . . rebuilt this bastion S. Angelo and the whole perimeter of the parapets. He also dug a well inside [? the Fort] and carried out much work that was necessary because of crumbling [of walls].'

The lost inscription links the enlarged cavalier with the reconstruction of the parapet of the whole Fort. The captain referred to is possibly Joseph Botelho da Silva (1658–63) or Joseph Homem da Costa (1671–3), who are the only two Josephs in Boxer's list. The former is the more likely, in view of his longer tour of duty in the Fort, during which occurred an Omani raid on Mombasa (1661).

Besides the cavalier, remains of a few buildings of minor importance were found in the bastion. On the south side of the cavalier were stumps of three rough square pillars or pedestals, which may be the supports of the roof of the guardroom shown on the Lopes de Sá plan. At the same level, but ignoring the pillars, were the foundations of an equally rough square enclosure built up against the retaining wall of the raised parapet walk, which must be Arab.

High up in the wall above the re-entrant angle was a round-arched window. The building to which it belonged has disappeared and is shown on no Portuguese plan nor on the 1899 plan. It may be part of the eighteenth-century house at the south end of the west parapet walk, mentioned above (p. 22).

The west side of the bastion, between the cavalier and the projection facing S. Filipe, has not been investigated. However, it would seem to be identical with the similar area in S. Filipe, with a narrow Arab wall on top of the Portuguese wall on the west face, leaving a space behind to be used as a sentry walk. At the end of the

[3] C. C. von der Decken (1869), appendix following p. 335. Diary of Richard Thornton, unpublished. By courtesy of H. A. Fosbrooke.

projection was a small square-headed gun-port, also Arab. Subsequently a turret or watchtower was built, rather smaller than the other turrets, which was entered from the sentry walk against the west face of the bastion. The roof was conical with a 'golf-tee'-shaped finial on a short stem. The reason for siting the turret in this position is obscure, and the square-headed gun-port is masked by it. It is probably nineteenth-century.

At the east end of the bastion, against the east parapet walk with the top flush with it, was a sunken enclosure with a lime-concrete floor, which had been used as a tank. One internal corner was reinforced by a semicircular moulding, as occurred in the cistern of the Great Mosque at Mnarani.[4]

On the Guillain sketch there is a building on top of the cavalier, which appears on von der Decken's drawing with two windows or doors high up in the east wall. This is represented today by the additions to the east and west walls and the niches in them. In the early prison period a magazine was built on the site, with new north and south walls but using the east and west walls of the Arab building. On the 1899 plan it is shown with a flight of steps on the east side. Today the flight of steps is on the north side, leading to a platform, 1·91 m wide, with the entrance to the magazine in the middle of the north wall.

The building of the magazine involved the construction of a south wall at right angles to the east wall to make a proper square. The earlier Arab wall would have been built over the south parapet, which would have produced an odious quadrilateral, unacceptable to the new regime. One is reminded of the statement, said to have been made by a Swahili builder to a discontented European client: 'Before you came here there were no right angles.' The result of the new building was that a triangular space was left between the magazine and the corner of the bastion, which could only be reached over the roof of the magazine because there was no door in the south wall. In this space, below the floor of the Arab house, were found three cannon: an early-seventeenth-century English 5 in. cannon (Fig. 81. 1), another possibly early-seventeenth-century 4 in. cannon (Fig. 81. 6), and a late-seventeenth-century English 4½ in. culverin (Fig. 81. 3). The condition of the iron of the culverin was good; in the others it was bad. These guns could have been part of the defences of the south-west corner of the Fort, and been buried to save the trouble of moving them when the magazine was built.

In the third quarter of the nineteenth century a house was built along the south side of the bastion (Fig. 18 A), with its outer wall on top of the wall of the musket-slits. This building is not shown on the sketch of the Fort made by von der Decken in 1861, and must therefore be subsequent to it, which is confirmed by the finds of Saarguemines ware (post-1858) below the lime floor. It may have been one of the buildings for which materials were being collected, mentioned by Thornton. It reached as far as a later destroyed turret, shown on the plan of 1899, where it is

[4] Kirkman (1959).

designated as the hospital. Subsequently it was used as a store, a warder's quarters, and finally as the carpenter's workshop.

At the east end of the bastion near the junction with the south parapet walk was a kitchen for European prisoners. Against the re-entrant angle a 'hangman's drop', consisting of a revetted and plastered pit with a flight of steps leading to the bottom, was built in the twentieth century. It was hardly ever used because killings on the coast seldom merited a capital sentence, and in any case there was no resident hangman in Mombasa.

The stratification in the bastion (Fig. 18 A) was confused by hollows, pits, and post-holes without any coherent pattern. In the upper part of the coral-chip filling were sherds of K'ang Hsi and eighteenth-century porcelain and nineteenth-century china mixed with Ming porcelain. Above this was red earth from buildings, and grey earth from refuse of the eighteenth and nineteenth centuries, on which the lime floor of the long building was laid. Most of the pits were unrevetted holes in the ground, between 1·22 and 1·83 m deep, but against or near the parapet walk three were revetted pits, 1·22 m deep, which were perhaps latrines. There were also pits in the parapet walk itself, showing that little regard was being paid to defensive considerations.

Eleven skeletons were found inside the bastion, six in early- and mid-seventeenth-century levels, three in late-seventeenth-century levels and two in eighteenth-century levels (Fig. 17 A, B). In addition, there were three outside the retaining wall. Twelve of the bodies, including the three outside the retaining wall, were buried on a north–south axis, six with head to the south and six with head to the north. The other two were normal Muslim burials with head to east, feet to west. The burials on the north–south axis I believe to be Portuguese, although the direction is unusual. The burials in the contemporary Portuguese cemetery at Dambarare in Mashonaland were east to west or west to east, but parallel with the line of a building which was probably a church.[5] In the Fort there was no building with which the burials could be aligned, although it would be natural, as was done, to put them in line with the angle of approach from the main court, rather than across it. No grave goods were found, though it is possible that the medallion illustrated on Plate 44. 1–2 can be associated with the middle burial of the three outside the wall.

[5] Garlake (1969).

7. *The Bastion of S. Filipe*

(Figs. 8 A and B, 18 B, 19 A and B, 20 A)

THE Bastion of S. Filipe was named after King Philip II of Spain, who inherited the throne of Portugal in 1580 and in whose reign the Fort was built. His arms, the castles and lions of Castile and Leon quartered and surmounted by an imperial crown, appear on a plaque on the west corner of the bastion (Pl. 14 C). On the Cienfuegos plan the bastion is named *La Raposeira* (the Foxhole), after the principal Portuguese street which is represented today by Ndia Kuu (High Street or Main Street). It was identical in plan with S. Alberto and, in so far as they have been excavated, the ramparts and defences follow the same pattern. Here it has been possible to excavate the inner projection of the bastion and to expose the original ramparts and their subsequent modifications. In the north-west corner is the cavalier of S. António which, according to the inscription, was built in 1648.

The inner projection was a solid platform faced with coral blocks, rising 1·96 m above the floor of the bastion with a parapet 1·14 m high on the outer face only (Fig. 18 B; Pl. 13 A). On the inner faces, looking east towards the curtain wall and north towards the interior of the bastion, there were no parapets, only a short slope rising 23 cm above the platform. Near the corner of the parapet at the end of the projection there was a pierced boss, similar to the bosses in S. Alberto. The platform, with its defences on one side only, presented the features of an earthwork redoubt, rather than a stone-built fortress. North of the projection there was the normal parapet, parapet walk, and firing-step, which ran round the bastion and north wall of the Fort at an average 1·23 m above its surface. Between the platform and the west parapet there was the same re-entrant angle and rough wall of unplastered masonry, with a roll moulding at the juncture of wall and coral, as was found in S. Alberto (Fig. 18 A). This wall had collapsed and been rebuilt. The repair was clean enough on the outside, but on the inside was spread inwards, like an untidy darn in a sock. Similar repairs (carried out after the bombardment of 1875) were found on the floor behind the north face of the rectangular projection and in S. Mateus. In the late nineteenth century the wall was raised and an arched window and alcove added. The repair may be part of the same building operation.

Against the inner face of the platform a wall was built running northwards, parallel to the parapet walk, and disappearing under the cavalier. Only two courses of this wall were found, and it may have served as a temporary retaining wall for the filling of the bastion until enough material could be collected to raise the whole level. When this was done the upper courses were removed and used elsewhere. It was covered with coral-chip fill and is certainly an early feature. How much of what was found in this part of the bastion could also be found in the unexcavated part of S. Alberto, is unknown, but it is reasonable to assume that the two bastions were built as a pair. The later fill in both was also similar: red earth and coral chips with Ming porcelain and Islamic grey- and manganese-glazed earthenware.

During the reconstruction of 1634–9 the bastion was raised to the level of the old parapet and a new parapet, 1·37 m high, built above it (Figs. 18 B, 19 B). Behind, and at the level of the old parapet, were patches of paving with thick coral blocks (Fig. 20 A). The best-preserved was 3·66 m wide and 1·22 m deep. There was no well-defined edge and the paving may have extended over the whole area of the bastion. The wall in front of the well-preserved patch was recessed 23 cm, which suggests that the recess and platform were connected. Later a 84 cm curtain wall with musket-slits was added above the second parapet, and some time in the nineteenth century a thin curtain wall with slits was built on top of the Portuguese wall, leaving a narrow sentry-walk behind it.

The inner face of the bastion projection, including the recessed length and crude gun-port, was rebuilt more than once (Fig. 19 A). On the inner side, lying on the sloping edge, there was one course of coral blocks which must be contemporary with the raising of the level of the parapet. Above it was a rubble wall with two seat latrines in it, opening into the re-entrant angle, probably late Portuguese. These also had been rebuilt.

During the Arab period the projection was divided in two, longitudinally, by a wall running south from the cavalier, and the space on the west was subdivided by two cross-walls into three rooms. On the east a single cross-wall made two large rooms on the inside of the bastion. A photograph[1] taken towards the end of the century shows a palm-frond roof over the two outer rooms on the west side (Pl. 5 A). This was replaced by a flat roof carried on mangrove poles, which was reached by an extension of the steps against the cavalier. In the 1899 plan it is described as the tailor's workshop. In spite of the windows which had been made in the west wall, it must have been dark, even by nineteenth-century standards.

The cavalier was built in 1648 by Captain António da Silva Menezes (1648–51 ?) to command the approach from Kilindini. The structure consisted of a raised platform, 2·74 m above the floor of the bastion, with a parapet wall 1·59 m high and 1·14 m thick. The foundations went down through the red-earth and coral fill but did not reach natural rock. In the north-west corner was a turret with a shallow dome and round cap (Fig. 26 K). In each face of the cavalier were three embrasures. The eastern embrasure of the south face served as the entrance, approached by a flight of steps (Pl. 13 B). Above the steps was an inscription on a tablet of red plaster made of powdered sherds (the *argamaca* referred to in Portuguese records),[2] which reads as follows:

[1] In Hinawy, Mbarak 'Ali (1950), and in Fort Jesus Museum.

[2] Michaelis, H., *A New Dictionary*, 8th ed. (1932): '*argamaca*: a kind of plastering made with sherds and tiles beaten to powder and tempered together with mortar.'

[NO ANO DE] 1648 VEO ENTRAR
[ANTONI]O DA SILVA DE MENEZES
NESTA FORTALEZA E ACHAN
DOA MUI DANIFICADA T[R] ATOU
DE A REPARAR FEZ CAZAS DE SOLD
ADOS E TRES ALMAZES E HUA
CAZA DOSPITAL E MANDOU F
QZER ESTE BELUARTE CAV
ALEIRO POR NOME S. ANTONIO.

This can be translated: 'In the year 1648 António da Silva de Menezes took over this fortress and finding it much damaged set about repairing it. He made quarters for the soldiers and three storehouses and a hospital and he ordered the construction of this cavalier bastion to be named S. António.'

This was the scene of the last stand of the Portuguese on the morning of 13 December 1698, of which the following is a description taken from the Portuguese archives.[3]

> The Captain seeing that they were assailed on two sides and that they could not fight on both fronts, retired to the cavalier of S. António where they defended themselves through the night with three cannon, an *espalhafato*,[4] and a few muskets. The day of St. Lucy dawned and they fought until the seventh hour, by which time all ten men were exhausted. The Captain, seeing that the enemy were on top of them and that they could no longer resist, sallied out a little way with his blunderbuss in his hands to drive them off. In this short sortie he received two balls from a *caitoca*[4] in his chest and fell dead. The Arabs called on the rest to surrender and hand over their arms, which they did. They approached the Captain with the intention of taking the blunderbuss from him, but as his hands still grasped it and could not release it, they cut off his head and slashed his body with a sword. Thus he ended his life gloriously in the service of his King.

On the Lopes de Sá plan a guardroom is shown against the east wall of the cavalier, and part of it may have survived in the walls of the Arab building which succeeded it. In view of its width it must have been divided by a wall, or by a row of pillars which were removed or incorporated in the later walls.

The bastion, apart from the corner covered by the cavalier, remained open in the later Portuguese period. The most interesting deposit was found in a large pit which had been dug in the coral-chip fill to obtain gravel. It had been filled up with black earth from a rubbish dump and contained a fine collection of sherds of K'ang Hsi porcelain, Portuguese blue-and-white, seventeenth-century Islamic wares, and beads.

Towards the end of the eighteenth century (the slight evidence for dating comes from the sherds found in repairs to the original lime floor) a house was built on top

[3] *Arquivo Português Oriental* (new ed.), iv (ii) II, p. 331.

[4] *espalhafato*: a bronze cannon, 6 palmos (3·65 m) long, weighing 90 quintals and firing a 90 lb (?) ball. *caitoca*: a type of musket used by the Omani Arabs and the Marathas. The ball had to be driven into the barrel with a hammer, so that it fitted more tightly and was discharged with greater force.
Communication from Prof. C. R. Boxer, quoting Pieris–Fitzler, *Ceylon and Portugal 1539–1552* (Leipzig, 1927); and Delgado, *Glossário Luso Asiático*, i (1919), p. 174.

of the cavalier inside the parapets. The internal plan was uncertain because it had been rebuilt more than once. The outer walls seemed to be original, but most of the subdivisions probably belonged to the succeeding rebuildings. In the north wall, between the gun-ports, there were two small square openings which may be Portuguese, and in the north-east angle an air vent to catch the north-east monsoon. The entrance was up the Portuguese steps and through the east embrasure in the south wall, into the east room. The east and south walls of this room were covered with a bluish lime coat with two lines of red ochre below the roof line. These painted lines extended only half-way across the east wall, so it would appear that in the past there had been a party-wall bisecting the room.

This house was rebuilt and the roof line raised 32 cm. There were now four rooms: a long room on the north side, with an east, a west, and a middle room south of it. The entrance continued to be at the top of the Portuguese steps, and there were three interior doorways: two with round archways at the south end of the east and west rooms, and one, square-headed, leading into the north room. There is no evidence of other openings, apart from the small square windows in the north wall. However, they may have been destroyed when the door in the middle embrasure of the south wall and the large windows in the west wall were added. Against the south wall over the old guardroom, was an extension, apparently without windows at least in the north and east walls, as shown on the Guillain sketch. It could only have been entered by a door at the east end of the north room. The junction of this room and the house is shown on the Guillain sketch in a ruinous condition, and it is possible that the whole building was in ruins when the Fort was taken over in 1895. A worn-out cannon, perhaps seventeenth-century English, similar to that in Fig. 81. 6, was found below a party-wall. It may have been used by the Akida when he fired on the town in 1875; it seems unlikely that it would have been hauled up from the court for use merely as a foundation.

The Protectorate authorities reduced the status of the north room by dividing it into two by a party-wall, and used the east section as a bathroom and latrine, with the drains issuing over the wall into the ditch. The old door into the north room was blocked and two new doors made, one from the west room into the lavatory and the other from the middle room into the new room at the north-west corner. The latrine consisted of a semicircular recess in the easternmost embrasure, with a square vent. In front of the opening was a drain for flushing with a jar of water. This is probably the building in which, according to the Mombasa district files,[5] the Principal Medical Officer lodged and was evicted with the utmost difficulty. The new arrangement appears on the 1899 plan.

Later, as is shown on a photograph of 1905,[6] a second floor was added, probably when it became the chief warder's quarters. A flight of stairs to the new storey was built through the round-arched doorway between the middle and west rooms. The

[5] In the Kenya National Archives. [6] In Fort Jesus Museum.

other round-arched doorway opposite, leading from the east room to the middle room, was blocked. New doorways were made opposite each other in the middle of the two long walls of the middle room. Another outer door was made through the middle embrasure of the cavalier on the south side of the middle room, which was reached by a bridge from the top of the Portuguese steps. The end of the bridge rested on the wall of the room which ran down the middle of the bastion, mentioned above.

The guardroom was rebuilt and divided by a thick wall. Doorways were made at the east end of the west wall and in the middle of the south wall. In the outer room an oven, extending the width of the room, was sunk in the floor with a flue running up the outer wall. In the floor were found sherds of late-eighteenth-century porcelain and a Deutsch–Ostafrika one-heller piece, dated 1912. Subsequently, this room became a woodstore, which at one time caught fire. The inner room had been used as a kitchen, and a flight of steps led from a court outside it up to the platform on the roof and then into the east room of the house. The mechanics of feeding the warder must have been complicated at this time. In the 1899 plan, three enclosures are shown with a flight of steps leading up to what must have been a platform extending over the room with the oven. Later an office was built over this room, which is shown on a photograph taken in 1906.[7]

The development of the defences of the bastion along its north side was similar to that on the south side of S. Alberto. An excavation beside the wall of the room with the oven exposed the old parapet, parapet walk, and firing-step, which were subsequently covered by the filling of the bastion. The wall on top of the old parapet was preserved best in the room of the oven, where a line of musket-slits has survived, and on the east flank, in which were sited the two vital gun-ports covering the main gate (Fig. 28 A, B, C). Above the Portuguese wall on the north side was a thin Arab wall with a sentry-walk behind it. At some time the Portuguese wall was reduced in height for two-thirds of its length, and raised to the height of the Arab wall for the remaining third at the north-east end of the bastion. A gun-port is shown at this point on the Guillain sketch, but it was later blocked. On top of both thin and thick sections of the wall was a gable-coping.

The eastern part of the bastion has not been excavated. It is shown on the 1899 plan as occupied by ten rooms or houses, and a latrine, all of which were removed between 1899 and 1922. A difference in level is also indicated by a flight of steps rising to a room at the junction of the bastion and the north curtain wall, mentioned in Chapter 2 in the paragraph dealing with the north barrack block.

[7] In Fort Jesus Museum.

8. *The Bastion of S. Matias*

(Figs. 8 C and D, 20 B, 21 A)

THE Bastion of S. Matias was named after Matias d'Albuquerque, Viceroy of India, during whose regime the Fort was built, but the shield on the outside wall, which would have borne his coat-of-arms, has disappeared. On the Cienfuegos plan it was named Baluarte del Mar, the bastion of the sea, and on the Lopes de Sá plan, Baluarte S. António, referring to the harbour of Mombasa which it overlooked. As I have suggested above, there may be some confusion in the naming of the bastions in the Cienfuegos plan. Baluarte del Mar would have been more appropriate for the Bastion of S. Mateus, the nearest to the open sea.

The bastion was built with a long swept-back rampart facing the creek, a short flank towards the town, and a straight flank at right angles to the north curtain, facing S. Filipe. The ramparts on the north and west flanks follow the pattern already described. At the north-east corner was a triangular flight of steps leading to the parapet walk, and at the east end of the north wall the parapet was interrupted to provide access to a corner turret, which disappeared later. Round the corner, and at the north end of the sea wall, the parapet and parapet walk were resumed at a slightly lower level, with no firing-step (Fig. 8 D). They terminated at what appears to be the flank of an embrasure, with a bed 23 cm above the level of the floor of the bastion. However, it is possible that the bed was actually the north end of a plastered kerb, 82 cm wide, which extended as far as the rectangular projection. The height of the kerb at the north end was 23 cm and at the south 76 cm above the ground behind it; the height from the top of the kerb to ground level outside the building varied between 6 m and 7·6 m. Similar kerb parapets occurred in the later forts in West Africa[1] and, as at Fort Jesus, their justification would appear to be that the height above the ground made any stronger defence superfluous. Subsequently normal parapets were often built on top of them.

Between the initial building of the Fort and the reconstruction of 1634, a wall was built on top of the kerb with a series of arched gun-ports, 92 cm wide and 70 cm high, with double splays (Fig. 28 D, E, F). This is an early type of gun-port and it is surprising that it should appear here. They were blocked when the passage between the house behind them and the wall was filled in, in accordance with the recommendations of Marinho.

There was a natural difference in level of 91·4 cm between the north and south end of S. Matias. When the elliptical bastion was added and the north end of the original

[1] Lawrence (1963), p. 162.

bastion was filled in, this difference was increased to 2·44 m. A retaining wall was built across the bastion, which was approached by a ramp beside the gatehouse.

The elliptical bastion was built against the west face of S. Matias at the time of the reconstruction of the Fort, leaving a space of 6·1 m for the entrance passage. It rose 3·96 m above the coral skirt of the hill on which the Fort was built. The foundations were 3·2 m thick on the outer side and 2·44 m thick on the inner side. The outer or north wall was strengthened by two buttresses, or cross-walls, 1·52 m thick, which did not, however, reach the opposite wall on the side of the entrance. The gaps between were filled with the usual red earth and coral chips, in which were found a few early-seventeenth-century sherds. Below the east buttress was a plastered wall, 91 cm thick, which may have been a kerb on the outer side of the approach to the original gate.

When the new bastion was added, the old parapet was removed and a wall, 1·85 m high and 1·30 m wide, was built along the north side of the bastion above the old wall and the addition (Fig. 8 c). There were three open gun-ports in this wall, 1·22 m by 84 cm, two covering the harbour and one the Portuguese town. At the apex of the ellipse was an arched gun-port, 1·14 m by 54 cm, covering the slope to the north-west of the Fort. The wall continued along the inner flank, then turned at right angles, where it met the old parapet, to run over it to the gatehouse. There was no structural means of access to the court above the outer passage, and the only approach from bastion to court would have been by a wooden ladder.

During the Arab period, a narrow wall, 1·12 m high with a gable-coping, was built on top of the Portuguese wall between the north-east corner of the bastion and the beginning of the curve of the ellipse, leaving an 89 cm wide space behind it as a sentry walk (Fig. 8 c). In the apex of the ellipse was found the stump of the flagstaff which appears on the Owen sketch.

On the Cienfuegos plan a building is shown in this part of the bastion called 'the house of the governor', but no trace of walls of that period was found. Subsequently, a rectangular building was erected against the north wall, leaving inaccessible the curved space at the west end behind the gun-port. This devotion to rectangles is more likely to be European than Arab, and the building was probably put up in the early prison period. It was used later as a hospital. In one wall was found a broken late-eighteenth-century Chinese snuff-bottle. Along the east wall of the bastion was a small building which replaced the latrine marked on the 1899 plan. Against the gatehouse, and over the old west parapet and parapet walk, was built a small room, used as a medical store.

In the prison period a tunnel was driven under the gatehouse and beneath the old west wall of the bastion, as a drain from the main court. The drain was on average 1·14 m in section and ran at the level of a grating in the north wall, then fell through a shaft behind the wall to emerge at a lower grating in the ditch. It is mentioned as a project in the 1899 plan.

In the lower, or south end, of the bastion was an L-shaped building, which is shown on the Lopes de Sá plan, but on none of the other plans. It is described as barracks. An excavation in the north room exposed an earth floor on which were lying a number of pieces of fine-grained coral, and below it the hard plastered floor of the original room, level with the lower section of the bastion. Fine-grained coral was used for borders and decoration, such as the achievement above the Portuguese inscription over the gate, but these pieces had never been used. Nothing of dating value was found below the floor or with the coral. The present building, except for a minor modification at the north end, probably to provide a space for steps to the roof, follows the Portuguese plan, although the veranda is a late prison addition.

One of the recommendations of Marinho (1633) was that 'an inner wall [i.e. a wall on the inside of the outer wall] should be built from the Captain's quarters to the bastion of S. Matias'. This wall was to be 'large enough [*sic*] in the opinion of the Council, for the space between the new wall and the old to be filled in and the old wall raised to the necessary height. A parapet should be made on top of it to render it defensible, so as to screen the houses in the Fort from anyone in the harbour.' This space would appear to be that between the back wall of the L-shaped building and the outer wall, and the new wall to be the wall which ran from the north-west corner of the room over the inner section of the Passage of the Arches. As built, this wall joined the inner wall of the L-shaped building, not the outer wall, but it may nevertheless be the wall in question (Fig. 20 B). If so, Marinho's plan was modified, in that a narrow parapet walk with rooms behind it was built, instead of a platform. The L-shaped building then would belong to the reconstruction period.

In Guillain's account of the Fort the rooms in the L-shaped building and the filled-in space behind them are described in the following words: 'The Portuguese buildings have been destroyed, except the rooms set in the thickness of the wall of the bastion of S. Matias, now used to store powder, shot, etc. They were intended to be stocked with sufficient grain for fifteen or eighteen months, supplies being renewed annually . . .'[2] An obvious inference from this description is that in 1846 the space between the back wall of this building and the outer wall was filled in, and that part of Marinho's recommendations had been executed.

The east wall of S. Matias received the full force of the guns of the Royal Navy during the bombardment of 18 January 1875, and the upper part was destroyed. It was restored in the old Arab style, but the musket-slits with the blocked and pierced apex are irregular and badly executed. The L-shaped building behind the wall suffered equally, and in order to rebuild it the filling was removed and a passage made behind it. At the end of the L-shaped building a flight of steps in concrete was later constructed to reach the upper level of the bastion. The north end of this wall in the upper level of the bastion is better built and may have been restored by the prison authorities. The

[2] Guillain, vol. iii, p. 254.

present north-east corner turret is not shown on the Guillain sketch of 1846, but it appears without a cupola on a photograph of 1902.[3]

The south room of the L-shaped building was the scene of one of the better-authenticated ghost stories, in which a rational explanation is as improbable as the story itself. It was related to me by Mr. N. A. Cameron, when Commissioner of Prisons in Uganda, who was at one time a prison officer in Fort Jesus. One evening in December 1938 he was in his quarters in S. Mateus, on the point of sitting down to his evening meal at about 9 o'clock, when he heard screams coming from the direction of the main gate. He hurried to the spot and found an African warder in hysterics. He said he had been lying on his bed in this room and that a European had stepped out of the wall and tried to strangle him. When asked to describe the European, he said that he had a beard and mad eyes; he wore a stiff, sticking-out collar, a jacket and breeches, and 'stockings like a memsahib'. The description would appear to fit a Portuguese gentleman of the early seventeenth century. In 1623 sumptuary legislation was passed in Portugal to prohibit the *gran gola*, or large ruff, but it might have lingered on in the colonies. 'Stockings like a memsahib' could well be woollen hose worn to above the knee. An African warder could have known nothing about old-style costume, and the conclusion can only be that a Portuguese had been seen who had ceased to exist 300 years before. An Arab warder told Mr. Cameron that there had been a similar happening ten years previously. Since the Fort ceased to be a prison, there has been no apparition, although a watchman now sleeps in the same room.

[3] In Fort Jesus Museum.

9. *The Bastion of S. Mateus*

(Figs. 21 B, 22 A and B, 23 A and B)

THE Bastion of S. Mateus was named after Mateus Mendes de Vasconcelos, the last Captain of the Coast to be stationed at Malindi and the first Captain of Mombasa. His arms, a phoenix quartered with bendlets wavy, surmounted by a phoenix, were carved on a plaque on the south-east corner of the Fort (Pl. 14 D). He was the ablest Portuguese to serve in East Africa: a resolute and successful soldier, a clever diplomatist who could make Arabs, Africans, and Portuguese co-operate, and the builder of Fort Jesus. The only occasion on which he was involved in an undignified dispute was that of an argument over the embarrassing matter of prize money with his superior officer, the Admiral Tomé de Sousa Coutinho. On the Cienfuegos plan the bastion is named *de la Banderas*, 'of the flags'. It is the lowest bastion in relation to the ground outside, and it was here that the storming parties climbed into the Fort on the night of 12 December 1698. The corner where it met the south curtain wall was subsequently the favourite place for escape when the Fort was a prison.

The plan was similar to that of S. Matias on the south and west, with parapet, firing-step, and parapet walk, but in the east wall was a large gate at a distance of 8·84 m from the apex of the bastion. On the south and west sides, at the level of the firing-step, was a platform, making solid the projection of the bastion (Fig. 22 B; Pl. 17 A). During excavations, a cutting was made on the west side of the bastion to expose the original surface at the base of the parapet walk. It did not appear to have been used and it is possible that the platform was constructed soon after the outer walls of the Fort were completed. It would seem to be contemporary with the gate, which is similar in style to the gate at the bottom of the Passage of the Steps.

The platform was about the same distance from the west wall as from the apex. On the east of it a sunken court extended to the outer wall. This was 3·05 m below the platform and, at its lowest point, about 91 cm below the level of the main court. The gate was reached by a flight of five steps cut in the coral, which was set in the wall about 3 m above the ground outside the Fort. This gate was 2·13 m wide and 2·59 m high, almost as large as the main gate of the Fort. It was spanned by a semicircular arch with radius 1·30 m and with centre 38 cm below the springing line. This arch was recessed below an arch made of an arc of a circle 2·59 m radius. The second arch was made with voussoirs 12 cm broad and 69 cm long, and was set at an angle of 45° to the face of the gate. There was a sill in front of the gate but, unlike the tunnel at the end of the Passage of the Arches, there was no drain below the sill by which storm water could get away (Fig. 24 A, B, C). The reason for the construction of a gate at this point, facing the guns of any enemy entering the harbour, is difficult to understand. The wall along the seaward face of the bastion, except at this point, has been so damaged and restored that it is impossible to see what was its original height, but it is unlikely to have been less than the height of the gate.

The platform had a fine plastered face, superior to any other plaster work in the Fort, and even to the fine plaster of the Palace of Gedi. It was covered with sketches of Portuguese ships, buildings, groups of men, fish, an animal, a cross, and symbols, drawn in carbon black and red ochre (Pls. 15, 16, 18). They did not form a composition and were not by a single hand, but were casual drawings by momentarily artistically-minded soldiers or sailors. The artist of the ships was clearly the most gifted or perhaps was better at ships than anything else but he was probably correct in realizing that he would make a better soldier than artist. The symbol of the heart pierced by an arrow, which appears on the sail of the best-drawn of the ships (Pl. 18 C) and also by itself, may be the symbol of St. Augustine. A woodcut of a heart with aorta, pierced by two arrows, appears in the *Sermonum opera*, published at Basle by John de Auerbod in 1494–5 illustrated in *Schrieber Manuel*, no. 3395. Closer in date is a painting of Jesus and St. Margharita Alacoque by Carlo Muccioli, in the Vatican, in which the heart of Jesus is shown pierced by an arrow. The allusion to St. Augustine would be appropriate in view of the existence of the Augustinian convent in the town, but I should be more certain if I could find some contemporary examples of the same motif. The ship on which it is shown was probably an actual ship, the *S. Agostinho da* ——, and caught the attention of the artist because of its association with the convent. Besides the drawings there was a crudely incised inscription, of which the only legible words were *São Baoque*, perhaps the name of a ship, and *Lemos*, a Portuguese surname (Pl. 17 B).

In the south end of this wall were a number of holes which might have been made by musket-balls. The sunken court was 18·29 m long and 12·24 m wide at the entrance, narrowing to 4·27 m at the south end, and might have been used for firing practice, though I should have supposed that the ditch would have been more convenient. At the Fort of S. Sebastião, Mozambique, the firing-range and place of execution were outside the fort between the walls and the sea.

During the 1634–9 reconstruction, a platform 4·52 m high was built along the seaward face of the bastion (Fig. 23 A). The new platform extended from the junction of the bastion with the rectangular projection and ran over the old platform at the south end. Under it a passage to the gate was constructed, 3·05 m square and 2·97 m high, with a vault of coral blocks, in which were square vents along the central axis, and a door on to the court. In the jambs of the door were two large holes for a beam to bar it. The court sloped down to the passage, a drop of one in twenty, with two steps at the end. Across the entrance to the court from the main court was a room with a narrow doorway, 71 cm wide.

The outer gate was subsequently narrowed to 91 cm, the width of a postern, by the construction of square pillars within the arch. Later, the postern gate was blocked and the steps filled up to the level of the court, converting the passage into a room. In the soft grey earth-filling were found sherds of coffee-coloured cups, with panels in rose pink, which cannot be from earlier than the second half of the eighteenth century. It may be that these sherds found their way in from the pit that was dug in the filling of the court at the time of the repair after the 1875 bombardment.

On the west side of the court a stout wall, 91 cm thick, with a pronounced batter, was built at a distance of 15 cm from the painted wall at its north end, but widening to a metre as it ran south and finally over it in front of the passage to the gate. The space between was filled in with the usual coral chips and contained Ming porcelain. The same filling was carried across the bastion over the old platform to the south and west walls. A gun-port was made in the west wall to cover the south curtain and the east face of S. Alberto. It was to this gun-port and the gun-ports in S. Alberto that the dying Portuguese were carried to the guns by African women, to fire on the Arab scaling ladders during the assault of 20 July 1697. The assault was broken off with heavy losses to the attackers, and the gunners died soon afterwards, one hopes with a soldierly sense of satisfaction in duty well done, at least at the journey's end.

The new wall of the court curved round at the north end to meet the wall of the room A across the gorge of the bastion. The room is marked on the Lopes de Sá plan as 'Provisions Store', but this may be a transposition from another building on the west side of the bastion marked 'Guardroom'. Its position is more suitable for a guardroom than a store, and the narrow doorway in the south wall is clearly a defensive rather than a utilitarian feature. In addition to the small door leading to the court, there must have been another in the north wall of the room opening on to the main court.

In the middle of the sunken court, between the two gun-platforms, but eccentrically positioned in relation to the side walls, were the remains of a masonry structure which might have been an oven, from what appeared to be a flue on one side of it. The original surface of the court, belonging to the period of the painted wall, was found below the present surface. Between the two surfaces were many sherds of K'ang Hsi porcelain. On the Lopes de Sá plan no gate is shown, but a sunken court is indicated. It would appear that by this time (1728) the door from the guardroom was already blocked and the court partially filled with rubbish. The filling-up was a slow process of accumulation lasting nearly a hundred years.

Against the west wall of the court was a thick deposit of ash containing 135 crucibles. These were an average of 10 cm deep and 9 cm across, with a pinched mouth (Fig. 83. 1, 2). The majority had no residue in them, but copper was found adhering to the sides of a few broken pieces. On the outside of some there were patches of a red glassy substance or bloom. With the crucibles were found fragments of *tuyéres* with 2 cm channels, and slag. The wall was scorched and cracked along the ash line, and it must have been subjected to considerable heat. Sherds of rose-pink porcelain which were found with the crucibles showed that the operations in which they were used did not take place before the middle of the eighteenth century.

Subsequently, a small mosque was built at the north end of the bastion against the wall of the guardroom, which was raised to the necessary height (Fig. 23 B). The only feature was a plain narrow *mihrab* with a rounded top in the north wall. The door was in the middle of the south wall and there was a window on the west side of it. The mosque was approached round the south-west corner of the guardroom and over the battered wall, which was broken down to make an even slope. Two steps led up to the entrance, at right angles to the slope, and the steps continued in front of the mosque to the gun-platform facing the sea. There was a masonry bench along the front of the building, divided by the steps. The mosque was not built before the nineteenth century.

At the south end of the filled-in court was a funnel-shaped pit to seat a flagpole. This pit must also date from the same period, since it was dug partially into the battered wall, and it is clear that the outside was not intended to be seen. A similar revetted pit was made for the flagstaff in S. Matias (p. 55).

The parapet along the gun-platform may be Portuguese, but the details are certainly Arab. The Owen sketch shows gun-ports but no musket-slits, and no corner turret. The majority of the slits are of the concave-headed type, resembling those in the east face of S. Matias, and are believed to be nineteenth-century (Fig. 29 K, L). The turret at the apex of the bastion was built as the fire-control position, from which the officer in charge would give the order to fire the guns lined up along the platform, when a hostile ship passed his line of sight. It was probably one of the measures taken to put the Fort in order during the struggle between the Mazrui governors and the Sultan of Muscat and Zanzibar in the early nineteenth century. An older turret is shown in this position on the Teixeira plan.

A large gun-port in the south wall near the turret (Fig. 27 E, F) is angled to fire on a ship as it rounded the point below the Katharine Bibby Hospital. It seems to be unrelated to and probably earlier than the turret. On the Owen sketch there was no gun-port in this position, but the von der Decken sketch showed three arched ports in a row. The rounded arch may be Portuguese, but the square opening with a mangrove-pole lintel is certainly Arab.

In the make-up of the final surface of the bastion was found a piece of fine-grained coral, 18 by 7 cm, with a magical text in Arabic, mentioning the angel Israfil. The text reads:

[*in centre*] The amulet of Al-Juba al Hindi.
Israfil, ʻUthman, O Guardian.

[*around the edge*] Go away, thief from [my] house.
May all the hyenas and lions eat him,
every one of them, and every member
of his band and his relatives [likewise]
who cross over the threshold.
(Trans. B. G. Martin)

By the style of writing, the amulet may not be older than the nineteenth century. The sentiment would be acceptable at any period other than the second half of the twentieth century.

The bombardment of 1875 breached the seaward wall of the bastion. A cutting against the middle of it exposed a sleeve wall which had been built against the old wall and continued almost as far as the turret. Part of a shell was found in the foundation trench of the sleeve wall, proving that the damage was due to the bombardment. Another shell went through the middle of the blocking of the old Portuguese gate, hit the opposite wall, cracked the barrel-vault of the passage, and was found in pieces on the floor. The breach was repaired from the inside as well as the outside, a pit being dug through the filling of the court behind it to get the masons out after they had finished their work.

On the 1899 plan the provisions store, or guardroom, was marked as a military cell, and the mosque as a lunatic cell. Men in authority in those days were not unduly sensitive or tactful. In front of the cell a square enclosure was indicated. The set-up was reminiscent of the accommodation for a cherished animal in a well-kept zoo, but it was none the worse for that. The bastion was entered by a doorway between the military cell and the south barrack block and was described as a wood-yard. At the north end of the gun-platform, at the junction with the rectangular projection, a warder's quarters were built, which were occupied by the matron after the installation of a women's gaol.

Some time after 1899 the bastion was modified. The west side was lowered, and a retaining wall built above the original painted wall, with a flight of steps at the south end, leading up to the platform. Against the west wall a kitchen was constructed, reaching as far as the Portuguese gun-port. A laundry tank was sunk in the platform against the east wall, near the turret.

10. *The Perimeter Wall, Ditch, and Outwork*

(Figs. 1–5 and 16 B)

THE Herédia and Teixeira plans show a perimeter wall with turrets on the counterscarp. No traces of the wall have survived, but it would have followed the line of the present low wall, which runs a few yards back from the counterscarp, between the ditch and the Law Courts and Municipal Offices.

The Ditch (Figs. 1–5) is frequently mentioned in the early references before the 1631 revolt. After the recovery of the Fort, work continued but it was never in fact finished. The only part which was completed was between the re-entrant angles on the landward side. Here it was levelled and plastered at a depth of 1·52 m below the present surface. This gave a height of 10·19 m to the top of the old parapet, or 12 m when the curtain wall was built. The counterscarp, which would normally be finished with a vertical face, was virtually untouched. In it are caves in which lived a number of the inhabitants of Mombasa during the siege.[1] They had invited the Omani Arabs to deliver them from the Portuguese, but when they saw their liberators they preferred their old oppressors. There are modern parallels, but the choice has not normally remained open, even for a short period of two years.

On the north, the town side, the ditch was 9·14 m wide, probably as a result of quarrying operations, but the counterscarp may never have been so high on this side. It was crossed by a wooden bridge or gangway opposite the old main gate, and by a similar structure after the new gate had been built. In Owen's sketch the new gate appears to be approached by a sloping causeway, but Guillain in his description mentions a bridge:

> The height of the scarp [*sic*] is about 17 m, including the ditch which is 4 or 5 m deep and of equal width, and surrounds the fortress on the three landward sides. On the side of the counterscarp below the salient of the north bastion the ground has been cut away in order to extend the ditch as far as the shore, and the channel resulting from this operation has been blocked by a wall in which an opening with an arched entrance has been made. A bridge thrown across the ditch gives access to the duty gate opening into the left side of the northern bastion.[2]

'Duty gate' (*porte de service*) is an odd way to describe the main gate of the Fort, but there is no alternative explanation. The 'opening with the arched entrance' is the water-gate. Today the main gate is approached by a sloping causeway, which curves

[1] Strandes (tr. Wallwork), p. 215. [2] Guillain, vol. iii, p. 252.

round the elliptical bastion. A photograph taken in 1905[3] shows a bridge over the ditch and not the present culvert.

On the south of the Fort the counterscarp followed rather closely the south wall of S. Alberto, but beyond the south-east corner was broken by the natural condition of the ground. It was resumed at the south-east corner of S. Mateus, also rather close to the wall. Marinho in his recommendations wrote: 'In the Bastion of S. Mateus is a gate which is very low in the wall. The natural rock should be cut back with picks, as it has been cut back at other exposed places, so that it will not be possible to climb into the bastion.'

The outwork, or *couraça*, below the rectangular projection between the seaward bastions, would seem to be shown on the Herédia and Teixeira plans and is mentioned in the Bocarro/Rezende description. It was made to provide a position as close to sea level as possible—actually about 7·32 m above water level—for the heavy guns, the twenty-, twenty-four-, and thirty-six-pounders, which were the 'ship-breakers'. It would also have served to protect supplies landed by boat, until they could be taken into the Fort through the narrow tunnel to the Passage of the Arches. An outwork with a polygonal shape appears for the first time on the Cienfuegos plan, and is described as the 'external fortification in form of a *couraça*, unfinished'. In the Lopes de Sá plan it is shown with the same polygonal shape but with a partition wall and gate in the middle, dividing it into an outer and inner ward. In the south wall was a gate towards the small bay where supplies could be landed, but there was no gate on the north side, facing the town. The polygonal shape may be due to the collapse of the cliff on which the outwork stands. It may originally have been rectangular, as shown on the earlier plans. The existence of the partition has not been proved by excavation.

The east wall facing the sea was rebuilt in the early nineteenth century. Below the surface, running under it, were found sherds of porcelain with the comb pattern, which cannot be earlier than the second half of the eighteenth century. Beneath the wall was found a plastered retaining wall, similar to the wall on the north and south sides of the rectangular projection, which was carried down to the original coral of the slope a depth of 63 cm. There was no surface where the wall ended, and the outwork must have been filled in immediately to a level 15 cm below the top of the retaining wall and about 30 cm below the level of the later outwork. In the filling Ming porcelain was found.

The nineteenth-century wall was 2·44 m high and 1·03 m wide, with a gabled top, decorated at each end with a pyramid on a cube base. It was pierced by four gun-ports, three spy-holes at standing level in the main face, three spy-holes in the diagonal section at the level of the parapet walk, and a doorway. The gun-ports were splayed on the outside and recessed in the wall; the outer arch was rounded, but the inner arch had an ogival nick (Fig. 28 J, K, L). The ogival nick occurs in Portuguese

[3] In Fort Jesus Museum.

architecture, but it is a common feature of the Arab architecture of the coast of East Africa.[4] The finest example is in the tower of the Great Mosque at Mogadishu (thirteenth-century). One gun-port had been rebuilt with a plain gable arch on the inside. Seats were subsequently added inside the gun-ports. The three-way spy-hole was peculiar in itself, without being in any way peculiar in the context of Arab building. There was no field of fire or vision, and its only use would appear to be to listen to people amiably conversing on the ledge outside the wall. The arched doorway was approached by a flight of steps from the shore, and led into a square pit with a galvanized-iron roof, which is shown on a photograph of 1902.[5] It could have been used for storing lime for building and is probably nineteenth-century.

Behind the wall on the north side of the outwork, which slopes downwards from the face of the Fort, was a firing-step, raised 1·67 m above the surface of the outwork, and an arched doorway. East of the doorway, the wall appeared to be contemporary with the east wall. The section west of the north doorway, the south wall, the firing-steps on both sides, and both the entrances, had been rebuilt, probably after the 1875 bombardment. During the bombardment the outwork was raked with fire from the rigging of the attacking ships, so that the guns could not be manned. This was a defect in design which had been noticed by Guillain.[6]

South of the gap in the coral where the Passage of the Arches emerged, was a small, square, plastered block, below which were found sherds of K'ang Hsi porcelain. It is Portuguese and might have been an altar, but it may have had some mundane use—as a table, for example.

Outside the outwork, on the north side, a wall extended along the top of the cliff to the water-gate. Only the foundations remain, but it may have been the battery mentioned by Guillain: 'An opening at one corner [i.e. the north entrance of the outwork] provides communication between it and a battery at ground level, parallel to the wall of the Fort, erected on the shore.'[7] The battery is not shown on the accompanying sketch, but this does not invalidate it, as Guillain was not himself the artist. The water-gate is shown on the Krapf and Guillain sketches, but not on Owen's, so it would have been built between 1824 and 1844, in the late Mazrui or early Zanzibar period. The arch is a true arch built with voussoirs, which is unknown to the building tradition of the coast. Its construction is interesting as showing that western building techniques were being adopted by Arabs at the beginning of the nineteenth century.

[4] Garlake (1966), Pls. IV, V, and pp. 8, 27, 45–6, 72.
[5] In Fort Jesus Museum.
[6] Guillain, vol. iii, p. 252, and p. 75 below.
[7] Guillain, vol. iii, p. 252.

11. Building Materials and Methods

THE building material of the Fort is coral, either coursed coral blocks or coral rag set in red earth and lime mortar, with plastered face. Small, coursed blocks, with an average 13 cm face, were used in the earliest stone buildings on the East African coast in the Kilwa area. However, the use of blocks was abandoned at the end of the thirteenth century for random rubble, which continued as the normal building material until the end of the nineteenth century.[1]

The Portuguese preferred to use large coral blocks of an average height of 22 cm set in courses. However, they sometimes had to fall back on the traditional Arab materials. The choice would appear to have depended on availability of material, rather than the importance of the building: the church and part of the Captain's House were built of rubble; the barracks of coral blocks. The church and the entrance passages had the flat Arab-type roof, carried on beams. All the other buildings were covered with semicircular Spanish tiles 33 cm long and 11 to 13 cm wide, made in Portugal or India. A few complete tiles and thousands of broken pieces have been found in the excavations, mostly in late-seventeenth- and early-eighteenth-century levels.

The original parapet and parapet walk were built of blocks with a lime and concrete filling, but the later curtain walls were made of rubble, although with larger stones and stronger mortar than were normally used in Arab buildings. At its best, as in the curtain walls, it was almost lime concrete. There were considerable variations in the thickness of the walls, even in walls which were obviously contemporary. In the case of the Captain's House and the south barrack block there was a variation of 8 cm in walls of the same building. It might be justifiable to say that a Portuguese outer wall would be about 1·14 m, as opposed to a similar Arab wall which would not exceed 84 cm. A Portuguese house wall would be about 61 cm as opposed to 54 cm, but even then the barrack rooms were an exception. So far as the width of the buildings was concerned, there was a similar lack of uniformity. The Portuguese structures were considerably wider—the church, for example, 7·16 m—than the Arab, which did not exceed 2·44 m. This was about the maximum length for supporting the heavy lime-concrete roofs, often 38 cm thick, and also the maximum length for large mangrove poles that were procurable in quantity.

The Portuguese building units were the *braca*, or fathom, and the *palmo* or span, in a relation of 10 to 1. The *braca* is reckoned at 2·22 m, the *palmo* at 22 cm.[2] However, as can be seen from the table, these measurements do not fit the actual walls very closely, and even less the measurements given in Bocarro/Rezende. The Arab building

[1] Chittick (1966). Garlake (1966), Pl. I, pp. 16, 54, 60.

[2] Mitterwallner (1964).

unit was the cubit,[3] 43 cm, but again, as can be seen in the actual buildings, there was no high degree of accuracy. One feels that the individual mason cut his piece of stick to his own hand as a measure for the wall he was building.

The arches of the doorways and gun-ports were semicircular, whether they were Portuguese or Arab. The only two-centred arches were those over the Passage of the Arches. Arches with the ogival nick at the apex—a common feature on the East African coast—occurred in the windows of the room over the gatehouse (Fig. 24 J) and in the gun-ports of the outwork (Fig. 28 J, K, L), both rebuildings of the eighteenth, possibly nineteenth, century.

Mouldings occurred on the capitals and bases of doorways and pillars, on the turrets on the cavaliers and north curtain wall, and on the pinnacles over the main gate (Figs. 26, 27). All, except the upper moulding of the turret on the north curtain (Fig. 26 L), are Portuguese. Three can be dated: viz. the arch of the outer gate (Fig. 26 F) and the pinnacles over the gate (Fig. 27 A) to 1634; and the turret on the cavalier of S. António (Fig. 26 K) to 1648. There is a similarity between the moulding on the lower part of the turret on the north curtain (Fig. 26 L) and the outer gate (Fig. 26 F), and the pillar of the portico of the Captain's House (Fig. 25 B); and between the half pillar of the inner passage (Fig. 26 D) and the jamb of the doorway of the portico (Fig. 26 E). These are useful comparisons, since it would appear to establish that the lower part of the turret on the north wall is Portuguese, and that the pillars of the portico are early-seventeenth-century. It does not help, however, in the dating of the half pillar or the reconstruction of the portico. The upper moulding of the turret on the north curtain, the half keyhole, is typical Omani.[4]

Copings of the walls and parapets and the treatment of the gun-ports and musket-slits varied. In the Portuguese period the coping of the parapets consisted of a flat top with a sloping outer edge. In the Arab period the copings were either a double slope or gable or a single slope, usually inwards.

The gun-platform and gatehouse were crowned by crenellations with vertical sides and gable tops. Two varieties can be distinguished: one large, 46 cm wide; the other small, 33 cm wide with clear-cut outline. The former is represented by the two rows on the gun-platform, the upper a copy of the lower; the other by the crenellations on the gatehouse, which include a number as much as 61 cm wide. The upper row on the gun-platform has a rounded profile, which also occurs on the castle at Kilwa, restored in the early nineteenth century.[5]

Both Portuguese and Arab gun-ports vary considerably, and include the open, square-topped embrasure and the closed type with a rounded arch. Many of them have been damaged or modified. Plans and sections of representative examples are drawn on Figs. 27 and 28. The open type was used in S. Alberto, in the cavalier of S. António, and probably in S. Matias, though here the embrasures were later capped

[3] Chittick (1959).

[4] Garlake (1966), Fig. 2 D, pp. 43, 72.

[5] Chittick (1959), pp. 179–203.

with poles forming an architrave. The gun-ports in the projections of S. Alberto and S. Filipe had similar architraves.

The bed of the ports generally sloped downwards, and the soffit of the arch in the closed ports upwards (Figs. 27 and 28). An upward slope is an indication of Portuguese work; a level slope, a perhaps not infallible presumption, of Arab work.[6] The downward slope of the bed was more pronounced in the Portuguese gun-ports, which also tended to be larger, or rather, included large as well as small ports. All ports, except those in the east wall of S. Matias, had a single outward splay starting from the inner face of the port. Recessed ports, generally with a small opening were made in the two important ports covering the main gate (Fig. 28 A, B, C), in the square-headed port at the apex of S. Mateus (Fig. 27 E, F), and in the Arab ports of the outwork (Fig. 28 J, K, L). The bed of the port was generally 38 cm or more in the Portuguese ports, and 15 to 23 cm in the Arab ports, above the ground behind them.

Arab and Portuguese musket-slits and spy-holes both had an inward splay, but otherwise showed more consistent differences than the gun-ports (Fig. 29). The Portuguese slit usually had a square face, an average of 43 cm on the inside, and a rectangular face on the outside, 99 cm high, and sloped down at a gradient of about one in three (Fig. 29 C, D, E, F). They covered the counterscarp and the ditch immediately below it. The characteristic Arab slit was pointed, with an internal width of 25 cm and height of 53 to 69 cm, with a similar downward slope (Fig. 29 G–L). The outer face of the apex was blocked, and pierced by a spy-hole. The execution of the slits was irregular, but two treatments of the gable can be distinguished, one with concave, the other with straight sides. The straight-sided slits are to be seen on the gun-platform (Fig. 29 I, J), in the north curtain (Fig. 29 G, H) and in S. Matias; the concave slits in S. Mateus (Fig. 29 K, L) and the east wall of S. Matias. The straight-sided slits are probably earlier. The plain slits of the Portuguese type continued to be used in the Arab period, notably in the turrets. Occasionally another type appears, with a rounded head which was sometimes blocked and pierced, but these may be modern repairs.

Only one Portuguese window has survived, the round-arched window in a square frame in the north wall of the Captain's House (Fig. 29 A, B). This was at a height of 56 cm from the floor and would have had a wooden shutter on the inside.

[6] I owe this tentative guide to R. Lewcock.

12. *Literary and Iconographical Material*

(Figs. 4–6; Pls. 3–5)

THE principal cartographical and iconographical material for the Fort consists of seven plans dating from 1610 to 1954, seven sketches made between 1824 and 1861, and a number of photographs taken at the end of the nineteenth or in the early twentieth century. The most important literary material is an inspection report of 1633 and three descriptions of the Fort in 1635, 1846, and 1861. In addition there are four inscriptions, of which three have survived *in situ* and the other in a copy, and a number of references to specific buildings which have been discussed in the relevant chapters.

The plans offer considerable difficulties, particularly by the omission of features which one has every reason to suppose existed. The omission of any buildings at the east end of the main court in the Lopes de Sá plan is particularly puzzling, since the room over the inner section of the Passage of the Arches and some structure along the line of the portico of the Captain's House and the later prison 'lamp' room, must have been in existence at that time. There is also the degree of reliability regarding scale and detail which, even in the case of the most convincing plan (Lopes de Sá), cannot be very high. The texts are more reliable, but are not without their perplexities. The descriptions are not exhaustive: the omission of any reference to the church in Bocarro/Rezende is surprising. Similarly, Thornton does not mention the audience room of the Mazrui or the L-shaped building in S. Matias. Perhaps he could not visit them, as they may have been occupied by Tanggai's family, but it seems strange that he makes no reference to what must have been the largest structures in the Fort.

The earliest of the documents are the Herédia and Teixeira plans (Fig. 4 A, B). They are in atlases, one published in 1610, the other between 1620 and 1630. They show the Fort as it was first built on the plan of Cairato. The Teixeira plan is based on the Herédia plan, but it is both simplified and embellished, and thereby made less accurate. The landward bastions are shown with their re-entrant angles in the Herédia plan, but are cut straight in the Teixeira. Both appear to have been drawn to a scale of 25 mm to 41 m and are reasonably true to scale. An outwork is shown as an extension of the rectangular projection, and the Passage of the Arches as a flight of steps. Cannon are placed in S. Matias and S. Mateus and in the outwork and, in the Teixeira plan, also in the re-entrant angles of the landward bastions. The Herédia, but not the Teixeira, plan shows buildings inside the Fort, but it is difficult to reconcile them with what was found in the excavations.

The report of Balthasar Marinho (4 April 1633) contains recommendations for the improvement of the defences after the loss and recovery of the Fort, some of which were carried out. The report also contained injunctions regarding the maintenance of the weapons, the administration of the accounts, and the defences of the Makupa ford between the island and the mainland.

First and foremost it is necessary to fill up the spring which is inside the cistern and to make the bottom of the cistern level with *mate*[1] and lime, well tamped with honey or molasses, so that it will not absorb water; then, when it is level, two or three layers of *argamaca*[2] plaster should be put all over the bottom of the cistern and also the sides (if there is enough *argamaca*), as much as seems necessary to make it watertight so that it will not leak.

Secondly, an inner wall should be built from the Captain's quarters to the Bastion of S. Matias, a distance of twelve standard *braca* (7·22 m). This should be large enough, in the opinion of the Council, for the space between the new wall and the old to be filled in and the old wall raised to the necessary height. A parapet should be made on top of it to render it defensible and to screen the houses in the Fort from anyone in the harbour.

For the service of Your Majesty and the defence of the Fort a wall should be built from the curtain of the gate of the Fort, at a place which I have marked, and a strong door with a good lock made. A guardroom should be made for use during the day, with a flat roof over it as protection from rain and sun, and seats below where the soldiers of the guard can sit.

As for the gate which is below the Fort in the outwork, by which the enemy entered who made themselves masters of the Fort, this gate also should be secured against incursion by means of a cannon set in the mouth of the passage.

In the Bastion of S. Mateus there is a gate which is very low in the wall. The natural rock should be cut back with picks, as it has been cut back at other exposed places, so that it is not possible to climb into the bastion.

These expenses should be covered from the one per cent duty which in the past was paid to the Customs.

The Rezende plan (Fig. 5 A) in the *Livro do Estado da India Oriental*, compiled by António Bocarro at Goa in 1635, and revised by Pedro Barreto de Rezende,[3] shows the Fort after the reconstruction of 1633–4, with the elliptical bastion covering the new gate, and towers in the angles of the rectangular projection. It also shows the church with a flat roof and with a baptistery at the south-west corner. The other buildings, and a tower at the south-east, had tiled roofs, apparently of the pent type. No trace of the buildings in the centre of the court has been found. As de Azevedo points out, they might have been copied from the Herédia plan and 'made more convincing'. The Passage of the Arches is not shown, but, from the text, the gun-platform shown in front of the Captain's House can only be the outwork, not an open space at the same level as the house. The text which accompanies the plan, ambiguous or incomprehensible as it sometimes is, is to be preferred to the grotesque plan, although the measurements are quite unreliable and there is confusion between the original

[1] A Konkani–Marathi word meaning a fine clay used for making pots and tiles. *Glossario Luso-Asiatico*, ii, pp. 42–3.

[2] See p. 50, n. 2.

[3] Boxer and de Azevedo (1960), p. 136.

parapets and the later curtain walls on top of them. The Portuguese *braca* or fathom is generally reckoned to be 2·22 m, which would make a *palmo* 22 cm; the *passo geometrico* is 1·52 m, and the *passo andante* 62 cm.[4] After the measurements in the text, the actual measurements are given in brackets.

The shape of the fortress is a quadrilateral, longer than it is broad, with four bastions in the four corners, which are called by the names inscribed on them. It can be seen also from the figure in the text that the two bastions on the landward side have a triangular plan, shaped like a spike, and the two on the harbour side are obtuse. This fortress has, as can be seen from the plan, an outwork which goes down to the harbour and which can be defended by soldiers who leave the fort by a concealed gate which emerges in the middle of the outwork. The outwork is 15 geometrical paces (14·64 m) in width, running along the length of the fortress, and 20 paces (26·82 m) in length running down to the harbour. In the two corners of the outwork on the harbour are small towers like sentry boxes, with loopholes.

The fortress has a ditch on the landward side, which has been excavated to a width of 3 fathoms (3·05–9·14 m) at the top and about the same width at the bottom or a little less. It is cut down into the rock to a depth of 2 or 3 fathoms (4·57–6·10 m). The ditch is a little narrower at the places where the two bastions are thrown out like spikes, because they are not exactly the same, but the contour of the ditch conforms with the angles of the bastions and the depth with the depth of the bastions.[5] The walls and parapets of the fortress are suitable and adequate because the blacks of the country are not accustomed to climbing walls with ladders.

The four bastions of the fortress are built up to the height of a man above the other walls. The two on the harbour side, which are larger, have a parapet walk of 15 walking paces, and those on the landward side of 12 walking paces.[6] Moreover, the projections are all open to the sky; the parapets on top of them are breast-high, 3 spans [*sic*] (83 cm–1·37 m) thick, and are made with loopholes.

The stretch of wall between the bastions of S. Filipe and S. Matias is the longest and is 12 standard fathoms (34·14 m) in length; the other is shorter and is 10 fathoms (43·9 m) in length.[7] These measurements are distinct from the bastions, the dimensions of which are given above.

The Captain's quarters are in the stretch of wall above and adjoining the outwork on the inside, overlooking the harbour.[8] They are large enough to accommodate a married man and his family.

Inside the fortress there are many single-storey houses arranged in squares, roofed with tiles, to accommodate the soldiers. Along the wall above the gate there is a quadrangular building with a flat roof in which are two store-rooms, where the powder is kept. Further within the walls is a magazine cut in the rock itself, to keep provisions and munitions. This

[4] Mitterwallner (1964).

[5] The text is obscure, but I think this is what it means. Actually, it is untrue, because the ditch was never finished, and against the wall of the Fort it is 1·52 m deeper than it is against the counterscarp.

[6] The parapet walks run round two sides of the bastions on the seaward side, and three sides of the bastions on the landward side. They are much larger than the measurements given.

[7] A glaring example of the inaccuracies of this text.

[8] I understand by this that the wall of the Captain's quarters was flush with the back wall of the outwork, i.e. the wall of the Fort.

is very damp because it is deep below the ground, and for this reason it is seldom that the foregoing articles are kept in it.

There is also in the fortress a cistern for water, cut in the rock, but it is not at present in order and never has been. Instructions have now been given to repair it because there is no water in the fortress. However, outside at a distance of 4 fathoms, there is a well which, although brackish, could be used in time of emergency. The way[9] to the well could be fortified, as was done by the King of Mombasa, the traitor Dom Jeronimo.[10]

The Cienfuegos plan (Fig. 5 B) is schematized, like the Herédia and Teixeira plans. It is accompanied by a brief and flowery description of East Africa and Mombasa, made and dedicated to Cardinal Mota, on the occasion of the recovery of Mombasa in 1728. The account of the Fort is adapted from Rezende and adds nothing to the key to the buildings attached to the plan. The Captain's House is described as a *casa mediana para o governader* (a moderate-sized house for the governor), and the church as *sua egreja parochial* (its parish church). The west barrack block is shown as a single line extending to the north end of the curtain wall. The omission of the steps is probably only a simplification, but the existence of the north section of the barracks is incompatible with the well, and the plan must therefore be earlier than that of Lopes de Sá. The elliptical bastion is shown, so the plan must be post-1634, but the cavaliers do not appear, so it may have been made before 1648, the date of the construction of the north-west cavalier, S. António. A large building in the upper level is described as the *casa del gobernador* (governor's house); this is the only occasion when the term 'governor' is applied to the captain. The layout of the east end of the court differs from that of all the other plans. The Captain's House and the Passage of the Arches are omitted, but a building marked 'barracks' is shown in this area, which would have been over the inner section of the passage. South of it are two square structures, one marked *magazine de polvero* (powder-magazine), the other *puerta souranca quebra a la couraça* (blocked door overlooking the outwork). No trace of the powder-magazine has been found, but the *puerta* may be the door in the east wall of the prison 'lamp' room. The outwork is shown accurately as a five-sided polygon, as in the Lopes de Sá plan and as it is today.

The names of the bastions have all been changed: S. Alberto to S. António, S. Filipe to *la Raposera* (the foxhole), S. Matias to *Baluarte del Mar* (bastion of the sea), and S. Mateus to *Baluarte de las Banderas* (bastion of the flags). The appearance of the name S. António does not refer to the cavalier S. António, which is sited in S. Filipe not in S. Alberto. In the Lopes de Sá plan it is applied to S. Matias, which is the logical place for it since this is the north-east bastion and overlooks the *Barra de S. António*, the name given by the Portuguese to the harbour of Mombasa. Changes in the names of towers and bastions in fortresses is a common practice. In the Tower of London

[9] This well has not been located.

[10] Translation by the author with the assistance of Prof. C. R. Boxer, from the Evora text in the *Arquivo Português Oriental*, iv (ii), I (1937), pp. 43–5.

the names of the towers were changed and transferred many times and, more relevant, at the Fort of S. Sebastião, Mozambique, the bastion of S. António became S. Barbara.

The only explanation I can offer for the anomalies in this plan is that it was an old project plan, showing the Fort with existing buildings to be retained and proposed new constructions. It was found in Goa or, more likely, Lisbon by the dubious 'Marquis' of Cienfuegos, and used to illustrate the report to his prospective patron, Cardinal Mota. The names may be the invention of a radical-minded draughtsman who preferred functional to honorific names. I can understand that in the mood of Portugal of the 1640s there would have been an antipathy to the Spanish Habsburgs, like King Philip and the Archduke Albert, but not to true Portuguese like Vasconcelos and Albuquerque—the latter one of the most famous names in Portuguese imperial history.

The Lopes de Sá plan (Fig. 5 C) was made by an Engineer Lieutenant-Colonel and shows the Fort and the buildings in it as they were in 1728, after thirty years of Arab occupation. It has a scale of 200 feet to 2·16 inches, and is the most professional of the Portuguese plans. However, the attention paid to accuracy can be judged from the difference between the length of the two sections of the scale. The difference in level between the central court and the bastions, the two cavaliers, the L-shaped building in S. Matias, and the sunken court in S. Mateus are all shown. At the west end of the main court the northern section of the barrack block has been replaced by the well. At the east end the Captain's House has disappeared and a platform is shown running round the projection and into the bastions on each side of it. In S. Mateus there is a guardroom in the same position as the later prison kitchen. The bastions, except for S. Matias, called S. António, have gone back to their original names. Nevertheless, the plan suffers from schematizations and simplifications which are grounds for distrust. The length of the chapel is certainly curtailed and I have grave doubts of the void at the east end of the Fort.

There is then a gap in records and plans for 170 years, which is broken by the visit recorded in Captain Owen's *Narrative of Voyages to Explore the Shores of Africa*, with two sketches of the Fort (Pl. 3 A).

The castle is of a quadrangular form and, notwithstanding its great size and dilapidated state, it might, with little expense, be rendered strong, especially those parts which the Arabs have allowed to remain untouched; for so wretched is their masonry that their attempts to repair the Portuguese work have in general taken away from its strength. The interior of Mombasa fort is a mass of indiscriminate ruins, huts and hovels, many of them built wherever space could be found, but generally formed from parts of the ruins matted over for roofs. When seized from the Portuguese every building within the outer wall was thrown down, and the foundations torn up to search for treasure supposed to have been hidden here. The fine tank, which once contained water enough for two or three years, can not now be traced without great difficulty. But, wretched as the place is, it is now used as the residence of the reigning family whose retainers constitute the garrison, amounting to about two hundred men, women and children.[11]

The sketch of the Fort from the sea shows the ruinous condition of the walls and the absence of turrets on the corners of the rectangular projection and the south-east bastion. The tower in the south-east angle is shown with a door at its base. Latrine shafts were used in storied Arab buildings on the coast, but there is no evidence of such an opening at the base of the tower today. Inside the Fort, two towers are shown, one on the south-west, the other either in the north-west bastion or over the gate, but they are exaggerated in height and look like English Perpendicular church towers. The tall flagstaff is in the elliptical bastion. Along the south wall are two buildings with palm-frond roofs on the line of the old barracks. The other illustration shows the main gate with the armorial feature above it.

There is no account of the Fort during the British Protectorate of 1824–6. The British representative, or rather the representative of Captain Owen, because he had no other authority for his position, was not permitted to live in the Fort and apparently was not invited to examine it.[12]

The next piece of information is in Dr. Krapf's *Travels, Researches and Missionary Labours*. It is a sketch of the Fort from the other side of the creek (Pl. 3 B), made presumably between 1844 and 1859, although the book was published in 1860. As one might expect, it is the best and most convincing sketch of the seven. It shows the turrets at the corners of the rectangular platform, the turret in S. Mateus, the house in the south-west bastion, the gatehouse, two palm-frond roofs over the barracks on the south curtain, and a palm-frond roof on the gun-platform in the position of the house on the 1899 plan, probably Tanggai's *baraza*. It would appear that Krapf did not enter the Fort and he gives no description of it.

The two sketches by Captain Guillain belong to the same period. One of them shows almost the same view as Krapf's; the other the Fort from the north (Pl. 4 A). The latter is more interesting, and although something has gone wrong with the drawing, the details are obviously authentic. The palm-frond roof of the L-shaped building in S. Matias is shown, but no buildings along the north face, nor any turret in the north-east corner. The turret in the middle of the curtain wall appears, but not the upper storey with the conical top. On top of the cavalier of S. António is a house with a flat roof. The roof is a little above the blocked merlons, and the dome of the turret in the north-west corner is just above the roof line. This house extended over the room of the oven, and provided the lower part of the walls of the later prison office. The flagstaff is shown in the middle of the main court, as it is today. The approach to the Fort is obscured by a circular tomb with a palm-frond roof in the cemetery of the Mazrui, which has now disappeared. Guillain went over the Fort with Tanggai, and his description is translated below:

[11] Owen (1833), vol. i, p. 406. [12] Gray (1957).

The object of the morning expedition, for which I had stayed ashore the previous evening, was to visit the fortress and the south-east part of the island. The former lies 1,200 metres beyond the entrance to the north-east port, at the extreme south of the town. It is built on a rocky piece of rising ground, which has been quarried, not only to serve as the foundations but also to form the lower part of the walls. This building is a bastioned square of about 110 metres on the outside, the bastions corresponding approximately to the four points of the compass. Only the side facing west-south-west has been laid out according to professional principles—that is to say, so as to present no uncovered corner. The lines of the other three faces have been kept almost exactly parallel to the sides of the square, in order no doubt to make the most of the space inside and to lessen the chances of the bastions being destroyed by making them too acute. Then, to avoid the weakness in the plan resulting from the defective outline, the engineers have built round half towers at the shoulder angles and on the bastions.

The east-north-east face, which commands both the entrance to the harbour, the anchorage below the town and the opposite shore on the mainland, has a more curious arrangement. In order to cover the positions of attack and ensure the maximum of firing power, the bastion plan has not been followed on this side. The flanks and the curtain wall, to conform with the imaginary line joining the two corners of the shoulder, take up a line in proportion to that which would have been given them in a regular plan, so that the curtain wall juts out, instead of being a re-entrant. At the base of this there is a gate protected by a sort of crenellated *tambour* or outwork. The side parallel to the curtain wall has been pierced with gun-ports to make a small shore battery. By reason of the slope of the land, however, this outwork is completely unprotected from fire directed against it by ships or boats anchored in the harbour. An opening at one corner provides communication between it and a battery at ground-level, parallel to the wall of the Fort, erected on the shore itself. The fortress thus has on this front three fire positions. The artillery flank on the north-north-west protects the town, known as Gavana, and the other two defend the approaches to the fortress on the landward side.

The height of the scarp is about 17 metres, including the ditch, which is 4 to 5 metres deep and of an equal width, and surrounds the fortress on the three landward sides. On the side of the counterscarp below the salient of the north bastion the ground has been cut away in order to extend the ditch as far as the shore, and the gap resulting from this operation has been blocked by a wall in which an opening with an arched entrance has been made. A bridge thrown across the ditch gives access to the duty gate opening into the left side of the northern bastion.

Built by the Portuguese in 1594, this fortress was restored in 1635 and, apart from the effects of weather on the masonry, the walls remain as they were at that time. This is confirmed by the description given by Rezende at the latter date. At the corners of the western and southern bastions it is still possible to read the names on the coats-of-arms carved in the stone: Bastion of St. Philip on the western, Bastion of St. Albert on the southern. According to Rezende the northern bastion was called St. Mathias, meaning that it was under the protection of the patron saint of the Viceroy Mathias d'Albuquerque, during whose governorship the Fort was built. But this coat-of-arms as well as that on the south-east, having been inscribed on the front of the fortress which was the most exposed to enemy fire, have no doubt been effaced by cannon fire and were not put back when the breaches were repaired.[13] As often as not most of the fresh breaches made during the various attacks by Saiyid Said against the stronghold, then in the hands of the Mazrui, have remained open. The revetment walls with their deep cracks have shrubs growing out of the fissures in several places. The embrasures are almost all broken down and the guns in the upper and lower batteries are pitted by rust or fallen from the worm-eaten gun-carriages, so that even the least damaged would be incapable of sustaining an hour's fire. To restore the fortress to a respectable state of defence, as much work would have to be carried out inside as on the walls. The arrangement of the place demonstrates the Arabs' ignorance of the military techniques. Here and there are piles of boxes covered with straw, which could catch fire very easily. The Portuguese buildings have been destroyed, except the passage cut out of the thickness of the walls in the bastion of St. Mathias, now used for storing powder, cannon-balls, etc. They were intended to receive a consignment of grain, twelve or eighteen months' provisioning, replenished every year. The cistern is out of use, but there is a well with drinkable water which would serve the needs of the garrison in case of siege.

The garrison, composed of Baluchis and Hadraumis, numbers two hundred men, I am told. The *jemadar*, Tanggui, claims that he has four hundred, but as through the customs contract he draws 700 to 800 piastres monthly for his pay and that of his garrison, and as each man receives 2½ to 5 piastres a month, it is evident that he is in fact paid for a force of 250 men at most. Baluchis are in the majority; Said's preference for this foreign militia, which contributed largely to his rise to power, is well known. At the time when this prince took possession of the Fort of Mombasa, he decreed that there should be a garrison of 500 men; this has diminished as the Sultan's authority grew. It supplies 15 to 20 men to the Governor, to ensure that his orders are carried out; the remainder live in the Fort and never sleep out without the permission of the commandant. From 11 a.m. to 1 p.m. the Fort is closed for rest and prayer, and from sundown to sunrise there is no communication with the town.[14]

The next record of the Fort is the water-colour sketch in Baron von der Decken's *Reisen in Ost-Afrika*, published in 1871, probably drawn in 1861 at the time of the Baron's visit. It was made from the high ground south of the Fort, near the Katharine Bibby Hospital (Pl. 4 B). The palm-frond roof of the building on the gun-platform is shown, but at right angles to the parapet. A similar roof at the same angle is shown behind the south angle tower and another, perhaps the mosque, in S. Mateus.

The turret at the west end of the south curtain is missing, but the house in the south-west corner of S. Alberto is shown with a flat roof and, apparently, with the south-west corner of the bastion excluded, as it is today. The drawing of the von der Decken sketch is competent and seems to be accurate, but some of the details, such as the two windows high up in the house in S. Alberto, the three gun-ports in the south wall of S. Mateus, and the direction of the roofs athwart the platform instead of head-on, may be the consequence of completing the drawing away from the subject. In the

[13] This is not quite correct. The coat-of-arms of Mateus Mendes de Vasconcelos has survived on the Bastion of S. Mateus.

[14] Guillain, vol. iii, pp. 251–5.

same book is another sketch of the gate, which may be a re-drawing of the sketch in Owen.

The description of the Fort in the *Reisen* is brief and mentions only the entrance and the rectangular projection. The Baron was, however, accompanied by an Englishman, Richard Thornton, who gives in his diary a more detailed picture, and also the transcription of a Portuguese inscription, which has disappeared (page 46). The text of Thornton's references to the Fort is given below.

> Before breakfast we took the theodolite and went to the Fort to go over it. Had a little delay at the door; then old Tanggai came out to us and in we went. The doorway is large and leads into a large right-angled passage which opens into the centre of the Fort from under the high house which is seen from the outside. We first went to the sea front of the Fort where old Tanggai has his *baraza*, passing on the way an old subterranean passage leading to the sea, now choked up with rubbish. The guns were nearly all English eighteen-pounder ship guns, dated 1802, 1803, 1811, etc. The *baraza* was a good large room with a fine view of the sea, etc. Tanggai showed us his guns then took us to see an old bronze Portuguese gun at the north-east corner. Then returned to the *baraza* where we had tea and sweets, then off round the Fort along the east side to the centre, where there is a deep square well and a large cistern by its side. All the interior of the Fort is filled with small *makuti* huts and very dirty. All the families and slaves of the Beleuchis live inside it. Then went on to the south-west [*sic*] corner where there is a stone house with a small mutilated stone tablet let into the wall on one side of the door. Whilst the Baron copied this tablet, I went on to the top of the house and from it took observations with the theodolite.[15]

The report on the damage to the Fort caused by the bombardment with shell and Hale rockets in 1875, which was requested by the British Admiralty and which would *ipso facto* have given a most valuable account of buildings in the Fort, has disappeared. It may have been a secret document, eventually destroyed by some distracted official to make room for current papers. It may come to light in some foreign archives if, at some time, somewhere, it has been able to shed its stamp of secrecy and so pass into the hands of an archivist and be preserved.

The next document relating to the Fort is the Public Works Department plan of 1899 (Fig. 6) which shows the new prison buildings as well as the buildings, mostly Arab, existing when the Fort was taken over in 1895. Originally, only the seaward side which included the bastions of S. Matias and S. Mateus and the gun-platform between them, was used as the prison. This was also the area which had suffered most from the bombardment of 1875 and had probably been patched rather than restored in the intervening twenty years. The buildings here are, therefore, more likely to be prison constructions than those in the other parts of the Fort, which were converted later when it became necessary to enlarge the prison.

The P.W.D. plan shows the Fort 171 years after its predecessor, the Lopes de Sá plan of 1728. Almost all the Portuguese buildings have collapsed or been destroyed,

[15] The tablet is the inscription on the cavalier in S. Filipe (see p. 51).

but sometimes, as in the case of the south barrack block and the L-shaped building in S. Matias, the Arab and prison builders have used the walls as foundations.

There are a number of early photographs of the Fort in the possession of the family of Sir Mbarak ʿAli Hinawy, probably taken in the last decade of the nineteenth century. The most interesting is the view along the west wall (Pl. 5 A), showing the buildings with palm-frond roofs in S. Filipe, and the platform behind the west curtain. The photograph of the sea front taken in 1894, in the National Maritime Museum at Greenwich (Pl. 5 B), shows the upper row of crenellations still incomplete. These photographs illustrate the Public Works Department plan of 1899.

A re-survey of the prison was made in 1922 and revised in 1954,[16] and a comparison between this and the 1899 plan (Fig. 6) shows the extension of prison accommodation all over the area of the Fort. In the final arrangement of the prison which lasted until 1957, European prisoners were accommodated in the south-west corner, Asian along the south curtain wall, African along the north curtain, juveniles in the north-east bastion, women in the area of the Audience Room of the Mazrui, and lunatics on the gun-platform above them. Some sign of gradation between the sexes had to be shown, even in conditions of well-deserved misfortune. The lunatics should not, of course, have been in Fort Jesus at all, but there were always so many local lunatics in the Nairobi mental asylum that there was never room for anybody from the coast.

[16] Plan in Fort Jesus.

Part II. The Finds

In the course of the excavations at Fort Jesus large quantities of unglazed earthenware, glazed earthenware, porcelain, and beads were found. The ceramic and bead pattern of the Kenya coast, which had stopped at Gedi and other sites at the end of the sixteenth century, is now carried forward to the end of the nineteenth.

The fullest descriptions of the individual pieces accompany the drawings (Figs. 30–86), except in the case of the Islamic glazed wares (Pls. 21–3), the Chinese porcelain (Pls. 24–38), and the Portuguese religious medallions (Pls. 43–4), in which the decoration is of greater significance than the form. An attempt has been made to classify the Islamic glazed wares and the Chinese porcelain, and numbers have been given to the different types for convenience of reference.

References to Gedi, The Great Mosque, are to my book *The Arab City of Gedi, Excavations at the Great Mosque, Architecture and Finds* (Oxford University Press, 1954). The change has been made to distinguish the Great Mosque from the other publications on Gedi (see bibliography). In these references Cl. for 'class' indicates the groups in which the ceramic has been classified.

Other finds included glass, cannon, cannon-balls, crucibles and stone vessels, implements, ornaments, fittings, and coins. Of these the most interesting were the Portuguese medallions, referred to above, and the Arab moulds for ornaments (Pl. 42).

A number of animal bones were found, mostly in the Passage of the Arches. Among those which could be identified, cow bones greatly predominated. The list was made up as follows: cow, 147; ovicaprids, 31; buffalo, 12; sheep, 11; goat, 7; hippopotamus, 3; camel, 2; ostrich, 2; giant monitor lizard, 1; donkey, 1.[1]

[1] Identified by Margaret Leakey.

13. *The Ceramics*

THE ceramics found in the Fort included wares from China, India, Persia, Portugal, England, and other countries of western Europe and Asia, as well as the local earthenware. They indicate the cosmopolitan culture which prevailed on the coast of East Africa and around the Indian Ocean during the seventeenth, eighteenth, and nineteenth centuries.

The types of vessels found are described in the following eleven sections, and are illustrated in Figs. 30–75 and Plates 19–41.

The treatment of the European china could have been fuller, but the cost of illustration—and without illustration comment has little meaning—was not considered justified by the importance of any conclusions which could be drawn from it. Similarly, the usefulness of the chapters on the local earthenware would have been enhanced by more photographs, and the beads by coloured photographs, but these would have raised the book's selling price.

UNGLAZED WARES

LOCAL EARTHENWARE (Figs. 30–56; Pl. 19)

The local earthenware was made of hard-baked reddish clay without grits, similar to the wares found in earlier levels at Gedi and Ungwana and other sites north of Mombasa. The only variations were a few sherds with the sandy-buff body, published in *Gedi, The Great Mosque*, Cl. 34–40, Fig. 21.[1]

The categories of pots consisted of cooking-pots, large and small, deep (*chungu*) or shallow (*kaango*), rounded or carinated; relish bowls (*bunguu*), large and small, deep or shallow; a large bowl with turned-out lip (*bia*) for holding coconut milk and, as a subsidiary use, for serving up food; jars or pitchers with short or long necks (*kuzi*); lamps (*taa*), lids, charcoal stoves (*mziga*); and miniature pots and bowls used as toilet articles or toys. Large jars for holding water (*nzio* or *jirambo*) were not common. However, this type of vessel was probably imported from Portugal, India, and Persia.

Among the cooking-pots I have been unable to obtain any clear information that there was a difference in use between the rounded and carinated pots. Generally, but not always, the rounded pots were deep, their depth equalling or exceeding half the diameter, while the carinated pots were shallow, their depth being less than half their diameter. The tall appliqué-ornamented pots are an exception.

The food of the coast consisted of millet, rice, and bananas, which would be cooked in the deeper pots. Arab and Arab–African cooking is normally a matter of grilling

[1] Kirkman (1954).

9200351

on a spit or boiling. The *samoosa*, which is fried in deep fat is an exception. Malicious people say that the Arab *samoosa* are crisper than the Indian because Arabs are more generous with the fat, but this may be no more than racial bitchiness. However, in the matter of boiling there are dishes which have to be stirred and others which can be left to stew. The carinated bowls, particularly those with inward sloping necks and sharp carination, would seem to be less suitable for millet porridge, which was the staple cereal dish of the coast and must be stirred. They would have been used for meat or fish which was eaten as a relish with it. The small rather deep pots would be used for heating oil, generally ghee. Milk of goats or cows does not seem to have been an article of general consumption in the Arab world of the coast. There were no special utensils in earthenware made for it, though the Omani copper milk bowl may have been used.

Besides cooking, there would be the preparation of medicines, snuff, and poisons, which would demand a kind of mortar for pounding and a small bowl for boiling. The tall bowls, commoner in the Arab–African sites and called *kidumo*, as well as some of the *bunguu* with vertical sides, were used as mortars. The small deep bowls for heating oil were also used for the preparation of arrow poisons.

Other vessels were made of wood, such as the eating bowl called *hero*, and the mortar called *kinu*. These terms are sometimes employed for clay vessels used for a similar purpose.

The surface was sometimes painted with red oxide, which was frequently burnished, on the inside of the bowls and on the outside of the pots and jars. In East Africa this technique goes back at least to the thirteenth century. At the end of the seventeenth century the burnishing was often perfunctory, and by the end of the eighteenth was no longer in general use. It is, however, still employed in the village industry at Marjoreni, and why it should be rare in the later levels in Fort Jesus is unknown.

Besides an over-all internal burnish, there was an alternative treatment by which only the lip was painted and burnished. This treatment was in use throughout the seventeenth century but was never popular, except in the case of the pots in Fig. 30. 21–6, and the carinated pots in Fig. 30. 5–10. It was uncommon after the seventeenth century except on the pots with swan-necks and chamfered outer lip (Fig. 50. 29–36).

Another treatment was the coating of part of the pot with red oxide but without the extra labour of burnishing. This had occurred in late-sixteenth-century levels at Gedi, but at Fort Jesus was particularly common on the necks of jars and above the carination on large carinated bowls in eighteenth- and nineteenth-century levels (Figs. 42. 12–17; 49. 3 and 6).

There were also a few examples in eighteenth-century levels of burnishing on the raw body without the red coat. The object of burnishing was utilitarian rather than aesthetic, so that the vessel should be less porous and should be given a harder surface on places where it would receive most wear, such as on the lip.

However, there were other treatments which were purely for embellishment, such as incised, appliqué, and/or moulded ornament (Pl. 19. 1–5), and also a form of painted decoration with broad red vertical stripes. Appliqué and moulded ornamentation are variations of the same decorative purpose which was to achieve the effect by a raised pattern. When simple, as generally in the early seventeenth century, it was sufficient to press out the soft clay. Later a taste developed for more prominent patterns which could only be executed by adding strips of clay. The incised and appliqué ornament was found principally on cooking-pots and occasionally on lamps and jars; the moulded ornament on cooking-pots only; the red stripes on bowls, carinated bowls, and jars.

The distinction between bowls, cooking-pots, and jars is not always easy to make when only the rim is available. A vessel with a base is classified as a bowl, but there are a few vessels without bases which have obviously never served as cooking-pots and should be considered as eating-bowls. There are also vessels with the carination proper to a cooking-pot but with a base which makes it into a bowl. Cooking-pots and jars can sometimes only be separated by size and, somewhat arbitrarily, by the existence of a neck. The distinction between the bag-shaped pot and the shouldered jar is often difficult to make.

The local ceramic pattern of both pots and bowls changed at the end of the seventeenth century. It changed again in respect of the cooking-pots in the middle of the eighteenth and again at the beginning of the nineteenth century. The burnished bowls continued in the same forms from the end of the seventeenth to the end of the eighteenth centuries. The cause of these changes has not yet been discovered. The new types belonged basically to the coast ceramic and were not related to the ceramic of the hinterland. The jar forms were, as they had always been, less liable to change than the other forms.

Today the industry is in decline. There is still a demand but the making of pots is only an additional, not a basic source of income. The industry is carried on at Marjoreni near Shimoni, fifty miles south of Mombasa, and at Kwa Jomvu near Mombasa, on a small scale by women, usually elderly, where there is suitable clay. It may not survive another decade.

The cooking-pots, bowls, and jars made up ninety per cent of the sherds of earthenware found in the Fort, but there were also a few sherds which had belonged to other vessels.

Lids

Lids, or *kia*, were of two types. One was the conventional type of lid with a knob on the top, sometimes frilled round the edge and never carbonized. It occurred in late-seventeenth-century levels but was commonest in the early nineteenth century (Fig. 54. 15).

The other type had a turned-up rim, like a hat, and sometimes a handle in the middle. It was invariably carbonized. Handles have not been found in the same numbers as lids, and it is possible that not all lids had them. The earliest example of this type was found in a late-seventeenth-century level (Fig. 39. 30). They were still rare in the eighteenth century and were commonest in the nineteenth.

Lamps

The open boat-shaped lamps, or *taa*, which had been made in the Semitic world for over two thousand years, continued with the same forms that had been found in fifteenth- and sixteenth-century levels at Gedi. In the seventeenth and eighteenth centuries they tended to be a regular oval with very little pinch at the lip. In the nineteenth the pinch was more pronounced and the base was sometimes flattened in the middle (Fig. 54. 13). Unusual forms include types with internal flanges (Fig. 45. 16, 17) from eighteenth-century levels; with three spouts and perhaps a handle (Fig. 54. 12), and a type with a pedestal base (Fig. 54. 14), both from nineteenth-century levels. They were also found with a red burnish on the inside or on the rim, or with a frill on the lip and a line of dots or nicks on the carination. A nineteenth-century example with appliqué ornament is shown in Fig. 51. 3.

Horned Bowls

Horned bowls, or *mziga*, were found in all levels in the Fort, including some with a pierced horn (Fig. 43. 25). There was an example with parallel lines of ribbing round the flange from a nineteenth-century level (Fig. 54. 11). They were used as charcoal stoves and were first made for use on dhows, so that the crew could cook their food without setting fire to the ship. This type of vessel was first found in late-fifteenth-century levels at Gedi, and until recently was made at Kwa Jomvu, near Mombasa. It was also made in south Arabia, where the form was probably invented, and in the eastern Congo, where it was introduced by the Arabs when they started to build boats on Lake Tanganyika and Lake Victoria.

Sectioned Bowls

A curious type of bowl, always carbonized, was made with one or more raised egg-shaped receptacles in the bottom (Plate 19. 6–8). No complete section was found and it is impossible to reconstruct the form of the vessel. The receptacles may have been moulds for holding a residual substance after the liquid, in which it had been held in suspension, had boiled away or evaporated. They were found in nineteenth-, rarely eighteenth-century levels, but no recollection of them has survived among the people of the coast.

Flanged Bowls

Another type of bowl was flanged with projections set horizontally at intervals round the rim. It occurred in early-seventeenth-century levels with a red rim (Fig. 32. 21, 22), plain in late-seventeenth-century levels and burnished in early-nineteenth-century levels.

Handled Bowls

Allied to the flanged bowls were bowls with handles, sometimes burnished, which have been found in early-seventeenth-century levels (Fig. 32. 20)

Mortars

The mortar was a stout straight-sided bowl with cordons, perhaps in imitation of wooden bowls, which was used for powdering snuff or herbs. It had been found in late-sixteenth-century levels at Gedi, and occurred at Fort Jesus in a different form in eighteenth- (Fig. 43. 24) and nineteenth-century levels (Fig. 54. 10).

In the key attached to the figures the terms 'common', 'uncommon', and 'single specimens' are used. The term uncommon means that not more than two or three examples have been found and not necessarily all in the same period. The forms shown in figures of one period are not repeated if they were found—as they often were—in the succeeding period. It is impossible to say whether sherds which occur sporadically in later levels are the result of actual survival of a pot or the survival of a tradition. The occasional late appearance of the odd red-striped sherds is particularly puzzling. It should be borne in mind that we are dealing with very simple forms and ornamentation and there is no reason why they should not recur. There is also, compared with pottery of the Roman Empire or the Near East, only a small amount of material from an even smaller number of sites on which to make pronouncements.

Ornament

The most interesting feature about these pots should be the ornament, but most of it consists of a variety of incised patterns of chevrons, curves, and lines (Pl. 19. 1–5), which had been used on the coast for hundreds of years. Normally it took the form of a continuous band above the carination, or a series of single motifs with intervals between them, such as Figs. 55. 37–42 and 56. 57–61 and 67–76. Occasionally there seem to have been isolated marks which have no decorative function, such as nos. 43–5, 48, and 49. These marks may have a magical significance or may be trade marks. In almost all cases only part of the pot was found, and the motifs believed to be in series with intervals may in fact be isolated marks. Today certain potters among the Kamba and Taita, two Bantu tribes of the hinterland, mark their pots. The Kamba duplicate the mark on the opposite side of the pot.[2]

The ornament is found usually on the carinated cooking-pots, less commonly on the rounded and shouldered pots and bowls. There would be a natural preference for single motifs on the rounded bowls because of the difficulty of keeping a horizontal line without the help of the carination. The distribution of the types of incised ornament, numbered 1–108, among the types of pot in the four periods is shown in the table below. (Numbers refer to Figs. 55–6 unless otherwise stated.)

[2] Communication from Jean Brown.

The numbers of different types of ornament vary over the four periods of the history of the Fort. In Period I there were thirteen varieties; in Period II, twenty-one; in Period III, fifteen, and in Period IV, sixty-four. The increase in variety is also matched by an increase in interest. Of the more elaborate and possibly significant motifs there were none in Period I; three (nos. 24, 25, and 29) in Period II; five (nos. 38–42) in Period III, and twelve (nos. 57, 58, and 67–76) in Period IV.

	17th cent.: Period I	late 17th cent.: Period II	18th cent.: Period III	19th cent.: Period IV
Small thin-walled rounded pots	1, 6–10	12		
Rounded pots with turned-out lip	Fig. 30. 4	13, 16, 23, 24	33, 41–3	50, 58, 73, 74
Rounded pots		15		59, 75
Shouldered pots		22	37, 39, 40, 44	47, 49, 56, 57, 72, 76
Small carinated pots	2–5 Fig. 30. 3	14	34	55
Carinated pots with smooth surface	11	17–20		
Carinated pots with red neck		26–32	46	60–70
Carinated pots with rounded neck			36	53, 55
Carinated pots with straight neck				50–2, 77
Carinated pots with slight concave neck		21, 25	35	
Carinated pots with deep concave neck				54, 78, 79–108
Bowls			38, 43, 45	48
Lamp				71

Virtually nothing is known about East African decorative motifs, and it is possible that eventually some meaning may be found to the groups of vertical wedges and dots (nos. 24, 25, 29, 38–42, and 57–76), which appear on pots, usually with a red neck or rim, from the late seventeenth century onwards. They seem to have a numerical significance. No. 24 could be the number 6 and no. 29, the number 9. No. 25 is more difficult to explain but could represent indefinite quantity, and no. 62, with its groups of 12 and 8, could also belong to the same set. Ignoring the central strokes in nos. 69, 70, 71, and 72, there is a representation of 4, 6, 2, 5. Both sets could be inspired by the designs on playing-cards, which were used by the Europeans in the

Indian Ocean countries and were no doubt noticed by Arabs and Africans. No. 59, the inverted pyramid of dots, probably represents the pudendal triangle. The number of dots is not constant and no significance attaches to it. Other marks, such as nos. 27 and 49, seem to be reminiscent of characters on Chinese porcelain, while nos. 55, 56, and 60 recall European heraldic bearings. No. 77 is an unusual combination of vertical lines and punch-marks on a pot (Fig. 48. 4) which is itself unusual, and it must be an import from another African ceramic area. No. 78 was made by the impression of a small scallop shell and is a unique example of this kind of ornament.

The other two modes of ornament are less interesting. The appliqué or moulded patterns (Figs. 31. 14; 36. 29–33; 37. 2; 43. 1–16; 51. 14, 18, 20–4; Pl. 19. 1–3) are limited to strokes and arcs, and the painted patterns (Figs. 31. 16–22; 37. 1, 2; 42. 19, 20) to broad red vertical stripes above the carination, similar to the burnished lines.

Today, ornament of any kind is seldom used and the only habitual embellishment is painting with red ochre and burnishing.

The main periods in the Fort are defined by Chinese porcelain which continues to be the most precise method of dating East African sites. The levels in which relatively large and so representative collections of sherds were found are listed below. No significant variations were found between deposits in the same period.

Period I—Ming and Transitional Ming, 1593–*c.* 1670.

Make-up of the rectangular projection, perhaps as early as 1596.
Filling of S. Filipe, S. Matias, and the gun-platform in S. Mateus, 1634.
Make-up of Elliptical Bastion, 1634.
Make-up of Cavalier S. António, 1648.
Filling over Passage of the Steps. No K'ang Hsi types; perhaps as early as 1650.

Period II—K'ang Hsi, *c.* 1670–*c.* 1730.

Gravel pit in S. Filipe.
Filling of Captain's House.
Room of the stands.
Lower filling of court in S. Mateus.
Lower filling of Passage of the Arches.

Period III—Famille rose, *c.* 1730–*c.* 1840.

Court on north side of Captain's House.
Area of the main court, the west barrack block, and the church.
Upper filling of court in S. Mateus.

Period IV—European china, *c.* 1840–*c.* 1895.

Upper filling of Passage of the Arches.
Area between Captain's House and audience room of the Mazrui.
Area of south barrack block.

PERIOD I. EARLY SEVENTEENTH CENTURY (Figs. 30–3)

The typical forms of early-seventeenth-century local earthenware, which were found in the Fort associated with Ming porcelain, were the cooking-pots with lips turned out and upward, sometimes carinated (Fig. 30. 3, 4, 13–32), and bowls usually burnished (Fig. 33, 1–17) some with sloping outer lip (Fig. 33. 1–4) or thickened, rounded inner lip (Fig. 33. 7–10). Other types were the basic rounded cooking-pot (Fig. 30. 1), plain carinated pots (Fig. 30. 2, 5–11), burnished carinated bowls (Fig. 33. 18–22 and 26–30), and shallow pots like dishes, sometimes with projecting lips (Fig. 31. 1–6). Jars were less common and consisted of the water pot with a long or medium neck, burnished or unburnished (Fig. 33. 31–4, 36, 37), and the jar with a short neck, almost a collar (Fig. 32. 2, 3, and Fig. 33. 35), which may have been used for some kind of pickled or dried substance. Other vessels were rare but included a few sherds of lamps and horned bowls, similar to those which had been found at Gedi. New forms were the unguent bowl (Fig. 33. 23), the platter (Fig. 33. 25), and the handled and flanged bowls (Fig. 32. 20–2).

Besides the ordinary classes of earthenware there were three groups distinguished by their decoration. One was characteristic of the early seventeenth century and the others made their appearance in this period but were prominent later. The first was a class of carinated and shouldered pots with a broad red stripe above the carination on the outside (Fig. 31. 16–22). This type of decoration had been found at Ungwana in sixteenth-century levels and in a slightly different form, with narrow instead of broad stripes, at Kilwa in fourteenth- and fifteenth-century levels. A few sherds of the Kilwa variety have been found at Gedi, probably left by visitors.

The other two classes were the deep pots with appliqué or moulded ornament in the form of vertical stripes above the carination (Fig. 31. 12–14) and normally proportioned pots with a smoothed surface often a near-vertical neck above the carination and carved, or rather sliced, ornament like Fig. 55. 11 on the carination (Fig. 31. 10).

PERIOD II. LATE SEVENTEENTH CENTURY (Figs. 34–9)

The late seventeenth century is represented by four large deposits and one small deposit, which are associated by the presence of the same type of *famille verte* and blue-and-white porcelain and the absence of *famille rose*. Three of the four deposits can be dated by circumstantial evidence. The filling of the Captain's House must have been carried out soon after the capture of the Fort by the Arabs in 1698. The filling in the court of S. Mateus may be the next, as the gate is not shown on the Lopes de Sá plan of 1728. The deposit in the Passage of the Arches must be later than 1728 because the gate to the outwork is mentioned on the plan. The date of the filling of the gravel pit in S. Filipe is unknown. From the high proportion of pots with turned-out lips, like Fig. 30. 31, 32, it could have been the earliest of the four deposits. On the other hand, the shallow pots with turned-out lips (Fig. 31. 1–6), a common pot of Period I, were rare in S. Filipe although found in quantity in S. Mateus, which was linked by other ceramic features more to the eighteenth than to the early seventeenth century. The sherds which were found on the floor of the room of the stands were similar to those from S. Filipe. This floor was covered at the time of the demolition of the north end of the west barrack block and the construction of the courts behind the church, which occurred before the siege. In all these deposits was a quantity of Portuguese blue-and-white which, unlike the Chinese, was of no interest to anybody except the Portuguese. The sequence of Portuguese blue-and-white has never been worked out, and it is not yet possible to distinguish between late-seventeenth- and early-eighteenth-century types. However, it is unlikely to have reached Mombasa after the beginning of the siege in 1696. The occupation of 1728 was a military expedition, which would not have had more than the minimum of household goods.

The pots with turned-out lips (Fig. 30. 13–22) and the shallow pots with projecting lips (Fig. 31. 1–3) continued to be made. The pots with appliqué ornament became more numerous and the ornament more distinctive (Fig. 36. 29–33; Pl. 19. 1–3). Shouldered and rounded pots were still relatively uncommon, except in S. Mateus. A variant which continued throughout the eighteenth and into the nineteenth century was a shouldered pot, often painted red on the rim (Fig. 34. 7, 8).

There were two new groups of pots, similar in form but with alternative decoration. One had a smooth black surface and carved diamond-shaped ornament on the carination and occasionally a bead rim (Fig. 35. 4–7, 19 and 26). This type had appeared in Period I (Fig. 31. 10) but was characteristic of Period II and the eighteenth century, though uncommon later. The other was painted red above the carination but not burnished. The carination was usually marked by a line of indentations, large or small, horizontal or vertical, with one or two lines above them (Fig. 35. 4, 6, and 22). The neck above the carination was often ornamented with an incised pattern (Fig. 55. 26–32). This type continued into the nineteenth century.

The jars of early-seventeenth-century type, apart from the collared form (Fig. 32. 2, 3), continued. The jar with the medium-sized 'hole' mouth, which had occurred occasionally at Gedi (see *Gedi—The Palace*, Fig. 11. 0)[3] now reappeared and continued to be made during the eighteenth century.

Unburnished bowls were uncommon and, in the case of the smaller bowls, followed the types of Period I (Fig. 32. 10–16). The heavier bowls included some forms (Fig. 38. 10–16) which had not been found in Period I but had occurred at Gedi and Ungwana. The burnished bowls and jars of Period I continued, but a new form with an inward-sloping or hollowed, thickened lip (Fig. 39. 6–15, 19–23) was introduced.

PERIOD III. EIGHTEENTH CENTURY (Figs. 40–5)

In the eighteenth century, i.e. between 1730 and 1837, the period defined by the presence of *famille rose* porcelain and the absence of European china, the forms of cooking-pot introduced at the end of the seventeenth century continued. The rounded,

[3] Kirkman (1963).

shouldered, and carinated pots shown on Figs. 40–2 do not differ significantly from those shown on Figs. 34–6. Among the carinated pots most of the old forms, such as Fig. 35. 11, 13, 14, 20–3; and Fig. 36. 1, 5, and 23–5, continued. Incised ornament, except on the pots with red necks, was uncommon. There was more variety of form and ornament in the class of appliqué-ornamented pots (Fig. 43. 1–16). The red-striped pots (Fig. 42. 19–20) were rare. The commonest forms of cooking-pot were the carinated pots with a smooth black surface and the pots painted red above the carination.

The jar forms were the same as in the previous period.

Among the bowls, burnished and unburnished, the old shapes continued to be made, but a wide shallow bowl with a chamfered or tapered lip (Figs. 44. 7, 11; 45. 2) was the characteristic form. The burnished bowls with the grooved lips (Fig. 45. 3) were uncommon.

Boat-shaped lamps continued in the usual forms (Fig. 45. 15). Large lamps were made with internal flanges (Fig. 45. 16, 17). This design was possibly an economy measure, and it would be interesting to know if it was a success and how much dissatisfaction it caused among the staff.

PERIOD IV. NINETEENTH CENTURY (Figs. 46–54 and Pl. 19.)

In the nineteenth century, the period between 1837 and 1895 defined by the presence of European, mainly English china, a new interest in pottery was apparent. This was shown by the changes in form and the more general use of incised and appliqué ornament. There was also an increase in the numbers of rounded and shouldered cooking-pots, in comparison with the carinated pots which had predominated in the previous period. The forms (Figs. 46 and 47) were similar to those in use in the eighteenth century, but with this type of pot there is little scope for creativeness.

Among the carinated pots the forms in use in the eighteenth century—notably the large pots with red necks, usually with incised ornament (Figs. 49. 3, 6; 50. 8–11), and the appliqué wares (Fig. 51. 14–24)—continued with a renewed diversity of form and ornament. The wares with a smooth black surface (Fig. 47. 12) were uncommon. Pots with bead rims, both rounded and carinated in the case of the smooth black wares, had occurred sporadically in all periods (Figs. 31. 11; 35. 26; 36. 24, 29) but they were more common in the nineteenth century, particularly in the pots ornamented with the pudendal triangle (Fig. 47. 5).

However, the characteristic cooking-pots of the nineteenth century were the pots with deeply concave and swan necks, often with chamfered edge to the lip (Fig. 50. 29–36) and a variety of incised ornament (Figs. 55, 56). This new profile had appeared in the eighteenth century with the pots with appliqué ornament (Fig. 43. 4, 7, 8), but it was only in the nineteenth century that it came into general use.

Among the eating-bowls, the old types which had appeared in the late seventeenth century continued. The only innovations seem to have been the use of an external groove below the lip (Fig. 54. 7), and the introduction of a class of sturdy bowls with a flat as opposed to a disk base and a thick bottom (Figs. 52. 1, 2, 4, 6; 54. 8). These bowls may also have been used for grinding tobacco or some other dried plant. The burnished bowls (Fig. 54. 1–8) follow the eighteenth-century types but were found only in the lower levels of the period. This was particularly noticeable in the large deposit of nineteenth-century wares found in the Passage of the Arches.

IMPORTED EARTHENWARE, INDIAN, ISLAMIC (Figs. 57–67; Pl. 20)

Besides the locally made earthenware there were a number of groups which belonged to different ceramic traditions. The red-polished, the quartz-studded, and the large pink jars have been identified as Portuguese; the round, red water pots with black circles are of Indian origin, but the origin of the other types has not yet been securely established.

In Figs. 57–9 there are two groups and in Figs. 60, 61 one group of carinated pots, jars, dishes, flasks, and, rarely, bowls, which are related by form though differing in fabric and treatment. They were made on the wheel and show a regularity and a professional touch which is absent from the local wares.

The carinated pots in Fig. 57. 1–9 and Pl. 20. 1, were made of a hard-baked earthenware. They appeared in the early levels in the Fort and continued until the end of the seventeenth century. The jars (Fig. 57. 10–19 and Pl. 20. 2, 3) and the bowls (Fig. 57. 20, 21) were covered with a pink slip, and belonged principally to the later seventeenth century. The jars, bowls, and pots in Fig. 58 were made in a thin, hard-baked, red earthenware, often with a metallic sheen, probably mica. They were also mostly late seventeenth century.

In Figs. 59 and 60 are drawn the black-bodied counterparts of Figs. 57 and 58. They follow the same sequence. The carinated pots appear in the early-seventeenth-century levels of the Fort, and the jars and other forms, with a few exceptions, later. The bottles (Fig. 61. 1, 2 and 4–6) were found in early-seventeenth-century levels; most of the other forms were late seventeenth century. Associated with them were a few sherds of similar bottles and bowls in a fine cream, grey (Pl. 20. 4–6), or pink earthenware. The bottle (Fig. 75. 5), in spite of its similarity to the others, is considered, with some reservation, to be Portuguese, in view of the identity of the fabric with the other red polished pieces.

The forms, except the heavier black-bodied pieces in Fig. 59, derive from contemporary metalwork. The resemblance is most striking in the case of the small jars (Figs. 58. 5, 11; 60. 1–3, 7), the larger jars or water-pots (Fig. 58. 12–16), the bowls (Fig. 58. 17–18), the dishes (Fig. 60. 11–13) and the bottles with the fragile bases (Fig. 61. 4–6). The metallic sheen on the red-bodied pieces of Fig. 58 and Pl. 20. 7–13 may be part of the same pretension. Decoration was limited to the roulette and wavy line slip patterns shown on Fig. 58. 5, 19–20.

All these forms have a general likeness to the Baroda wares.[4] However, the most distinctive types found in Fort Jesus were absent from the Baroda series and there were no perfect identities. I believe that the wares found in the Fort belong to a collateral branch of the ceramic tradition which prevailed in Gujurat and the surrounding areas. Their appearance in the early seventeenth century, their multiplication in the late seventeenth, and their disappearance at the time of the loss of Mombasa by the Portuguese, suggests that they came from one or other of the northern Portuguese possessions, such as Diu or Damão.

Besides these wares was another group which appears to be distinct, which occurred mostly in early-seventeenth-century levels. It consisted of flasks with two handles (Fig. 61. 9) in pink earthenware with a stamped design of circular medallions with the same metallic sheen which occurred on the red-bodied wares in Fig. 58 mentioned above. The stamped patterns (Pl. 20. 9–13) were typical Arab geometrical designs, resembling the designs found on pots from excavations in Iraq.[5] Similar sherds had also been found at Ungwana,[6] but neither at Ungwana nor Fort Jesus were they at all common. In addition to the flasks, there were a number of carved bosses (Pl. 20. 7–8), which were presumably knobs of lids. Knobs such as these were found in Bahmani levels (A.D. 1435–1581) at Kolhapur.[7]

In Fig. 62 there are three groups of hand-made pots which are cruder and coarser in execution than most of the local pots. The jugs (Fig. 62. 1–4) are eighteenth- and nineteenth-century and belong to a ceramic tradition apparently derived from leather prototypes. The high-pitched handle is reminiscent of the jar found at Baroda,[8] but the execution is so crude that it is unlikely to have been made there. It may have been made at a port in south Persia or Oman[9] which was in constant touch with Mombasa. The rounded flask (Fig. 62. 5) shows better workmanship and is the only example of this form which has been found. The jug of Fig. 62. 6 is entirely different, both in fabric and style, and with its imperfectly baked body, recalls the jars of Fig. 67. 11, 12. A cup of the same ware was found on the surface near Ngomeni, a well-known dhow anchorage eighteen miles north of Malindi.

A large number of fragments of the Indian water pot, commonly known as the *chatty* (Figs. 63, 64) were found in the Fort. This was a thin red ware, painted with black cordons and occasionally bands of hatching on the raw biscuit or, less commonly, on a white slip. Most of the sherds came from nineteenth-century levels, but there were sufficient numbers from earlier levels to show that this type of ware was being made and imported from the end of the seventeenth or the beginning of the eighteenth century. It was manufactured at Muscat, presumably by Indian potters who had come from a different part of India from the makers of the red-and-black wares

[4] Subbarao (1953), Figs. 16–23.
[5] Iraq Government Dept. of Antiquities (1940), Pls. XXXVI–XXXVII.
[6] Kirkman (1966), Fig. 25. W. [7] Sankalia and Dikshit (1952), pp. 79–81.
[8] Subbarao (1953), Fig. 18. 53.
[9] Potteries at Saham near Sofar are mentioned by Miles (1966), p. 456.

of Figs. 58–61. Similar pots, but with a heavier body, were also made in Zanzibar by Indian potters at the end of the nineteenth century.

The characteristic form was the water pot, but there were also dishes (Fig. 63. 16), bowls (Fig. 64. 18–20), jars (Fig. 64. 3, 4), and incense-burners (Fig. 64. 21). There were five different shapes among the water pots. The basic form had a rounded profile and an upright neck with a cupped mouth (Fig. 63. 1, 2, 7). This was the standard form of pot in all periods. The first variant was a similar vessel but without the cupped mouth (Figs. 63. 3, 4, 8, 9, 11; 64. 1, 2). The second had a flared-lip, often hollowed at the back where the lip met the neck (Figs. 63. 5, 6, 10; 64. 5–9). The third had an upright or long flared neck with a median ridge (Figs. 63. 12, 13; 64. 10–14). The fourth was a carinated pot with a projecting lip (Figs. 63. 14, 15; 64. 15–17).

The basic form and variations one and two appeared in K'ang Hsi levels; the other variants with dishes, bowls, and incense burners in the eighteenth-century levels, and the jars in those of the nineteenth century. The hollowing at the back of the upright and flared pots tended to be omitted in nineteenth-century examples, but all forms, once they had appeared, continued to be found in all subsequent levels.

Jars

Sherds of unglazed jars with handles, of the *amphora* type but with flat bottoms or the *pithos* type with near straight sides and without handles were found in all levels. The bottoms of the jars found in the Fort were flat and generally smaller in diameter than the body at its greatest width. The rims displayed a number of varieties of the rolled or projecting rim. The handles, unlike the handles on Chinese jars which are generally horizontal, were vertical.

There were three principal groups of large jars: one a group of pink wares which can be identified as Portuguese (Fig. 74. 14–23); second, of grey- and buff-bodied wares, sometimes with grits (Figs. 66 and 67), which were probably from the Persian Gulf or southern Persia; third, another group of pink wares (Fig. 65. 1–17) which appeared in late-seventeenth-century levels, but were commonest in those of the eighteenth and nineteenth centuries. These are the most difficult to classify but, except for nos. 1–3, they appear to belong to the same ceramic tradition as the grey wares.

Within the main classifications, the principal differences are to be seen in the degree of attention paid to the lip, the use of a white or black slip, and the presence of grits in the clay. A white slip was used on both Portuguese and Arab jars and over any type of body. The black slip was confined to the grey and buff wares (Figs. 66. 1; 67. 11–14). The mauve slip was unusual and occurred on the pink wares (Fig. 65. 6) and the grey wares (Fig. 67. 5, 6).

The addition of black grits to the clay was uncommon and only occurred in eighteenth- and nineteenth-century jars (Figs. 66. 6, 7; 67, 5–10, 12). This is a normal practice with potters and its relative scarcity among these wares may provide evidence for their place of manufacture. Similarly, the mauve slip has significance. It occurred also on Chinese jars (Fig. 70. 10, 11), and Fig. 65. 6, may be Chinese.

Associated with the jars by their fabric were the heavy bowls (Fig. 67. 15) found in nineteenth-century levels. The two basins in a pink ware (Fig. 65. 18, 19) may be Portuguese, although they were found in later levels.

A large number of bowls for water pipes (*narghili*) in red, buff, or black earthenware were found in nineteenth-century levels, principally in the Passage of the Arches. Another type of ware found in these levels was the square incense-pot on four legs with simple, red-painted panels. These two ceramic forms are found in sites all over the Arab world, but they may also have been made in India.

A few sherds of the white porous earthenware made for cooling liquids were found in seventeenth-century levels, similar to those found at Gedi[10] and Ungwana.[11] However, it was only in the nineteenth-century levels of the Passage of the Arches that they were at all numerous. There were three main forms: rounded flasks with wide or narrow necks, and a carinated flask with a wide neck. They were normally decorated with zones of hatchings, interrupted diagonal lines, or other simple linear patterns.

ISLAMIC GLAZED EARTHENWARE (Figs. 68, 69; Pls. 21–3)

The Islamic glazed earthenware which has been found in the Fort may be divided according to the composition of the body, into four groups.

A. A hard-baked red ware with both alkaline and lead glazes (Cls. 1–7). Fig. 68, 1–7, 9, 10; Pl. 21. 1–4.

B. A hard grey-buff ware with a lead glaze (Cls. 8–12). Fig. 68. 8, 11; Pls. 21. 5; 22. 2.

C. A fine sugary white ware with an alkaline glaze (Cls. 13–19). Fig. 68. 12–15; Pls. 22. 3–4; 23. 1–3.

D. A soft buff ware with a lead glaze (Cls. 20–6). Fig. 69; Pl. 23. 4–10.

The alkaline glazes have generally disintegrated; the lead glazes, particularly in the fourth group, have tended to flake. The only consistently stable glazes were Classes 4–12, 16, 20, and 23–6. The instability of the glaze need not have affected the normal use of the ceramics—they were not made to be buried for excavation by archaeologists.

The typical Islamic glazed ware of the early seventeenth century, which was found with Ming porcelain, consisted of dishes and bowls with a simple floral decoration on a red or grey-buff body, groups A and B. Identical sherds were found in surface levels at Gedi, Ungwana, and Kilepwa. Class I is the same ware as at Ungwana (Kirkman, 1966, Pl. xiv D, 5–8); Class 2 as at Gedi (Kirkman, 1954, Cl. 8, Fig. 24 d–l), Kilepwa (Kirkman, 1952, Fig. 3 j), and Ungwana (Kirkman, 1966, Pl. xiv D, 1–4); Class 3 as at Ungwana, Pl. xiii; Class 9 as at Gedi (Kirkman, 1954, Cl. 11, Fig. 24 y) and at The Palace (Kirkman, 1963, Pl. x, 6–7) and Ungwana Pl. xiv D, 11.

[10] Kirkman (1954), Fig. 28, and (1963), Fig. 13 R.

[11] Kirkman (1966), Fig. 25 X–AC.

The dishes, bowls, and jugs with single-coloured glazes, Classes 5 and 10, were by no means as common as they had been on these sites.

Another type, Class 20, which has also been found at Ungwana (Kirkman, 1966, Fig. XXV A–D), was the small cup without handles, with a watery-green glaze on the outside and yellow on the inside over a soft buff body, which may have been made at Alexandria.[12]

A few sherds of the blue-and-white bowls with a sugary white body (Classes 13–19) were also found in these levels.

In the late seventeenth century the earlier types continued, but the characteristic ware was the blue-and-white just mentioned in its various forms (Classes 13–19). This is the ware similar to that described as Kashan in Gedi (Kirkman, 1954), but is in fact more likely to have been made in Kerman, where famous potteries existed in the sixteenth and seventeenth centuries.[13] However, the sherds found in the Fort, except Class 17 in which the leaves are identical with the leaves in Lane, Pl. lviii B, do not resemble very closely the vessels which have been published. It is possible that they came from other potteries in Kerman or even Makran, whose products have escaped notice.

The commonest types were bowls and dishes with floral and landscape designs in blue-and-white, in imitation of Wan Li porcelain, Class 13. This is the ware which was traded round the markets of the Indian Ocean to make up for the scarcity of porcelain after the destruction of the Ching-tê Chên factories in 1673.[14] Actually, the increased export to East Africa did not set in until it was no longer a necessity ware, since it was found with K'ang Hsi porcelain from the rebuilt factories. It was most plentiful in the filling of the Captain's House, in the court in S. Mateus, and in the lowest levels of the Passage of the Arches. The truly Persian types of this ware (Classes 16–18) were less common. All varieties disappeared after the first quarter of the eighteenth century.

The thin bowls and small dishes with blue, red, green, and yellow glazes on the outside, and yellow inside over a soft buff body (Class 22), were found only in late-seventeenth-century levels and particularly in the filling of the court in S. Mateus. They did not occur in the pit in S. Filipe or in the Captain's House. A curious feature of these bowls and dishes was the vertical scoring below the glaze, giving a fur-like finish. The intention was probably to make the glaze adhere to the body, but this object was seldom attained. They have also been found at a site in Trucial Oman.[15]

A few sherds of bowls with blue-and-white decoration in Chinese style but over a soft buff body (Class 21) were also found. The glaze has tended to detach itself from the body. Some sherds of this ware were found at the seventeenth-century site of Antsoh in Madagascar.[16]

[12] Kirkman (1966), footnote, p. 44.
[13] Lane (1957), pp. 88–100.
[14] Volker (1954), pp. 113, 224.
[15] Communication from B. de Cardi.
[16] Excavated by Dr. P. Vérin.

The characteristic wares of the eighteenth and nineteenth centuries were the platters in pale green (Class 24) and the bowls and dishes with the same kind of schematized floral and geometric motifs as Classes 1, 2, 4, 8, and 9, but on a soft buff body (Class 25).

The dishes with a red body and decoration in the same style as Class 1, but with a harder surface slightly crackled or an incised design of straight and wavy lines in old *sgraffiato* technique (Classes 6 and 7), were invariably found in nineteenth-century levels, and must be a revival, rather than a survival. Similarly, the jugs and bowls of Class 26, with their archaic Sassanian–Islamic glaze, were found in eighteenth- and nineteenth-century levels.

The jug with vertical handles and trellis decoration (Class 12) may be a survival from the past. The style of decoration is closest to the bowls and dishes of *Gedi, The Great Mosque*, Cl. 10, Fig. 24, v–t. A complete vessel of this type is in the Zanzibar Museum.

CLASSES OF ISLAMIC GLAZED WARES

A

1. Large plates with flanged lip and ring base, glazed on inside only and decorated with a zigzag border and formalized flowers, and a round or foliate motif in the bottom, sometimes in imitation of Chinese designs, in three colours, green, blue, and black, on a white or yellow ground over a hard red body. Common. Early and late seventeenth century. Fig. 68. 3, 4; Pl. 21. 1, 2.
2. Similar plates but with design in one colour, blue on white, or black on white or yellow. Common. Early seventeenth century. Fig. 68. 2, 7.
3. Similar plates but with more elaborate designs under a transparent glaze on outside as well as inside. Common. Early seventeenth century. Fig. 68. 1; Pl. 21. 3.
4. Plates and bowls with a short lip, border of chevrons, tendrils, or rounded arcade, single motif in bottom, in black on blue. Common. Early seventeenth century. Fig. 68. 5; Pl. 21. 4.
5. Plates, bowls, and jugs with a plain black, blue, celadon, grey, or turquoise glaze. Uncommon. Early seventeenth century. Fig. 68. 9, 13.
6. Plates with blue glaze and incised design in old *sgraffiato* style. Uncommon. Nineteenth century.
7. Plates with flat bases and decoration in same style as Class 1 under a crackled white glaze. Uncommon. Nineteenth century. Fig. 68. 10; Pl. 22. 1.

B

8. Plates with designs similar to Class 1 but in a hard grey-buff earthenware. Common. Early seventeenth century.
9. Plates and bowls with design similar to Class 4 in black on a grey-buff or pale lilac ground. Common. Early seventeenth century. Fig. 68. 8; Pls. 21. 5; 22. 2.

10. Plates and jugs with a plain black, green, or lilac glaze. Uncommon. Early seventeenth century. Fig. 68. 6.
11. Small bowls, plates, and platters with a hard white glaze. Uncommon. Early seventeenth century. Fig. 68. 11.
12. Jug with two vertical handles and trellis decoration in green and aubergine on white. Single specimen. Nineteenth century. Fig. 69. 12.

C

13. Bowls and plates with floral and landscape designs in blue-and-white, in imitation of Wan Li wares, on a sugary white body. On the base there was often a 'tassel' mark or Chinese square mark. Common. Late seventeenth century. Fig. 68. 12; Pl. 22. 3.
14. Bowl with blue glaze inside and outside. Single specimen. Late seventeenth century. Fig. 68. 14.
15. Bowls and heavy plates with celadon-coloured glaze and incised radiate ornament. One bowl had traces of overglaze blue on outside. Uncommon. Late seventeenth century.
16. Bowls and plates with bands of chevron ornament on outside incised under a plain white glaze. The glaze had decayed, leaving a surface like muslin over the bowl. Uncommon. Late seventeenth century. Fig. 68. 15; Pl. 22. 4.
17. Bowls, plates, and small pots, plain or with willowy floral design in turquoise green on white, sometimes stained by green. Uncommon. Late seventeenth century. Pl. 23. 1–2.
18. Bowl with floral design in blue, olive-green, and red on white. Single specimen. Late seventeenth century.
19. Plate with schematized floral design in chocolate on white. Single specimen. Late seventeenth century. Pl. 23. 3.

D

20. Small cups without handles, incised bands and zigzags on outside under a watery green glaze, on inside yellow glaze over a soft buff body. Uncommon. Early seventeenth century.
21. Small bowls with blue-and-white decoration in Chinese style. Uncommon. Late seventeenth century.
22. Thin bowls and small plates with blue, green, red, or yellow glaze on outside and yellow inside, vertical scoring on outside below glaze. Uncommon. Late seventeenth century. Fig. 69. 1–3; Pl. 23. 4, 5.
23. Bowls and jugs with yellow-brown glaze. Uncommon. Late seventeenth and nineteenth centuries. Fig. 69. 10.
24. Bowls and platters with slightly concave disk bases, jars and pedestal cups with green, pale green, or grey-blue glaze on inside of the bowls and on outside of the jars and cups. Common. Eighteenth century. Fig. 69. 4–7, 11.

25. Bowls with chevron border, schematized leaves, geometrical motifs in black on a pale blue or turquoise ground; or bands of pale green and blue on inside and on the upper part of the outside; sometimes with a moulding like a cable 5 cm below the rim on the outside. Common. Eighteenth century. Fig. 69. 8, 9; Pl. 23. 6–10.
26. Bowl and jar with a bright blue glaze over shallow diagonal grooving. Single specimen. Nineteenth century. Fig. 69. 13.

CHINESE PORCELAIN (Pls. 24–38)

The Chinese porcelain found in the Fort included examples of most of the common wares of the seventeenth, eighteenth, and nineteenth centuries. The forms were ninety per cent bowls, dishes, and cups; bottles and vases were rare. They have been classified according to style of decoration, in three periods: Ming, K'ang Hsi, and eighteenth/nineteenth centuries. Tables showing the minimum number of specimens in each class in the Ming and K'ang Hsi periods, and a list of marks, follow the class lists at the end of this section.

In the fill levels of the bastions and in the filling of the Passage of the Steps there were numerous sherds of Wan Li blue-and-white. The bastions were filled in during the reconstruction of the Fort between 1634 and 1639, but the date of the extension of the Captain's House over the Passage of the Steps is unknown. Another building of the first half of the seventeenth century was the cavalier of S. António, built in 1648, but there were very few sherds in the cuttings below the floor. The porcelain which was found was, however, of Wan Li type. These sherds, notably Classes 1*a*, 6*a*, and 6*b*, were similar to those which had been found in the uppermost levels at Gedi, Ungwana, and Mnarani. The thin-bodied bowls were uncommon at these sites, but the significant difference was the absence at all Arab–African sites of the plates with elaborate panelled borders, Class 2, Pl. 24. 3.

These towns all came to an end about the same time, when the coast was overrun by the Galla from Somalia. Mnarani, the old Kilifi, was in existence in 1612, but it could not have lasted much longer.[17] Gedi, twenty-seven miles north of Kilifi, is mentioned by no Portuguese author, but it could not have survived longer than Kilifi. In all probability it would have been abandoned earlier, in view of its exposed position two miles from a harbour. At Ungwana, on the shore, 150 miles further north—the Oja of the Portuguese—no porcelain later than Wan Li was found in the excavations. It must have ceased to be an urban centre at about the same time as the others. The only explanation of the absence of the panelled plates is that they had not arrived. Their appearance in East Africa would have been between 1612 and 1634, and the date of manufacture need not have been much earlier, in view of the regular monsoon trade between India and East Africa.

[17] Strandes (tr. 1968).

Few marks were found in the early levels: one Ch'êng-Hua, three hallmarks, and two two-character marks of commendation.

The bowls with slip decoration on the inside (Class 19) were interesting; also the fine lid of a white jar with incised floral design (Class 20; Pl. 26. 1), and the polychrome bowl with a blue-and-white design on the inside (Class 17). Swatow polychrome plates (Class 22; Pl. 26. 2) were more numerous in the K'ang Hsi levels.

Transitional, as opposed to Wan Li pieces, were uncommon. Apart from the dishes with elaborate panelled borders, which are not generally considered Transitional, the only types which can be distinguished from Wan Li are the small bowl with a lion in the bottom (Class 8*a*), the vase with birds in two shades of blue (Class 13*b*; Pl. 25. 6), and the curious bowls with tendrils on a cream ground (Class 16; Pl. 25. 7). All these would appear to belong to the immediate post-Wan Li period, i.e. 1619–34.

The next group of porcelain consisted of Transitional and K'ang Hsi types, which were found in one large, two medium, and two smaller, homogeneous deposits in the Fort. The largest collection came from the filling of the pit in S. Filipe; the two medium collections from the filling of the Captain's House and the court in S. Mateus and the smaller groups from the rebuilding of the room of the stands against the west, parapet walk and the bottom of the Passage of the Arches.

The date of the filling of the Captain's House cannot be much later than the fall of the Fort in 1698, since the fortress would hardly have been left for long with a gap in the defences. In the account of the storming of the Fort, the gate in S. Mateus is mentioned, so it would appear that the court behind it was still open. The gate in the Passage of the Arches is referred to as late as 1728 and shown on the Lopes de Sá plan; presumably, therefore, the deposit cannot be earlier.

The rebuilding of the rooms against the west parapet walk is connected with the rebuilding of the church, which would be before the beginning of the siege of 1696. The most important deposit, however, the pit in S. Filipe, cannot be associated with any event. The need for gravel for roofs and floors would have occurred in either the Portuguese or Arab period.

A comparison of the deposit in S. Filipe with the other two large deposits, allowing for a proportional difference in totals of three to one (Captain's House) and two to one (S. Mateus) shows, surprisingly, a closer relation between the deposits in S. Filipe and S. Mateus than between either of them and the deposit in the Captain's House. The deposit in the room of the stands was closer to the deposit in S. Filipe, and the deposit in the Passage of the Arches to that in the Captain's House.

The most striking difference between the groups is the abundance in S. Filipe of the pieces of two shades of blue (Class 5), the cups of Class 10, the bowls of Class 11, the dishes with the artemisia leaf (Class 13), the badly drawn aster bowls (Class 14), and the coffee-coloured bowls (Class 20), with their scarcity in the Captain's House; and, on the other hand, the abundance of the polychrome bowls and dishes (Class 1), the *café-au-lait* (Class 21), the white bowls and dishes (Class 27), and the *blanc de chine* (Class 30) in the Captain's House, compared with the deposit in S. Filipe.

The most significant of these discrepancies is perhaps the bowls in two tints of blue, particularly Classes 5*a* and 5*b*, which are survivals from the Transitional period, and which did not occur in the Captain's House. This, I believe, indicates that there is a difference in date between the deposits of between ten and twenty years. Assuming that the deposit in the Captain's House was closed in 1698, which is not unreasonable on both circumstantial and typological grounds, the deposit in S. Filipe would have been closed between 1678 and 1688. During the intervening period the earlier K'ang Hsi types had become less common. The predominance of Classes 1, 21, 27, and 30 in the Captain's House could also be explained by the fact that these were quality wares, which one would expect to find there and perhaps nowhere else. At the Portuguese fair of Dambarare, destroyed in 1693, sherds of yellow and green (Class 3), coffee (Class 20), white (Class 27), cream (Class 29), and celadon (Class 30) were found, but no *café-au-lait*.[18]

The royal marks were about equal in number in all three deposits, but hallmarks were more numerous in S. Filipe, and symbols in the Captain's House. In S. Mateus hallmarks were few and symbols limited to one fungus and one two-fish mark. The links and two-fish marks were not found in S. Filipe, and presumably are later than the others. The style of writing royal names in most examples followed Garner, nos. 99*e* and 99*h*, and particularly the dated 1690 plate, Garner no. 68. The earlier stocky type of character was found in Ch'êng-Hua marks in Classes 3 and 14, both from S. Mateus.

The bowls and dishes followed the traditional forms, except for the wide shallow dishes with the artemisia leaf (Class 13), which seem to be a new form on the coast, or at least only newly in general use.

Sherds which can be recognized as early eighteenth century were uncommon in the Fort, and it is probable that there was a decline in the importation of Chinese porcelain during the first half of the century, indicating a decline in trade. There is no evidence of recovery until the third quarter of the century, to which I believe belongs most of the eighteenth-century porcelain found in the Fort. The levels in which it was represented were the north court of the Captain's House and the upper part of the filling in S. Mateus. In the area of the main court, the church, and the west barrack block, eighteenth-century porcelain was common, but was found with European china, which I do not believe was imported in quantity before the expulsion of the Mazrui in 1837.

The characteristic eighteenth-century types were the small bowls with a border of rosettes (Class 12*a*; Pl. 35. 6), the dishes with 'cod roe' decoration (Class 17; Pl. 37. 1), the bowls with trellis and spray (Class 15; Pl. 36. 5, 6), the chrysanthemum (Class 16*a*; Pl. 36. 7, 8), and the comb or character (Class 19*a*; Pl. 37. 3–5), the bowls and

18 Garlake (1969), pp. 39–40.

dishes with incised ornament and blue bands (Class 27*a*; Pl. 38. 4, 5) and the blue bowls (Class 30). A few sherds of some of these forms, notably Classes 12*a*, 19*a*, and 27*a*, and also the polychromes of Classes 1 and 2, were found in the Captain's House and the filling in S. Mateus. The other types were new.

In the nineteenth century all these classes continued to be imported. The largest deposits were the upper filling of the Passage of the Arches and the upper filling of the platform against the south wall of the rectangular projection; the first of the third quarter, and the second of the last quarter of the century.

The second destruction of the porcelain factories of Ching-tê-Chên by the Taiping rebels in 1853 may have been the blow from which the export trade never recovered. The factories were not rebuilt until 1864, and by that time European wares had established their position in the market. The characteristic nineteenth-century wares were the polychrome bowls and cups (Classes 7 and 8; Pl. 35. 2–4) and blue-and-white (Classes 16*b*, 22; Pl. 38. 1, 2; and Classes 23 and 25).

Marks, other than square marks, were less common than in the preceding period. There was one grotesquely written Ch'êng-Hua mark on a coffee-coloured bowl with panels (Class 9); a few marks of commendation on Classes 13, 14, and 15; one symbol on a bowl of Class 13, and a large number of square marks on Classes 9, 10, 15, 16*a*, 19*a*, 19*b*, and 21, mostly meaningless. The only significance which can be applied to these marks is that they associate different types of bowl with similar marks. It may merely be that in some factories marks, such as the mark of commendation and Chê'ng-Hua, were permissible but not obligatory, while in others it was never the practice to use marks. Only in Class 19*a* are marks habitual.

The white of the background of both the polychrome and the blue-and-white was frequently a grey-white, sometimes mottled grey-white, or a light grey. The 'blue' of the blue-and-white was frequently a grey-blue, or even black or sepia. There was obviously an indifference to standards in production or an inspection tolerance, which shows that the Chinese potters of the nineteenth century were ahead of their time in one respect, if not in others.

CLASSES OF MING PORCELAIN

Blue-and-White

1*a*. Small plates with landscape in the bottom, often including two does and, less commonly, birds, aquatic scenes with ducks, or floral sprays; running border of similar motifs on rim, or panels extending over cavetto. A thick- and thin-bodied type. Mark including character Fu. Common. Pl. 24. 1.

1*b*. Similar plates, sometimes with the seven precious things, or gadroons in panels extending over cavetto. Thick and thin types. Uncommon. Pl. 24. 2.

1*c*. Plate and aquatic scene on a hatched ground. Single specimen. Pl. 24. 4.

2. Large and small plates with landscape designs or the seven precious things in the bottom; elaborate decoration on rim, consisting of sprays or seven precious

things in panels, foliate or plain border between panels and design in bottom A thick- and thin-bodied type. Common. Pl. 24. 3.

3. Heavy plates and bowls with thick foot-ring, similar designs and also the lotus blossom of Cl. 6*a*, often with border of trellis and cross on inside of rim of bowl. Common. Pl. 24. 5.

4. Heavy bowl with heavenly horse in bottom. Single specimen.

5*a*. Large bowls with landscape and aquatic scenes, similar to 1*a*. Mark T'ung-tê-t'ang chih. Common. Pl. 24. 6.

5*b*. Large bowls with broad tendril band below rim on outside. Uncommon.

6*a*. Bowls with open lotus blossoms. Mark Ch'êng-Hua and Ch'ang-shou. Common. Pl. 25. 1.

6*b*. Similar bowls with grotesque animal, similar to those published in *Gedi—The Palace*, Pl. XV. Common.

6*c*. Bowls with floral design in bottom. Mark illegible. Common.

7. Bowls with formal floral or geometric motif in bottom. Common.

8*a*. Small bowl with lion in bottom, deep blue. Mark Yü-t'ang chia ch'i. Uncommon.

8*b*. Small bowls with phoenix in broad band on outside. Single specimen.

9*a*. Bowls with doe in bottom and panels with does outside. A thick- and thin-bodied type. Common. Pl. 25. 2.

9*b*. Bowls with bird in bottom and birds on outside. Thick- and thin-bodied type. Common.

9*c*. Bowls with landscapes, birds, lizards, and butterflies. Thin fabric. Common. Pl. 25. 3.

10. Bowls with seven precious things in fluted panels. Thin fabric. Common. Pl. 25. 4.

11*a*. Lids of jars with phoenix or tendrils in white on blue ground. Uncommon. Pl. 25. 5.

11*b*. Lids with seven precious things and sprays in panels. Single specimen.

12. Large jars with floral designs and panels at base. Common.

13*a*. Vases with dragons and horses. Uncommon.

13*b*. Vases with birds in two shades of blue. Single specimen. Pl. 25. 6.

14. Bottles, some with long neck, floral designs in dark blue. Uncommon.

15. Lid of square box in grey-blue. Single specimen.

16. Bowls with tendril design on a cream ground, bare ring in bottom. Uncommon. Pl. 25. 7.

Polychrome outside, blue-and-white inside

17. Small bowl with yellow petals on white above base and panels with sprays in green and blue on a red ground, inside a lion in blue-and-white. Mark Miao-ching t'ang. Single specimen.

White outside, blue-and-white inside

18. Bowls with trellis and cross border on inside. Uncommon.
19. Bowls with slip design on inside, sometimes with spray in bottom or on outside. Common.

White

20. Lid of jar with incised floral design in *jui* frame. Single specimen. Pl. 26. 1.

Yellow

21. Plates and bowls with yellow glaze inside and outside. Uncommon.

Swatow ware

22. Plates with floral design in red-and-green on a white body. Uncommon. Pl. 26. 2.

CLASSES OF K'ANG HSI PORCELAIN

Polychrome (iron-red, aubergine, green, yellow)

1*a*. Bowls usually with out-turned lips, one with brown rim, principal decoration of peony, plum, pineapple motifs on outside, motif repeated in bottom and in border on inside of lip. Marks: Ch'êng-Hua, Hua-yu-t'ang ch'ing ya chih, Yung-fa-hao chih, and a meaningless mark in a square. Common. Pl. 26. 3–5.

1*b*. Bowls with plain lip, principal design of tendrils with border of tendrils on inside, outside plain or with individual sprays, border repeated on outside.

1*c*. Plates with grooved ring base, blossoms on a red trellis ground on inside, curling waves and classical borders on outside. No marks. Common. Pl. 26. 6.

1*d*. Similar plates with floral designs and border of petals, alternating red and green on outside, *jui* border or undulating striped lines in green and yellow on inside. Marks: Hsüan Tê, K'ang Hsi, and illegible hallmark.

1*e*. Jars with necks and small handles on shoulder in same colours and also underglaze blue, bands of petals round neck, alternating blue and red, floral decoration on shoulder and in panels round jar. Pl. 27. 1.

2. Small bowls, thin fabric, yellow or green ground on outside with border below rim in alternate colour, with quatrefoils in aubergine and red, separated by small leaves in green, border of petals above base. Inside white with border same as outside. No marks. Pl. 27. 2.
3. Cups and saucers with mottled green and yellow 'egg-and-spinach' decoration. Mark: four-character Ch'êng-Hua.

Blue-and-white

4. Small dish with horses on background of waves. Mark: probably Chia Ching.

5*a*. Bowls, cups, and small bottle with decoration of flowers or fruit in dark and light blue, perhaps Transitional. Pl. 27. 4–6.

5b. Bowls with design of horses in similar two tints of blue.

5c. Bowls and plates with series of sprays above base in two tints of blue. Marks: six- and four-character Ch'êng-Hua and K'ang Hsi. Pl. 28. 1.

5d. Fine bowls with figures in a garden and broad fluted panels above base on outside in two tints of blue, plain inside except for broad trellis and quatrefoil border below rim, similar to border on *café-au-lait* plates. Mark: Ch'êng-Hua. Pl. 27. 7.

5e. Fluted bowls, plates, and saucers with floral designs in two tints of blue. Mark: Hsüan Tê.

6a. Bowls with turned-out lips and lotus tendrils on outside, lotus in bottom, in single tint of blue. Marks: K'ang Hsi. Pl. 28. 2.

6b. Bowls and cups with various floral designs, sometimes smudged, some similar to designs on coffee-coloured bowls. Marks: Ch'êng-Hua, K'ang Hsi, and Mei-yü t'ang chih.

6c. Similar bowls with figures in a garden. Mark: K'ang Hsi. Pl. 28. 3.

6d. Bowls, lids, and saucers with chrysanthemum, lotus, or peony blossoms and formalized tendrils. Marks: artemisia leaf and two fishes. Pl. 28. 4–6.

7. Plates with grooved foot-ring and phoenix with long tail, or neatly drawn floral design. No marks.

8. Bowls with floral design in outline and solid blue. Mark: two fishes. Pl. 28. 7.

9. Jar and miniature pot with lotus blossoms in solid blue.

10a. Cups with chevron border, quatrefoil in bottom. Mark: fungus.

10b. Similar cups with neatly drawn floral motifs in bottom. Marks: Ch'êng-Hua, K'ang Hsi, Ch'i yen t'ang chih; conch, twisted leaf. Pl. 29. 1.

11a. Small bowls with ying-yang and pa-kua design, pa-kua in bottom. Marks: K'un shan mei yü and - - ya chih. Pl. 29. 2.

11b. Similar bowls with sprays and tendrils, spray in bottom. No marks. Common. Pl. 29. 3.

11c. Similar bowls with dancing boys, rocks in bottom. Marks: K'un yu ya chih, - pi t'ang chih. Common. Pl. 29. 4, 6, 12.

11d. Similar bowl with immortal, landscape in bottom. Mark: K'un yu ya chih. Pl. 29. 5.

11e. Similar bowl with clerk reading letter in bottom. Mark: K'un shan mei yü.

11f. Similar bowl with design of trees, 'the three friends', grassy tuft in bottom. Marks: K'un shan mei yü, Jui-yün t'ang chih, Cheng chi pao yü, Cheng yü t'ang chih, - - ya chih. Common. Pl. 29. 7, 8, 11, 13–15.

11g. Similar bowls with schematized lotus design, lotus in bottom. No mark. Pl. 29. 9.

11h. Similar bowls with lotus blossoms, lotus in bottom. No mark. Pl. 29. 10, 16.

11i. Similar bowls with floral design in medallion. Marks: K'un shan mei yü.

11j. Similar bowls with cash in bottom. Mark: Cheng yü t'ang chih.

11*k*. Similar bowls with dancing boy in bottom. Mark: Mei-yü-ya-ko.
11*l*. Similar bowls with flower and rock, cash in bottom. Mark: Ching chih pao yü.
11*m*. Similar bowls with landscape in bottom. Mark: K'un shan mei yü.
11*n*. Similar bowl with lotus on stem in bottom. Mark: K'un shan mei yü.
12. Similar small bowls and miniature pots with floral designs in outline. Mark: Ch'êng-Hua in square. Pl. 29. 17.
13. Shallow plates with blotchy design, usually an artemisia leaf and branch with buds on a bluish-white ground, brown lip. No marks. Common. Pl. 30. 1.
14. Bowls with roughly drawn flowers, perhaps an aster, usually in a grey-blue. Marks: Ch'êng-Hua and square. Pl. 30. 2.
15. Bowls with landscape and floral designs in similar rough style in grey-blue. Pl. 30. 3, 4.
16*a*. Bowls with poems, usually in grey-blue. Mark: Ch'êng-Hua in square.
16*b*. Bowls with large characters and medallions, border of rosettes. Pl. 30. 7.
17*a*. Plates with pavilion scene in deep blue. Marks: Ch'êng-Hua and K'ang Hsi. Pl. 30. 5.
17*b*. Plates with floral designs, brown edge to lip. Marks: Ch'êng-Hua and K'ang Hsi.
18. Small plates and stem cups with water-weed design in solid blue. Pl. 30. 8, 9.
19*a*. Bowl with a design of symbols, resembling Garner no. 67, on a dead white ground. Mark illegible. Tê-Hua or Annamese. Pl. 30. 6.
19*b*. Bowl with character and leaf in grey on white ground, thick uneven glaze. Perhaps Tê-Hua ware.
19*c*. Bowls with floral designs, sometimes in grey on a cream ground, sometimes crackled, resembling 34*b*.

Coffee outside, blue-and-white inside

20*a*. Bowls with tendrils and blossoms, border of chevrons or trellis. Marks: Ch'êng-Hua and illegible. Common. Pl. 31. 1.
20*b*. Bowls with phoenix with long tail, similar to no. 7. No marks. Pl. 31. 2.
20*c*. Bowl with long broad leaves in Hsüan Tê style.
20*d*. Bowl with formalized tendril scroll in bottom, like no. 23.
20*e*. Bowls and cups, plain inside. Marks: Ch'êng-Hua, leaf.
20*f*. Cups plain with trellis and dot border.
20*g*. Cups plain with landscape in bottom. No marks. Pl. 31. 3.
20*h*. Cups plain with naturalistic or schematized floral design in bottom. No mark.
20*i*. Cups plain with fruit basket in bottom, trellis-and-dot border. No mark.
20*j*. Saucer with brazier and incense-burner in bottom. No marks. Pl. 31. 4.
20*k*. Bowls and cups with coffee glaze inside as well as outside. No marks.
20*l*. Bowls with dark coffee or chocolate glaze on outside, floral design in bottom. No marks.

Café-au-lait *outside, blue-and-white inside*

21*a*. Bowls, cups, and plates with floral sprays. Marks: Ch'êng-Hua, K'ang Hsi, illegible, and leaf. Common. Pl. 31. 5, 6.
21*b*. Plates with schematized lotus design similar to 9. Marks: Chia Ching, K'ang Hsi. Pl. 31. 7.
21*c*. Plates and bowls with various borders. Pl. 31. 8.
21*d*. Bowls and plates with incised tendril ornament, border of swastikas. Mark: Ta Ming.

Celadon outside, blue-and-white inside

22*a*. Bowls with formalized *jui* motif in bottom. No mark.
22*b*. Cup with landscape, similar to 20*g*, in bottom. No mark.
22*c*. Cup with fruit basket, similar to 20*i*, in bottom. No mark.

Mottled green and yellow outside, similar to 3, blue-and-white inside

23. Cups with schematized floral design in bottom. No mark. Pl. 27. 3.

Powder blue outside, blue-and-white inside

24. Plates with sprays in white on blue ground outside, floral design with band of sprays below and *jui* border above bottom on inside. Pl. 31. 9.

Coral red outside, white inside

25. Bowls plain, double ring in blue on base. No mark.

White outside, blue-and-white inside

26. Plates in thin white porcelain with floral design in bottom, similar to 21*a*. No mark.

White

27*a*. Plates, similar to 26, in plain white porcelain. Marks: Ch'êng-Hua, conch, winged links.
27*b*. Similar bowls and cups. sometimes thin. Mark: Ch'êng Hua. Common.

Bluish white

28*a*. Plates with grooved foot-ring, similar to 1*c*, 1*d*, and 7. No mark.
28*b*. Bowls and cups. No mark.

Cream

29. Bowls, cups, and plates, coarser fabric often scorched in kiln. No mark.

Blanc de chine

30*a*. Bowls and cups with carved tendril ornament either over-all or in bands. Pl. 32. 1, 2.

30*b*. Plain cups.
30*c*. Figurines of birds, dogs of Fao, and elephants. Pl. 32. 3.
30*d*. Kidney-shaped boxes with lids, carved tendril, or phoenix ornament. Pl. 32. 4.
30*e*. Palettes, incense-burners, and spoons.
30*f*. Bowls with incised floral designs in panels. Pl. 32. 5.

Celadon

31*a*. Plates with glossy glaze, incised ornament of cloud scrolls, foot-ring with external chamfer. Pl. 32. 6.
31*b*. Similar plates but crackled over a coarse body.
31*c*. Pale yellow-green bowls, bare circle in bottom, partially glazed on outside, over a coarse buff body.

Dark blue

32. Plates with incised design on inside over a coarse body. Pl. 33. 1.

Swatow wares

33. Bowls and plates with floral designs in solid red and green, often in panels on a transparent, sometimes crackled, celadon or grey-white body. No mark. Pl. 33. 2, 3.

Plates with matt surface, perhaps Annamese

34*a*. Plates with similar decoration on a buff ground and body. Pl. 33. 4.
34*b*. Similar plates with large flowers in solid red and green in bottom on same buff body. Pl. 33. 5.

Japanese blue-and-white

35. Plates with broad flat rims decorated with coarsely executed panels in Wan Li style. Arita ware. Pl. 33. 6.
36. Basin with prominent volutes around rim, landscape design in rich blue. Pl. 33. 7.

CLASSES OF EIGHTEENTH- AND NINETEENTH-CENTURY PORCELAIN

Polychrome (iron-red, rose-pink, green, yellow, and gold leaf).

1*a*. Cups and plates with floral designs in iron-red, green, and gold leaf. Eighteenth century. Pl. 34. 1.
1*b*. Bowls and plates with floral or landscape designs in underglaze blue in bottom with borders in green, red, and gold leaf. Eighteenth century. Pl. 34. 3.
2. Bowls and plates with floral designs in red, green, gold, and underglaze blue. Eighteenth century. Pl. 34. 4.
3. Bowls and plates with floral designs in rose-pink, green, blue, and yellow. Eighteenth century, most from Passage of the Arches. Common. Pl. 34. 2.

4*a*. Bowls and plates often with floral designs in panels or trellis in rose-pink, green, and red. Eighteenth century, most from Passage of the Arches. Common. Pl. 34. 5.

4*b*. Small bowls, cups, and plates with floral designs, often with broad bands below lip in red, green, aubergine, and blue. Eighteenth century, most from Passage of the Arches. Pl. 35. 1.

5. Bowls, cups, mugs, and plates with floral designs in green and rose-pink, often within borders of iron-red and overglaze blue, one sherd with Arabic letters in gold on a blue band. Eighteenth century, most from Passage of the Arches and later fill over Passage of the Steps. Common.

6. Small bowls and saucers with alternate bands of tendrils in red and mock Arabic letters in black. Nineteenth century.

7*a*. Bowls with medallions with green trellis outlined in red, and red sprays. Nineteenth century. Common. Pl. 35. 2.

7*b*. Bowls with broad red border of water-weeds and close trellis in red, reminiscent of Swatow wares (K'ang Hsi 33), often with red chrysanthemum on base. Nineteenth century. Common. Pl. 35. 3.

7*c*. Cups with red trellis border or festoons in red and green. Nineteenth century. Common.

8. Bowls, cups, plates, and lids with floral designs in green, yellow, and pink with incised outlines on a grey-white ground. Nineteenth century. Common. Pl. 35. 4.

9. Bowls, cups, and lids of jars with coffee-coloured glaze on outside with quatrefoil and star-shaped panels with sprays in rose-pink, blue, green, and red. One from an eighteenth-century level with Ch'êng-Hua mark, another from a nineteenth-century level with square mark similar to mark on 10. Inside usually plain but sometimes grey-white, occasionally with sprays in panels in rose-pink or blue in style of 3. Common. Eighteenth and nineteenth centuries.

10. Bowls with coral-red, green, or yellow ground, and foliate panels with sprays in red and rose-pink on outside. One red with square mark on base. Nineteenth century. Common. Pl. 35. 5.

11. Small snuff bottles with a green ground and panels with sprays in red and green. Nineteenth century. Common.

Blue-and-white

12*a*. Bowls generally small with rosette band below rim on outside and tied spray or series of cones above base on outside, in blue on bluish-white ground, or black on white ground. Eighteenth century. Common. Pl. 35. 6.

12*b*. Similar bowls with trellis and spray border below rim and a series of cones above base. Eighteenth century. Common. Pl. 35. 7.

12*c*. Similar bowls with mosaic and spray border. Nineteenth century. Common.

12*d*. Similar bowls with border of classical scrolls. Nineteenth century. Common.

13*a*. Bowls and plates with horses, or dragons, or floral designs, in solid without outlines. One or two characters on base, including *ch'ang*, 'long life' and *ch'un*, 'enduring spring'. Eighteenth and nineteenth centuries. Pls. 35. 8, 9; 36. 2.

13*b*. Bowls with floral designs in similar style with similar marks. Eighteenth and nineteenth centuries, mostly the latter. Pl. 36. 1.

13*c*. Bowls with floral designs, sometimes with border below lip. Marks on base similar to 13*a*. Nineteenth century. Common.

13*d*. Plates with coarsely executed floral designs. Nineteenth century. Pl. 36. 3.

14. Plates with landscapes and elaborate borders, or floral designs without borders, one with two-character mark. Eighteenth century. Common. Pl. 36. 4.

15. Bowls, rarely plates, with trellis and spray on outside, spray or concentric circle in bottom. Mark: K'un yu ya chih and square mark on base. Eighteenth and nineteenth centuries. Common. Pl. 36. 5, 6.

16*a*. Bowls with chrysanthemums on outside, single spray in bottom. Square mark on base. Eighteenth and nineteenth centuries. Common. Pl. 36. 7, 8.

16*b*. Plates with similar chrysanthemum design, unglazed base. Eighteenth and nineteenth centuries. Common.

17. Plates and jars with over-all design of blossoms and buds and the 'cod-roe' design, often with brown rims. Eighteenth century. Common. Pl. 37. 1.

18*a*. Jars of ginger-jar type with bare rims and chevron band on shoulder, lids with sketchy landscape design. Eighteenth and nineteenth centuries.

18*b*. Small jars with lids and similar designs. Nineteenth century.

18*c*. Basin with landscape design. Nineteenth century. Pl. 37. 2.

19*a*. Bowls, cups, and plates with over-all character (?) or comb pattern on outside, similar character or symbol in bottom. Usually with unglazed base and square mark, some bases with chamfered ring similar to 30 from eighteenth-century levels. Eighteenth and nineteenth centuries. Common. Pl. 37. 3.

19*b*. Plates with similar design on inside and large character in white on blue ground in bottom, two with square mark on base. Nineteenth century. Common. Pl. 37. 4.

19*c*. Bowls and cups with similar but degenerate design, bottom sometimes bare, or with bare ring and comb mark in middle, often with transparent glaze on a grey-buff body. Eighteenth but mostly nineteenth century. Common. Pl. 37. 5.

20. Bowls and plates with sketchy floral design similar to 13*b* in greyish-blue on bluish-white ground, sometimes with bare bottom or bare ring in bottom, body often grey-buff. Eighteenth but mostly nineteenth century. Common.

21. Bowls with *shou* character in panels on outside, bare ring with *shou* or square mark in bottom. Nineteenth century. Pl. 37. 6, 7.

22. Heavy bowls with two rows of differing versions of *shou* character on outside, sometimes sepia under a transparent glaze on a grey-buff ground. In bottom, *ch'uan* in petal-shaped mark. Nineteenth century. Common. Pl. 38. 1, 2.

23. Heavy plate with two lines of schematized characters on inside, bare ring in bottom, sometimes in sepia under a transparent glaze over a grey-buff body. Nineteenth century.
24*a*. Bowls and lids with random sprays in grey-blue with unglazed bottom, or in sepia on cream, sometimes with sprays on inside and concentric circles in bottom. Nineteenth century. Common.
24*b*. Bowls and cups with tendril scrolls, sometimes in sepia on a grey ground. Nineteenth century. Pl. 38. 3.
25. Cups, saucers, small plates with the Fitzhugh design. Nineteenth century. Common.
26*a*. Small cups with floral design or band below rim. Eighteenth but mostly nineteenth century. Common.
26*b*. Stem cups with floral design. Eighteenth and nineteenth centuries.
26*c*. Spoons with sketchy floral design. Nineteenth century.
27*a*. Bowls with incised floral design, blue borders with diamond pattern below rim and above base on outside. One from Captain's House and one from S. Mateus, but mostly eighteenth century. Pl. 38. 5.
27*b*. Plates with similar incised designs and blue borders. One from filling of court in S. Mateus but mostly eighteenth century. Common. Pl. 38. 4.
27*c*. Plates with similar blue borders but incised ornament omitted, often sexfoil motif in bottom. Eighteenth century. Common. Pl. 36. 6.

Blue-and-white and aubergine

28. Plates with tall ring base and birds or dragons in blue-and-white and aubergine, unglazed base. Eighteenth century. Pl. 38. 7.

White

29*a*. Bowls with turned-out lips and tall thick ring bases, sometimes with foliate edge. Eighteenth or nineteenth century. Common.
29*b*. Small cups and saucers in grey-white. Nineteenth century. Common.

Monochromes

30. Bowls and cups, dark blue on outside, bluish-white inside with distinctive chamfered unglazed foot-ring, five bowls in a light blue with normal glazed foot-ring. Eighteenth and nineteenth centuries. Common.
31. Bowls and small jars with grey glaze. Nineteenth century.
32. Fluted lids, greenish-white with brown edges. Nineteenth century.
33. Snuff bottles in dark blue and celadon glazes, embossed concentric or rectangular patterns below glaze. Nineteenth century. Common.

MINIMUM NUMBER OF VESSELS

MING

Class No.	*S. Filipe*	*Passage of Steps*	*S. Matias*	*S. Mateus*	*S. Alberto*	*Other*	*Total*
1*a*	54	35	31	17	47	15	199
1*b*	2	2	3		2		9
1*c*				1			1
2	17	5	3	10	8	9	52
3	8	3	4	1	1	1	18
4	1						1
5*a*	1	1				1	3
5*b*		1		1			2
6*a*	4	6	8	2	3		23
6*b*		1			1		2
6*c*			1				1
7	4		5	1	2		12
8*a*	1						1
8*b*	1					1	2
9*a*	3		2		1		6
9*b*	6	9	3	4	4	1	27
9*c*	1	1	1				3
10	1	2					3
11*a*		1				1	2
11*b*	1				2		3
12	2		2	6	3	7	20
13*a*	1						1
13*b*	1			1		1	3
14		1					1
15				1	1		2
16				2	2	1	5
17				1			1
18					1		1
19	4		4	2	1		11
20					1		1
21	4			1			5
22	1				1		2
	118	68	67	51	81	38	423

K'ANG HSI

Class No.	*S. Filipe*	*Captain's House*	*S. Mateus*	*Other*	*Total*
1*a*	14	4	5	1	24
1*b*	1	2		3	6
1*c*	2	3	2	1	8
1*d*	2	2	1	1	6
1*e*	2	2		1	5
2	3	2			5
3		1	2	1	4
4			1	1	2
5*a*	2		2		4
5*b*	2			1	3
5*c*	12	1	2		15
5*d*	1				1
5*e*		2			2
6*a*	9	2	1	2	14
6*b*	4	2	1	8	15
6*c*		2		1	3
6*d*	6		3	5	14
7		1	1		2
8			1	1	2
9	2			2	4
10*a*	4	6	1	9	20
10*b*	4			1	5
11*a*	3	1	1		5
11*b*	14	3	8	15	40
11*c*	7	1	1	3	12
11*d*	3		1	1	5
11*e*		1			1
11*f*	16	5	4	13	38
11*g*	2				2
11*h*	4	5		5	14
11*i*	3		1	1	5
11*j*		1		2	3
12				5	5
13	127	20	61		208
(small)	12	3	1	8	24
14	46	5	44	9	104
15	3	3	3		9
16*a*	1	1	1	1	4
16*b*	1		1		2
17*a*	2	1		3	6

K'ANG HSI (*cont.*)

Class No.	*S. Filipe*	*Captain's House*	*S. Mateus*	*Other*	*Total*
17*b*			4	14	18
18				1	1
19*a*				1	1
19*b*		1			1
19*c*				10	10
20*a*	20	1	4		25
20*b*	6	1	4	1	12
20*c*				1	1
20*d*				2	2
20*e*			2		2
20*f*	2	1	1		4
20*g*	4	1	1		6
20*h*				1	1
20*i*	1		1		2
20*j*	2				2
20*k*			2		2
20*l*			1		1
21*a*	3	13	1	1	18
21*b*	2	4	1	2	9
21*c*	1	2		3	6
21*d*	4			1	5
22*a*				1	1
22*b*	1				1
22*c*		1			1
23	1				1
24	2			2	4
25			1		1
26				1	1
27*a*	1	3	1		5
27*b*	2	10	3	6	21
28*a*	1	1			2
28*b*	3		6	3	12
29	3	1			4
30*a*	2	1	1		4
30*b*	4		1		5
30*c*	1	2			3
30*d*		4	3		7
30*e*	1	1	1		3
30*f*		2	1		3
31*a*	3	1	1		5

K'ANG HSI (*cont.*)

Class No.	S. Filipe	Captain's House	S. Mateus	Other	Total
31*b*	3	2	2		7
31*c*	1				1
32	1	1	3	1	6
33	2	1	3	1	7
34*a*			3		3
34*b*	2	2	2		6
35	4	2	6		12
36			1		1
	397	141	211	158	907

INDEX OF MARKS

MING

	Class No.	S. Filipe	Passage of the Arches	S. Alberto	Total
Royal Name					
Ch'êng-Hua	6*a*			1	1
Hallmarks					
Miao-ching t'ang chih	17	1			1
T'ung-tê t'ang chih	5*a*			1	1
Yü t'ang chia ch'i	8*a*	1			1
Marks of Commendation					
Ch'ang-shou	6*a*		1		1
Fu and illegible character	1*a*			1	1
		2	1	3	6

K'ANG HSI

	Class No.	S. Filipe	Captain's House	S. Mateus	Other	Total
Royal Name						
Ch'êng-Hua	1*a*	2		1		3
	3			1		1
	5*c*	4				4
	5*d*		1			1
	6*a*	1				1
	6*b*		1			1
	10*b*	5	2	3		10

K'ANG HSI (*cont.*)

Royal Name	*Class No.*	*S. Filipe*	*Captain's House*	*S. Mateus*	*Other*	*Total*
(in square)	12				1	1
	14		2	1		3
	17*a*				1	1
(in square)	16*a*				1	1
	20*a*				1	1
	20*e*	1				1
	21*a*	1	5	3		9
	27*a*	1				1
	27*b*				2	2
		15	11	9	6	41
K'ang Hsi	1*d*			1		1
	5*a*	1				1
	5*c*	5				5
	5*e*				1	1
	6*a*	8	2			10
	6*b*	1				1
	6*c*	1		1		2
	10*b*				1	1
	17*a*		1			1
	17*b*				1	1
	21*a*				1	1
	21*b*	1				1
		17	3	2	4	26
Chia Ching	4			1		1
	21*b*	2	1		1	4
		2	1	1	1	5
Hsüan Tê	1*d*				1	1
	5*e*	1				1
		1			1	2
imperfect		3				3
Grand Total		38	15	12	12	77

K'ANG HSI (*cont.*)

	Class No.	S. Filipe	Captain's House	S. Mateus	Other	Total
Hallmarks						
Hua-yu-t'ang ch'ing ya chih	1*a*	4			1	5
Yung-fa-hao chih	1*a*			1		1
Mei-yü t'ang chih	6*b*	1				1
Ch'i yen t'ang chih	10*b*	3				3
- - ya chih	11*a*	1				1
K'un yu ya chih	11*c*	2				2
	11*d*	1				1
- pi t'ang chih	11*c*				1	1
K'un shan mei yü	11*a*	1				1
	11*d*	1				1
	11*e*		1			1
	11*f*	8	4		5	17
	11*i*	1				1
	11*m*				1	1
	11*n*		1	1	1	3
Cheng-yü-t'ang chih	11*f*			1	1	2
	11*j*	2	1		1	4
Mei-yü-ya-ko	11*k*				1	1
Cheng chi pao yü	11*f*		1	1	1	3
	11*l*				1	1
illegible	11*d*	1				1
	19*a*			1		1
	20*a*	2				2
	21*a*				1	1
		28	8	5	15	56
Symbols						
conch	10*b*	4			1	5
	27*a*		4			4
fungus	10*a*	4	6	1	9	20
leaf	6*a*	2				2
	20*e*				1	1
twisted leaf	21*a*				1	1
links	27*a*		2		1	3
two fishes	6*d*			1		1
	8				1	1
group of five red dots	1*a*				1	1
square mark	14				1	1
		10	12	2	16	40

EIGHTEENTH AND NINETEENTH CENTURIES

	Class No.
Hallmarks	
Ch'êng-Hua	9
K'un yu ya chih	15
square mark	9, 10, 15, 16*a*, 19*a*, 19*b*, 21
Commendation	
ch'ang	13*a*, 13*b*, 13*c*
ch'un	13*a*, 13*b*, 13*c*
shou	21
illegible	14, 15

CHINESE AND RELATED STONEWARE (Fig. 70, Pl. 39)

A number of sherds of glazed earthenware were found in the Fort which had belonged to jars of varying size: large, 53 cm high, medium, 38 cm, and small, 25 cm. They were covered with a glossy black or yellow-brown glaze, and were made with four small horizontal handles for the cords by which the lid would be attached. The body of the large and medium-sized jars was grey, rarely pink; that of the smaller was yellow, rarely grey. These jars occurred in early-seventeenth-century levels but were commonest in those of the late seventeenth century. The large jars continued to be imported or to survive throughout the eighteenth century, but the smaller jars were replaced by imitations (Fig. 71. 1–10) at the beginning of the century.

The commonest were the medium-sized black jars with a rolled rim and an illegible stamp on the shoulder (Fig. 70. 13 and 14). Complete jars of this type, and of the larger type with studs below the shoulder, were recovered from the frigate sunk off the Fort in 1697, and are in Fort Jesus Museum.[18A]

The large black storage jars (Fig. 70. 1–4), similar to those published in *Gedi—The Palace*, Fig. 14 M, were less common. They were pear-shaped, standing about 1·22 m, with a mouth 30 cm wide and a body 61 cm wide. The largest, with a row of studs on the shoulder, occurred in eighteenth- and nineteenth-century levels; complete examples exist in private hands and in the Lamu Museum. Other large jars had grey bodies with mauve slips (Fig. 67. 5 and 6), similar to the unglazed earthenware jar on Fig. 65. 6.

A third form, of which only one example was found, was the large jar with a grey-purple body, brown glaze, and horizontal handles on the shoulder (Fig. 70. 16; Pl. 39. 1).

Among the medium-sized jars were sherds of vessels with green ground and carved ornament of acanthus leaves and *jui* borders in yellow, similar to the jar in the Victoria

[18A] Kirkman (1972)

and Albert Museum, London, illustrated by Honey, Pl. 81. These occurred in early- and late-seventeenth century levels. Sherds of a similar type of jar, but with carved dragons and phoenixes, were found in late-seventeenth- and eighteenth-century levels, but the motifs were normally in the same dark green as the background. The body was yellow, similar to the small jars, often with streaks of brown varnish on the inside.

A few sherds were found of a jar with the same yellow body, yellow-brown glaze, incised ornament, and a twisted 'barley-sugar' handle. They occurred in early- and late-seventeenth-century levels, but not afterwards.

The smaller jars (Fig. 70. 18) are commoner in late-seventeenth-century levels, but are similar to the types found in late-sixteenth-century levels at Gedi (*Great Mosque*, Fig. 32 s, t, E). In the earlier specimens the body was generally grey, while in the later it was usually yellow and only rarely pink or grey.

Most of these wares were made in Kwangtung, and belong to Eine Moore class 3 A, E, F, G, but the jars with a mauve slip (Fig. 67. 5 and 6) and the unique heavy brown glazed jar (Fig. 70. 16) are probably Kalong (Siamese) ware, Moore class 6 C.[19] It would appear that these Ming type jars continued to be made in the seventeenth century.

UNIDENTIFIED GLAZED WARES (Figs. 71–3; Pl. 39. 2–6)

In addition to the small stoneware jars, there was another group of small jars with a rolled rim and a poor brown or black glaze on a grey, pink, or, in the later levels, buff earthenware (Fig. 71. 1–2; Pl. 39. 2, 3). The glazes varied between a smooth brown to a rough grey-brown or neutral tint, similar to the bowls in Figs. 72 and 73. A characteristic of these jars was two pairs of horizontal handles, set close together on the shoulder. This is a feature which I have not seen on any unquestionable Chinese pieces. They appeared in the late seventeenth century and continued into the nineteenth century. The larger jars (Fig. 71. 4, 7–10) were numerous in the nineteenth-century levels and the glaze tended to cover less of the body.

A prominent feature of the ceramic pattern of the late-seventeenth-, eighteenth-, and nineteenth-century levels was a class of heavy bowls and, less commonly, plates with tapered or flanged lips and ring or disk bases (Figs. 72 and 73; Pl. 39. 4, 5, 6). The bodies varied from grey or grey-pink to buff. The seventeenth- and eighteenth-century specimens were generally grey or grey-pink; the nineteenth-century pieces pink or buff. However, occasional specimens with buff bodies occurred in the early-seventeenth-century levels, and grey and grey-pink specimens in the later levels. The glaze also varied from green, rarely iridescent, and brown, through successive stages of degeneration to neutral or brownish-grey. Similarly, the surface declined from a smooth green or glossy brown to a rough matt, sometimes only on the inside and

[19] Moore (1970).

upper part of the outside of the vessel. By this time it is clear that no aesthetic element was present, but merely the utilitarian wish to make the bowl less porous. Green was the popular colour of the seventeenth century, particularly for the wide-mouthed bowls, and the least common in the nineteenth century. The nondescript tints and poor surface began to prevail in the eighteenth and predominated in the nineteenth century. The seventeenth-century forms continued into the eighteenth, though the plates with flanged lips, usually with a green glaze (Fig. 72. 6–10 and 13) were commonest in late-seventeenth-century levels and rare later. The cordoned bowl or beaker (Fig. 72. 5) is reminiscent of the jar on Fig. 74. 3, considered to be Portuguese, but the fabric is similar to these bowls.

This brown- and green-coloured stoneware had occurred in the upper levels at Gedi (*Great Mosque*, Cl. 7, 8, p. 132), and a few sherds of Fig. 72. 7 were found in the lower levels in Fort Jesus. However, it is the characteristic ware of the late seventeenth, eighteenth, and early nineteenth centuries. It has been found in Malaya at Johore Bahru,[20] but has not, so far as I know, been recorded from India, Indo-China, or Indonesia. The forms of the lips follow the forms of both Islamic and Chinese wares. A peculiar feature is the groove on the inside of the lip, as shown on Fig. 72. 12, 14 and Fig. 73. 6, 16. The forms of the lips and bases are to me more Far Eastern than Near Eastern, which would argue a factory somewhere on the eastern side of the Indian Ocean in Indo-China or Indonesia.

PORTUGUESE AND OTHER EUROPEAN WARES (Figs. 74 and 75; Pls. 40 and 41)

The Portuguese ceramic found in the Fort consisted of demijohns and basins in a green or yellow salt-glazed ware; large jars in a hard-baked red earthenware; small bowls, dishes, and flasks in a polished red ware; and dishes, small jars, and flasks in a blue-and-white maiolica.

The salt-glazed ware consisted of demijohns, jars, and basins, some with vertical handles, with a green, yellow, or brown glaze on a red body (Fig. 74. 1–3; Pl. 41. 10, 11). There was frequently a change of colour, such as green outside and yellow inside, as was found on Islamic wares Classes 20, 22. A curious feature is a blister or blob of glaze which occurs on top of the flat-topped bowls and basins (Fig. 74. 6, 9). This is probably adventitious and of no significance, except as an indication of indifferent workmanship. Associated with these vessels is the unglazed demijohn (Fig. 74. 13) with a similar neck and rim to Fig. 74. 1. They were found in early- and late-seventeenth-century levels.

Large jars made in a red earthenware, sometimes with a white slip (Figs. 74. 14–23; 75. 1, 2) resembling Spanish olive-oil and water jars, were also found. Nos. 22 and 23, although they occurred in the Passage of the Arches, are probably Portuguese.

[20] Private communication from B. A. V. Peacock.

A jar is a substantial vessel which performs a static role in a house and would have a longer expectation of life than a cooking-pot or an eating-bowl. There is no reason why it should not survive 100 years of use. Some of the pink-bodied jars of Fig. 65 may also be Portuguese.

Both the jars and demijohns belong to the same ceramic tradition as the Spanish olive-oil jars from the Caribbean.[21] In the museum at Fort Jesus there is a tall red earthenware water jar with a rolled rim, flange handles, and a monogram, in Iberian tradition. Its history is unknown, other than that it is of local provenance. No sherds of similar jars have been found in the Fort, though its hard-baked, pitted outer surface is similar to that of the smaller vessel of Fig. 74. 23.

The basins, Fig. 65. 18, 19, may also be Portuguese, although they were found in eighteenth- and nineteenth-century levels.

The thin red, pink, or *terra sigillata* ware consisted of small bowls, flasks, and jars (Fig. 75. 3–7; Pl. 40. 1–8, 12, 15), sometimes finely polished and sometimes without polish but studded with quartz chips (Pl. 40. 9–14). Unfortunately, apart from the tall flask (Fig. 75. 5), only fragments were found. It was impossible to reconstruct the vessels with angel heads (Pl. 40. 12, 15). This ware occurred principally in early-seventeenth-century levels but continued in use until the end of the century. Similar wares, both the red-polished and quartz-studded types, are still made in the Alemtejo in and were on sale in the market at Estremoz in 1964.

Portuguese maiolica occurred in the filling of the bastions but was more frequent in late-seventeenth-century levels. This was a hard buff-bodied ware, plain white, or more often blue-and-white or blue-and-aubergine-and-white. The designs on the blue-and-white are frequently childish, consisting of solid strokes or little spiky objects which could be leaves, birds, or snowflakes. The design on the blue-and-aubergine-and-white are slightly more sophisticated (Pl. 41. 1–8).

The commonest form was a bowl with straight sides, like a child's porridge plate (Fig. 75. 10; Pl. 41.7, 8), 12·7 cm across and 5·08 cm high, plain white, or with a pattern on the outside consisting of a series of pyramidal heaps with apex alternatively at top and bottom. In the bottom, not on the base, was frequently the unidentified symbol 三, 扌, 3 in aubergine, possibly an imitation of the tassel mark found on Persian blue-and-white. Other forms were plates with flat lips, 21 cm across (Fig. 75. 11), sometimes with a fan border, as on the dish with the cross of the Order of Christ found at Takwa.[22] The most interesting sherd, however, was the base of a plate with a shield with the arms of Cardoso (first and third quarter) impaling Teixeira (second quarter) and perhaps de Matos (fourth quarter), surmounted by an episcopal hat with six tassels on each side (Pl. 42. 1). This is the coat of arms of a bishop who has not been identified. It was found at the bottom of the Passage of the Arches.

Besides the plates there were small jars or potiche, 6·35 cm in diameter, often with the letters 'I H S' within a radiate cartouche. In the pit in S. Filipe was found a small

[21] Goggin (1960); Ashdown (1972). [22] Kirkman (1957), Fig. 8.

flask with the monogram 'HP R DG' within a radiate cartouche, which might mean *Hospitale Reale Deo Gratias* (Fig. 75. 12; Pl. 41. 9). It probably held a purge and may have come from the famous hospital at Goa.

There were a number of potteries in Portugal, of which the largest were at Lisbon, Coimbra, and Oporto. In the Museum at Coimbra is a fine collection of Portuguese blue-and-white maiolica. The radiate cartouche and the fan-shaped border occur on these vessels, but none of the other motifs. Portuguese blue-and-white has never been studied exhaustively, and it is not yet possible to date or attribute individual pieces.

A few sherds of the German stoneware jugs, with a dark brown salt glaze and a bearded face below the lip, known in England as Bellarmines, were found in the Captain's House, in the Passage of the Arches, and in the west barrack block. The rosette on one of these sherds was similar to the rosette on a jug found in the ruins of Basing House in Hampshire, England, destroyed in 1645 during the Civil War.[23] A small grey stoneware jug, which is probably German, also came from the Captain's House (Fig. 75. 13).

A green glazed jug, probably English, was found in a nineteenth-century level in the Passage of the Arches, and a few sherds of brown glazed earthenware, perhaps Rouen ware, occurred in eighteenth- and nineteenth-century levels.

NINETEENTH-CENTURY ENGLISH AND EUROPEAN PORCELAIN AND CHINA

A large quantity of European china and a few sherds of porcelain were found in the Fort, particularly in the Passage of the Arches. This collection is a representative example of the types which were sent to East Africa in the nineteenth century. It can be seen from the marks that the majority belong to the third quarter of the century.[24] It is most unlikely that any quantity of European china would have reached Mombasa before its absorption in Saiyid Said's dominions in 1837. European china was, of course, well known all over the Indian Ocean by the end of the eighteenth century and was in use in Zanzibar in the 1820s. Cups and plates even reached the Kabaka of the Buganda in the middle of the eighteenth century,[25] but this was something exceptional. There would, however, have been little interest in European china in such a stronghold of the past as the Mombasa of the Mazrui. Guillain, referring to the whole of the coast, gives an impression that European china in 1846 was no more than a future rival to Chinese porcelain. Most of the English china came via Bombay, since direct trade between Britain and East Africa, except in muskets, was slight for most of Saiyid Said's reign and stopped completely between 1848 and 1855.[26]

Crockery—In this category are comprised articles of pottery and porcelain which come, each in its class, from different countries. China (faience) of English manufacture is brought

[23] Moorhouse (1970) no. 226.
[24] Chaffers (1952); Cushion and Honey (1956).
[25] Ingham (1962), p. 57.
[26] Nicholls (1971), pp. 335–8.

mainly by ships of this nation which trade with Zanzibar. Most of the procelain is of Chinese origin and comes almost entirely via Bombay, whose annual export of this commodity to the African coast is worth about 12,000 rupees. A little porcelain comes also in American ships. Most of the porcelain [*sic*] imported is of English manufacture. However, all the crockery imported into the country is of very mediocre quality and priced accordingly. Among the pottery, most of which comes from India, are great quantities of water pots made at Muscat [these are Indian chatties]. A few pieces of crockery (faience and porcelain) of French origin have lately been imported from Maiotte.[27]

China first appeared in the rubble level overlying the eighteenth-century mud in the Passage of the Arches and continued with increasing quantities in the succeeding levels. The commonest pieces were plates and dishes, later bowls and cups. In the print wares, blue was the most popular colour, but other colours, black, brown, green, mauve, pink, purple, sepia, and salmon, were also found. A few sherds of English flowered porcelain and French gilt white porcelain appeared in nineteenth-century levels.

In the second half of the nineteenth century there were large imports of European china from the Saar, notably the flowered cups and bowls manufactured by Utzschneider & Co., Saarguemines, and, less common, by Villeroy & Boch, Wallerfangen.

The lustred bowls made by Frank Beardmore & Co., bearing the name Peera Dewjee, Zanzibar were an interesting import. Peera Dewjee was a Customs Master of Zanzibar who retired and set up an importing business.

The principal varieties are listed below, followed by a list of potters and potters' marks.

CLASSES OF EUROPEAN WARES

1. Plates and large dishes and, less common, bowls and cups in creamware.
2*a*. Plates in a creamware with foliate edge coloured blue or green, sometimes carved on rim.
2*b*. Same, but with pink edge, moulded rosette pattern on rim.
3*a*. Plates and a few cups with 'willow pattern' design in a blue print. The thickness varied from 0·42 cm to 0·96 cm. In the lowest levels the thinnest predominated but some sherds of 0·96 cm were also found.
3*b*. Similar, but with floral designs, sometimes reversed, white on blue ground.
3*c*. Similar, but with classical decorative patterns.
3*d*. Similar, with landscape designs.
3*e*. Plates with copies of Chinese comb and chrysanthemum patterns in blue.
4*a*. Plates with panels in blue on a bluish-white ground.
4*b*. Dish with Chinese landscape design in blue, red, and gold on the same bluish-white ground.

[27] Guillain (1856–7), vol. iii, p. 347.

5*a*. Small plates or saucers in white or cream.
5*b*. Similar, with printed floral patterns in outline blue or grey on white ground.
6*a*. Shallow bowls with painted floral patterns in two shades of pink and green with black blobs.
6*b*. Bowls and cups decorated with large blossoms in red, blue, dark and light green, yellow, and mauve, on white ground.
6*c*. Similar, but with geometric or schematized floral motifs in bands.
7. Cups and bowls with printed trellis pattern imposed on a chequer ground of dark blue or light blue on white.
8. Small bowls with turned-out lips, outside pale blue above white near base.
9*a*. Banded bowls and mugs with rope mark with strands of different colours and green border.
9*b*. Similar, with mark like a monogram and border in blue.
9*c*. Similar, yellow with raised white cordons.
9*d*. Similar, with variations of grey, brown, black, or blue 'mocha' decoration on white.
9*a*. Similar, with impressed chequers in light blue or green on white.
10. Bowls with floral designs in brown or gold lustre.
11*a*. Coffee cups without handles, pink printed on white and lustred.
11*b*. Similar, green or old rose printed on white.
11*c*. Similar, green and gold or gold on white, fluted.
11*d*. Similar, dark blue and gold on white.
11*e*. Similar, red on white, fluted.
11*f*. Copper and blue on bluish ground.
11*g*. Pink on white, fluted.
11*h*. Similar, dark blue, iron red, or green on white.

MARKS ON EUROPEAN WARES

W. Adams & Sons 1880–	a Stag	Cl. 5*a*
	an Eagle SUPERIOR WHITE GRANITE W. ADAMS & SONS.	
Frank Beardmore & Co. 1903–14	A Crown above a Shield across shield F. B. & Co. around PEERA DEWJEE ZANZIBAR	Cl. 10
G. F. Bowers 1842–68	a Twisted Rope (impressed)	Cl. 3*d*, 6*b*
J. & W. Brameld	BRAMELD (impressed)	Cl. 3*d*

R. Cochran & Co.	a Britannia R. COCHRAN & Co. GLASGOW	Cl. 5*b*
Copeland 1847–67	COPELAND LATE SPODE	Cl. 3*a*
	COPELAND	Cl. 3*a* (also in green) and 3*c*
J. Defrie	J. DEFRIE	Cl. 3*b* in sepia
T. I. & J. Emberton	an Anchor in Garter (inscribed) T. I. & J. EMBERTON	Cl. 3*e*
	LILLY in circle (inscribed) T. I. & J. EMBERTON	Cl. 3*e*
Harrop & Burgess 1895–1904	a Crown WARRANTED H & B	Cl. 3*a*
J. & M. P. B. & Co.	ARCADIA J. &. M. P. B. & Co.	Cl. 3*d*
Jackson & Gosling (?)	J. G. & Co. STOKE UPON TRENT	Cl. 3*d*
William Ridgeway 1830–54	W. R. & Co. ALBION	Cl. 3*b* in purple
Société Céramique Maastricht	a Lion around SOCIETE CERAMIQUE MAASTRICHT	Cl. 6*b*
Spode 1800–33	SPODE	Cl. 3*d*
Tell & Co.	an Anchor (impressed)	Cl. 3*c*
Utzschneider & Co. 1858	a Coronet above a Shield around OPAQUE DE SAARGUEMINES	Cl. 4*a*, 6*b*, 6*c*
Villeroy & Boch 1789	a Winged Head VILLEROY AND BOCH WALLERFANGEN	Cl. 6*b*, 6*c*
Vouzin Legat & Co.	a Lion around MONS. VOUZIN LEGAT & Cie. NIMY	Cl. 6*b*

Maker	Mark	Class
Wileman & Co. 1892–1925	DICE W & Co	Cl. 1
Wiltshaw & Robinson	STONEWARE W & R STOKE UPON TRENT	Cl. 3*e*
Thomas Wood & Co. 1897–1904	T. W. & Co. in Garter Garter inscribed ORCHARD	Cl. 1
	a Ship F. P.	Cl. 3*b*
	CALCUTTA (impressed) STOKE UPON TRENT	Cl. 3*a*
	IRONSTONE CHINA Royal coat of arms ETON COLLEGE	Cl. 3*d* in sepia
	a Crown PARIS in Garter	Cl. 3*b*
	an Anchor LONDON (impressed)	Cl. 3*c*
	an Anchor in Garter inscribed LEVANT	Cl. 3*c*

Patent Marks

Mark	Class
1844	Cl. 1
1847	Cl. 3*c*
1862 (Copeland)	Cl. 3*c*

14. Glass

(Figs. 76–9)

THE glass found in the Fort, with few exceptions such as Fig. 76. 13, consisted of bottles and flasks. The Arab glass vessels were mostly necks of *marasha* or rose-water sprinklers. The earliest had an irregular cup mouth with tucked-in lip (Fig. 76. 1). These were found in early-seventeenth-century levels. In the late seventeenth century a more regular vessel was imported (Fig. 76. 2, 3) with a knopf below the lip or half-way down the neck, sometimes with a sharply turned-out lip. The normal colour of the metal was green, but this last variety was in white. The flask with a pinched lip (Fig. 76. 5) was found in an eighteenth-century level. The other flasks with multiple strings (Fig. 76. 6, 8, and 9) were found in eighteenth- and nineteenth-century levels, although this is an old ornamental device which goes back to the twelfth century.[1] None of these flasks was complete, but both oval and round ring bases have been found.

Also found in early-seventeenth-century levels were necks of vessels with a rolled rim and a rounded border with a flat base (Fig. 76. 7), similar to Haynes, Plate 12 d. These were less common than the sprinkler vases. The curious vessels with roughly twisted-off neck and wide band (Fig. 76. 10, 11) occurred only in eighteenth- and nineteenth-century levels, and may be lamp glasses, like Fig. 76. 12.

The European glass consisted of the base of a Venetian *tazza* (Fig. 76. 13), case bottles (Figs. 77. 1–5; 78. 1–3 and 8; Pl. 42. 2) and round bottles (Figs. 77. 6–11; 78. 4, 7, and 9). No European glass other than the Venetian *tazza*, was found in the early-seventeenth-century levels, but in those of the late-seventeenth century, case-bottles, both large and small, with turned-out lips occurred. This is surprising because in America these bottles occurred in early-seventeenth-century levels and were rare later.[2] The large case-bottles had pewter screw necks and caps (Fig. 77. 1–3). The small bottles (Figs. 77. 4, 5; 78. 8) were sealed with corks. Also in the late-seventeenth-century levels were found round bottles with thick concave bases with shallow 'kicks' and conical necks with strings (Figs. 77. 6; 78. 9), similar to Hume, Fig. 3.

In the eighteenth century, case-bottles and round bottles continued to be imported and must have been one of the most acceptable European manufactures. The forms of the round bottles followed to a great extent the forms of the English and French bottles published by Hume and Sutermeister.[3] The French bottles (Figs. 77. 8, 10, 11; 78. 7; 79. 4, 5, 8, 9) were probably a by-product of the French slave trade with Mauritius and Reunion. These bottles are not evidence of any great taste for wine in

[1] Haynes, (1948), Pl. 8 d. [2] Hume (1961). [3] Sutermeister (1968).

East Africa; they would have been used for storage and would have had a scarcity value which they did not enjoy in their own country. In addition to the marks shown on Fig. 79. 1, 2, there were: 'Vieux Cognac', 'St. Julien Medoc', 'Châteaux Giscours', and 'P.M.D.S.' The case-bottles found in eighteenth-century levels all had a strong rounded lip intended for a cork. The forms with a raised band (Fig. 79. 5, 7) were unusual. All European glass, except for a few nineteenth-century types, was a medium smoky variety.

15. *Beads*

(Fig. 80)

GLASS

GLASS beads have been classified as wound, moulded, and drawn or cane beads. Another classification would make a distinction between the individually made (wound and moulded beads) and the mass-produced drawn or cane type. Moulded beads are the least common of the three types. The modern stamped beads can sometimes be recognized by a median line, showing that they were made in two halves.

The difference between individually hand-fabricated and drawn beads is a distinction of production and quality, not necessarily of time and place. Originally all beads were wound, but at a time unknown the idea of making a long tube out of a bubble enclosed in glass dawned on somebody, and an industry was born.

The place of manufacture of these beads has still to be established. It was believed that the small opaque beads were made in India, since they have been found all round the Indian Ocean, some in levels in Malaya which were considered to be as early as the eighth century. However, they are extremely scarce in museums in India.[1] In Portuguese stock inventories beads are frequently mentioned, but seldom with the place of origin. In the early-sixteenth-century records of the Sofala factors, small red-and-black beads of Cambay are listed, and also beads of Cambay of all sorts. These would appear to be the small opaque beads of classes A.2 and A.6 (see p. 143). It is strange that the similar blue, green, and yellow beads should not be specified, although small yellow and green beads are often referred to but without the ascriptions to Cambay. The *contas azuis de vidro vindas de Portugal*[2] may imply a Portuguese factory whose products should be distinguishable from the others.

Two types of Venetian beads are mentioned: *contas de Venezia azuis compridas e finas* and *cristaliho azul fino de Venezia*.[3] The first could be class B.2 and the second class B.5. *Contas cristalinhas* appear frequently in the records but without place of origin. Few of these three types were found in early-sixteenth-century levels, and they only became common in the late seventeenth century. They, and in fact all the types of glass beads except classes A and D.1–3 have been regarded as European, made in Venice, Amsterdam, and other places. However, none of them has been found in sixteenth-century levels at the Arab–African sites in Kenya. It seems extraordinary that they should not have been found if they were in existence at this time, and that

[1] Communication from Claire Davison.

[2] Lobato (1960), list C, following p. 313.

[3] Lobato, op. cit., p. 45.

there should be this difference in imports between the two captaincies of Malindi and Sofala, both drawing their supplies from the same source. Such anomalies also occur with the beads found in sites in Rhodesia, such as Dambarare.[4]

The form of the beads depended on the process of manufacture. There was considerable scope for variety in the wound and moulded types, while the drawn beads were limited to variations on the cylinder. Among the wound beads the variations were based largely on the sphere and its modifications: the bicone; the sphere flattened on two opposite faces, called oblate; and the barrel, usually so attenuated as to be better described as an ellipse. The moulded beads comprised the melon, the star, the oblong, and the cable—all extremely uncommon; and spheres with multiple facets, which were a little more common. Among the drawn beads there is a distinction between the reheated beads with rounded smooth edges, and the crude chopped or broken beads. The final form of both types was either the disk or short cylinder, greater across than on the axis of the perforation; the standard cylinder, with diameter and axis equal; and the long or true cylinder. The disk and standard cylinder were the usual forms in East Africa.

The true cylinder, except among the light blue beads, was by no means popular in East Africa, unlike the beads which have been found in contemporary contexts in West Africa and North America. Of all objects found in excavations, isolated beads are the most dangerous to ascribe to the level in which they were found, unless it is a sealed level and there can be no possibility of their having fallen from the cutting above. Confusion of this kind is the reason, I believe, for the extraordinary early dating sometimes ascribed to certain types of rosetta, chevron, and eye-beads. Dr. van der Sleen has done a great service by drawing attention to the bead factory or factories at Amsterdam and their varied production of beads, some of which have ended up in museums, described as Roman, Merovingian, etc. His jest, 'All beads were made at Amsterdam', should be in the mind of everyone who has to deal with glass beads.[5]

Many thousands of glass beads were found in Fort Jesus, mostly of the drawn types. There were 131,270+ drawn beads, as compared with 802+ wound beads. Tables 1–17 show the composition of the largest deposits. These are clearly not casual losses but the residue of stocks.

There is no significance in the minor variations in form of the mass-produced beads (classes A, B, and J), but the selection of colour in the various periods is of interest. Table 18 shows the occurrences of beads or groups of beads and Table 19 the over-all totals. A comparison of the two tables indicates that these two factors are not always in correspondence. The nineteenth-century numbers are inflated by the larger area excavated and the greater number of levels, due to greater disturbance, than in the earlier periods. A discount of thirty per cent in the frequency table would give a true factor of comparison. The eighteenth-century totals for class A may be

[4] Garlake (1969). [5] van der Sleen (1963).

inflated by the anomalous groups (Tables 9–11), in which the bead pattern was late-seventeenth century although the level was dated by eighteenth-century rose-pink porcelain.

In Table 20 are shown the percentages of each colour of class A according to period, and in Table 21 the percentage in each period of each colour, both by occurrence and by number. The differences are less in the occurrence lists than in the totals, and may give a more correct proportion.

In the earliest Transitional Ming porcelain levels the great majority of glass beads consisted of reheated beads, generally small, about 3·2 mm on axis and diameter, with opaque colours: dark blue, yellow, black, red, greenish-blue, green, pearl, and orange, in order of frequency (A.1–8). The first six of these colours had occurred at Gedi and other medieval sites.[6] The pearl and orange were not found on those sites, but are identical in manufacture. The number found in early-seventeenth-century levels was small. They were never very popular and it is reasonable to regard them as a variation of an old line, rather than a new product from a different source. I believe these reheated beads to be the *continhas muidas de Cambia* of the Portuguese lists, which were made in India.[7] In his account of the wreck of the Santo Alberto, J. B. Lavanha mentioned Negapatam as a source of red beads.[8] However, this probably means no more than the place from which they were exported; there is no tradition of bead manufacture in Negapatam today.[9] These were the principal beads of the early-seventeenth-century levels and all, except the red, continued to appear in substantial quantities in late-seventeenth-century levels beside the new types. The disappearance of the red beads has still to be explained. Negapatam was taken from the Portuguese by the Dutch in 1658, but this need not have meant the end of the industry, and even if the red beads were considered to be an illegal import, their illegality would have ceased after the fall of Fort Jesus in 1698.

During the early seventeenth century dark blue was the most popular colour; orange and pearl the least. However, these two colours were only beginning to arrive at the end of Period I, about 1634. In the late seventeenth century green, followed by yellow, and in the eighteenth and nineteenth centuries green and greenish-blue were the most popular colours. In the eighteenth and nineteenth centuries the beads of class A were less numerous than those of class B. In class B, the dark blue, B.2 and 2*a*, were by far the most numerous, followed by the opaque white, B.3 and 3*a*, and the red on white, B.1 and 1*a*.

A few examples of B.1, 2, and 3 occurred in early-seventeenth-century levels, which suggests that they were reaching East Africa a little before 1634. Among them were drawn beads larger than had yet occurred, an average 2 cm on axis and 1 cm diameter. This new fashion is interesting and may indicate that more beads were being worn as necklaces than sewn on cloth. Smaller beads continued to be made, especially

[6] Kirkman (1954), (1959), (1960), (1966).
[7] Lobato (1960), p. 58.
[8] Theal (1898–1903), ii, p. 303.
[9] Communication from Claire Davison.

in the blue, which occurred as small as 2·1 mm. These beads, whether large or small, were hardly ever reheated, but left with sharp edges, and often made with very little attempt at sizing.

Other new series of beads (B.4–10) appeared with the new K'ang Hsi types in the latter half of the seventeenth century. They consisted of light blue long cylinders; transparent white imitation crystal; and black, 6·4 mm on diameter and axis, often so irregular as to suggest that they might have been made in an open mould; transparent green, usually large, up to 9·6 mm on axis and diameter; transparent yellow or brown, usually small; large opaque green, darker than the usual tint of A.4; small 3·2 mm transparent beads with opaque lines parallel to the axis, and a few pink on white which do not become numerous until the eighteenth century. All these types of beads were often covered with a hard brown patina which was not found on the beads of class A. There were to be three more additions to this class of mass-produced drawn type. In the eighteenth century there appeared a coral pink opaque and a black on a white core; and in the nineteenth, light blue on white cylinders and large, roughly made, greenish-yellow cylinders often distorted in firing.

Besides the monochromes there were nine varieties of striped beads (class C.1–9; Fig. 80. 1–4), of which only one, the small white-on-black (Fig. 80. 1) was at all numerous. A few were found in eighteenth-century levels but the majority were in eighteenth- and nineteenth-century deposits. Some, notably C.1 and C.2 were similar to the Amsterdam beads,[10] but the place of manufacture of the coarser types, the poorest quality of trade beads, has still to be discovered. They would have reached East Africa from Diu or Goa and later from Surat and Bombay.

There were a few wound beads of the classical type, oblates or bicones with the strands clearly visible, sometimes with white strands mixed with the basic colours, green, yellow, and black (D.1–3; Fig. 80. 5). These had been common in fourteenth-century levels at Gedi and other sites, but were scarce later. In the eighteenth century this type was revived in dark blue and light blue (D.4–5). Another type of wound bead consisted of oblates and ellipses (Fig. 80. 6, 7), rarely bicones, with the surface marvered smooth (D.6–9 and E.1–7). The pink were the most numerous in the oblates and the white among the ellipses. The white, black, and pink appeared in late-seventeenth-century levels but were commoner in the eighteenth and nineteenth centuries. The bright blue, transparent green, and yellow did not occur in the Fort before the eighteenth century.

The ring bead (class F; Fig. 80. 8, 9) is one of the earliest forms of bead, but has not been found in East Africa before the end of the seventeenth century and was not at all common until the nineteenth. The commonest colour was yellow and there was a variant with a wide, almost strap ring (Fig. 80. 9).

Decorated wound beads (class G; Fig. 80. 10–23) were no commoner than the striped drawn beads. It would appear that there was little interest in the more

[10] van der Sleen (1963), pp. 261–3.

elaborate beads, which suggests that beads were used in mass with the idea of colour above everything else.

Only two decorated beads (G.6*a*; Fig. 80. 20 and G.6*c*: Fig. 80. 22) were found in early-seventeenth-century levels, but they were relatively numerous in later levels. Eye and chevron beads had been found in sixteenth-century levels at Gedi,[11] and their absence from the early levels in Fort Jesus is surprising.

The beads with a white spray on a pink, green, or dark blue ground (G.7; Fig. 80. 23) are Venetian; the other decorated beads may be Venetian or Dutch. The Dutch bead industry, like the glass industry, was founded by immigrants from Venice.[12]

The very large beads (class H; Fig. 80. 25) of the type used today in the Middle East on the necks of camels, apparently go back to the early seventeenth century.

A limited number of faceted cylinders and spheres (class I) were found in all levels except the early-seventeenth-century. The commonest colour was dark blue. Four small melon beads (I.8) and a curious 'cable' bead (I.9; Fig. 80. 27) were also found. In the nineteenth-century levels there were a number of stamped beads (class J), among which the gold-lustred spheres were commonest.

OTHER

Besides beads made from glass there was a much smaller number made from other materials, of which shell, ivory, and cornelian were the most numerous. Beads of these materials had also been found in the medieval Arab sites.[13]

The beads from the large land snail, *achatina*, consisted of slightly concave disks and varied from 9·6 mm to 32 mm in diameter (Fig. 80. 39). They appeared in all levels but were most numerous in the eighteenth and nineteenth centuries. They are the *caracois*[14] of the Portuguese inventories. Large strings of them were found in the Portuguese cemetery at Dambarare in Mashonaland.

Marine-shell beads were of two kinds: one, cylinders and bicones made from large shells such as clams and spider shells; the other, disks made from small bivalves, such as scallops. Among the cylinders and bicones the commonest forms were cylinders (Fig. 80. 40, 41) 6·44 mm to 12·7 mm long, with a diameter of between 3·2 mm and 6·44 mm. The bicones (Fig. 80. 42) measured 12·7 mm long, with a diameter of 6·44 mm. The material of the shell, often translucent, is known as aragonite, and can have a fine smooth surface like marble or alabaster. The disks are also commonly 6·44 mm in diameter and are not as well made as the cylinders and bicones. Shell beads occurred in all levels but were commonest in the late seventeenth century. They also occurred in quantity in the Arab–African sites.

Beads from the conus shell were similar, and were made from the top of the shell, cut off and pierced. They varied from 9·6 mm to 25 mm in diameter. In certain inland

[11] Kirkman (1954), Fig. 35; idem (1963), Fig. 15 k.

[12] van der Sleen (1963), p. 261.

[13] Kirkman (1954), (1959), (1960), (1963).

[14] Lobato (1960), list C, following p. 313.

parts of East Africa, and in Madagascar, the larger shells were worn singly on the head, but the few found in the Fort were probably used as true beads on a string.

The olives and cowries were merely pierced and strung. They were not very numerous. Cowries were apparently not used as currency in the Mombasa area.

Ivory beads were found in all periods and included two long strings, one early-seventeenth- and the other eighteenth-century, which were found in S. Alberto. The majority were spheres, but there were a few baluster-shaped and channelled specimens (Fig. 80. 28–32). Ivory beads were often carried by Arabs and used as praying beads. They were not common in medieval sites. One curious carved and inlaid bead (Fig. 80. 33) was found in a nineteenth-century level. They are not mentioned in the Portuguese inventories.

The commonest stone bead was the cornelian. These were either spheres, 6·4 mm to 9·6 mm in diameter, or polygons, about 2 cm long with five to seven sides of varying width which were sometimes rounded. The proportion of spheres to polygons rose in the later levels. In the late seventeenth century it was twelve to thirty-one; in the eighteenth, forty-four to sixty, and in the nineteenth, fifty-eight to sixty-nine. The only early-seventeenth-century cornelian was a bicone. Cornelians are probably the *contas grossas vermelhas* of Cambay.[15]

Crystal, coral, jet, and pewter beads (Fig. 80. 34–6) are mentioned frequently in the inventories; also amber beads, but of these last none has been found, unless the resin spheres that occurred in nineteenth-century levels were survivals.

Crystals were found in early-seventeenth-century levels, and ugly white agate polygons, similar to cornelians, occurred in all levels except the early-seventeenth-century. A third of the crystals were spheres; the rest were faceted cylinders and bicones. The spheres were probably of Indian manufacture, the others may be Venetian. In addition there were three specimens of onyx and one of lapis probably from India.

Cylindrical beads of Mediterranean pink coral were Portuguese imports. In diameter they were about 3·2 mm and varied in length between 6·4 mm and 1·27 cm. They were found mostly in late-seventeenth-century levels; they were rare in the eighteenth century, but in the nineteenth importing was apparently resumed.

Three jet beads have been identified, one star (late-seventeenth-century), one faceted disk (eighteenth), and one cylinder (nineteenth).

Beads of unusual materials were two spheres made of clay, one from a late-seventeenth-, the other from a nineteenth-century level, and three of resin from a nineteenth-century level.

Metal beads were extremely scarce, perhaps because more care was taken of them. The most numerous were rough standard cylinders of pewter (Fig. 80. 36). Two gold spheres and one copper cylinder were found. In the nineteenth century, iron and copper beads were in general use in the interior of East Africa, and glass beads were used sparingly.

[15] Lobato (1960), list C, following p. 313.

Among natural objects which may have been used as beads, there were the tube-like molluscs, *Dentalium* and *Teredo*. They are mentioned without commitment in case they should occur on some other site in a more convincing context. Six *Dentalium* were found in eighteenth-century and one in nineteenth-century levels. Five *Teredo* came from late-seventeenth-, eleven from eighteenth-, and seven from nineteenth-century levels.

GLASS BEADS—STOCKS

TABLE 1. EARLY SEVENTEENTH CENTURY: FILLING OF BASTION S. MATIAS

A.	*1*	*2*	*3*	*4*	*5*	*6*	*7*	*8*		
	262	774	47	101	20	605	2	2	1,813	
B.	*1*	*1a*	*2*	*2a*	*3*	*8*				
	4	1	4	1	2	2			14	
H.	*3*									
	1								1	1,828

TABLE 2. EARLY SEVENTEENTH CENTURY: PASSAGE OF THE STEPS

A.	*1*	*2*	*3*	*4*	*5*	*6*	*7*	*8*		
	1	27	1,150	5	18	5	1	1	1,208	
B.	*1*	*1a*	*2*	*3a*	*3a*	*4*	*6*	*7*		
	1	8	5	4	2	1	1	9	31	1,239

TABLE 3. EARLY SEVENTEENTH CENTURY: FILLING OF BASTION S. FILIPE

A.	*1*	*2*	*3*	*4*	*5*	*6*	*7*	*8*		
	551	59	60	55	308	96	18	9	1,156	
B.	*1*	*1a*	*2*	*2a*	*3*	*4*	*6*			
	8	4	2	1	8	1	1		25	
C.	*8*									
	1								1	
D.	*1*	*2*								
	1	1							2	
E.	*2*	*3*								
	1	1							2	1,186

TABLE 4. EARLY SEVENTEENTH CENTURY: DEPOSIT IN BASTION S. ALBERTO

A.	*1*	*2*	*3*	*4*	*5*	*6*	*7*	*8*		
	227	36	2	12	2	8	1			288

TABLE 5. LATE SEVENTEENTH CENTURY: PIT IN S. FILIPE

A.	*1*	*2*	*3*	*4*	*5*	*6*	*7*	*8*							
	208	100	143	267	187	36	41	44						1,026	
B.	*1*a	*2*	*2*a	*3*	*3*a	*4*	*5*	*6*	*7*	*8*	*10*	*11*	*12*		
	23	3	38	2	26	13	3	5	6	6	11	3	2	141	
E.	*3*														
	1													1	
G.	*2*a	*6*b													
	1	1												2	
I.	*1*	*6*	*8*a												
	1	1	1											3	1,173

TABLE 6. LATE SEVENTEENTH CENTURY: FILLING OF COURT IN S. MATEUS

A.	*1*	*2*	*3*	*4*	*5*	*6*	*7*	*8*							
	86	7	125	219	20	12	120	114						703	
B.	*1*	*1*a	*2*	*2*a	*3*	*3*a	*4*	*5*	*6*	*7*	*8*	*11*	*12*		
	10	25	10	63	13	36	11	1	13	5	1	1	3	192	
D.	*1*	*6*	*8*												
	1	1	1											3	
E.	*1*	*2*	*3*												
	2	1	2											5	
F.	*1*														
	1													1	
H.	*1*	*2*													
	1	1												2	
I.	*1*														
	1													1	
J.	*1*														
	1													1	908

TABLE 7. LATE SEVENTEENTH CENTURY: FILLING OF CAPTAIN'S HOUSE

A.	*1*	*2*	*3*	*4*	*5*	*6*	*7*	*8*						
	29	11	34	94	93	8	4	18					291	
B.	*1*	*1*a	*2*	*2*a	*3*	*3*a	*4*	*6*	*7*	*8*	*9*	*12*		
	21	108	46	165	19	99	61	37	4	1	5	1	567	
E.	*2*													
	1												1	
F.	*1*													
	1												1	860

TABLE 8. LATE SEVENTEENTH CENTURY: FILLING IN HOUSE OF VICAR FORANE

A.	*1*	*2*	*3*	*4*	*5*	*6*	*7*	*8*						
	274	277	434	274	32	36	162	77					1,566	
B.	*1*	*1*a	*2*	*2*a	*3*	*3*a	*4*	*5*	*6*	*7*	*8*	*9*	*10*	
	321	849	12	2,272	23	1,256	19	50	19	3	2	7	13	4,846
C.	*3*													
	2													2
E.	*1*	*3*												
	14	1												15
G.	*2*a	*7*a												
	1	1												2
I.	*1*	*8*a												
	1	1												2 6,433

TABLE 9. EIGHTEENTH CENTURY: DEPOSIT NEAR WELL. A

A.	*1*	*2*	*3*	*4*	*5*	*6*	*7*	*8*		
	138	9	142	79	4	1	25	8	406	
B.	*1*	*1*a	*2*	*2*a	*3*a	*5*	*9*			
	2	4	1	13	4	2			27	
D.	*6*									
	1								1	434

TABLE 10. EIGHTEENTH CENTURY: DEPOSIT NEAR WELL. B

A.	*1*	*2*	*3*	*4*	*5*	*6*	*7*	*8*								
	225	14	265	156	13	5	38	19							735	
B.	*1*	*1*a	*2*	*2*a	*3*	*3*a	*4*	*5*	*6*	*7*	*8*	*9*	*10*	*12*		
	4	41	15	75	14	93	3	4	4	5	1	3	3	1	266	
D.	*6*															
	1														1	
E.	*2*	*5*														
	1	1													2	
F.	*1*															
	1														1	1,005

TABLE 11. EIGHTEENTH CENTURY: DEPOSIT NEAR WELL. C

A.	*1*	*2*	*3*	*4*	*5*	*6*	*7*	*8*					
	221	29	303	191	21	14	87	23					889
B.	*1*	*1*a	*2*	*2*a	*3*	*3*a	*4*	*5*	*7*	*8*	*10*		
	4	86	5	120	24	169	1	8	3	2	3		425
D.	*6*												
	1											1	
E.	*2*												
	1											1	
G.	*2*c												
	1											1	1,317

TABLE 12. EIGHTEENTH CENTURY: NORTH COURT OF CAPTAIN'S HOUSE

A.	*1*	*2*	*3*	*4*	*5*	*6*	*7*	*8*								
	2	1,470	19	267	12	3	115	4							1,892	
B.	*1*	*1*a	*2*	*2*a	*3*	*3*a	*4*	*5*	*6*	*7*	*9*	*11*	*12*	*14*		
	339	5,975	536	11,689	621	5,670	170	276	191	250	107	1	223	13	26,061	
C.	*1*	*3*	*8*													
	92	1	2												95	
D.	*5*	*8*	*9*													
	20	13	1												34	
E.	*1*	*2*	*3*	*4*	*5*											
	21	16	6	1	2										46	
F.	*2*	*4*	*5*													
	1	3	1												5	
G.	*1*	*2*a														
	2	1													3	
I.	*9*															
	1														1	
J.	*1*															
	13														13	28,150

TABLE 13. EIGHTEENTH CENTURY: UNDER COURT OF CAPTAIN'S HOUSE

A.	*1*	*2*	*3*	*4*	*5*	*6*	*7*	*8*						
		105	14	96	3		1						218	
B.	*1*	*1*a	*2*	*2*a	*3*	*3*a	*4*	*5*	*6*	*7*	*8*	*9*		
	461	1,732	355	866	476	3,264	35	105	36	102	13	32	7,477	
E.	*1*	*2*	*5*											
	8	5	1										14	
I.	*1*													
	5												5	7,714

TABLE 14. NINETEENTH CENTURY: PASSAGE OF THE ARCHES

A.	*1*	*2*	*3*	*4*	*5*	*6*	*7*	*8*								
		40	5	4	6	4	101	24							184	
B.	*1*	*1*a	*2*	*2*a	*3*	*3*a	*4*	*5*	*6*	*7*	*9*	*10*	*11*	*12*		
	81	1,106	257	955	364	1,110	33	36	19	9	12	5	3	20	4,010	
C.	*2*	*9*														
	6	1													7	
D.	*6*															
	1														1	
E.	*1*	*2*	*5*													
	1	2	1												4	
F.	*1*	*3*														
	1	6													7	
G.	*1*a															
	1														1	
H.	*4*															
	1														1	
I.	*2*	*3*	*4*	*5*	*8*b											
	1	2	1	1	1										6	
J.	*1*	*2*	*4*	*8*												
	2	2	1	4											9	4,230

TABLE 15. NINETEENTH CENTURY: COURT OF CAPTAIN'S HOUSE

A.	*1*	*2*	*3*	*4*	*5*	*6*	*7*	*8*								
		83	4	18	4		4								113	
B.	*1*	*1*a	*2*	*2*a	*3*	*3*a	*4*	*6*	*7*	*9*	*11*	*12*	*14*	*15*		
	181	5,782	158	3,924	303	5,429	49	44	9	12	2	762	3	1	16,659	
E.	*5*															
	2														2	
F.	*1*															
	1														1	
G.	2b															
	1														1	
J.	*1*														1	16,777
	1															

TABLE 16. NINETEENTH CENTURY: SOUTH BARRACK BLOCK ON CORAL (ROOM 2)

A.	*1*	*2*	*3*	*4*	*5*	*6*	*7*	*8*			
			3		2					5	
B.	*1*	*1a*	*2*	*2a*	*3*	*3a*	*5*	*6*	*8*		
	101	24	421	64	382	17	6,520	6	1	7,536	
D.	*5*										
	1									1	
E.	*3*	*4*	*5*								
	1	1	20							22	7,564

TABLE 17. SOUTH BARRACK BLOCK ON FLOOR (ROOM 1)

A.	*1*	*2*	*3*	*4*	*5*	*6*	*7*	*8*		
		4		3	2		1		10	
B.	*1*	*1a*	*2*	*2a*	*3*	*3a*	*4*	*12*		
	43		429	182	265	106	3	159	1,187	
E.	*4*	*7*								
	1	3							4	1,201

TABLE 18. GLASS BEADS—NUMBER OF FINDS

		century				
		early 17th	late 17th	18th	19th	Total
Drawn Beads						
A.	1. Dark blue opaque	101	64	21	75	261
	2. Black	27	31	27	80	165
	3. Yellow	35	75	33	76	219
	4. Green	54	92	70	115	331
	5. Greenish-blue	72	64	57	93	286
	6. Red	51	38	19	32	140
	7. Orange	13	41	51	34	139
	8. Pearl	16	30	17	22	85
B.	1. Red on green (large)	23	38	75	170	306
	1a. —— (small)	11	57	90	200	358
	2. Dark blue transparent (large)	14	40	107	316	477
	2a. —— (small)	16	92	110	247	465
	3. Opaque white (large)	12	56	101	367	536
	3a. —— (small)	4	54	105	271	434

TABLE 18 (*cont.*):

			century				
			early 17th	late 17th	18th	19th	Total
	4.	Light blue	9	34	183	179	405
	5.	Transparent white	1?	18	136	112	267
	6.	Large black		9	27	59	95
	7.	Large transparent green	4?	27	59	82	172
	8.	Transparent yellow, and yellow-brown		11	16	24	51
	9.	Large green	1?	20	36	120	177
	10.	Transparent with opaque lines		13	12	6	31
	11.	Pink on white	8?	8	22	119	157
	12.	Light blue on white	1?	6	4	76	87
	13.	Pink opaque	3?	3	15	70	91
	14.	Greenish-yellow				10	10
	15.	Black on white core	1?		3	2	6
	16.	Bright blue				1	1
Striped Beads							
C.	1.	Small white on black			7	6	13
	2.	Red, white, and black			1	6	7
	3.	White on red		1	1	1	3
	4.	White pin stripe on dark blue				1	1
	5.	Red, white on green	1?			4	5
	6.	Red, bordered gold on white				2	2
	7.	Small blue on white				2	2
	8.	Small green on white			1		1
	9.	White on dark blue			1		1
Wound, Oblate							
D.	1.	Green	2	3	1	1	7
	2.	Yellow	1		1		2
	3.	Black		1		9	10
	4.	Dark blue		1?		5	6
	5.	Light blue		1	5	31	37
	6.	Pink		4	19	27	50
	7.	Transparent green			4	14	18
	8.	White		2	3	11	16
	9.	Small yellow			2	6	8
Wound, Ellipse							
E.	1.	White		4	10	26	40
	2.	Black	1?	5	9	23	38
	3.	Pink		6	12	31	49

TABLE 18 (*cont.*):

	century				
	early 17th	late 17th	18th	19th	Total
4. Yellow		1	5	29	35
5. Bright blue		1	7	33	41
6. Dark blue			1	2	3
7. Transparent green		1	2	18	21
Ring beads					
F. 1. Yellow		4	9	19	32
2. Blue	1 ?		3	11	15
3. Green		1		9	10
4. Aubergine			1		1
5. Black			1	3	4
6. Transparent		1		8	9
Decorated Beads, Oblates, Cylinders, and Ellipses					
G. 1*a*. Eye beads, black ground		1	3	8	12
1*b*. ——, blue ground		1			1
1*c*. ——, multiple or spotted pink, white, blue on black				1	1
1*d*. ——, red projecting eyes				1	1
2*a*. Chevron beads, white on black		2	1	1	4
2*b*. ——, black on white				1	1
2*c*. ——, white on pink			1		1
3. White trellis on black		1		1	2
4. Banded, white and black		1	1		2
5. White on transparent red ellipse				1	1
6*a*. Rosetta beads, green and white	1	1		2	4
6*b*. dark blue, light blue, and white		1			1
6*c*. red and dark blue	1				1
6*d*. red, white, and pale blue			1		1
7*a*. White spray on pink		1	2	2	5
7*b*. —— on green		2	1	1	4
7*c*. —— on deep blue				2	2
Large Camel or Donkey Beads					
H. 1. Blue and white rosetta barrel		1			1
2. Similar, heptagonal		1			1
3. Deep blue	1		1		2
4. Opaque white				2	2

TABLE 18 (*cont.*):

			century				
			early 17th	late 17th	18th	19th	Total
Moulded Beads, Faceted Spheres and Cylinders							
I.	1.	Black		3		2	5
	2.	Dark blue			2	14	16
	3.	Light blue on white		2		4	6
	4.	Green, usually transparent				3	3
	5.	Yellow transparent				5	5
	6.	Pink transparent		1		5	6
	7.	White transparent		2		2	4
	8*a*.	Melon, pink		2			2
	8*b*.	——, dark blue				2	2
	8*c*.	——, black				1	1
	8*d*.	——, transparent green				1	1
	9.	Cable yellow			1		1
	10.	Grooved tapered			1		1
Stamped Beads—Spheres							
J.	1.	Gold lustre				43	43
	2.	Red coated				15	15
	3.	Blue band on red				1	1
	4.	Blue, median line				8	8
	5.	Bright blue				18	18
	6.	Light blue				4	4
	7.	White, median line				6	6
	8.	White opaque				6	6
	9.	Milky white				4	4
OTHER BEADS—NUMBER OF FINDS							
	1.	Agate, hexagons and spheres		8	10	7	25
	2.	Clay, oblates		1		1	2
	3.	Copper cylinder			1		1
	4.	Pink coral cylinders	3	11	2	17	33
	5.	Cornelian, hexagons, spheres	1	23	21	42	87
	6.	Crystal, spheres and bicones	8	8	4	9	29
	7.	Gold spheres		1		1	2
	8.	Ivory cylinders and various	4	6	3	5	18
	9.	Jet, star, hexagon, cylinder		1	1	1	3
	10.	Lapis cylinder		1			1

TABLE 18 (*cont.*):

	early 17th century	late 17th century	18th century	19th century	Total
11. Onyx spheres			2	1	3
12. Pewter, standard hexagons		3	5	1	9
13. Resin spheres		1		2	3
14. Shell, *Achatina*	3	5	14	17	39
——, Marine	12	42	24	47	125
——, Conus		2		4	6
——, Cowry		1	1	2	4
——, Olive		1	2	6	9

TABLE 19. GLASS BEADS—TOTALS

	early 17th century	late 17th century	18th century	19th century	Total
Drawn Beads					
A. 1. Dark blue opaque	2,075	967	855	157	4,054
2. Black	922	562	1,784	406	3,674
3. Yellow	1,292	1,007	910	144	3,353
4. Green	348	1,111	978	405	2,842
5. Greenish-blue	738	465	138	132	1,473
6. Red	814	140	50	39	1,043
7. Orange	33	401	266	111	811
8. Pearl	25	296	107	52	480
					17,730
B. 1. Red on green (large)	44	466	1,152	505	2,167
1*a*. —— (small)	53	1,628	8,826	12,211	22,718
2. Dark blue transparent (large)	45	179	8,037	3,510	11,771
2*a*. —— (small)	45	5,415	15,653	11,434	32,547
3. Opaque white (large)	16	213	2,687	4,698	7,614
3*a*. —— (small)	52	2,413	10,213	10,287	22,965
4. Light blue	11	125	512	878	1,526
5. Transparent white	3	87	337	8,177	8,604
6. Large black	8	102	393	414	917
7. Large transparent green	14	53	502	255	824

TABLE 19 (*cont.*):

		century				
		early 17th	late 17th	18th	19th	Total
	8. Transparent yellow and yellow-brown		18	309	37	364
	9. Large green		23	177	174	374
	10. Transparent, with opaque lines		42	37	7	86
	11. Pink on white	8	11	49	370	438
	12. Light blue on white	1	7	4	141	153
	13. Pink opaque	6	6	69	241	322
	14. Greenish yellow				12	12
	15. Black on white core	1 ?		3	2	6
	16. Bright blue				2	2
						113,410
Striped Beads						
C.	1. Small white on black			98	6	104
	2. Red, white, and black			1	6	7
	3. White on red		2	1	2	5
	4. White pin stripe on dark blue				1	1
	5. Red, white on green	1 ?			4	5
	6. Red, bordered gold on white				2	2
	7. Small blue on white				3	3
	8. Small green on white			2		2
	9. White on dark blue			1		1
						130
Wound, Oblate						
D.	1. Green	3	3	2	1	9
	2. Yellow	1				1
	3. Black		1		14	15
	4. Dark blue		1		6	7
	5. Light blue		1	8	48	57
	6. Pink		8	51	30	89
	7. Transparent green			13	19	32
	8. White		7	34	15	56
	9. Small yellow			4	4	8
						274

TABLE 19 (*cont.*):

	century				
	early 17th	late 17th	18th	19th	Total
Wound, Ellipse					
E. 1. White		16	58	52	126
2. Black		5	28	32	65
3. Pink		6	16	35	57
4. Yellow		1	5	39	45
5. Bright blue			14	43	57
6. Dark blue		1	2	1	4
7. Transparent green		1	2	22	25
					379
Ring beads					
F. 1. Yellow		5	10	29	44
2. Blue	1		4	13	18
3. Green		1		11	12
4. Aubergine			3		3
5. Black			1	3	4
6. Transparent		2		8	10
					91
Decorated Beads, Oblates, Cylinders, and Ellipses					
G. 1*a*. Eye beads, black ground		2	4	8	14
1*b*. ——, blue ground		1			1
1*c*. ——, multiple or spotted pink, white, blue on black				7	7
1*d*. ——, red projecting eyes				1	1
2*a*. Chevron beads, white on black		2	1	1	4
2*b*. ——, black on white				1	1
2*c*. ——, white on pink			1		1
3. White trellis on black		1		1	2
4. Banded white and black		1	1		2
5. White on transparent red ellipse				1	1
6*a*. Rosetta beads, green and white	1	1		2	4
6*b*. ——, dark blue, light blue, and white		1			1
6*c*. ——, red and dark blue	1				1
6*d*. ——, red, white, and pale blue			1		1

TABLE 19 (*cont.*):

			century				
			early 17th	late 17th	18th	19th	Total
	7*a*.	White spray on pink		1	2	2	5
	7*b*.	—— on green		2	1	1	4
	7*c*.	—— on deep blue				2	2
							52
Large Camel or Donkey Beads							
H.	1.	Blue and white rosetta barrel		1			1
	2.	Similar, heptagonal		1			1
	3.	Deep blue	1		1		2
	4.	Opaque white				2	2
							6
Moulded beads, and Faceted Spheres and Cylinders							
I.	1.	Black		3		2	5
	2.	Dark blue			2	14	16
	3.	Light blue on white		2		4	6
	4.	Green, usually transparent				3	3
	5.	Yellow transparent				5	5
	6.	Pink transparent		1		5	6
	7.	White transparent		2		2	4
	8*a*.	Melon, pink		2			2
	8*b*.	——, dark blue				2	2
	8*c*.	——, black				1	1
	8*d*.	——, transparent green				1	1
	9.	Cable yellow			1		1
	10.	Groove tapered			1		1
							53
Stamped Beads—Spheres							
J.	1.	Gold lustre				52	52
	2.	Red coated				15	15
	3.	Blue band on red				1	1
	4.	Blue, median line				9	9
	5.	Bright blue				20	20
	6.	Light blue				4	4
	7.	White, median line				12	12
	8.	White opaque				6	6
	9.	Milky white				4	4
							123

TABLE 19 (*cont.*):

OTHER BEADS—TOTALS

	century				
	early 17th	late 17th	18th	19th	Total
1. Agate, hexagons and spheres		25	12	12	49
2. Clay, oblates		1		1	2
3. Copper cylinder			1		1
4. Pink coral cylinders	3	55	3	25	86
5. Cornelian, hexagons and spheres	1	33	61	79	174
6. Crystal, spheres and bicones	8	11	4	10	33
7. Gold spheres		1		1	2
8. Ivory cylinders and various	115	18	97	5	235
9. Jet, star, hexagon, cylinder		1	1	1	3
10. Lapis cylinder		1			1
11. Onyx spheres			2	1	3
12. Pewter, standard hexagons		4	5	1	10
13. Resin spheres		1		3	4
14. Shell, *Achatina*	22	21	123	18	184
——, Marine	23	290	101	62	476
——, *Conus*		2		4	6
——, Cowry	1		1	2	4
——, Olive		1	2	28	31

GLASS BEADS, CLASS A—COLOURS

TABLE 20. PERCENTAGES OF TOTALS BY PERIOD

	century				
	Total	early 17th	late 17th	18th	19th
A.1. Dark blue opaque					
by occurrence	261	38·69	24·52	8·04	28·73
by number	4,054	50·78	23·75	21·60	3·87
A.2. Black					
by occurrence	165	16·36	18·78	16·36	48·48
by number	3,674	25·09	15·29	48·57	11·05
A.3. Yellow					
by occurrence	219	25·98	34·26	15·06	34·70
by number	3,353	38·54	30·03	27·14	4·29

TABLE 20 (*cont.*):

	century				
	Total	early 17th	late 17th	18th	19th
A.4. Green					
by occurrence	331	16·31	27·80	21·14	34·75
by number	2,842	12·24	39·30	34·21	14·25
A.5. Greenish-blue					
by occurrence	286	25·18	22·37	19·93	32·52
by number	1,473	50·12	31·56	9·36	8·96
A.6. Red					
by occurrence	140	36·43	27·15	13·57	22·85
by number	1,043	78·06	13·42	4·79	3·73
A.7. Orange					
by occurrence	139	9·35	29·49	36·70	24·46
by number	811	4·06	49·47	32·79	13·68
A.8. Pearl					
by occurrence	85	18·82	35·29	20·00	25·88
by number	480	5·20	61·68	22·29	10·83

TABLE 21. PERCENTAGES OF TOTALS BY COLOUR

Period	Total	A.1	A.2	A.3	A.4	A.5	A.6	A.7	A.8
Early 17th century									
by occurrence	369	27·40	7·31	9·48	14·63	19·51	13·82	3·52	4·33
by number	6,247	33·23	14·75	20·69	5·57	11·81	13·03	0·52	0·40
Late 17th century									
by occurrence	435	14·71	7·12	17·25	21·16	14·72	8·73	9·42	6·89
by number	4,949	19·54	11·35	20·34	22·48	9·39	2·82	8·10	5·98
18th century									
by occurrence	295	7·11	9·15	11·18	23·74	19·33	6·44	17·29	5·76
by number	5,088	16·80	35·08	17·88	19·23	2·71	0·98	5·22	2·10
19th century									
by occurrence	527	14·23	15·18	14·42	21·84	17·64	6·07	6·45	4·17
by number	1,446	10·85	28·09	9·95	28·02	9·12	2·69	7·69	3·59

TABLE 22. NINETEENTH CENTURY: COLOURS IN ORDER OF POPULARITY

	1st	2nd	3rd	4th	5th	6th	7th	8th
Colours in order of frequency of finds	4	1	5	3	2	7	6	8
Colours in order of totals of finds	2	4	1	3	5	7	8	6
Stock Find Table 14	7	2	8	5	3	4	6	-
Stock Find Table 15	2	4	3/5/7	-	-	-	-	-
Stock Find Table 16	3	5	-	-	-	-	-	-
Stock Find Table 17	2	4	5	7	-	-	-	-

16. *Cannon and Cannon-balls*

(Figs. 81 and 82)

THERE were fifty-nine cannon in and around the Fort. Four, perhaps six, were seventeenth-century; eighteen were eighteenth-century, and thirty-five were early-nineteenth-century. One was French; one Venetian; one Swedish; one English, made in India; and the rest were made in England. Of the seventeenth-century cannon, nos. 1 and 2, and perhaps nos. 7 and 8, could have been in the Fort during the siege. It is possible that nos. 3, 4, and 5 were in the Fort when the Portuguese reoccupied it in 1728. The eighteenth-century cannon may well be the ordnance used by the Mazrui in their efforts to defend the Fort against Saiyid Said. The two brass cannon, nos. 58 and 59, came from H.M.S. *Leven* and *Barracouta*, and were left behind when the British Governor, Lieutenant Emery, R.N. was withdrawn in 1826.[1] The nineteenth-century cannon were probably placed in the Fort after its final recovery by Saiyid Said in 1837.

Most of them were lying without their carriages. Nos. 1, 3, and 7 were found below the nineteenth-century surface behind the magazine in the Bastion of S. Alberto, and had presumably been mounted on the cavalier until the construction of the Arab house shown on the Guillain plan of 1846. A battered cannon, no. 8, with iron flaking off in strips, was found below a prison party-wall in the cavalier S. António, and may have been mounted on the cavalier like nos. 1, 3, and 7. Another, no. 14, was below the top of the flight of cement steps in S. Matias. No. 6 was found in the Passage of the Arches, lying across the steps leading to the ammunition store, while a broken culverin, no. 4, similar to no. 3, was on top of the filling in the ammunition store.

In the Marinho list of artillery in the Fort (1635), the following armament is mentioned:

2	12 lb. bronze cannon
3	10 lb. bronze cannon
1	? bronze camelo
4	10 lb. iron cannon
2	6 lb. iron cannon
2	*c.* 4–6 lb. bronze sakers (at Makupa)
2	*c.* 2 lb. iron beveur (small short cannon)
1	10 lb. piece of 52 quintals (from Angaziga)

[1] Gray (1957), p. 165.

1	*c.* 10 lb. French brass culverin (from Angaziga)
1	*c.* 4 lb. brass falcon (from Pemba)
19	

613 . . .	iron shot
203 . . .	stone shot

In the Bocarro/Rezende account of the Fort (1636) the armament is mentioned as consisting of sixteen pieces, of which five were of iron between 6 and 10 lb. calibre. Of the rest, as many as twelve were bronze and included a 20-pounder from Angaziga (in the Comoro Is.) and two bronze sakers in the Fort at Makupa. The ammunition included 1,713 iron shot and the rest stone. This would appear to be another version of the Marinho list.

At the time of the siege, four 12-pounder cannon are mentioned as being mounted in Fort St. Joseph, which was situated between Fort Jesus and Kilindini harbour. An *espalhafato* in the cavalier S. António is referred to in the account of the fall of the Fort.[2] Three large Portuguese bronze cannon of early-sixteenth-century date are in front of the Government offices in Zanzibar. They were captured by the Persians when they recovered Ormuz in 1622, and then captured by the Muscat Arabs when they took Ormuz, probably in 1794, and brought to Zanzibar by Saiyid Said.

More than 2,700 iron cannon-balls were found in the Fort (see list). The majority weighed between 4½ and 6 lb. or rather heavier, allowing for loss of weight from oxidization. These would have been used in the field pieces or sakers. In the early-seventeenth-century levels only fifteen balls were found, of which eight were between 12·7 and 14 cm in diameter and 17 to 23 lb. in weight. There were 2,255 pieces in the ammunition store; the remainder were found in other late-seventeenth-, eighteenth-, and nineteenth-century levels, mostly nineteenth-century, around the Captain's House and the Passage of the Arches.

Hollow cannon-balls were uncommon. A few of the smaller type came from the ammunition store, but the larger and commoner type were found in nineteenth-century levels. One large broken ball was found in the pit in S. Filipe. The continued use of stone shot is surprising; they were commonest in late-seventeenth-century levels. In the filling of the Passage of the Arches there were three pieces which had been flattened on one side. In the upper part of the filling of the court in S. Mateus there were two pieces of bar shot. Both had been fired. Few of the other cannon-balls showed signs of use. In the Passage of the Arches there was a small number, mostly 5 cm, which had been fired, presumably during Saiyid Said's bombardment.

Lead shot were found in quantity in all levels, mainly 1·27 to 1·60 cm in diameter, with a few 2·24 cm.

In the court of the Captain's House there were a number of iron fittings of carriages,

[2] *Arquivo Português Oriental* (new ed.), iv (ii) II, pp. 75, 331.

such as the hinged plates which held the trunnions to the carriage, the rings on the sides, and the double plate with a spike at the end of the trail. These were the remains of broken carriages which were buried in the fill when the level of the court was raised some time after 1899. A broken port-fire cutter and linstock were also found but, like the other iron from excavations on the coast of East Africa, were in very bad condition.

CANNON

	Bore	Length[3]	Fig. No.
IRON			
1. English 18-pdr., about 1603 (from S. Alberto bastion)	5 in.	7′ 7″	81-1
2. Venetian, Bergamo, 32-pdr., about 1684	6½ in.	7′ 9″+	81-2
3. English 6-pdr., about 1696 (from S. Alberto)	4¼ in.	7′ 7″	81-3
4. Another from Ammunition Store	4¼ in.	7′ 7″	-
5. English 6-pdr., about 1706	4¼ in.	6′ 8″	81-4
6. English 18-pdr., 18th-century, touch with brass filling (from Passage of the Arches)	5 in.	6′+	81-5
7. English 6-pdr., possibly 17th-century (from S. Alberto)	4 in.	5′ 5″	81-6
8. Another (from S. António)	4 in.	7′ 8½″	-
9. English 6-pdr., about 1748	3¾ in.	5′ 1½″	-
10. French 24-pdr., about 1794	5½ in.	8′ 2″	82-1
11. English 42-pdr., 18th-century	7 in.	8′	82-2
12. English 4-pdr., 18th-century	3½ in.	3′ 8″	-
13. English 24-pdr., about 1803	5½ in.	8′ 3″	-
14. English 24-pdr., mark on left trunnion H for Harrison of Robertsbridge, 1760–80 (from S. Matias)	5¾ in.	7′ 8″	82-3
15. Another (from S. Matias), no mark visible	5¾ in.	7′ 8″	-
16. Another	5¾ in.	7′ 8″	-
17. Another	5¾ in.	7′ 8″	-
18. English 24-pdr., mark as no. 14 above	5½ in.	8′	
19. English 24-pdr., mark on right trunnion B for William Bowen of Bankside, Southwark, 1742–63	5½ in.	8′	82-4
20. Another	5½ in.	8′	
21. Swedish 18-pdr., mark near touch 3060, mark on right trunnion VB for Ulla Berchner, Stafso Works, on left trunnion 1752	5 in.	8′	82-5
22. English 24-pdr.	5½ in.	7′ 10″	
23. English 18-pdr., mark on right trunnion B for William Bowen, as no. 19 above	5 in.	5′ 1″	

[3] Measurements of length are from touch to muzzle; measurements of bore, owing to wear, accurate only within half an inch.

CANNON (*cont.*):

	Bore	Length	Fig. No.
24. English 18-pdr., mark on right trunnion W for Whitehead & Co., 1760–1820	5 in.	5′ 1″	
25. English 18-pdr., probably made in India *c.* 1820–40	5 in.	6′ 4″	
26. English 18-pdr., mark near touch Crown P 1798 W C, perhaps Samuel Walker & Co. of Rotherham, from 1746	5 in.	6′	
27. English 24-pdr., touch with brass filling	6 in.	7′ 10″	

English 18-pdr. cannon with lifting ring on cascibel—Bore 5″, Length 6′ 6″

	Marks on barrel					*Marks on trunnions* *L*	*R*
28.	Proof 8 lb. -	Service 4 lb. -	18 Crown	Pdr. -	PFK 1802	N 6	1 K
29.	,,	,,	,,	,,	,,	N 7	1 K
30.	,,	,,	,,	,,	,,	N 9	1 K
31.	,,	,,	,,	,,	PMM 1803	M	56
32.	,,	,,	,,	,,	,,	-	129
33.	,,	,,	,,	,,	,,	-	136
34.	,,	,,	,,	,,	PFK 1803	-	158
35.	,,	,,	,,	,,	PC & Co 1809	WC°	22
	Samuel Walker & Co., as no. 26						
36.	Proof 8 lb. -	Service 4 lb. -	18 Crown	Pdr. -	P 1811	BW	3
37.	,,	,,	,,	,,	MM 1811	-	2
38.	,,	,,	,,	,,	PMM 1812	-	4
39.	,,	,,	,,	,,	,,	M	6
40.	,,	,,	,,	,,	,,	M	8
41.	,,	,,	,,	,,	,,	M	23
42.	,,	,,	,,	,,	,,	-	41
43.	,,	,,	,,	,,	B & W	-	-
44.	,,	,,	,,	,,	P 1815	M	23
45.	,,	,,	,,	,,	P 1815	M	24
46.	,,	,,	,,	,,	B & W 1818	BW	20
47.	,,	,,	,,	,,	no date visible	-	8
48.	,,	,,	,,	,,	,,	M	5
49.	,,	,,	,,	,,		M	70
50.	Crown P - Service 3					-	-
51.	Charge Proof 8 - Service 4					M	30

English Carronades—Bore $6\frac{3}{4}$″, Length 4′ 6″

		L	*R*
52.	Crown P, Low Moor Ironworks of Messrs. Hood	Low Moor	2
53.	Crown P 1810	-	-

CANNON (*cont.*):

Marks on barrel	*Marks on trunnions* L	R
54. Crown P	-	-
55. Crown P	1	-
56. Crown P	-	21
57. No mark visible	-	-
BRASS		
58. English 6-pdr. from H.M.S. *Leven* or H.M.S. *Barracouta*, 1824—Bore 3½″, Length 4′ 3″	N 3	514
59. Another	-	-

CANNON-BALLS

Diam. cm	in.	Iron: Solid Weight	Ammn. store	Other areas	Hollow Weight	Ammn. store	Other areas	Stone Weight	Ammn. store	Other areas
2·5–5	1–2	2 oz.–1 lb.	-	34	-	-	-	-	-	-
5·7–7·6	2¼–3	,,	808	90	3 lb.	3	1	12 oz.–1 lb.	-	3
8·3–9·7	3¼–3¾	4½–6 lb.	1,124	59	4 lb.	-	2	2–3 lb.	-	4
10·2–11·5	4–4½	9–12 lb.	68	98	4 lb.	-	2	3–4 lb.	-	18
12·1	4¾	14–16 lb.	179	39	-	-	-	-	-	-
12·7–13·3	5–5¼	17–19 lb.	34	67	5 lb.	-	6	8 lb.	-	4
14	5½	22–7 lb.	42	15	14 lb.	-	1	8 lb.	-	4
14·6–15·2	5¾–6	-	-	-	-	-	-	10–12 lb.	-	8
15·8–16·4	6¼–6½	32 lb.	-	1	-	-	-	12 lb.	-	10
17·8–18·4	7–7¼	damaged		1	34 lb.+	-	3	16–20 lb.	-	1
19·1	7½	-	-	-	36 lb.+	-	2	20 lb.	-	2
21·6	8½	-	-	-	damaged	-	2	-	-	-
Fragments large										
12·7	prob. 5	-	-	-	-	-	-	-	-	-
17·8	some 7	-	-	-	-	-	25	-	-	-
small										
7·6	3	-	-	-	-	-	3	-	-	-
Totals			2,255	404		3	47		-	54

Iron Cannon-balls, distribution by levels

Diam.		Solid					Hollow				
cm	in.	early 17th cent.	late 17th cent.	18th cent.	19th cent.	Total	early 17th cent.	late 17th cent.	18th cent.	19th cent.	Total
2·5–5	1–2	2	4	15	13	34	-	-	-	-	-
5·7–7·6	2¼–3	-	820	28	50	898	-	3	-	1	4
8·3–9·7	3¼–3¾	1	1,139	16	27	1,183	-	2	-	-	2
10·2–11·5	4–4½	1	86	12	67	166	-	-	-	2	2
12·1	4¾	3	184	2	29	218	-	-	-	-	-
12·7–13·3	5–5¼	4	63	9	25	101	-	-	-	6	6
14	5½	4	45	4	4	57	-	-	-	1	1
14·6–15·2	5¾–6	-	-	-	-	-	-	-	-	-	-
15·8–16·4	6¼–6½	-	1	-	-	1	-	-	-	-	-
17·8–18·4	7–7¼	-	1	-	-	1	1	-	1	1	3
19·1	7½	-	-	-	-	-	-	1	-	1	2
21·6	8½	-	-	-	-	-	-	-	-	2	2
Fragments											
large											
12·7	prob. 5	-	-	-	-	-	-	-	3	22	25
small											
7·6	prob. 3	-	-	-	-	-	-	-	-	3	3
Totals		15	2,343	86	215	2,659	1	6	4	39	50

Stone Cannon-balls distribution by levels

Diam. cm	in.	early 17th cent.	late 17th cent.	18th cent.	19th cent.	Total
2·5–5	1–2	-	-	-	-	-
5·7–7·6	2¼–3	-	2	-	1	3
8·3–9·7	3¼–3¾	-	2	1	1	4
10·2–11·5	4–4½	-	11	3	4	18
12·1	4¾	-	-	-	-	-
12·7–13·3	5–5¼	-	4	-	-	4
14	5½	-	2	-	2	4
14·6–15·2	5¾–6	-	3	2	3	8
15·8–16·4	6¼–6½	-	8	1	1	10
17·8–18·4	7–7¼	-	1	-	-	1
19·1	7½	-	2	-	-	2
21·6	8½	-	-	-	-	-
Totals		-	35	7	12	54

17. *Minor Objects*

(Figs. 83–6)

OBJECTS other than ceramics, glass, beads, cannon, and cannon-balls were not numerous in the Fort. They can be classified, irrespective of material, under five headings:

1. Crucibles and stone vessels
2. Ornaments
3. Implements
4. Fittings
5. Coins

CRUCIBLES AND STONE VESSELS

Two types of crucible were found in the Fort. The commonest (Fig. 83. 1, 2) were, on average, 10 cm deep and 7 cm wide, with pinched mouths. There was one specimen in the pit in S. Filipe and more than 130 in the eighteenth-century filling of the court in S. Mateus (p. 60). Most of them were free of any substance inside, but had a purple gloss or bloom on the outside, presumably acquired during manufacture, because they did not appear to have been used. In some of the broken specimens were traces of green chloride, indicating that it was copper that was being melted. The other type (Fig. 83. 3) was much smaller. Only a few examples were found, including one in the pit in S. Filipe.

There were three stone vessels. The earliest in date was a small box in grey soapstone (Fig. 83. 4) from the late-seventeenth-century filling of the court in S. Mateus. The next was a large carved stone bowl (Fig. 83. 5) with a socket 5 cm deep for fixing to a stand. It appeared to be European in style, although it was found in the north court of the Captain's House. The third was a carved marble or alabaster bowl, probably also European, which was in a disturbed level in S. Alberto (Fig. 83. 6).

ORNAMENTS

The ornaments found in the Fort consisted of bracelets, glass bangles, rings, badges, lockets, pins, pendants, religious medallions, buckles, and belt ends—Arab, Indian, and Portuguese. In addition there were many small chains, similar to those found at Gedi and other sites. The majority had simple links, 3 mm long, and were found in nineteenth-century levels; but in an early-seventeenth-century level there was one with links 2 mm long, and in nineteenth-century levels chains with 12 mm and 19 mm links. Double- and treble-link chains with 6 mm links occurred in a late-seventeenth-century level. All these chains may have been used as bracelets carrying *herisi* or charms.

Bracelets consisted of brass strips between 5 mm and 8 mm wide, with incised or moulded ornament, usually Arab in style, although Fig. 84. 5, 6, and 7 have a European look about them. Only one, no. 1, is certainly Arab and occurred in a seventeenth-century level. Besides the strip bracelets there were two in other forms (nos. 9 and 10), from nineteenth-century levels. The plain rounded bracelet, which was also used as currency in parts of Africa, was uncommon in the Fort, but a group of eight was found in the early-seventeenth-century filling over the Passage of the Steps. They were 5 mm thick, with an average diameter of 5·7 cm, and weighed an ounce.

A quantity of fragments of glass bangles (Fig. 84. 11–16) was found, mostly in late-seventeenth-century levels, particularly in the pit in S. Filipe and in nineteenth-century levels. The seventeenth-century bangles were 1 mm to 3 mm in diameter. The section was normally rounded on the outside and flat against the arm, but a few were flat on the outside like a strap; cable bangles were rounded inside as well as out. The colour was normally black, but green and blue occurred and rarely yellow. Some of the bangles had a notched edge, others were twisted in the form of a wide or close cable (Fig. 84. 11, 12), or were ornamented with small knobs (Fig. 84. 13). Those with notches and knobs were invariably black; the cables black, green, or cream. They occurred occasionally in eighteenth-century levels, particularly in the north court by the Captain's House, but apparently were no longer being imported.

A larger type of bangle in black glass, 13 mm broad, was sometimes inlaid with red and yellow (Fig. 84. 15). The greater number came from the north court by the Captain's House and from the Passage of the Arches in nineteenth-century levels. However, one example was found in an early-seventeenth-century level in S. Filipe, and one black and one inlaid in late-seventeenth-century levels. There was one black glass ring in the filling of the Captain's House. Glass bangles are a particularly Indian ornament. A large number were found at Brahmapuri (Kolhapur) in fifteenth- and sixteenth-century levels, where there was also evidence of their manufacture.[1]

Brass and silver rings also occurred (Fig. 84. 17–22). The commonest were brass, 2 mm gauge and round in section, but there were also strips 3 mm gauge. There was one thin brass cable ring (Fig. 84. 21) and two bound wire rings (Fig. 84. 20). All were found in eighteenth-century levels and were Arab–African.

Of the two plain silver rings, one was 1 mm gauge and found in a late-seventeenth-century level, the other was 2 mm and found in an eighteenth-century level. In addition there was a silver strap ring with a double cockle-shell (Fig. 84. 18), a ring with a large serrated plate of base metal and an empty socket for a bezel (Fig. 84. 19), and a plain ring with a green glass bezel. The first two came from the filling of S. Alberto, the other from a nineteenth-century level. They were all probably Portuguese. A similar

[1] Sankalia and Dikshit (1952), p. 150, Pl. XXXV.

type of ring with embossed petals in base silver (Fig. 84. 22) was Arab and was found in a nineteenth-century level. There were two examples of coins mounted on rings, both nineteenth-century: a Maria Theresa dollar and an Indian Empire quarter-anna dated 1862.

In an early seventeenth-century level a bronze badge was found (Fig. 84. 23). It was in the form of an eight-pointed star with a device in the centre resembling a conventional grenade, and a tang at the back for fixing to a coat or hat. It would appear to be a military badge and, if so, is an early example of this type of insignia.

Also in early-seventeenth-century levels there were brass lockets in the form of a pod (Fig. 84. 25–7). In one case the pod was double-lobed with a flat plate behind, welded at the top and fastened with a small rivet at the bottom.

One brass pin with a rounded head, from an early-seventeenth-century level (Fig. 84. 28) was Portuguese; and a pin with a double loop from an eighteenth-century level (Fig. 84. 29) was Arab.

A brass pendant (Fig. 84. 30), three crescents (Fig. 84. 34, 35), one silver, the others copper, and a lead pendant (Fig. 84. 41), were found in nineteenth-century levels and were Arab.

The brass buckles of Fig. 84. 31, 32, and Fig. 84. 36, perhaps also a buckle, were Portuguese, as also the belt end, Fig. 84. 24. The buckle of Fig. 84. 33 was probably Arab.

The six religious medallions were of brass, some with traces of gilt. Four were in the form of an oval with a ring at the top (Pl. 43. 1–8) and two were crosses with pins (Pl. 44. 1–4). One (Pl. 44. 1, 2) may be associated with the burial outside S. Alberto (page 48); two (Pls. 43. 7, 8, and 44. 3, 4) were found in late-seventeenth-century levels in S. Filipe and in the Captain's House. The other three were in eighteenth- and nineteenth-century levels.

Two of the medallions (Pl. 43. 1, 2, 5, 6) are representations of the Virgin Mary contemplating her Immaculate Conception. The cult of the Immaculate Conception appeared at the end of the sixteenth century and was particularly developed in Andalusia in the seventeenth century, under the leadership of Don Pedro de Castro, Archbishop of Granada and later of Seville.[2] Similar medallions have been found in a Portuguese cemetery at Dambarare in Mashonaland.[3]

A bronze figure, 3 cm high, of a man holding a child, with a prong at the back for attachment to a hat or belt (Pl. 43. 9) was found in a disturbed level near the medallion of Pl. 43. 1, 2.

IMPLEMENTS

The implements found were made of brass, copper, iron, ivory, stone, and clay. Most of the iron was from nineteenth-century levels, although three iron keys came

[2] Moreno. [3] Garlake (1969), pp. 45–7.

from the Captain's House, but were so corroded that they could not be cleaned and drawn. The only other early iron which was recognizable was a barbed harpoon, 17·8 cm long, also from the Captain's House.

The brass and copper objects were in better condition. They included toothpicks and like instruments (Fig. 85. 1–5), needles (Fig. 85. 8–10), and eye pencils (Fig. 85. 11–14). Similar implements were found in fifteenth- and sixteenth-century levels at Gedi and Ungwana and were Arab. A Portuguese key and latch (Fig. 85. 6, 7) were found in the Captain's House, as well as a rounded copper shovel, 10 cm in diameter and 23 cm long, for gunpowder.

A Portuguese ivory peg (Fig. 85. 25) and bobbin (Fig. 85. 28) were found in late-seventeenth-century levels, and an ivory pawn (Fig. 85. 27) in an early-seventeenth-century level. Other articles of Arab manufacture were ivory and wooden knife handles (Fig. 85. 15–19), eighteenth- and nineteenth-century; a sickle-shaped razor (Fig. 85. 20), similar to the type found at Gedi; an ivory tube (Fig. 85. 26), perhaps a flute; solid earthenware disks, perhaps gaming pieces (Fig. 85. 29–31); and stoppers (Fig. 86. 16, 17). Pierced disks (Fig. 86. 12–15), varying from 1·9 cm to 6·9 cm across, were found principally in seventeenth-century levels but were scarce later.

There were a number of pipe bowls in clay, dating from the early seventeenth to the nineteenth century (Fig. 86, 18–22, 24). They were intended for the *narghili* or water-pipe, and were probably made locally. No. 23 was a pipe stem holder, similar to specimens found at Ungwana (Kirkman, 1966, Fig. 28, L, M, N). None was found in the Captain's House, but stems of clay pipes appeared in the lower filling of the court in S. Mateus, as well as in eighteenth-century levels, and may have been used by Portuguese soldiers.

A mould for making 13 mm shot, with handles (Pl. 42. 5), was found in the filling of the Captain's House and was probably Portuguese. Other moulds were for small ornaments and were Arab. One was made from a sherd of blue glazed earthenware and was late seventeenth- or early-eighteenth-century. The design was a flower with six petals surrounded by a border of small circles (Pl. 42. 6). Two were found in nineteenth-century levels, one of copper, the other of grey stone. The copper mould was used to make star-shaped ornaments (Pl. 42. 7); the stone mould, small circular plates with a series of concentric circles surrounding a dotted circle (Pl. 42. 8).

A square copper mould attached to a ring, with a design of a fish and palms (Pl. 42. 4) may have been used for stamping wafers or biscuits. It was on the floor of the Captain's House and was Portuguese. A pierced stamp (Fig. 85. 24), also from the Captain's House, may have had a similar purpose.

There were several rotary querns (Fig. 86. 26–8). One fine example was nearly 61 cm across and would have needed two persons to turn it. It was on the floor of the ammunition store and belonged to the early or mid eighteenth century; the others were in nineteenth-century levels. A basalt quern (Fig. 86. 28) may be earlier and was probably imported.

Arrow-heads were uncommon. Two shown in Fig. 85. 22, 23 were found in eighteenth-century levels. Portuguese documents of the sixteenth century mention the poisonous nature of wooden arrows. The adoption of iron arrow-heads in the eighteenth century is remembered as a notable event in Giriama tradition.[4]

Other iron implements from nineteenth-century levels in the Passage of the Arches were an adze with a hollow haft, 13·3 cm long and 5 cm wide, and a small anvil 8·2 cm by 6·35 cm and 10·2 cm high.

A gunpowder primer (Fig. 86. 25) of brass, probably nineteenth-century, was found in a surface level in S. Mateus.

FITTINGS

Besides the ornaments and implements there were a number of metal and ivory fittings for boxes and other articles, of both Portuguese and Arab manufacture.

A hinged ornament and key plate (Fig. 84. 40, 42), brass or copper stars (Fig. 84. 37–9), and an engraved copper plate (Pl. 42. 3) were seventeenth-century Portuguese; also a collection of brass nails and hooks (Fig. 86. 1–11).

Two ivory finials (Fig. 84. 43, 44) and a copper hinge strap (no. 45) were found in eighteenth- and nineteenth-century levels and were Arab.

A number of large iron nails, 17·8 cm long, such as are used today for dhows, and iron hasps for large carved doors, were found in the Passage of the Arches and other nineteenth-century levels.

Building materials of burnt brick consisted of tiles which were used on the Portuguese buildings, on average 12·7 cm wide and 30·5 cm long with a curve of 2·54 cm to 4·45 cm in depth, and firebricks, 11·47 cm broad and 3·28 to 3·91 cm thick, of uncertain length. Both were found in early- as well as late-seventeenth-century levels.

COINS

A large number of coins were found in the upper strata of the Fort, and these were useful for dating levels that might otherwise have been put fifty years earlier. Most of them were copper quarter-annas, East India Company or Indian Empire. The years and numbers are given in the table at the end of the chapter. Found with them were similar coins of the I.B.E.A. Company, Zanzibar, Oman, and Aden.

More interesting were the few odd coins from the earlier levels. They included only one Iberian coin: a four-reale piece, probably of Philip III, which was found in a disturbed level at the north end of the west parapet walk. In late-seventeenth-century levels were three small copper coins with Arabic legends, which seem to be the same as the recently published coins of Mogadishu. Two Persian local copper coins probably of Bushire and Tabriz, two Egyptian copper coins, and one Indian coin of Kutch were found in eighteenth-century levels.

[4] Prins (1952).

A Maria Theresa dollar had been made into a ring and was found in an eighteenth-century level.

Two Nuremburg tokens were interesting. Like Bellarmine jugs and Chinese porcelain snuff-bottles, they have found their way to the most unlikely places in the world. No. 11 was in the disturbed filling of S. Alberto and no. 12 in a nineteenth-century level in the main court.

It is clear, as had been supposed, that coins were not necessarily part of the exchange system of Kenya until the middle of the nineteenth century. In 1840 the Indian coinage was made official in Zanzibar, in an attempt to control the profiteering caused by the continual shortage of small change.

LIST OF COINS

Seventeenth and Eighteenth Centuries

1. Spanish silver four-reale; early seventeenth century, probably Philip III mint of Seville.

2–4. Three small copper coins with thin flans and Arabic letters, probably Mogadishu (cf. Freeman-Grenville, 1963, Pl. xviii).

5. Persian autonomous copper, probably Bushire (cf. Valentine, 1911, p. 129, no. 9).

6. Similar, Tabriz 1670 (cf. Poole, R. S., British Museum Catalogue, Pl. xx, 93).

7, 8. Two Egyptian copper, perhaps Ahmad II (1703–30).

9. Kutch copper, one dhuzla of Desaji I (1718–41).

10. Maria Theresa dollar (1780) made into a ring.

11. Nuremburg token, bust of Charles II of England around Carolus II DG. MAG. BR. FRA. ET HIB. REX. Shield quartering England, Ireland, Scotland, France around CONR LAUFFERS RECH PFENNIG COUNTERS.

12. Similar, ship with four masts around PLUS ULTRA, in exergue NISL. sunburst, crescent moon, and stars ÷ LAVER ÷ RECHE . . . TENIC ÷ TIC.

Nineteenth Century

	Total
East India Company:	
quarter-anna: 1830 .. 5; 1832 .. 2; 1833 .. 12; 1834 .. 35; 1853 .. 4; 1857 .. 7; 1858 .. 35	100
one pie: 1835 .. 2	2
one rupee: 1840 .. 1	1
Aden quarter-anna: 1833 .. 2; 1850 .. 1	3
Indian Empire:	
quarter-anna: 1862 .. 26; 1875 .. 1; 1876 .. 3; 1877 .. 3; 1882 .. 1; 1887 .. 2	36
quarter-rupee: 1862 .. 1	1
one rupee: 1880 .. 1; 1883 .. 2; 1886 .. 1; 1901 .. 1	5

Zanzibar:	
quarter-anna: Said bin Barghash (*sic*) 1881 .. 21; 1886 .. 1	22
Imperial British East Africa Company:	
quarter-anna: 1888 .. 49	49
East African Protectorate:	
one pice: 1895 .. 2; 1897 .. 3; 1898 .. 7	12
German Empire:	
one pfennig: 1876 .. 1	1
German East Africa Company:	
1891 .. 2	2
German East Africa:	
1912 .. 1	1
Oman and Muscat:	
quarter-anna: Faisal bin Turki 1897 .. 1	1

Appendix

CAPTAINS OF THE FORT

This list is taken from Boxer and de Azevedo, except for names marked with an asterisk, which are captains mentioned by Axelson. The incoming captains usually arrived from Goa at the beginning of the year (Boxer).

Mateus Mendes de Vasconcelos	*c.* 1593–1596
António Godinho de Andrade	1596–1598
Rui Soares de Mello	1598–?
*Constantino Castanho	*c.* 1601–1603
*Jorge Barreto	?
Gaspar Pereira	*c.* 1606
Pedro Gomes de Abreu	*c.* 1609
Manuel de Mello Pereira	1610–1614
Simão de Mello Pereira	1614–1620
Francisco de Sousa Pereira	1620–1625
*João Pereira Semedo	1624–1626
Marcel de Macedo	1626–1629
Pedro Leitão de Gamboa	1629–1631
Loss of the Fort	
Pedro Rodrigues Botelho	1632–1635
Francisco de Seixas Cabreira	1635–1639
Manuel de Sousa Coutinho	1643–1646
Diogo de Barros da Silva	1646–1648
António da Silva de Menezes	1648–1651
Francisco de Seixas Cabreira (second term)	1651–1653
Joseph Botelho da Silva	1658–1663
Manuel de Campos	1663–1667
João Santos (?) Cota	1667–1670
Joseph Homem da Costa	1671–1673
Manuel de Campos Mergulhão	1673–1676
Francisco Morais de Faria	1676–1679
Manuel Texeira Franco	1679–168?

Pedro Taveira Henriques	168?–168?
Leonardo da Costa	1682–1686
João Antunes Portugal	1686–1688
Duarte Figueiredo de Mello	1688–169?
Pascoal de Abreu Sarmento	1693–1694
João Rodrigues Leão	1694–1696
António Mogo de Mello	1696–1697
Sheikh Daud of Faza	1697–1698
Leonardo Barbosa Soutomaior	1698
Loss of the Fort	
Alvaro Caetano de Mello e Castro	1728–1729

VICEROYS AND GOVERNORS OF GOA

Vice-rei Matias de Albuquerque	1591–1597
Vice-rei D. Francisco da Gama (Conde de Vidigueria)	1597–1600
Vice-rei Aires de Saldanha	1600–1605
Vice-rei D. Marim Afonso de Castro	1605–1607
Governador D. Frei Aleixo ne Meneses (Arcebispo)	1608–1609
Governador André Furtado de Mendonça	1609
Vice-rei Rui Lourenço de Távora	1609–1612
Vice-rei D. Jerónimo de Azevedo	1612–1617
Vice-rei D. João Coutinho (Conde de Redondo)	1617–1619
Governador Fernão de Albuquerque	1619–1622
Vice-rei D. Francisco da Gama (Conde da Vidigueira) (second term)	1622–1628
Governador D. Frei Luís de Brito (Bispo de Miliapor)	1628–1629
Conselho { Nuno Alvares Botelho; D. Lourenço da Cunha; Gonçalves Pinto da Fonseca }	1629
Vice-rei D. Miguel de Noronha (Conde de Linhares)	1629–1635
Vice-rei Pedro da Silva	1635–1639
Governador António Teles de Meneses	1639–1640
Vice-rei João da Silva Telo de Meneses (Conde de Aveiras)	1640–1645
Vice-rei D. Filipe Mascarenhas	1645–1651
Conselho { D. Frei Francisco dos Mártires (Arcebispo); António de Sousa Coutinho; Francisco de Melo de Castro }	1651–1652

Vice-rei	D. Vasco Mascarenhas (Conde de Obídos)	1652–1655
Intruso	D. Bras de Castro	
Vice-rei	D. Rodrigo da Silveira (Conde de Sarzedas)	1655–1656
Governador	Manuel Mascarenhas Homem	1656
Conselho	Manuel Mascarenhas Homem Francisco de Melo e Castro António de Sousa Coutinho	1656–1661
Conselho	Luís de Mendonça Furtado D. Manuel Mascarenhas D. Pedro de Lencastre	1661–1662
Vice-rei	António de Melo e Castro	1662–1666
Vice-rei	João Nunes da Cunha (Conde de S. Vicente)	1666–1668
Conselho	António de Melo e Castro Luís de Miranda Henriques Manuel de Côrte Real de Sampaio	1668–1671
Vice-rei	Luís de Mendonça Furtado (Conde de Lavradio)	1671–1677
Vice-rei	D. Pedro de Almeida (Conde de Assumar)	1677–1678
Conselho	D. Frei António Brandão (Arcebispo) António Pais do Sande	1678–1681
Vice-rei	Francisco de Távora (Conde de Alvor)	1681–1686
Governador	D. Rodrigo da Costa	1686–1690
Governador	D. Miguel de Almeida	1690–1691
Conselho	D. Frei Agostino de Anunciacão (Arcebispo) D. Fernando Martim de Mascarenhas de Lencastre Luís Gonçalves Costa	1691–1692
Vice-rei	D. Pedro António de Noronha (Conde de Vila Verde)	1693–1698
Vice-rei	António Luís Gonçalves da Câmara Coutinho	1698–1701
Conselho	D. Frei Agostinho de Anunciacão (Arcebispo) D. Vasco Luís Coutinho	1701–1702
Vice-rei	Caetano de Melo e Castro	1702–1707
Vice-rei	D. Rodrígo da Costa	1707–1712
Vice-rei	Vasco Fernandes Cesar de Meneses	1712–1717
Governador	D. Sebastião de Andrade Pessanha (Arcebispo)	1717
Vice-rei	D. Luís de Meneses (Conde de Ericeera)	1717–1720
Vice-rei	Francisco José de Sampaio e Castro	1720–1723
Governador	D. Cristovão de Melo	1723
Conselho	D. Inácio de Santa Teresa (Arcebispo) D. Cristovão de Melo Cristovão Luís de Andrade	1723–1725
Vice-rei	João de Saldanha de Gama	1725–1732

KINGS OF SPAIN AND PORTUGAL

Philip I (II of Spain)	(1556) 1580–1598
Philip II (III of Spain)	1598–1621
Philip III (IV of Spain)	1621–1640

KINGS OF PORTUGAL

João IV	1640–1656
Alfonso VI	1656–1683
Pedro II	1683–1706
João V	1706–1750

WALIS OF THE FORT

Muhammad bin Mubarak	1698–?
Ahmad bin Zaid	? –1726
Nasir bin ʿAbdulla al Mazrui (acting)	1726–1728
Loss of the Fort	
Muhammad bin Saʿid al Maʿamiri	1730–173?
Salih bin Muhammad al Hadhrami	173?–1735
Muhammad bin ʿUthman al Mazrui	1735–1746
Saif bin Khalaf	1746–1747
ʿAli bin ʿUthman al Mazrui	1747–1762
Masud bin Nasir bin ʿUthman al Mazrui	1762–1787
ʿAbdulla bin Muhammad al Mazrui	1787–1789
Ahmad bin Muhammad bin ʿUthman al Mazrui	1789–1814
ʿAbdulla bin Ahmad bin Muhammad al Mazrui	1814–1823
Sulaiman bin ʿAli bin ʿUthman al Mazrui	1823–1826
Salim bin Ahmad bin Muhammad al Mazrui	1826–1835
Khamis bin Ahmad bin Muhammad al Mazrui	1835–1837
Rashid bin Salim bin Ahmad al Mazrui	1837
Loss of the Fort	

AKIDAS OF THE FORT

ʿAbdulla bin Mubarak al Bakshuwain	1842–1845?
Tanggai bin Shambe	1845?–1862?
Muhammad bin ʿAbdulla al Bakshuwain	1865?–1875

SULTANS OF MOMBASA

Ahmad *or* Muhammad	1593–1609
Hasan bin Ahmad	1609–1614
Muhammad bin Hasan	1614–1617 (or later)
Muhammad Yusif bin Hasan (Dom Jerónimo Chingulia)	1626–1632[1]

IMAMS AND SULTANS OF OMAN

YAʿARUBI IMAMS[2]

Nasir bin Murshid	1624–1649
Sultan bin Saif I	1649–1679
Belʿarab bin Sultan	1679–1688
Saif bin Sultan I	1688–1708
Sultan bin Saif II	1708–1718
Saif bin Sultan II (first time)	1718–1719
Muhanna bin Sultan	1719–1720
Yaʿrab bin Belʿarab	1721–1723
Saif bin Sultan II (restored)	1723–1724
Muhammad bin Nasir	1724–1728
Saif bin Sultan II (restored again)	1728–1738

BUSAID IMAMS AND SAIYIDS[3]

Ahmad bin Saif	1741–1783
Said bin Ahmad	1783–1791
Sultan bin Ahmad	1791–1804
Badar bin Saif bin Ahmad	1804–1806
Said bin Sultan	1806–1856

SULTANS OF ZANZIBAR

Majid bin Saʿid	1856–1870
Barghash bin Saʿid	1870–1888
Khalifa bin Saʿid	1888–1890
ʿAli bin Saʿid	1890–1893

[1] Sultan bin Hasan is the name this sultan is given by the Portuguese and also by the local history of Mombasa in Owen's *Narrative of Voyages*. However, a copy of a letter by him in the *Livros das Monções* No. 40, fol. 247, quoted by Strandes, is signed Muhammad bin Hasan. He may have changed his name after his reversion to Islam.

[2] From Boxer and de Azevedo (1960).

[3] Said bin Ahmad was the last Imam.

Hamid bin Thuwain bin Saʿid	1893–1896
Hamoud bin Muhammad	1896–1902
ʿAli bin Hamoud	1902–1911
Khalifa bin Harub bin Thuwain	1911–1960
ʿAbdulla bin Khalifa	1960–1963
Jamshid bin ʿAbdulla	1963–1964
REPUBLIC	1964

Bibliography

AL AMIN BIN 'ALI AL MAZRUI, 'History of the Mazrui', trans. by J. M. Ritchie (unpublished).

Archivo Portuguez Oriental, 8 vols. (Nova Goa, 1857–76), ed. J. H. Cunha Rivara.

Arquivo Português Oriental (new ed.), 11 vols. (Bastorá–Goa, 1936–40), ed. A. B. de Bragança Pereira.

ASHDOWN, J. 'Oil Jars', in *International Journal of Underwater Archaeology*, i (1972).

AXELSON, ERIC, *Portuguese in South-East Africa, 1600–1700* (Johannesburg, 1960).

BADGER, G. P. (ed. and trans.), 'History of the Imâms and Seyyids of Omân by Salîl-Razîk, from A.D. 661–1856', *Hakluyt Society Publications*, 1st series, vol. xliv (London, 1871).

BERG, F. J., 'The Swahili Community of Mombasa, 1500–1900', in *Journal of African History*, ix. 1 (1968).

—— and WALTER, B. J., 'Mosques, Population and Urban Development in Mombasa', *Hadith*, i (1968).

BOCARRO, ANTÓNIO, and BARRETO DE REZENDE, PEDRO, 'Livro do Estado da India Oriental', in *Arquivo Português Oriental* (new ed.), iv (ii) 1.

BOXER, C. R., and AZEVEDO, CARLOS DE, *Fort Jesus and the Portuguese in Mombasa* (London, 1960).

British Museum, Additional MS.—*see* Sir John Gray (1947).

AL BURI, FADHIL BIN SHAIKH 'UMAR, *Al Kawkabu 'd Durriyya li 'akhbar Ifriqiyya*, trans. by J. M. Ritchie (unpublished).

CERULLI, E., *Somalia I* (which incorporates text and Italian trans. of Kitab al Zenuj) (Rome, 1957).

CHAFFERS, W., *Collectors Handbook of Marks and Monograms on Pottery and Porcelain*, revised by F. Litchfield, 3rd ed. (London, 1952).

CHITTICK, NEVILLE, 'Notes on Kilwa', in *Tanganyika Notes and Records*, 53 (1959).

—— 'Kilwa: A Preliminary Report', *Azania*, i (1966).

—— 'Discoveries in the Lamu Archipelago', *Azania*, ii (1967).

—— 'A new look at the History of Pate', *Journal of African History*, x. 3 (1969).

CUSHION, J. P., and HONEY, W. B., *Handbook of Pottery and Porcelain Marks* (London, 1956).

DECKEN, C. C. VON DER, *Reisen in Ost-Afrika in den Jahren 1859–bis 61*, ed. O. Kersten (Heidelberg and Leipzig, 1869–71).

FREEMAN-GRENVILLE, G. S. P., *The East African Coast: Select Documents from the first to the earlier nineteenth century* (Oxford, 1962).

—— 'Coins from Mogadishu *c.* 1300 to *c.* 1700' in *Numismatic Chronicle*, 7th series, iii (1963).

—— 'The Martyrs of Mombasa, 1631', in *African Ecclesiastical Review* (October 1967).

GARLAKE, P. S., *The Early Islamic Architecture of the East African Coast* (Oxford, 1966).

—— 'Excavations at the Seventeenth-century Portuguese Site of Dambarare, Rhodesia', *Proceedings and Transactions of Rhodesia Scientific Association*, 54, pt. I (1969), p. 23.

—— and GARLAKE, M., 'Early Ship Engravings of the East African Coast', in *Tanganyika Notes and Records*, 63 (1964).

GARNER, H., *Oriental Blue and White* (London, 1963).

GOGGIN, J. M., 'The Spanish Olive Jar', *Yale University Publications in Anthropology*, 62 (Yale, 1960).

GRAY, SIR JOHN, 'Rezende's Description of East Africa in 1634', in *Tanganyika Notes and Records*, 23 (1947).

—— *The British in Mombasa, 1824–1826* (London, 1957, for the Kenya History Society).

GROTTANELLI, V. L., *Pescatori dell'Oceano Indiano* (Rome, 1955).

GUILLAIN, M., *Documents sur l'histoire, la géographie et le commerce de l'Afrique Orientale*, 3 vols. (Paris, 1856–7).

HARDINGE, A. H., *A Diplomatist in the East* (London, 1928).

HARTMANN, A., 'Augustinians in the Land of the Swahili', *Analecta Augustiniana*, xxv (1962).

HAYNES, E. BARRINGTON, *Glass through the Ages*, Pelican Books A. 166 (1948).

HINAWY, MBARAK BIN 'ALI, *Al Akida and Fort Jesus, Mombasa* (London, 1950; reprinted Nairobi, 1971).

HONEY, W. B., *The Ceramic Art of China and other countries of the Far East* (London, 1945).

HORNELL, James, 'The Sea-going *Mtepe* and *Dau* of the Lamu Archipelago', *The Mariner's Mirror*, xxvii (1) (1941).

HUME, I. N., 'The Glass Wine Bottle in Colonial Virginia', Corning Museum of Glass *Journal of Glass Studies*, iii (1961).

INGHAM, K., *A History of East Africa* (London, 1962).

Iraq Government Department of Antiquities, *Excavations at Samarra 1936–1939* (Baghdad, 1940).

KIRKMAN, JAMES, *The Arab City of Gedi—Excavations at the Great Mosque—Architecture and Finds* (Oxford, 1954).

—— 'Takwa, The Mosque of the Pillar', in *Ars Orientalis*, ii (1957).

—— 'Mnarani of Kilifi', *Ars Orientalis*, iii (1959).

—— 'The Tomb of the Dated Inscription at Gedi', Royal Anthropological Institute Occasional Paper No. 14, 1960.

—— *Gedi, The Palace* (The Hague, 1963).

—— *Men and Monuments on the East African Coast* (London, 1964).

—— *Ungwana on the Tana* (The Hague, 1966).

—— 'A Portuguese wreck off Mombasa', in *International Journal of Underwater Archaelogy*, i (1972).

Kitab al Zenuj—*see* Cerulli, E.

KRAPF, J. L., *Travels, Researches and Missionary Labours during an eighteen years residence in East Africa* (London, 1860).

LAMBERT, H. E., 'The Twelve Tribes and the Arab Community of Mombasa', *Mombasa Social Survey* (1958), unpublished.

LANE, ARTHUR, *Later Islamic Pottery: Persia, Syria, Egypt, Turkey* (London, 1957).

LAWRENCE, A. W., *Trade Castles and Forts of West Africa* (London, 1963).

LOBATO, ALEXANDRE, *A Ilha de Moçambique* (Lourenço Marques, 1945).

—— *A Expansão Portuguesa em Moçambique de 1498 a 1530*, Livro III, *Aspectos e Problemas da Vida Económica, de 1505 a 1530* (Lisboa, 1960).

MARINHO, BALTASAR, 'Lista das obras que o feitor Alcaide mor de S. Mgde ha de fazer nesta fortaleza e na fortificacão do paço de Macupa', Mombasa, 4 April 1633, in the *Arquivo Historico Ultramarino*, Lisbon, 'Documentos da India, 1634'.

MICHAELIS, H., *A New Dictionary of Portuguese and English Languages* (8th ed., Leipzig, 1932).

MILES, G., *The Countries and Tribes of the Persian Gulf* (London, 1919; 2nd ed., 1966).

MITTERWALLNER, G. VON, *Chaul* (Berlin, 1964).

MOORE, EINE, 'A Suggested Classification of Stonewares of Martabani Type', *Sarawak Museum Journal* (1970).

MOOREHOUSE, STEVENS, 'Finds from Basing House', Journal *Post-Medieval Archaeology*, iv (1970).

MORENO, G. M., *The Golden Age of Spanish Sculpture*,

MUNGEAM, G. H., *British Rule in Kenya, 1895–1912* (London, 1966).

NICHOLLS, C. S., *The Swahili Coast* (London, 1971).

OWEN, W. F. W., R.N., *Narrative of Voyages to Explore the shores of Africa, Arabia and Madagascar* (London, 1833).

POOLE, R. S., *The Coins of the Shahs of Persia in the British Museum* (London, 1887).

PRINS, A. H. J., *The Coastal Tribes of the North-East Bantu* (International African Institute, London, 1952).

—— 'Uncertainties in Coastal Cultural History: the *Ngalawa* and the *Mtepe*', in *Tanganyika Notes and Records*, 53 (1959).

—— *The Swahili-speaking Peoples of Zanzibar and the East African Coast* (International African Institute, London, 1961; new ed., 1968).

REGO, A. DA SILVA, *História das Missões do Padroada Português do Oriente India*, xi (Lisbon, 1955).

SALIL IBN RAZIK—*see* Badger, G. P.

SANKALIA, H. D., and DIKSHIT, M. G., *Excavations at Brahmapuri (Kolhapur), 1945–1946*, Deccan College Monograph, series 5 (Poona, 1952).

SAUVAGET, J., *Les Monuments historiques de Damas* (Beyrouth, 1932).

SLEEN, W. G. N. VAN DER, 'Ancient Glass Beads of East and Central Africa and the Indian Ocean', *Journal of the Royal Anthropological Institute*, 88, Part II (1958).

—— 'Bead-making in Seventeenth-Century Amsterdam', in *Archaeology*, 16 (4) (1963).

—— *A Handbook on Beads*, Journées internationales du Verre (Liège, 1967).

STIGAND, C. H., *The Land of Zinj* (London, 1913; new ed., 1966).

STRANDES, JUSTUS, *Die Portugiesenzeit von deutsch- und englisch-Ostafrika* (Berlin, 1899). English translation by Jean F. Wallwork, *The Portuguese Period in East Africa*, with annotations by James Kirkman (East African Literature Bureau, Nairobi, 1961; new ed., 1968).

SUBBARAO, B., *Baroda through the Ages*. Maharaja Sayajirao University Archaeology, series no. 1 (Baroda, 1953).

SUTERMEISTER, HELEN, 'An Eighteenth-Century Urban Estate in New France' [Louisbourg, Canada]. *Journal Post-Medieval Archaeology*, ii (1968).

THEAL, GEORGE MCCALL, *Records of South Eastern Africa* (London, 1898–1903).

VALENTINE, W. H., *Modern Copper Coins of the Muhammadan States* (London, 1911).

VASCONCELOS, E.—*see* below, PLANS—Cienfuegos.

VOLKER, T., *Porcelain and the Dutch East India Company*. Rijksmuseum voor Volkenkunde, no. 11 (Leiden, 1954).

PLANS

1610 HERÉDIA, MANOEL GODINHO DE, Atlas in Rio de Janeiro. Discussion in *Portugaliae Monumenta Cartographica*, vol. iv (Lisbon, 1960), pp. 39–48, and in Boxer and de Azevedo.

c. 1630 TEIXEIRA, JOÃO, in Munich, Paris, and Vienna. Discussion by O. Quelle in *Portugiesische Manuscriptatlanten in Abhandlungen des Geographischen Institutus der Freien Universitat Berlin*, Band II (Berlin, 1953), in *Portugaliae Monumenta Cartographica*, vol. iv (Lisbon, 1960), pp. 145–6, and in Boxer and de Azevedo.

1636 REZENDE, PEDRO BARRETO DE, in *Livro do Estado da India Oriental*. Discussion in C. R. Boxer, 'António Bocarro and the Livro do Estado da India Oriental' in *Garcia de Orta. Revista da Junta das Missões Geográficas e de Investigacões do Ultramar* (Lisbon, 1956), pp. 203–19, and in Boxer and de Azevedo.

1728 CIENFUEGOS, ALVARO DE, in *Junta das Missões Geográficas e de Investigacões do Ultramar* (Lisbon, 1956). Discussion in E. Vasconcelos, 'Um Mappa Antigo de Mombaça' in *Revista portuguesa colonial e maritima* (Lisbon, 1898–9), and in Boxer and de Azevedo.

1728 SÁ, JOSEPH LOPES DE, Engineer-Colonel, in 'Documentos da India', *Arquivo Historico Ultramarino, Lisbon*. Discussion in Boxer and de Azevedo.

1899 Kenya Public Works Department, nos. 2511 and 2512.

1954 Kenya Public Works Department, nos. 89 and 90.

PHOTOGRAPHS

Fort Jesus in 1894—National Maritime Museum, Greenwich, England.

Fort Jesus in 1905—Fort Jesus Museum, Mombasa, Kenya.

Figures

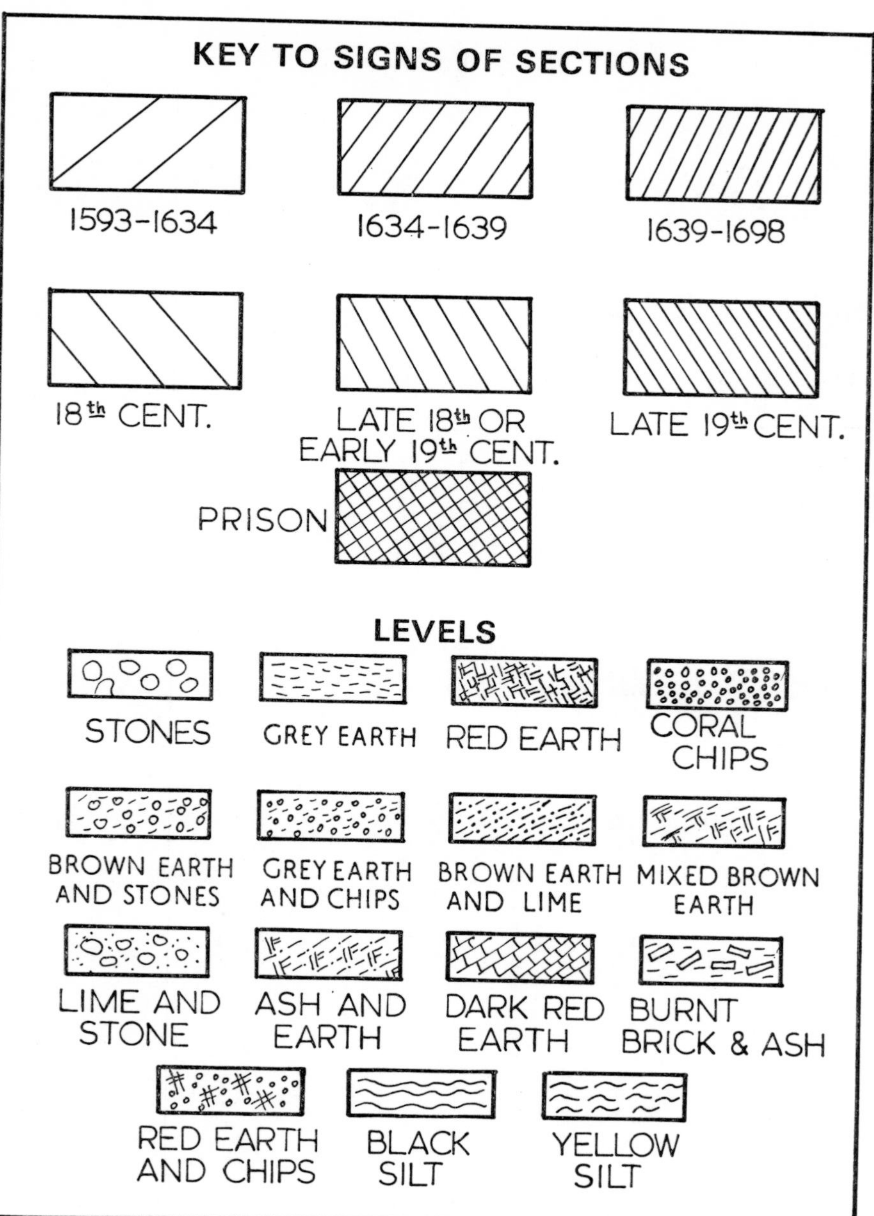

Key to Signs of Sections.

SHORE

LOW CLIFF

CORAL SLOPE

GATE

S. MATEUS

PAINTED
REVETMENT
WALL →

PARAPET, FIRING STEP, & PARAPET WALK

S. ALBERTO

LIME PIT

KERB

CAVE

LIME KILN

SOUTH BARRACK BLOCK

OUTLINE
OF
OUTWORK

GATE

PASSAGE OF THE STEPS

PILLARS OF PORTICO
OUTSIDE CAPTAIN'S HOUSE

COURT

GATE

PASSAGE OF THE ARCHES

HOUSE OF VICAR
FORANE AND
WEST BARRACK BLOCK

POSTS

ORIGINAL
CAVALIER

CHURCH

COUNTERSCARP

CORAL

OUTLINE OF CAPTAIN'S HOUSE

DITCH PARTIALLY
DUG

PILLAR

CISTERN

POSTS

PLATFORM

CORAL SLOPE

OUTLINE OF
HOUSE
MENTIONED BY
MARINHO

NORTH BARRACK BLOCK

KERB

S. MATIAS

LOW CLIFF

S. FILIPE

4 8 12m

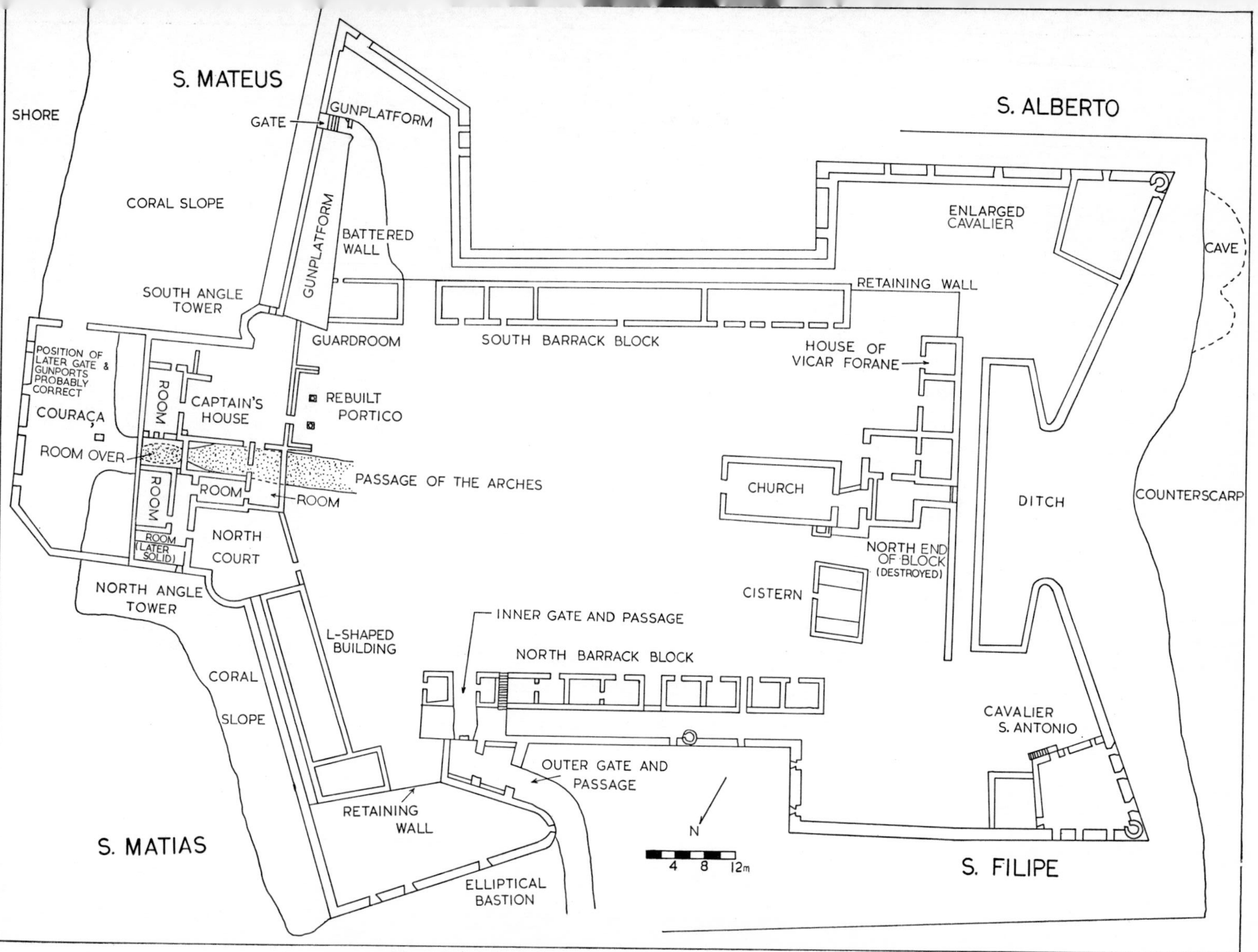

FIG. 2. Plan of Fort Jesus from excavations—The developed Fort, 1634–96.

The Arab Fort of the eighteenth and nineteenth centuries.

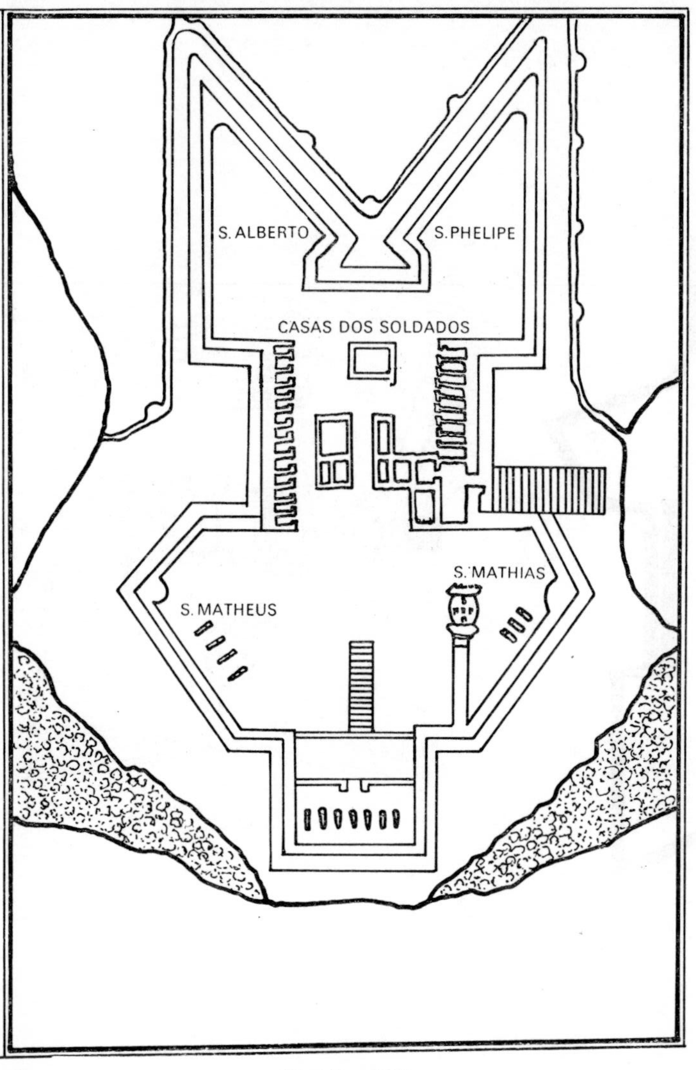

A

Herédia, 1610

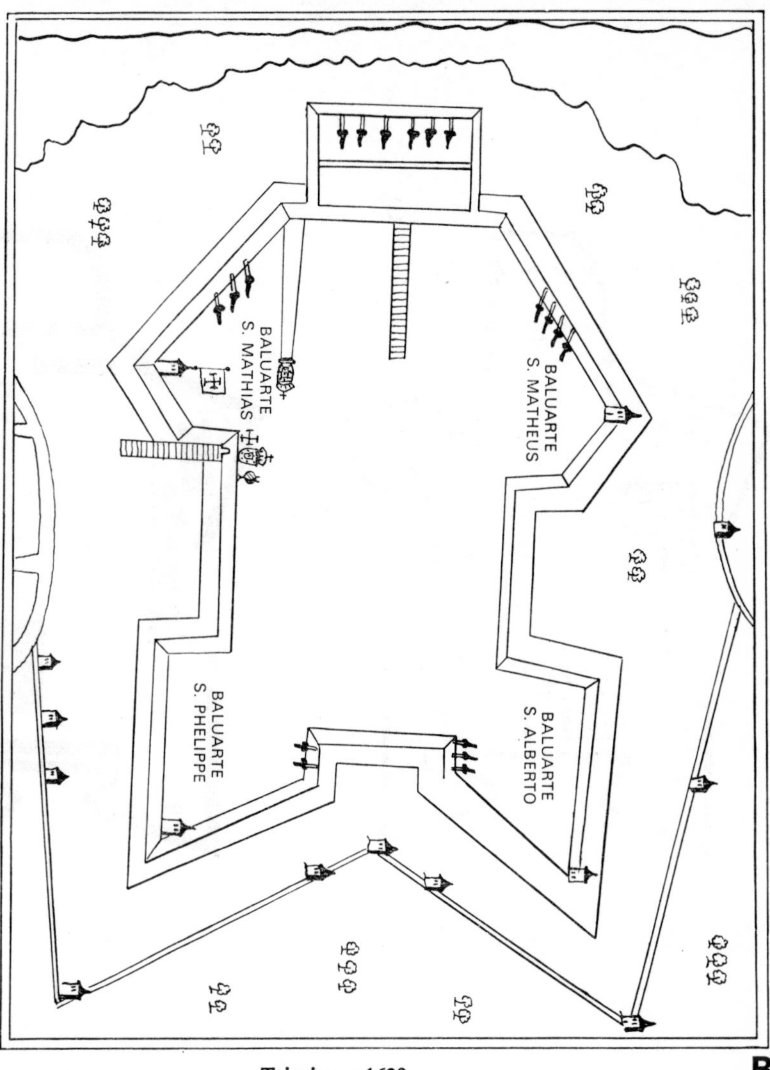

B

Teixeira, *c.*1620

FIG. 4. Portuguese plans of Fort Jesus.

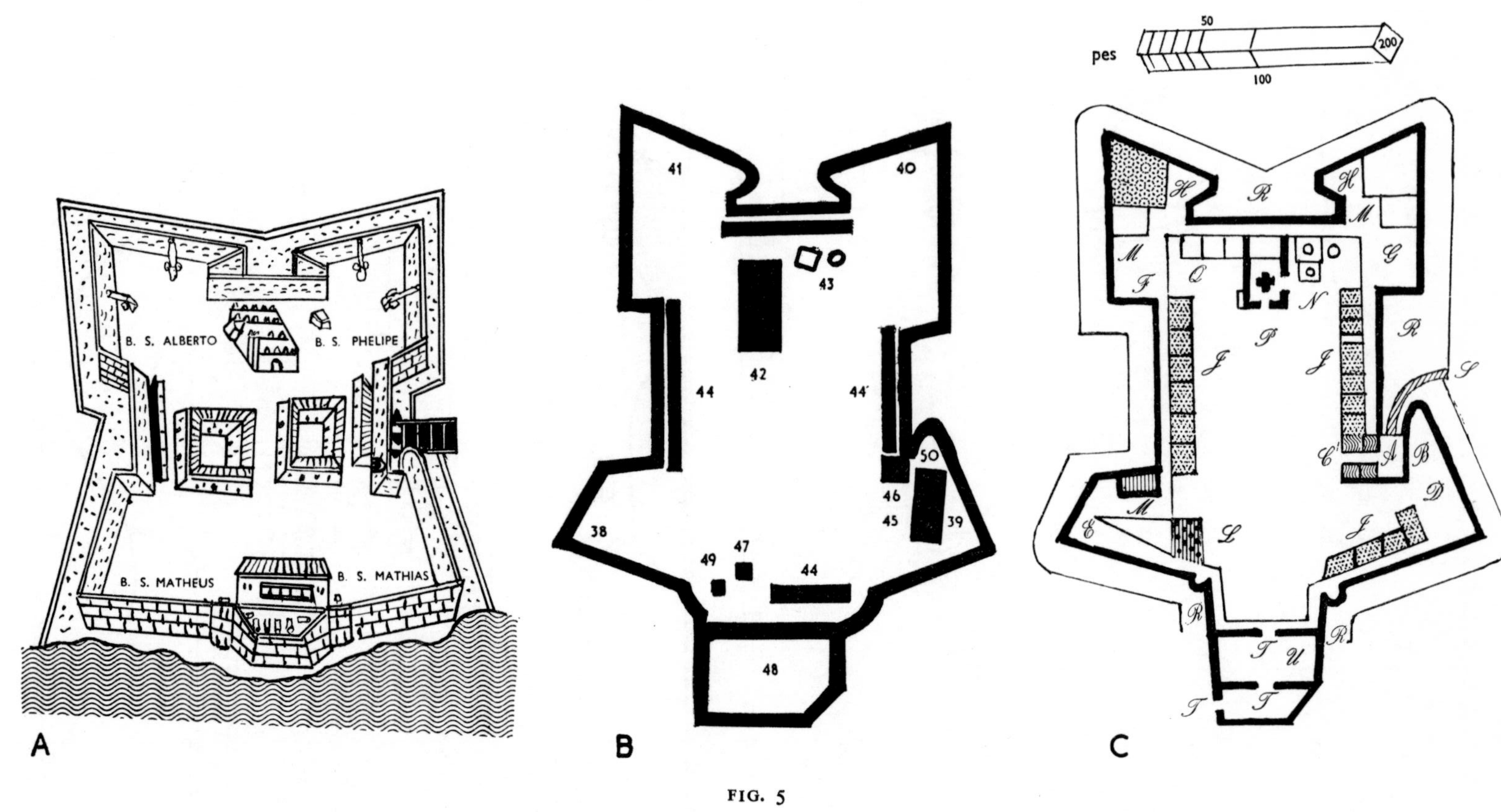
B. S. ALBERTO
B. S. PHELIPE
B. S. MATHEUS
B. S. MATHIAS
A
41
40
43
42
44
44'
50
46
45
39
38
47
49
44
48
B
pes
50
100
200
C

FIG. 5

Fig. 5. *Portuguese plans of Fort Jesus*

A. Bocarro/Rezende, 1636

B. Cienfuegos, 1728

38. Bastion of the Flags. 39. Bastion of the Sea. 40. Bastion de la Raposeira. 41. Bastion of S. António. 42. Church. 43. Cistern and Well. 44. Barracks. 45. House of the Governor. 46. Guardroom. 47. Powder-magazine. 48. External fortification in the form of a *couraça* unfinished. 49. Blocked door overlooking outwork. 50. Gate of the Fort.

C. Lopes de Sá, 1728

A. Main gate. B. Guardroom of the gate. C. Gate opening on the central court. D. Bastion of S. António. E. Bastion of S. Mateus. F. Bastion of S. Alberto. G. Bastion of S. Filipe. H. Cavalier bastions. J. Barracks. L. Provisions store. M. Guardrooms of the bastions. N. Cistern made by the Portuguese. O. Well in the shape of a cistern made by the Arabs. P. Cathedral church. Q. House of the *Vigario Forane*. R. Ditch unfinished in some places. S. Permanent bridge. T. Postern gates for the introduction of supplies from the shore. U. Low-level outwork on harbour to protect these supplies.

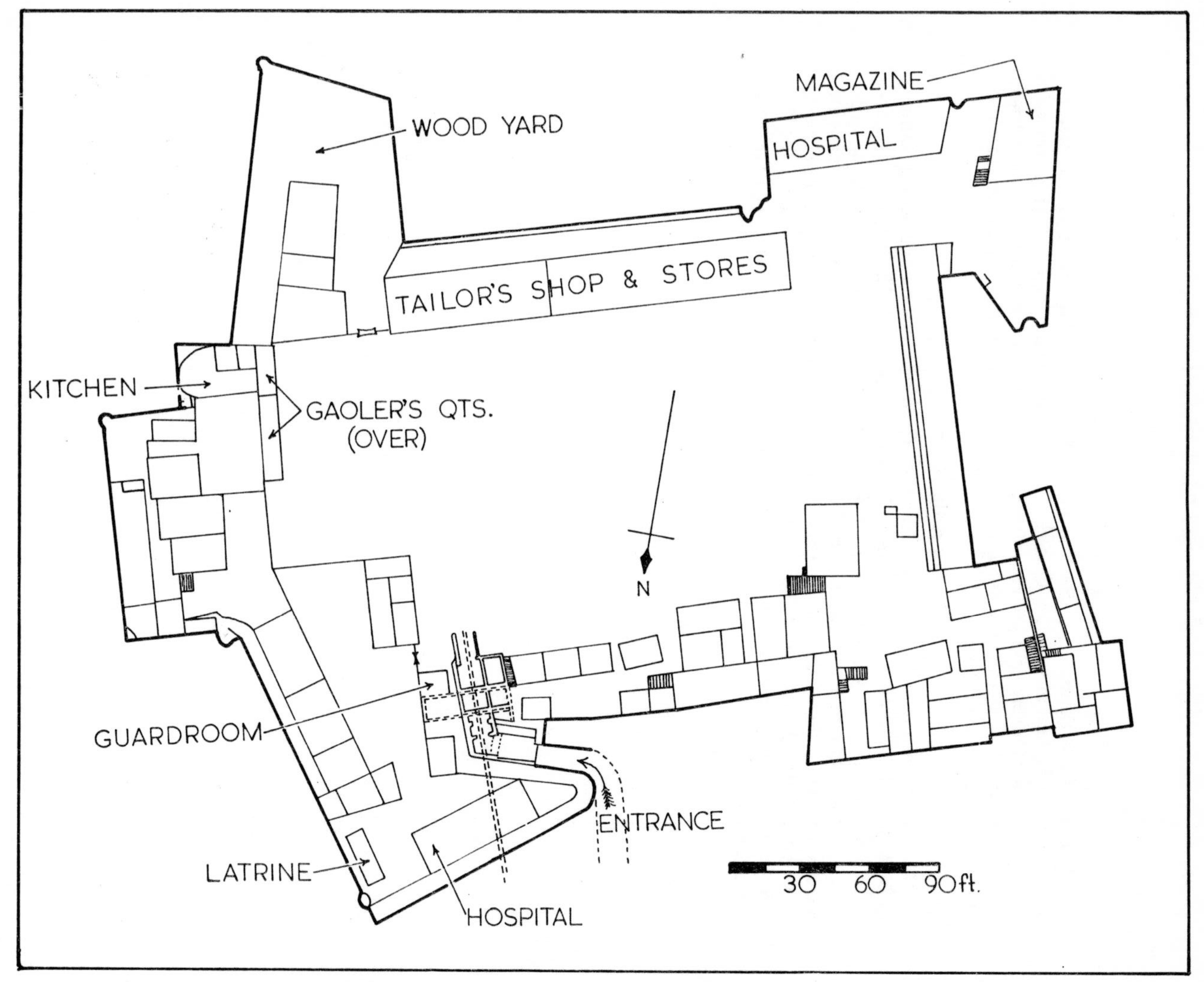

FIG. 6. Plan of Fort Jesus in 1899—Public Works Department No. 2511.

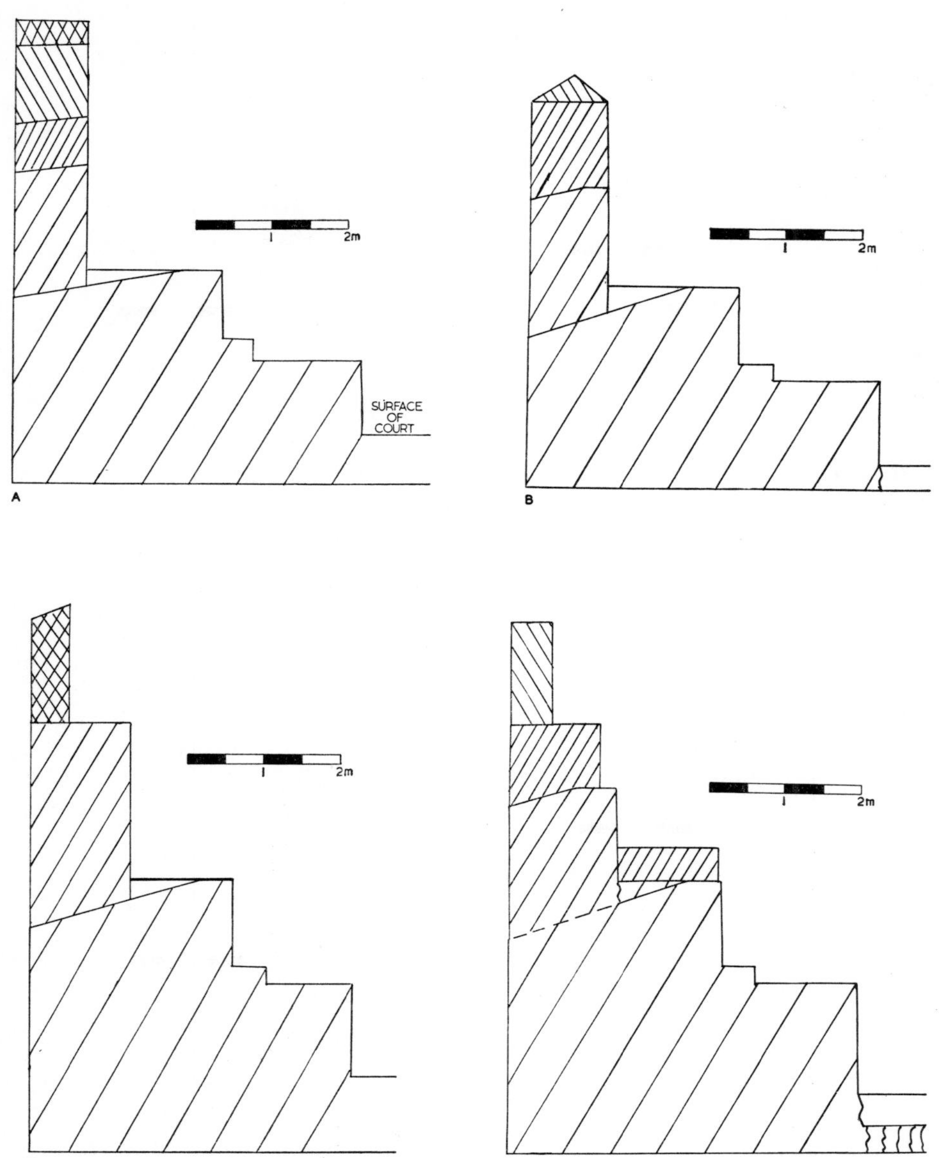

FIG. 7. Sections across the ramparts of Fort Jesus.
A. north curtain. B. west curtain. C. south curtain. D. S. Alberto (south).

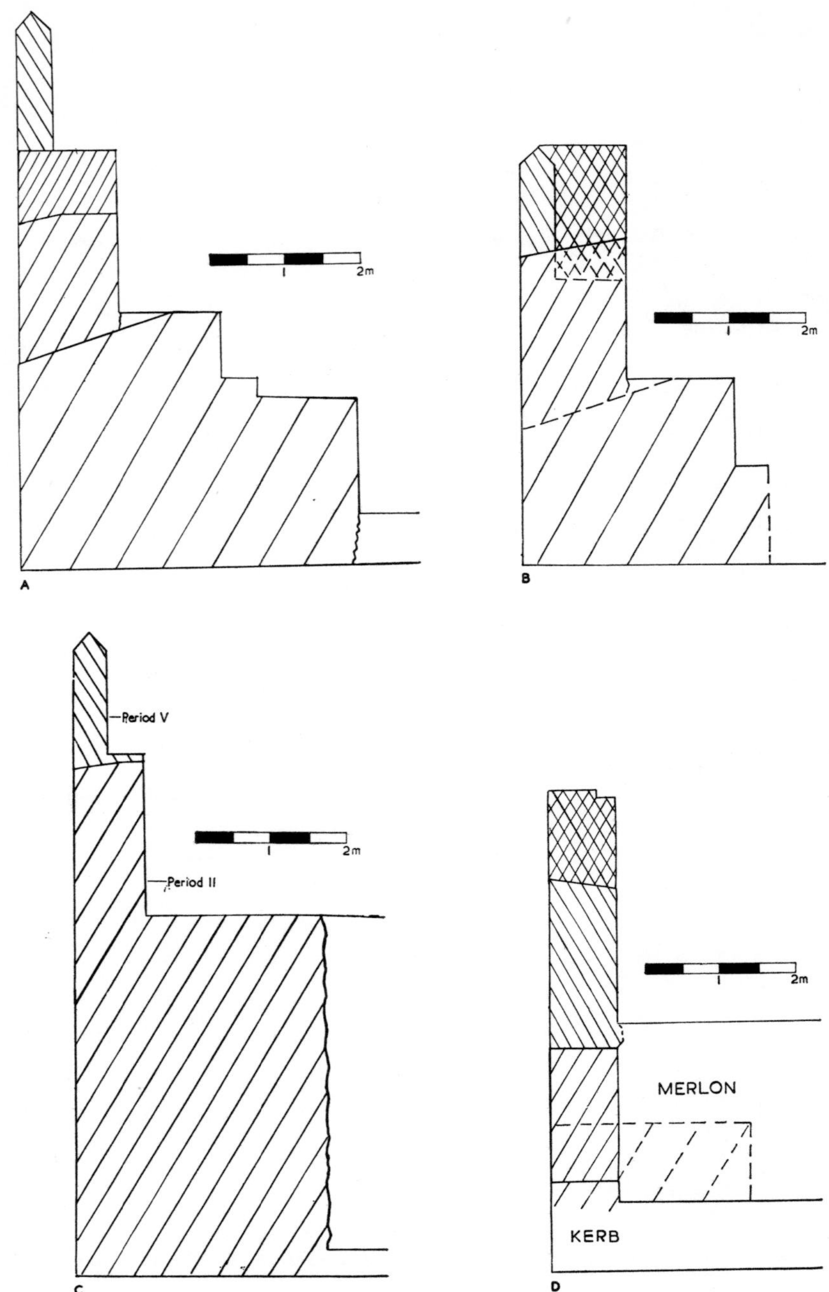

FIG. 8. Sections across the ramparts of Fort Jesus.
A. S. Filipe (west). B. S. Filipe (north). C. S. Matias (elliptical bastion, north). D. S. Matias (east).

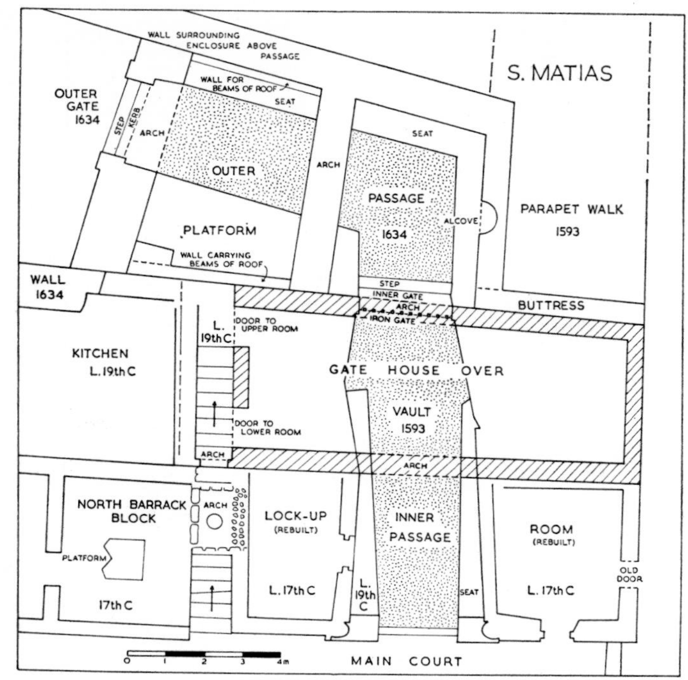

A

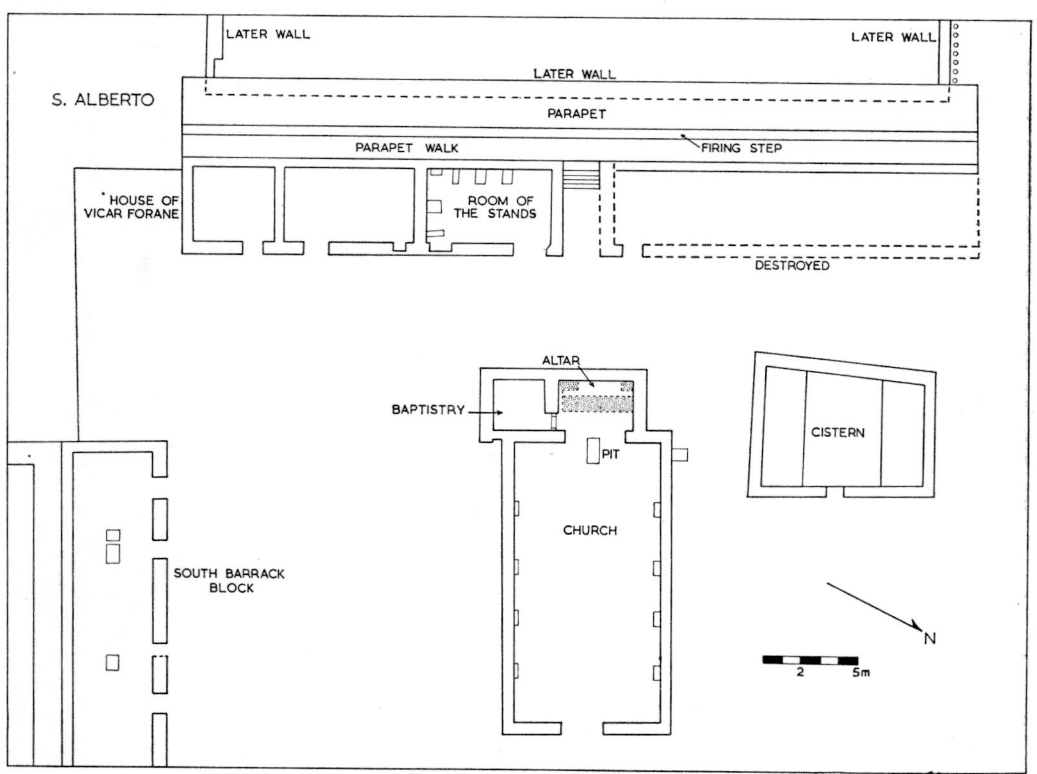

B

FIG. 9

A. Plan of gatehouse. B. West end of court during early seventeenth century.

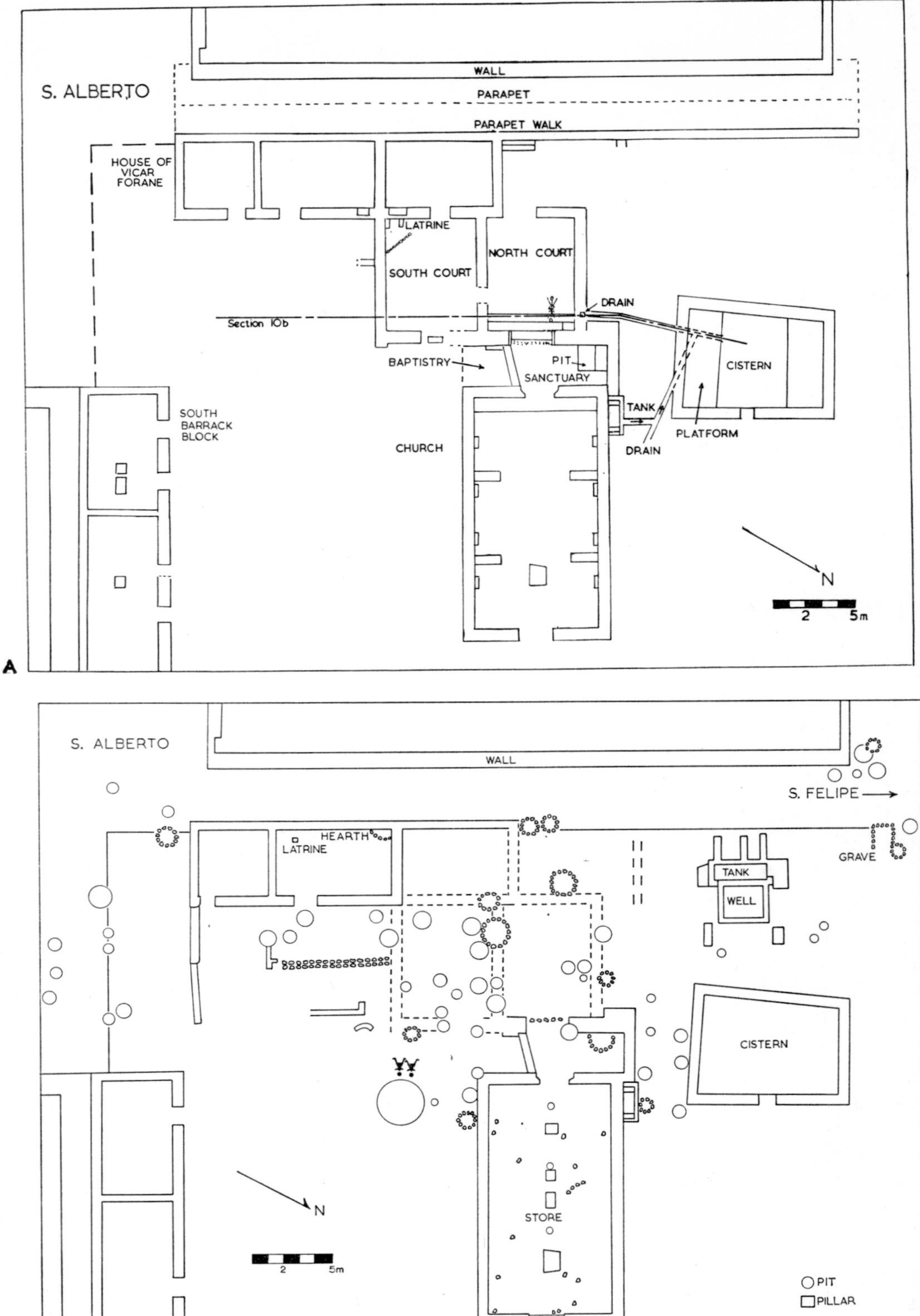

FIG. 10

A. West end of court, late seventeenth century. B. West end of court during eighteenth century.

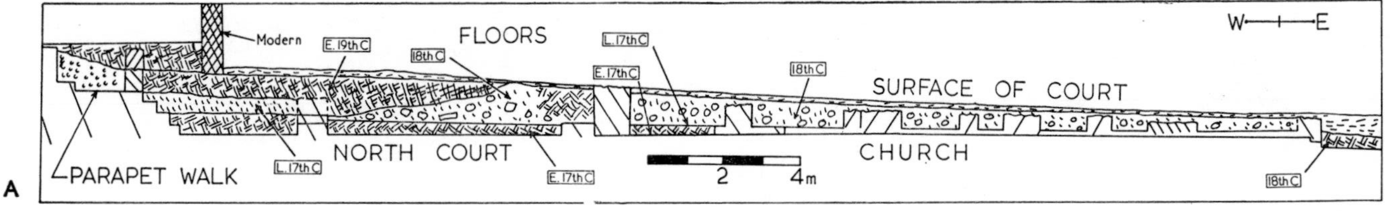

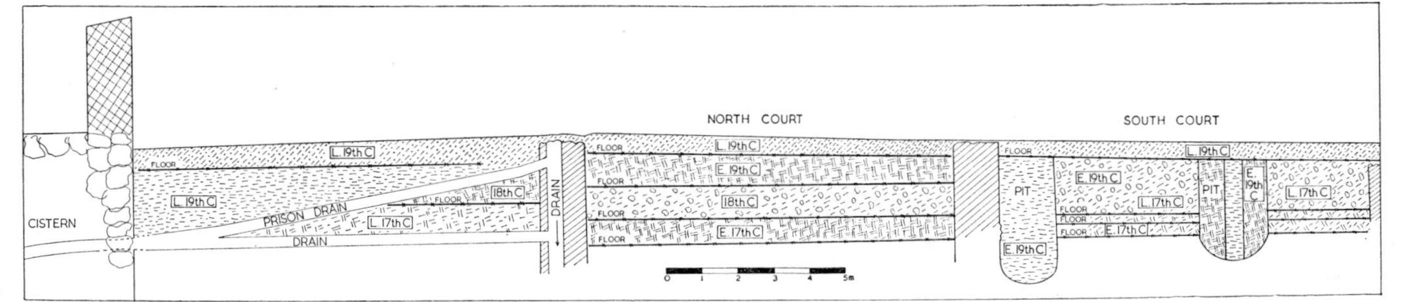

FIG. II

A. Section from west to east across church. B. Section north to south across courts behind church.

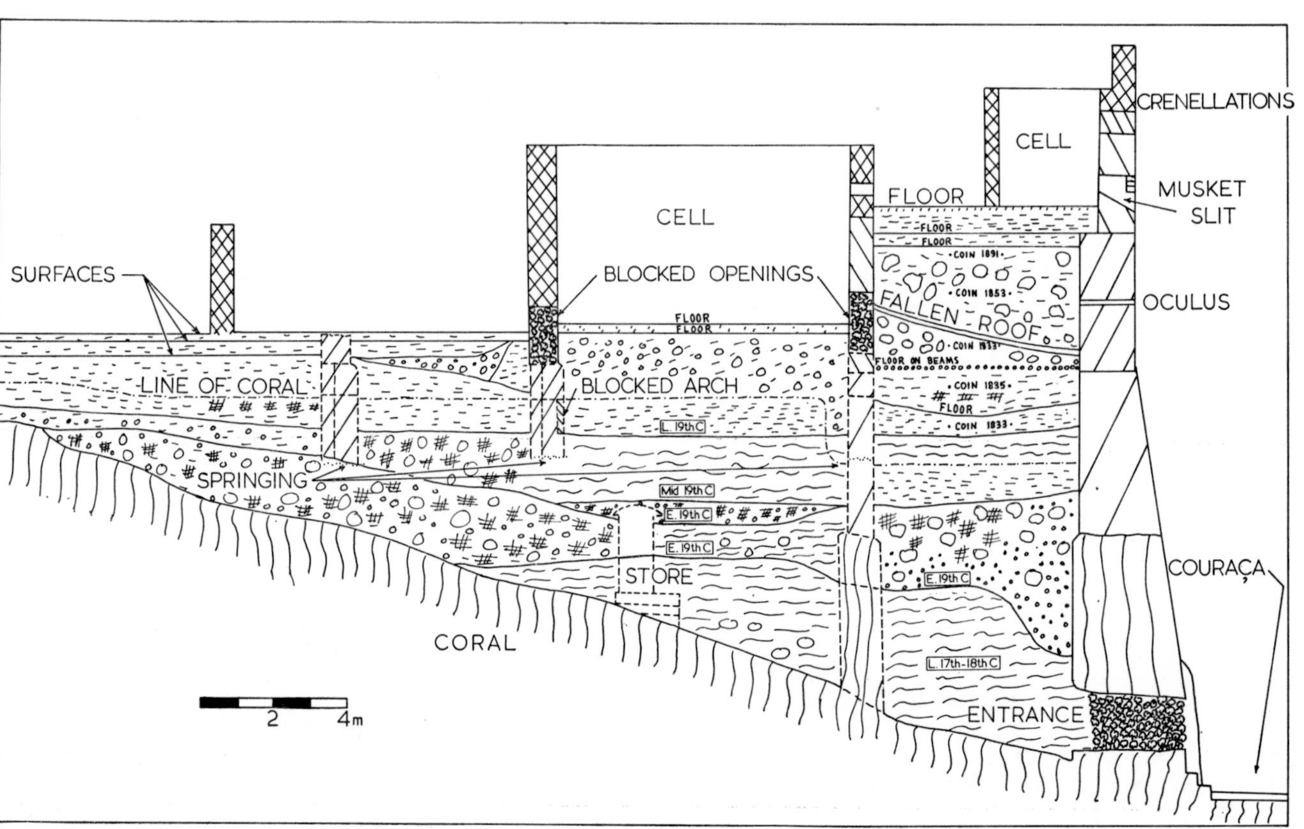

FIG. 12. Section along Passage of the Arches.

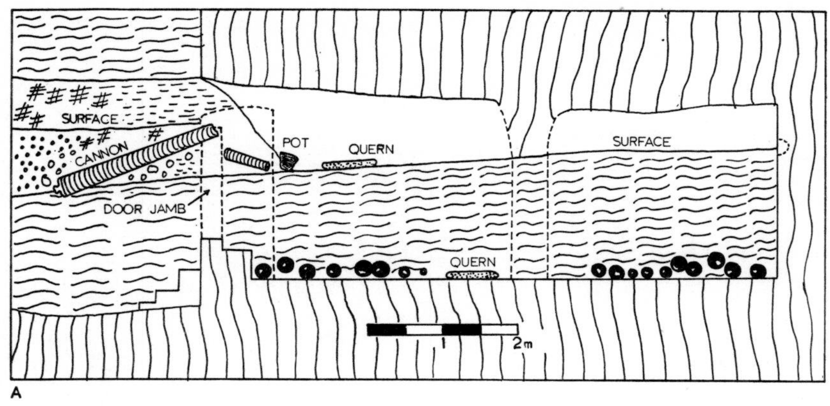

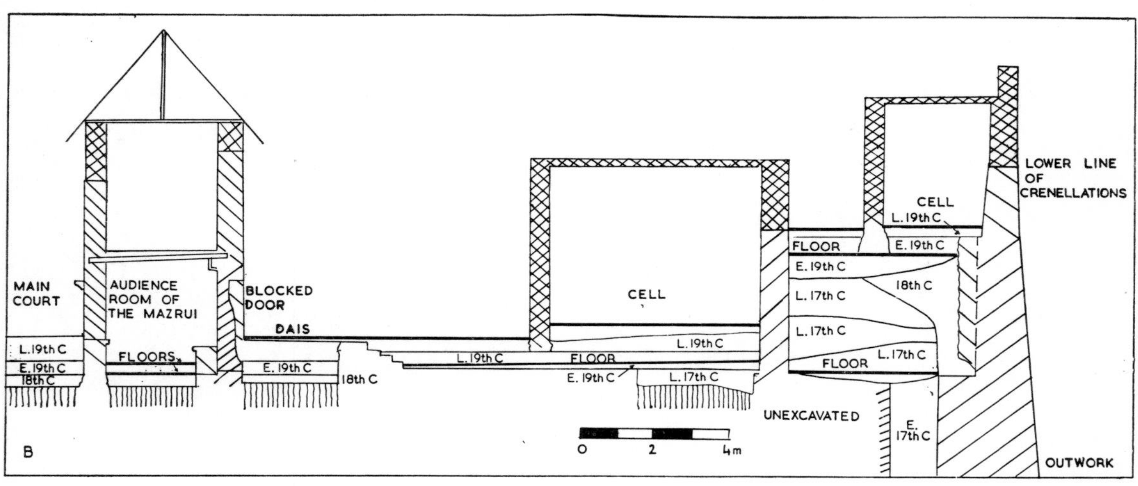

FIG. 13

A. Section through ammunition store. B. Section across court of Captain's House.

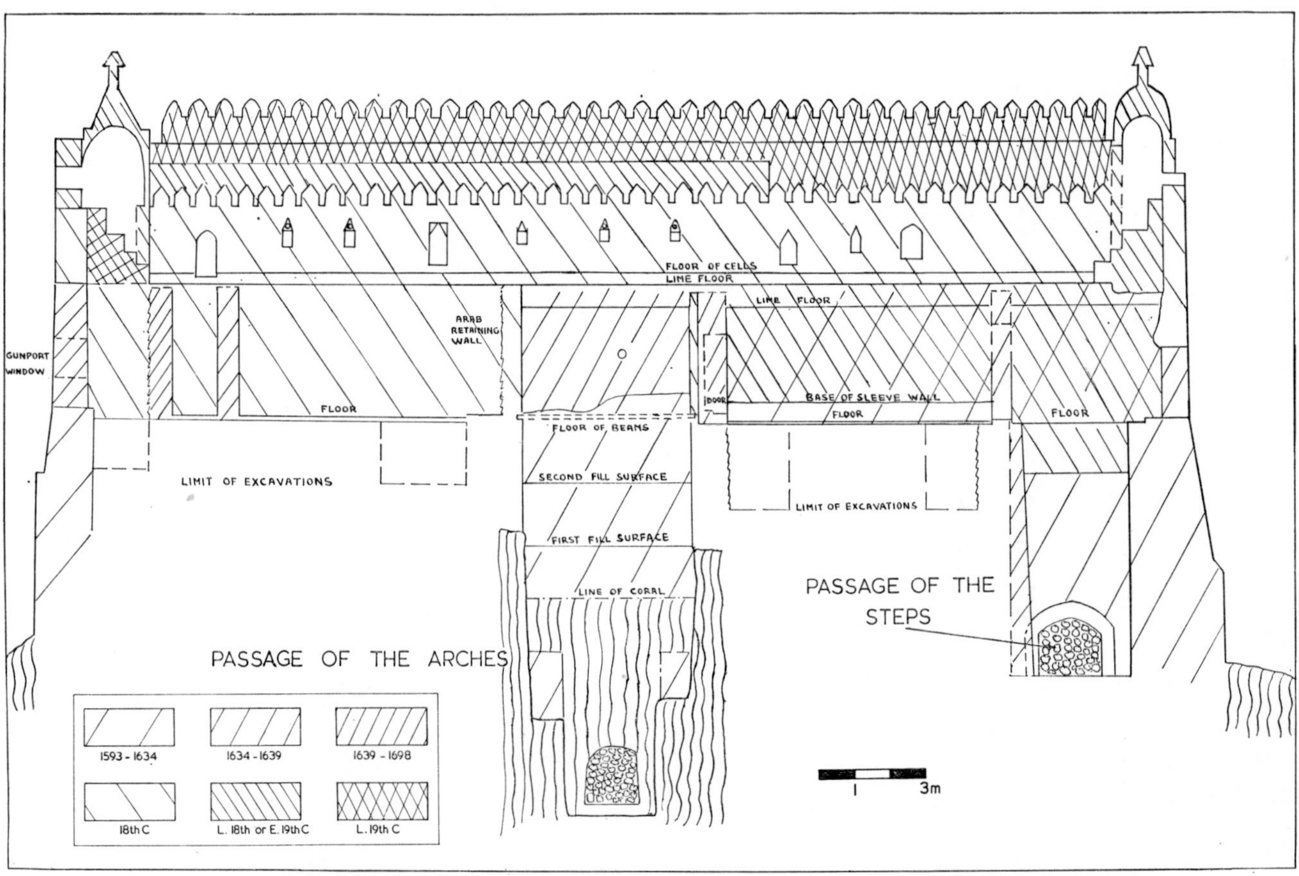

FIG. 14. Rectangular projection, internal elevation.

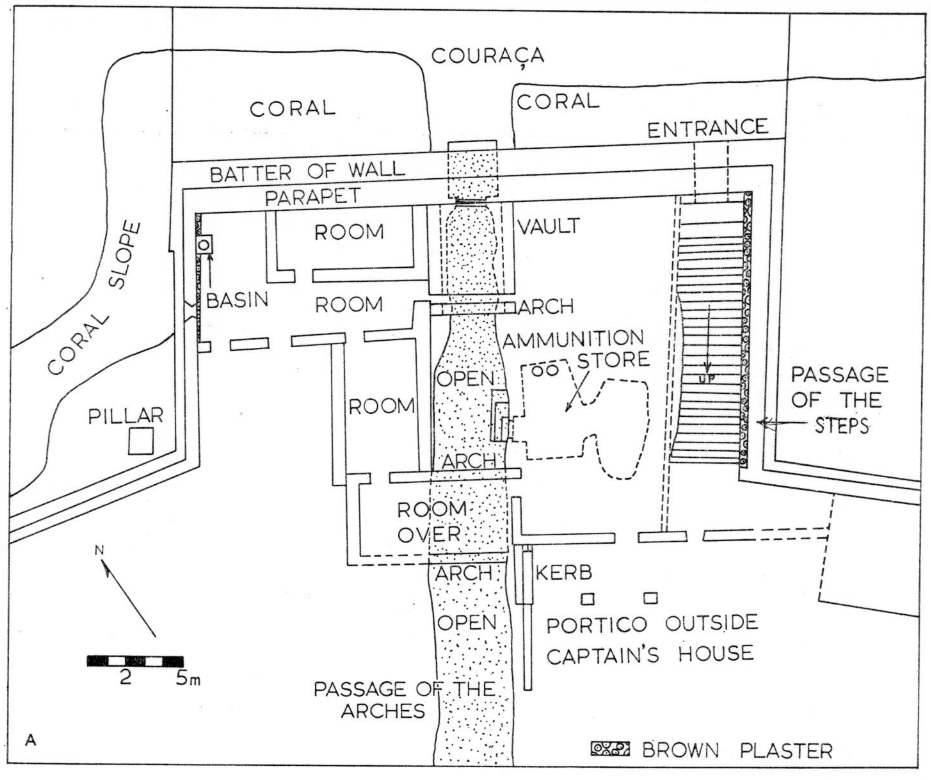

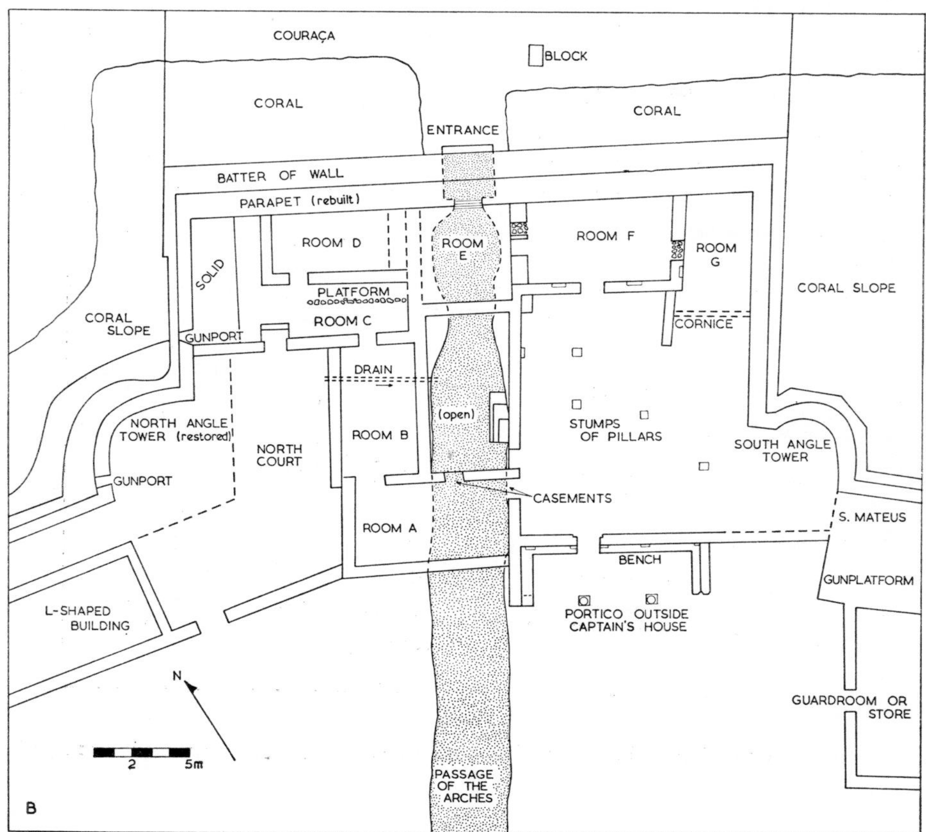

FIG. 15

A. Plan of rectangular projection showing passages and earliest buildings, 1593–1634.
B. Plan of rectangular projection in later Portuguese period, 1634–98.

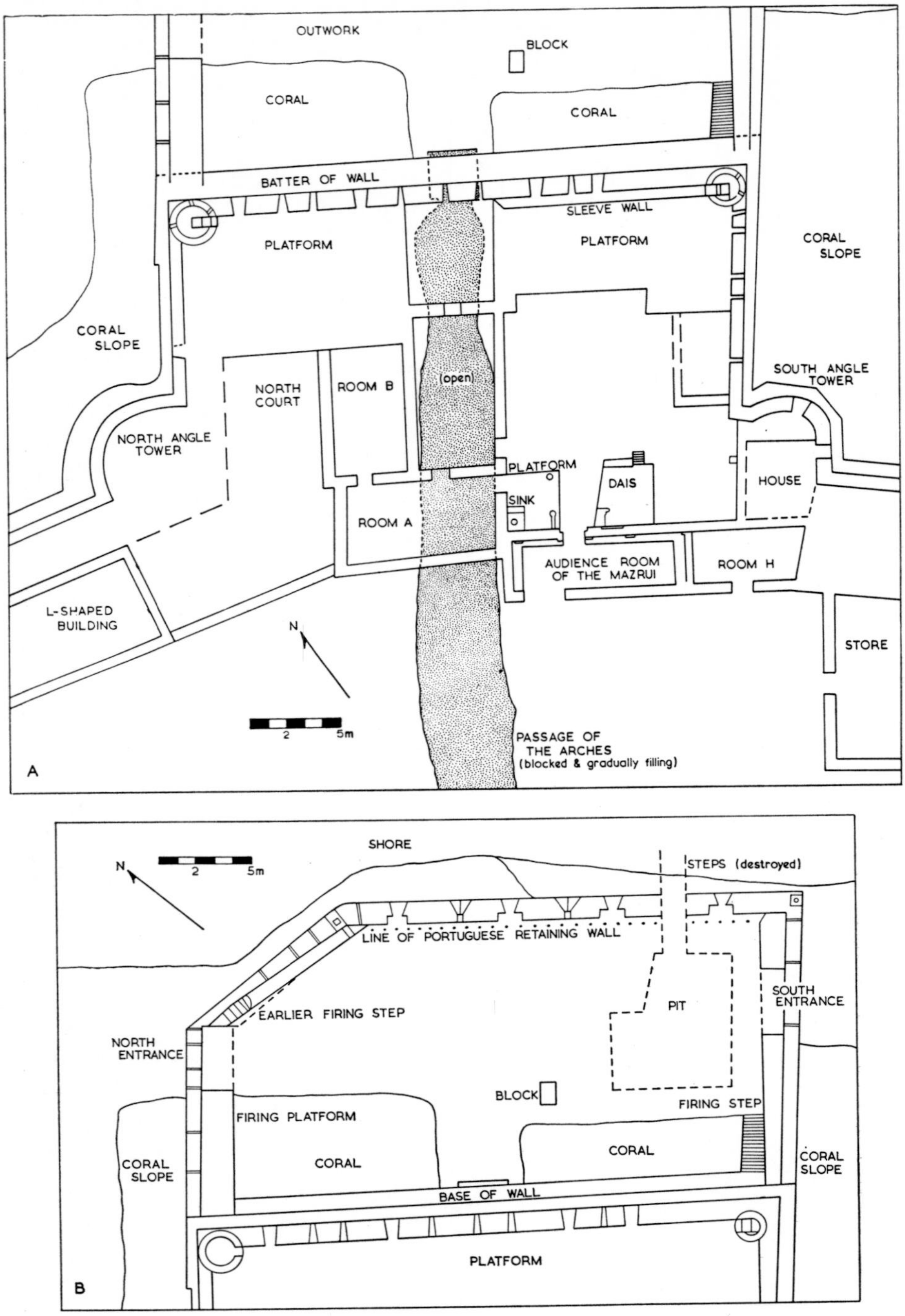

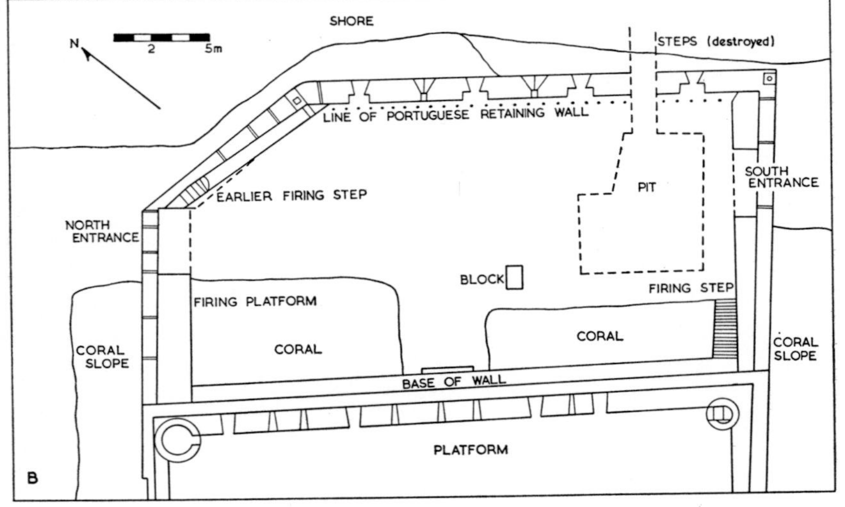

FIG. 16

A. Plan of rectangular projection in Arab period, 1698–1895. B. Outwork (*couraça*) in Arab period.

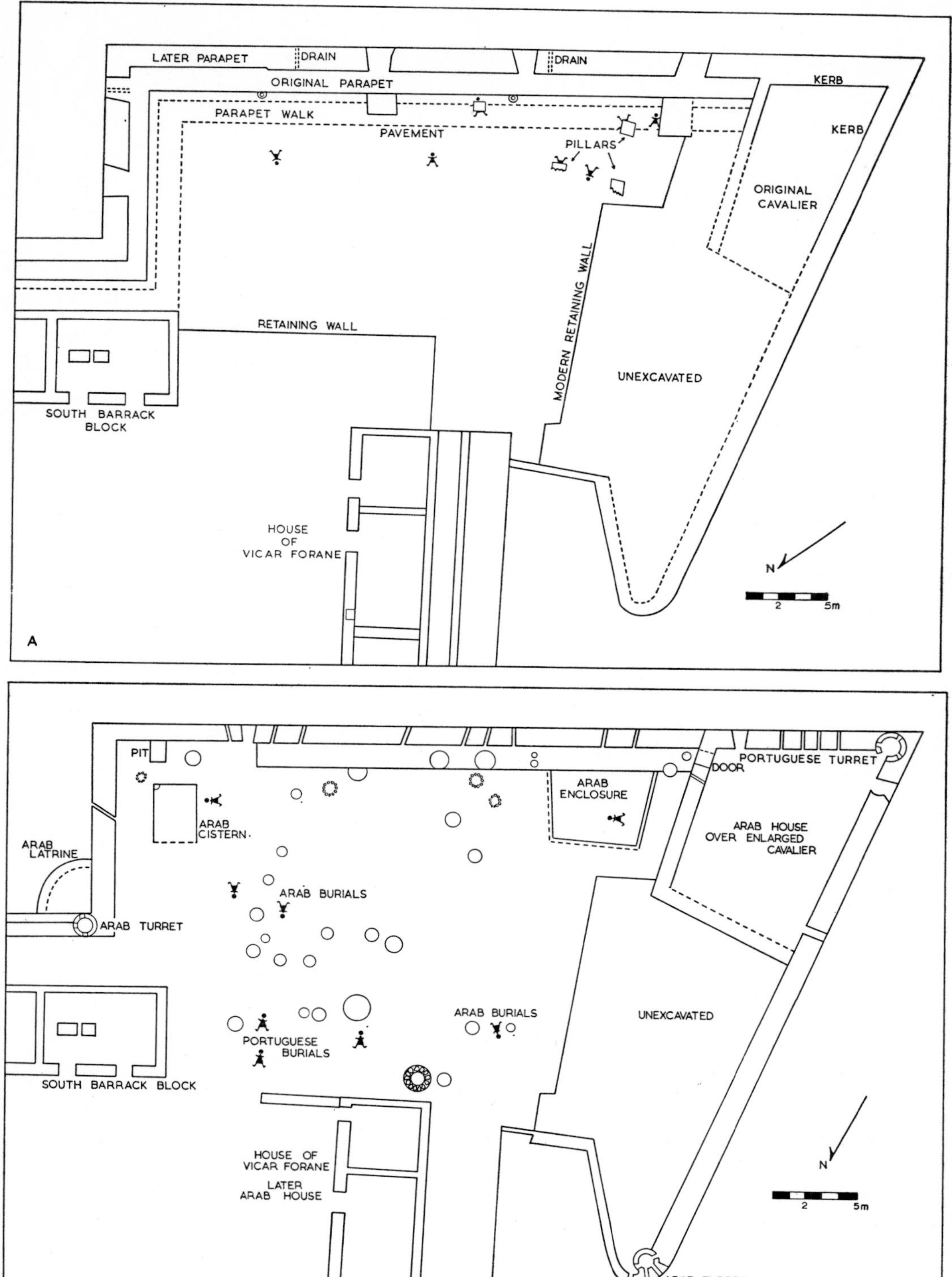

FIG. 17

A. Plan of S. Alberto in early and mid seventeenth century. B. Plan of S. Alberto late seventeenth (wall of musket-slits and cavalier) to early nineteenth century.

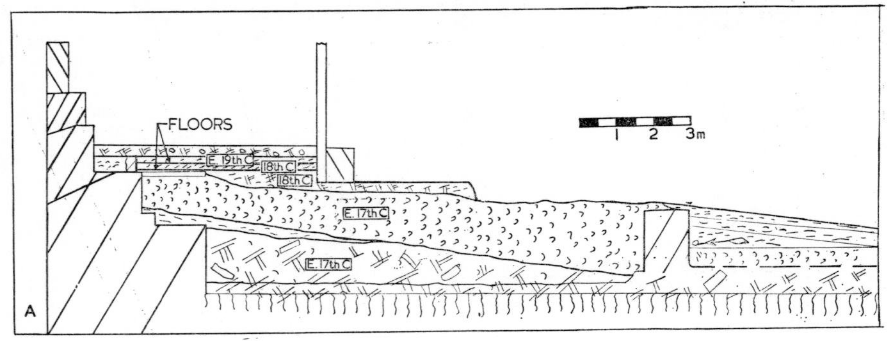

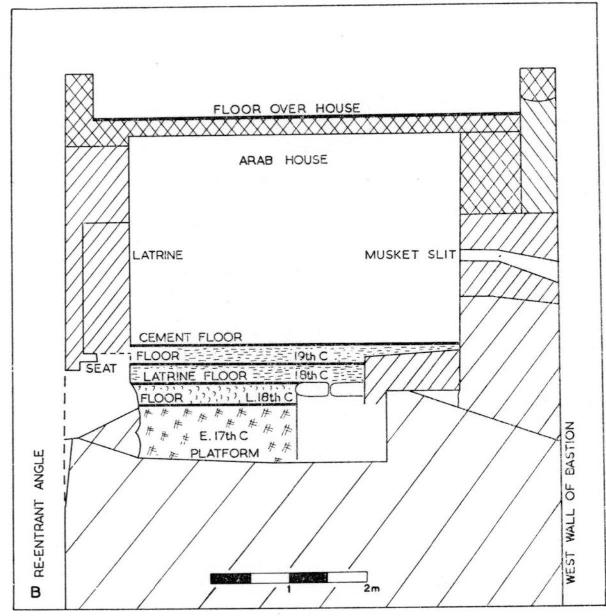

FIG. 18

A. Section south to north across S. Alberto bastion. B. Section across projection of S. Filipe.

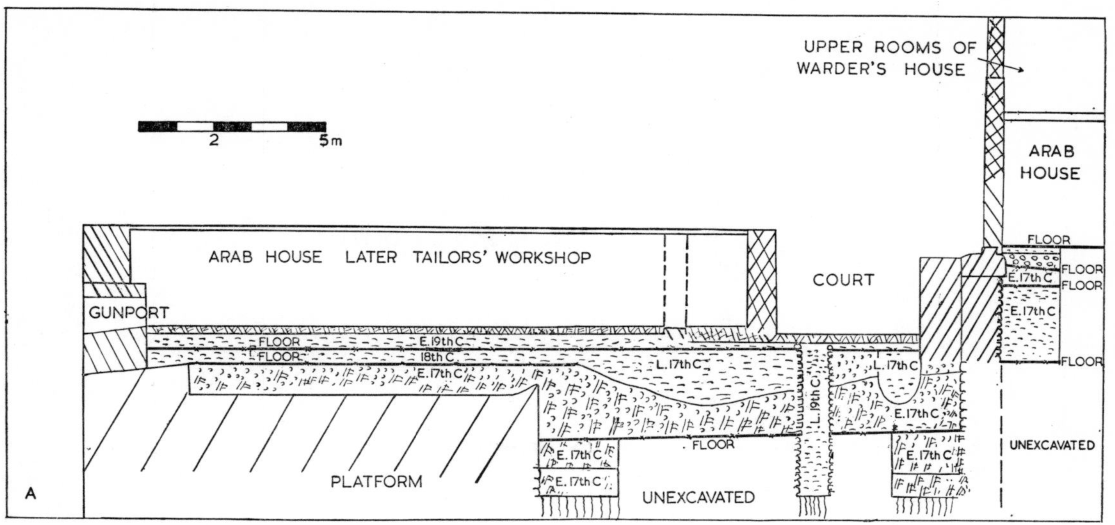

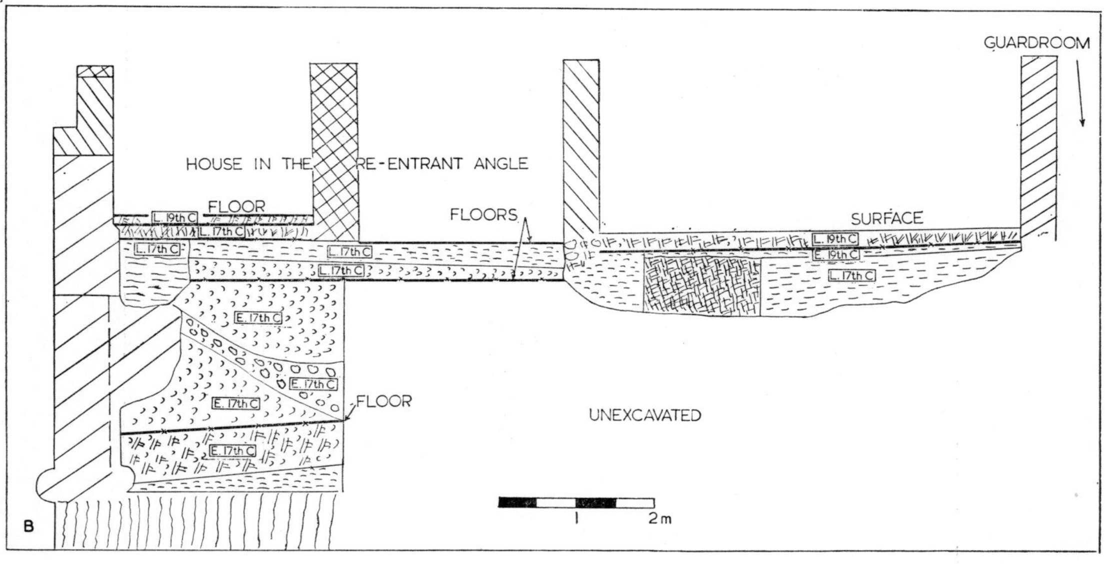

FIG. 19

A. Section south to north through projection of S. Filipe. B. Section against re-entrant angle of S. Filipe.

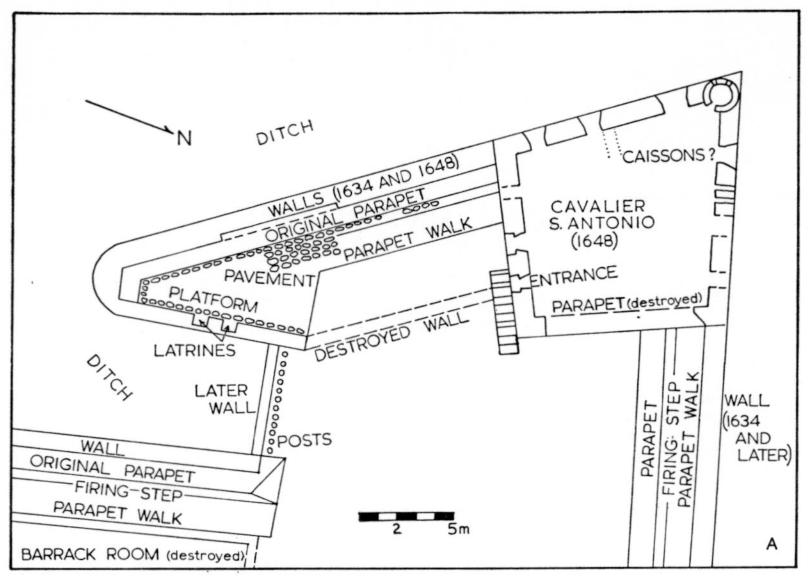

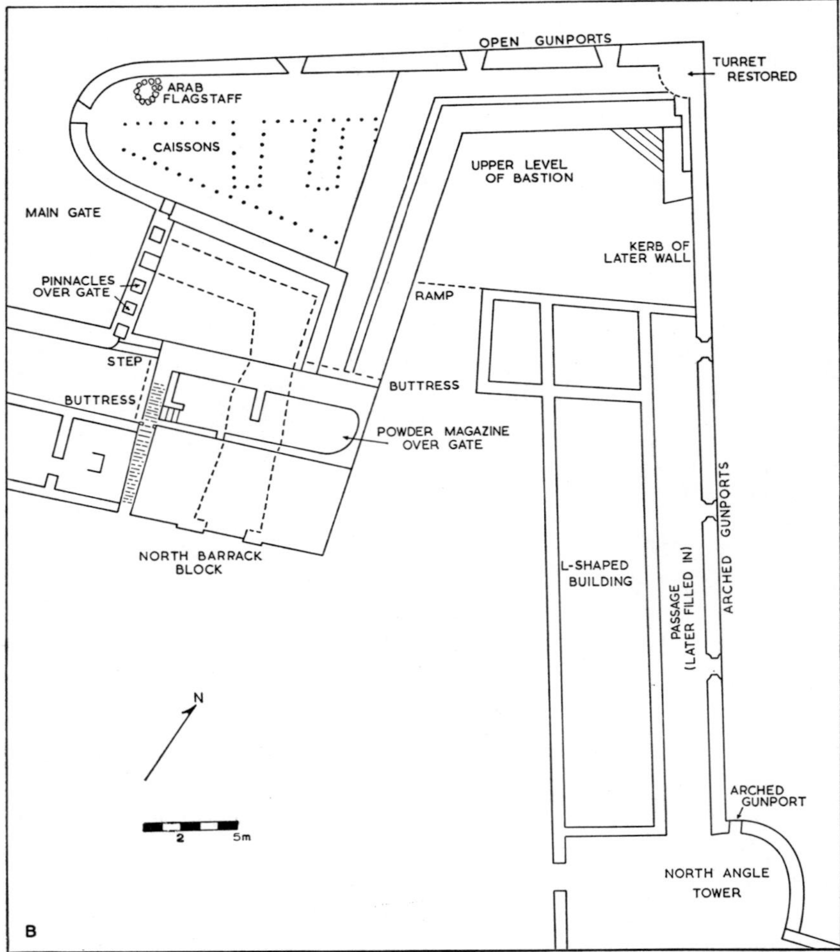

FIG. 20

A. Bastion of S. Filipe and cavalier in Portuguese period. B. S. Matias bastion and main gate in Portuguese period.

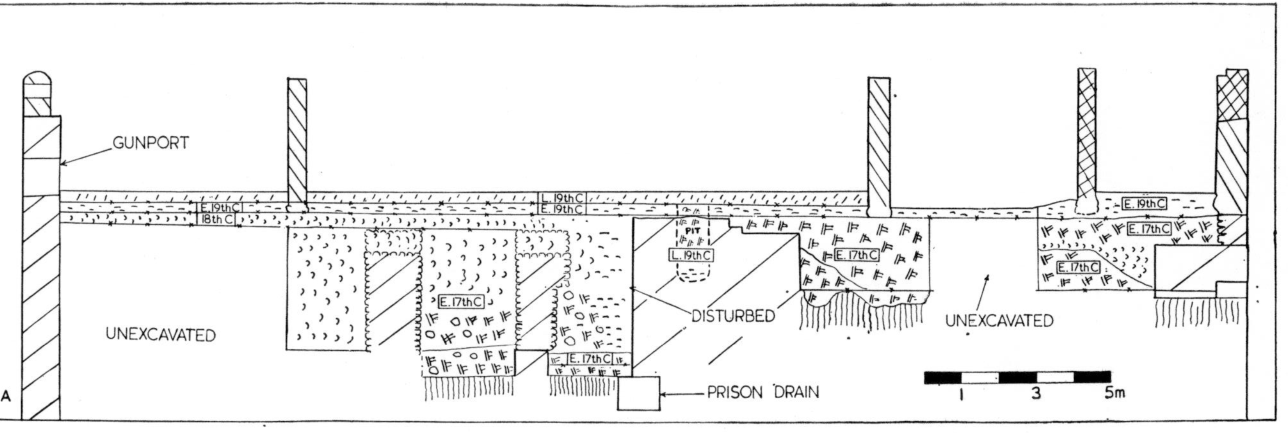

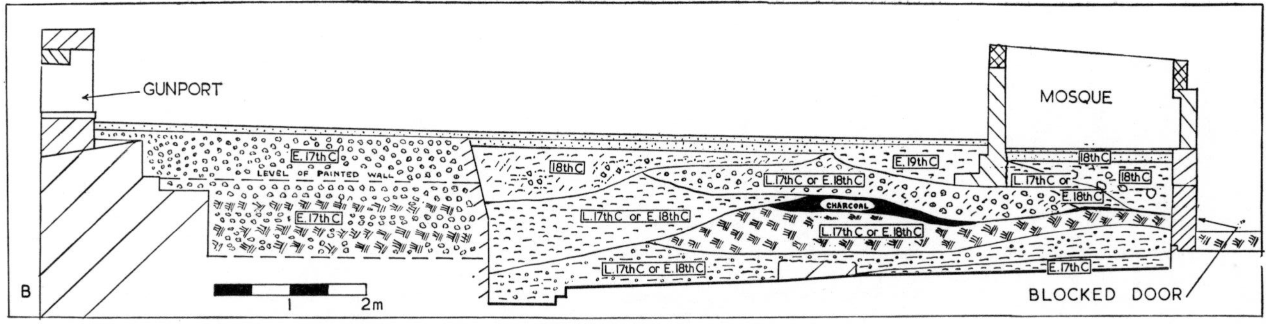

FIG. 21

A. Section west to east across S. Matias bastion. B. Section south to north across S. Mateus bastion.

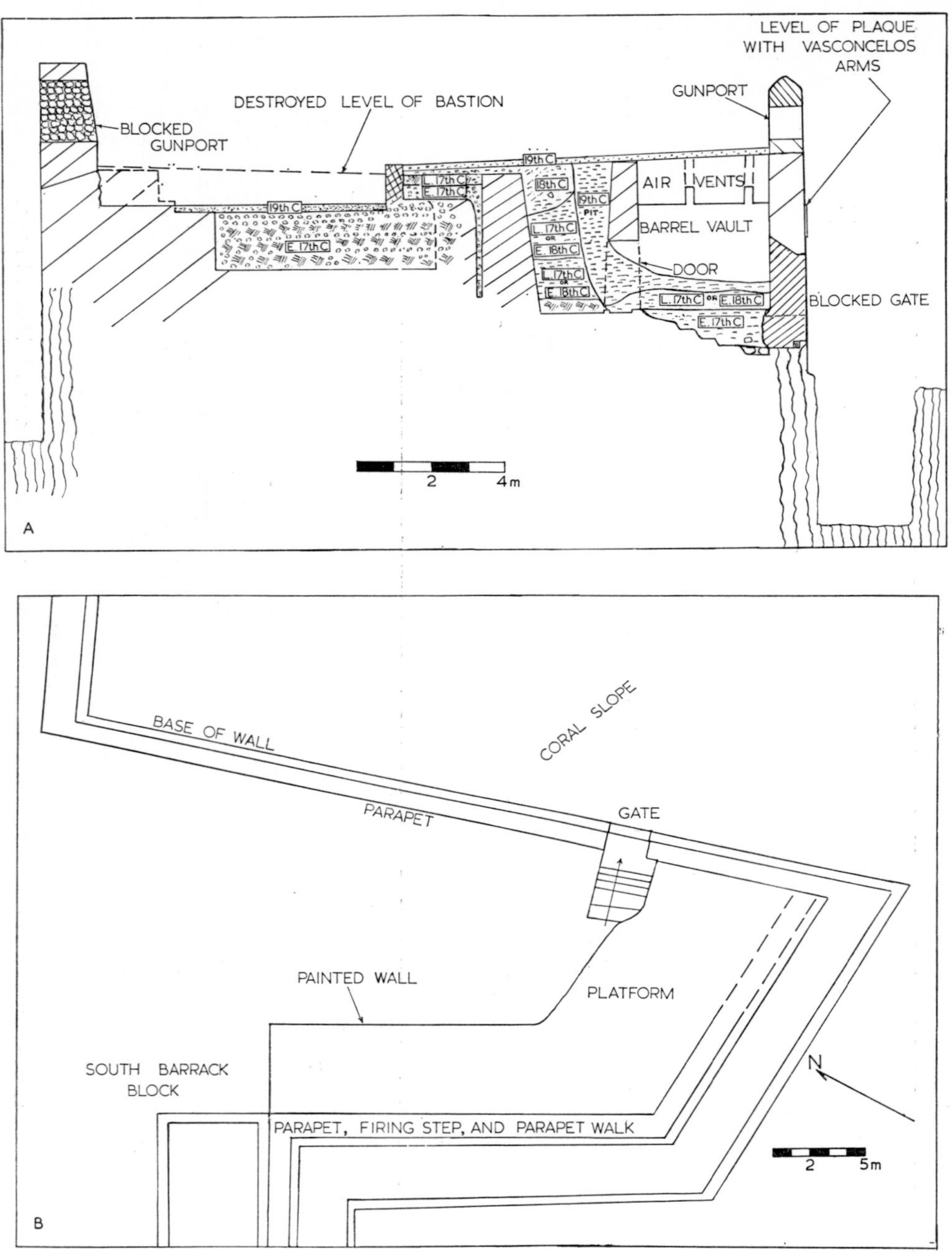

FIG. 22

A. Section west to east across S. Mateus bastion. B. S. Mateus bastion in early Portuguese period.

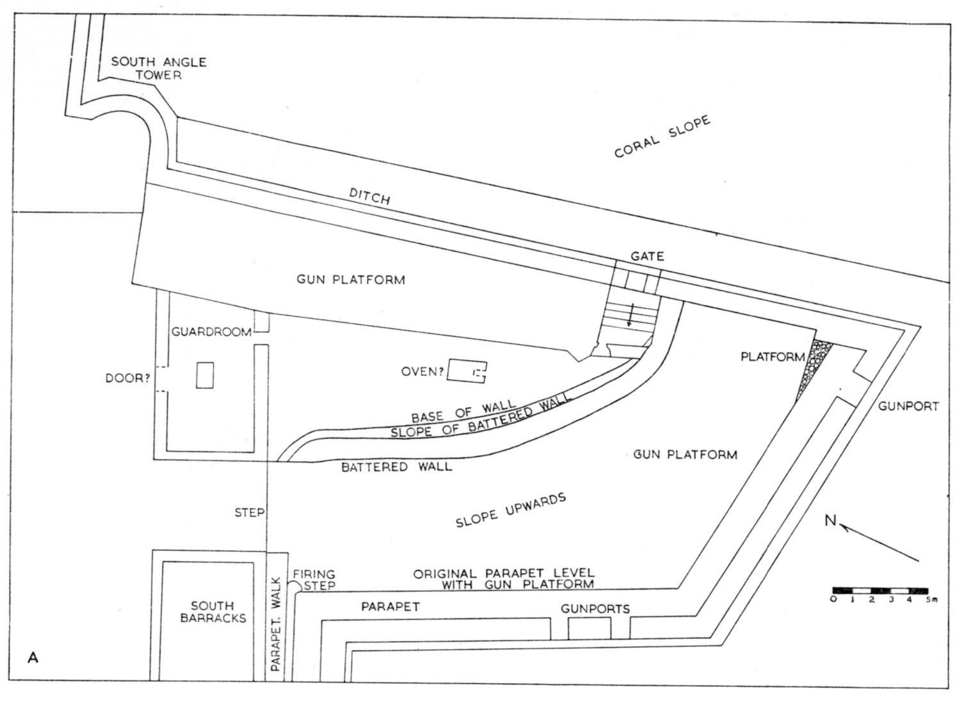

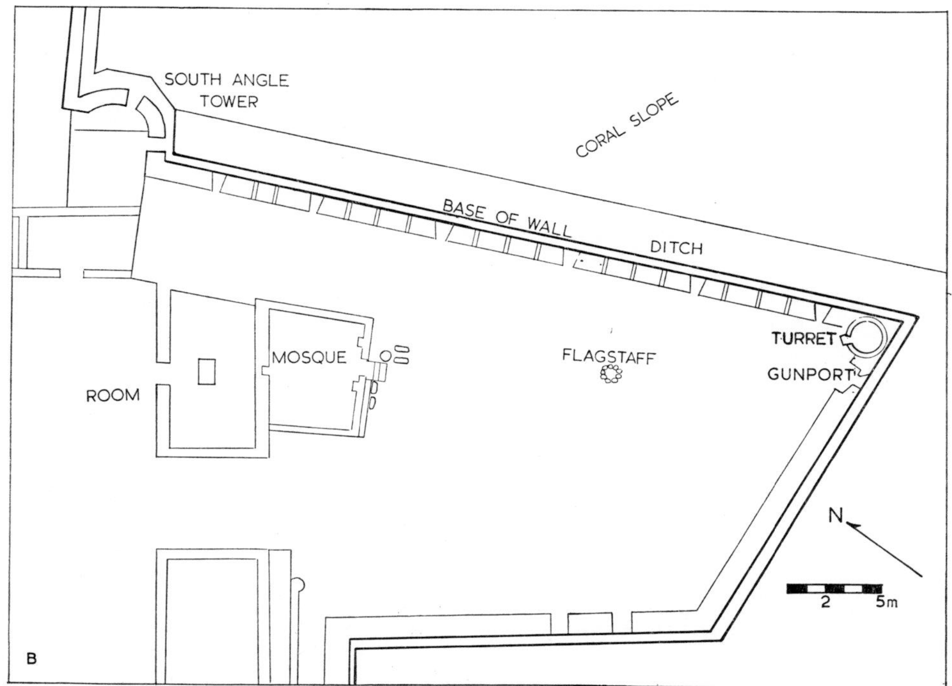

FIG. 23

A. Plan of S. Mateus in later Portuguese period, 1634–98. B. Plan of S. Mateus in Arab period.

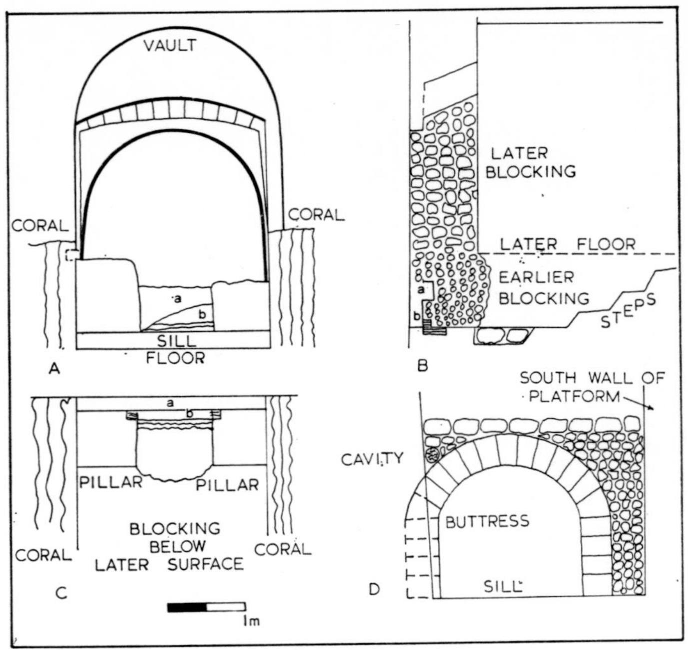

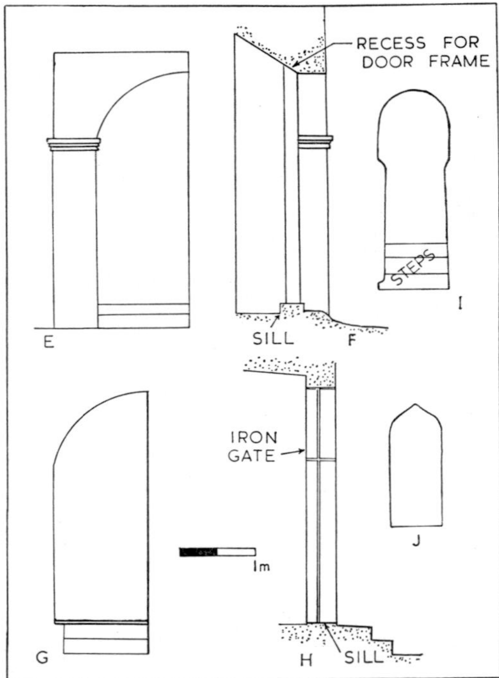

FIG. 24

A, B, C. Elevation, section, and plan of arch in S. Mateus. D. Elevation of arch at bottom of Passage of the Steps. E, F. Elevation and section of outer gate. G, H. Elevation and section of inner gate. I. Doorway over steps to gatehouse. J. Window in upper room of gatehouse.

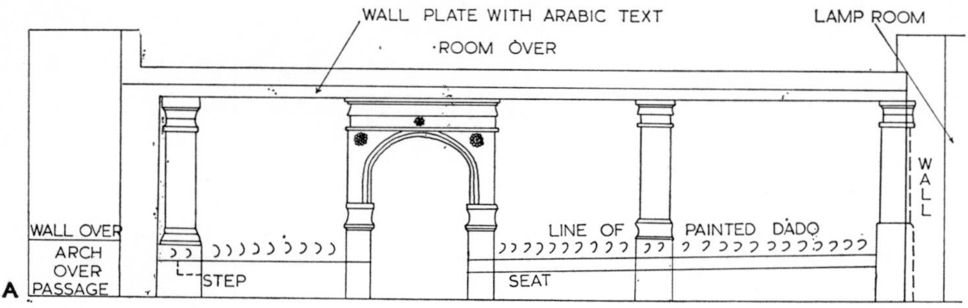

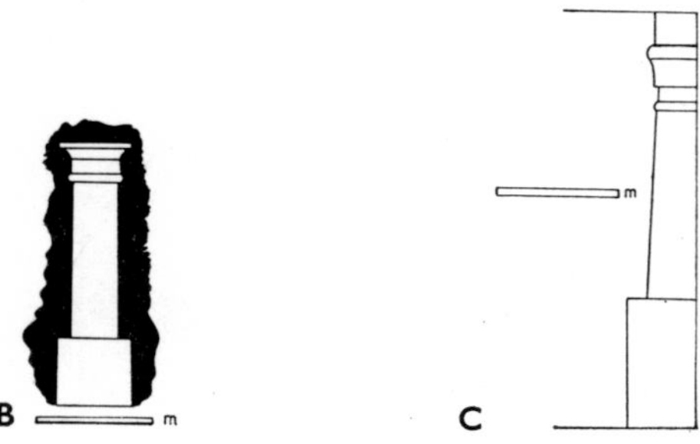

FIG. 25

A. Elevation of east wall of portico of Captain's House. B. Pillar of portico of Captain's House. C. Half pillar at end of inner passage of main gate.

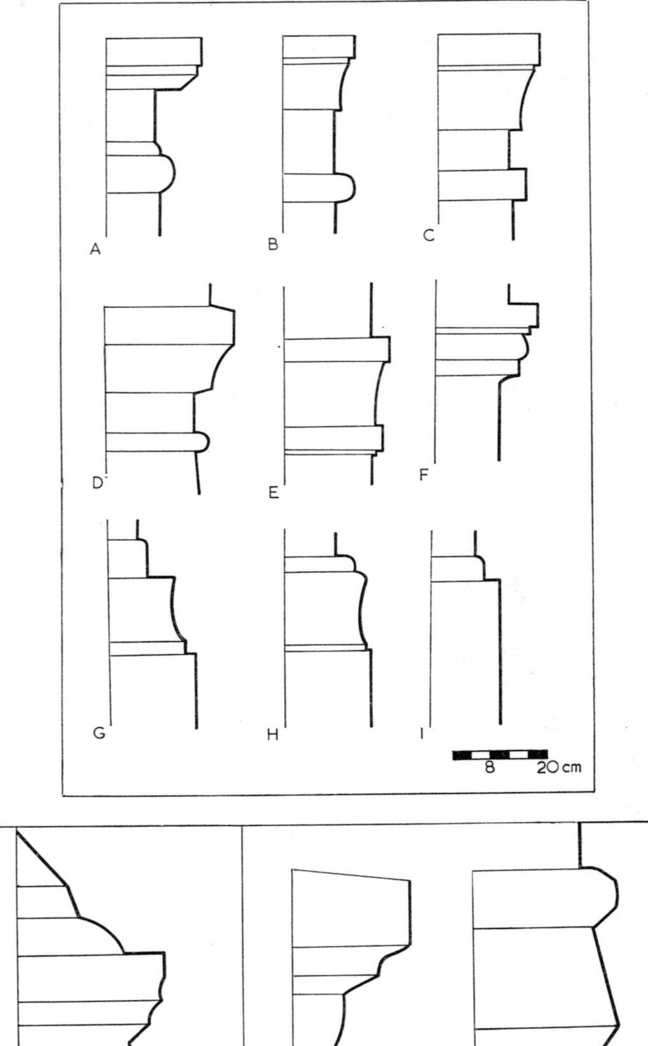

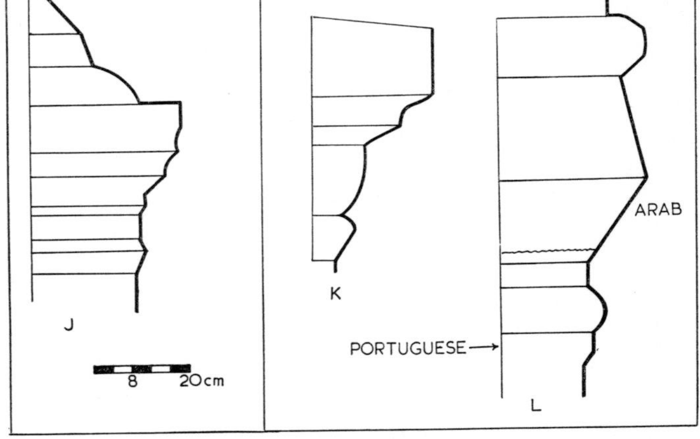

FIG. 26. Portuguese mouldings

Pillars of portico of Captain's House: A, set in west wall; B, of doorway; C, of east wall. D. Pillar of inner passage of main gate. E. Jamb of doorway of portico. F. Pillar of arch of outer gate. G, H, I. Bases of pillars of east wall of portico. J. Turret in cavalier in S. Alberto. K. Turret in cavalier S. António. L. Turret on north curtain.

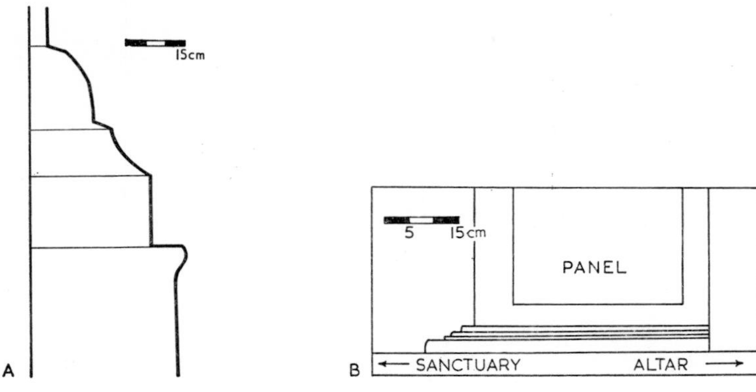

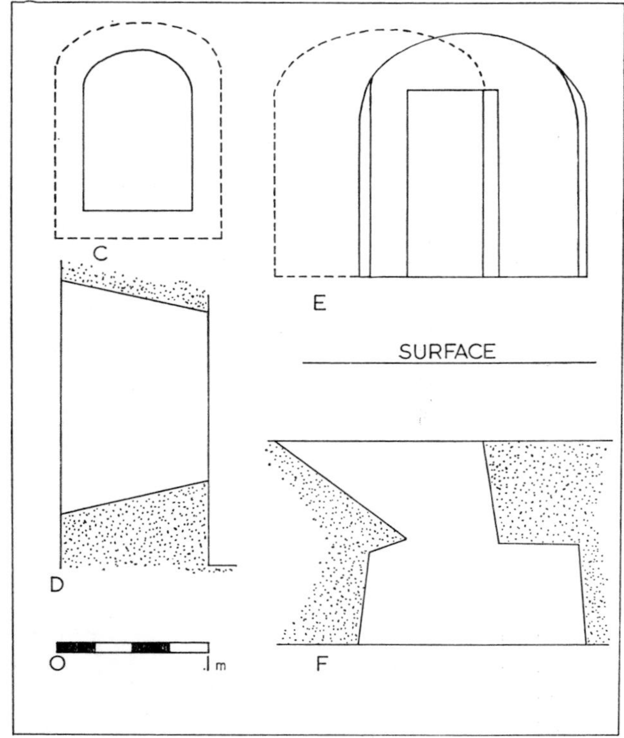

FIG. 27

A. Moulding of pinnacle over outer gate. B. Moulding at base of arch in front of altar in church. C, D. Gun-port in north curtain, 1634. E, F. Gun-port at apex of S. Mateus; angled opening probably Arab.

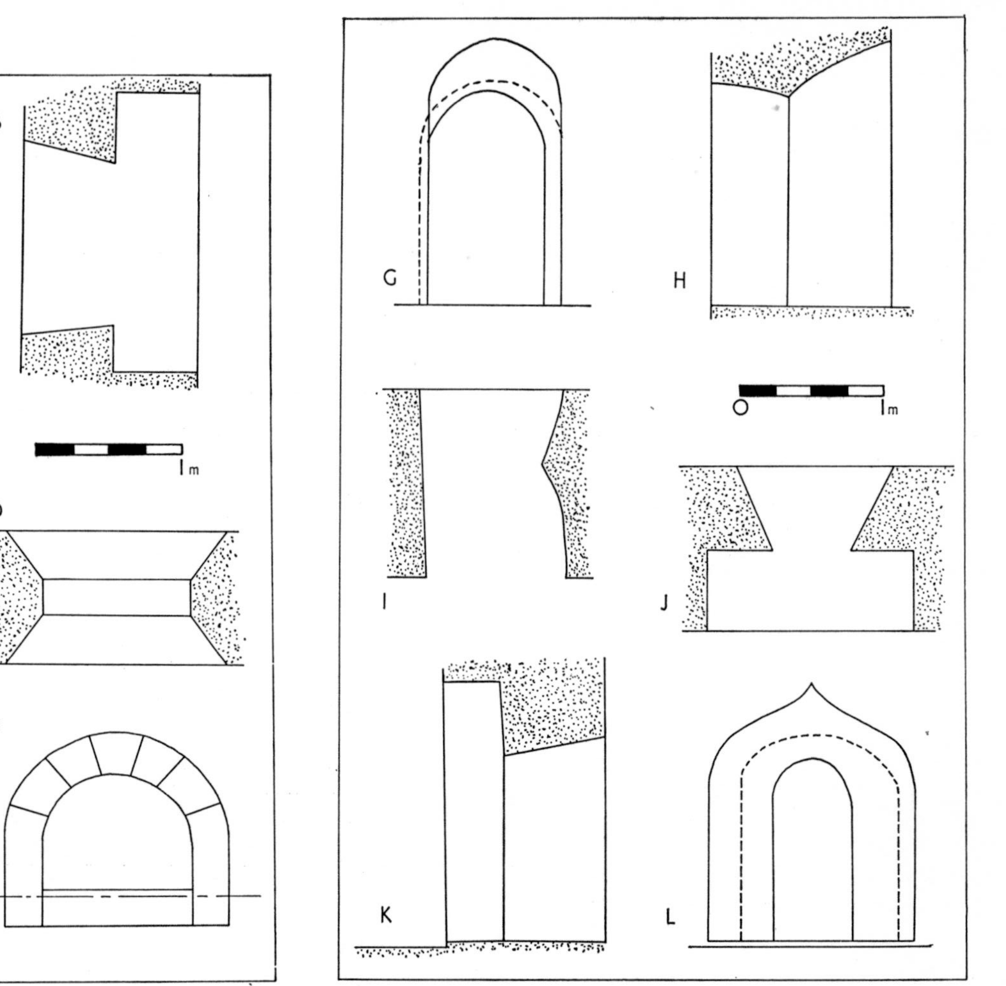

FIG. 28. Elevations, plans, and sections of gunports.

A, B, C, in east wall of S. Filipe, Portuguese. D, E, F, in east wall of S. Matias, Portuguese. G, H, I, in west wall of S. Alberto, Portuguese (?). J, K, L, in outwork, Arab.

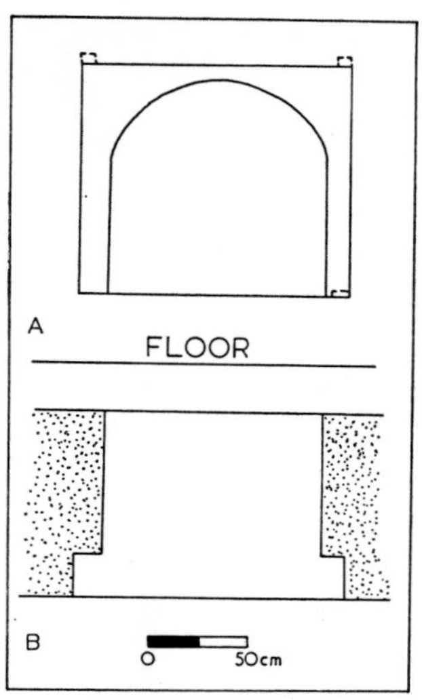

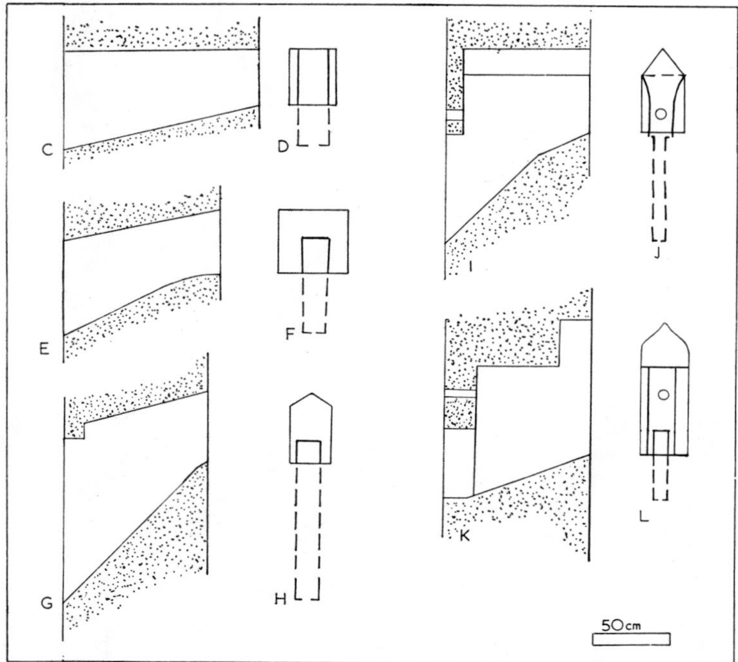

FIG. 29

A, B. Window port in Captain's House. C, D. Portuguese musket-slits, west curtain; E, F. North curtain. G, H. Arab musket-slits, north curtain; I, J. Gun-platform; K, L. S. Mateus.

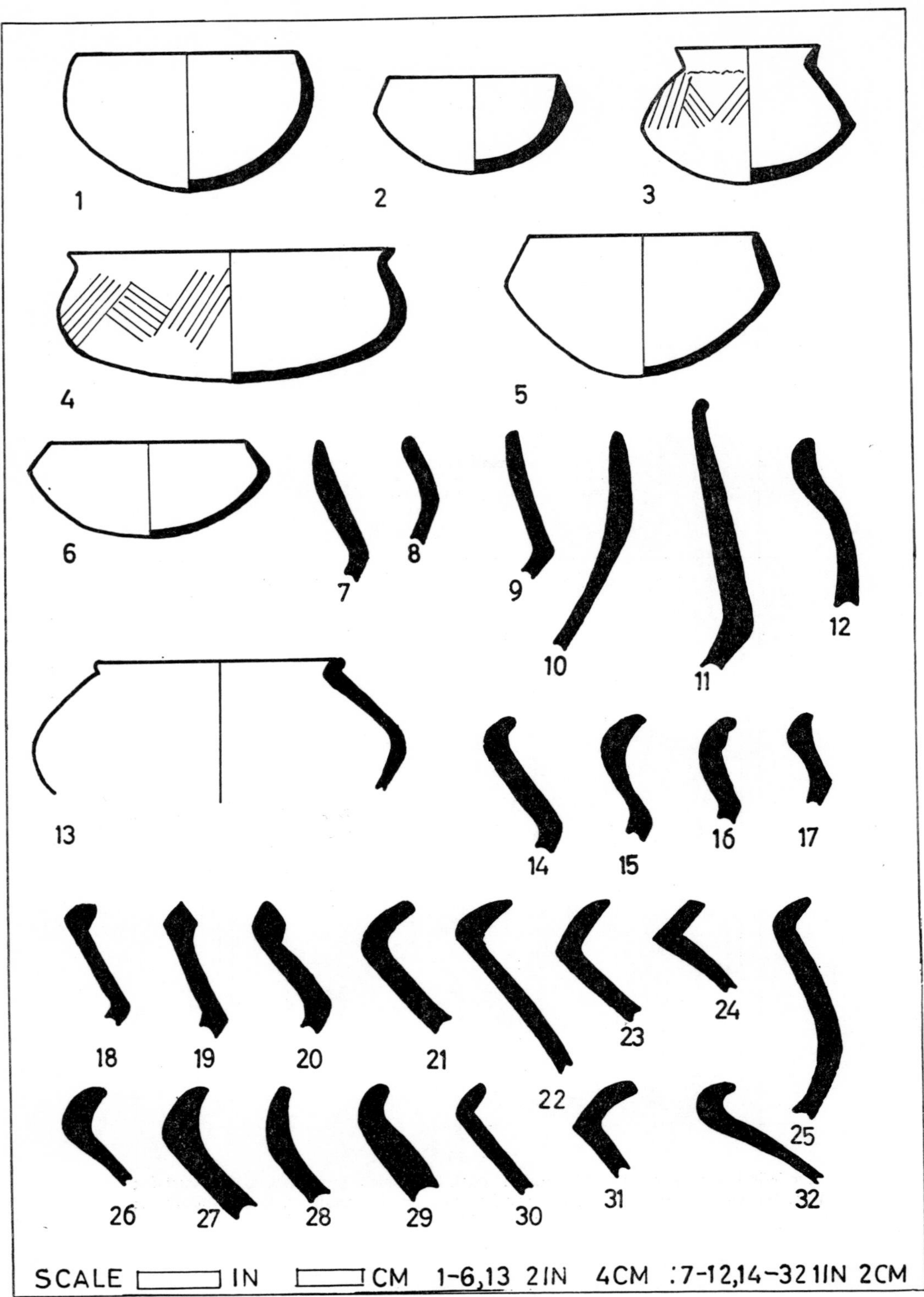
1
2
3
4
5
6
7
8
9
10
11
12
13
14
15
16
17
18
19
20
21
22
23
24
25
26
27
28
29
30
31
32
SCALE IN CM 1-6,13 2IN 4CM :7-12,14-32 1IN 2CM

FIG. 30

Fig. 30. *Fort Jesus. Local Earthenware. Early seventeenth century*

1. Rounded cooking-pot with incurved lip. Common.
2. Thick-sided carinated pot with tapered lip. Single example from filling of S. Mateus.
3. Small carinated pot with turned-out lip and unusual ornament. Single example from filling of S. Matias.
4. Rounded pot with turned-out lip and incised ornament. Single example from filling of S. Matias.

5–10. Carinated pots with straight or slightly convex neck above carination. Common.

11. Carinated pot with long neck, dotted ornament on carination with line above, beading on rim. Single example from filling of S. Mateus.
12. Shouldered pot. Single example from filling of S. Filipe.

13–32. Rounded and carinated pots with prominent everted lip. The common type of early seventeenth-century cooking-pot.

See pages 81–3, 88–9.

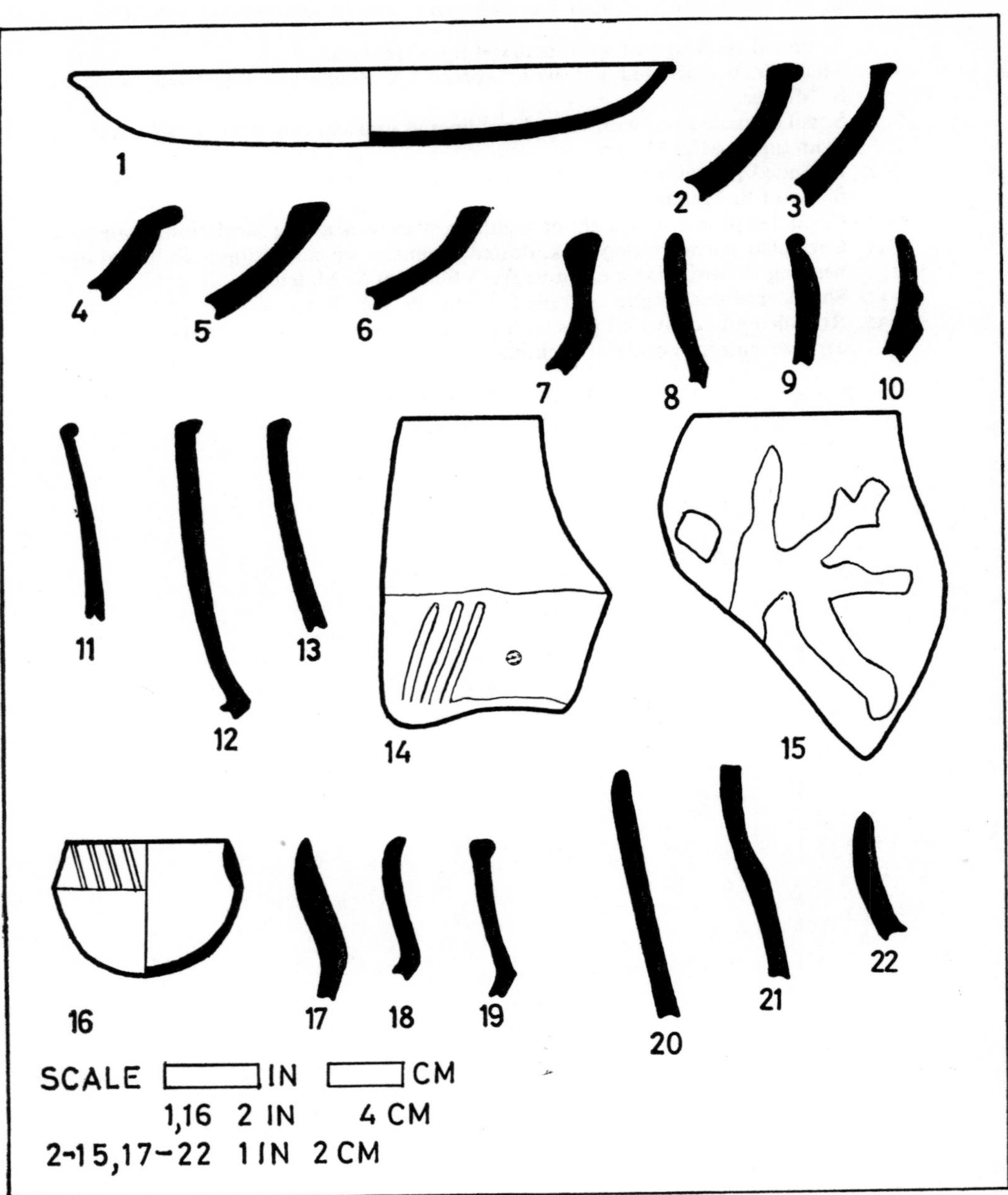
1
2
3
4
5
6
7
8
9
10
11
12
13
14
15
16
17
18
19
20
21
22
SCALE IN CM
1,16 2 IN 4 CM
2-15,17-22 1 IN 2 CM

FIG. 31

Fig. 31. *Fort Jesus. Local earthenware. Early seventeenth century*

1–6. Shallow pots with flat or projecting lip. Another common type of early seventeenth-century cooking-pots.

7. Carinated pot with thickened rim and concave neck. Single example from filling of S. Alberto.

8. Carinated pot with bead rim. Single example from make-up of Cavalier S. António.

9. Rounded pot with bead rim, smooth black surface. Single example from filling of S. Matias.

10. Carinated pot with cordon above and sliced diamond ornament below carination (see Fig. 55, ornament 17), smoothed surface. Single example from lowest level against west parapet walk. A form characteristic of late seventeenth-century levels.

11. Rounded pot with bead rim and rough surface. Single example from filling of S. Matias.

12, 13. Long-necked carinated pots with rough surface, projecting lip, and appliqué ornament like 14 below. Common.

14. Appliqué ornament on pots 12 and 13 above, with red coat above uneven line.

15. Similar pot but with motif in white pipe clay. Single example from filling in S. Filipe.

16–20. Carinated pots with broad red stripes above carination. Common.

21, 22. Shouldered pots with broad stripes above carination. Uncommon.

See pages 81–3, 87–90.

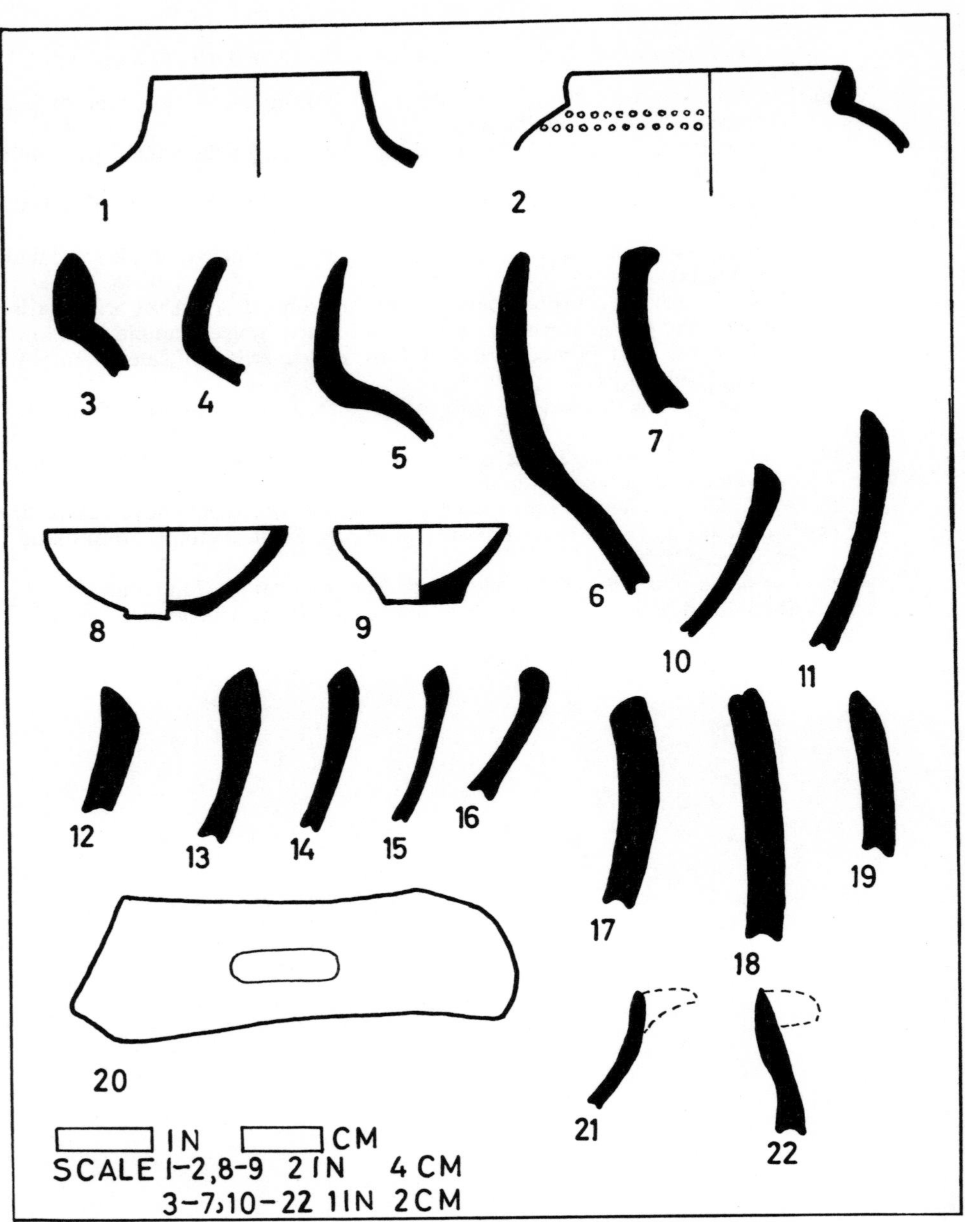
1
2
3
4
5
6
7
8
9
10
11
12
13
14
15
16
17
18
19
20
21
22
IN
CM
SCALE 1-2,8-9 2 IN 4 CM
3-7,10-22 1 IN 2 CM

FIG. 32

Fig. 32. *Fort Jesus. Local earthenware. Early seventeenth century*

1. Jar of thin fabric with vertical neck. Common.

2, 3. Jars with small stout neck like a collar and incised ornament on shoulder. A characteristic early seventeenth-century type.

4–6. Jars with slightly flared neck. The common type of jar in all periods.

7. Similar jar with projecting lip. Single example from filling over Passage of the Steps.

8. Small bowl with ring base, sometimes red on lip. Common.

9. Small bowl with thick flat base. Single example from filling in S. Filipe.

10–12. Bowls with outward sloping lip, sometimes red on lip. Common.

13–15. Bowls with inward sloping lip, sometimes red on lip. Common. These two forms are the characteristic bowl forms of the early seventeenth century.

16. Bowl with incurved lip. An old form, uncommon in these levels, from filling in S. Filipe.

17. Heavy bowl from filling over Passage of the Steps.

18. Similar bowl with serrated outer edge to rim. Single example from filling in S. Filipe.

19. Bowl with pointed lip. Single example from make-up of rectangular projection.

20. Handled bowl. Single example from filling of S. Filipe.

21, 22. Flanged bowls from filling of Passage of the Steps and S. Filipe.

See pages 81–5, 88–9.

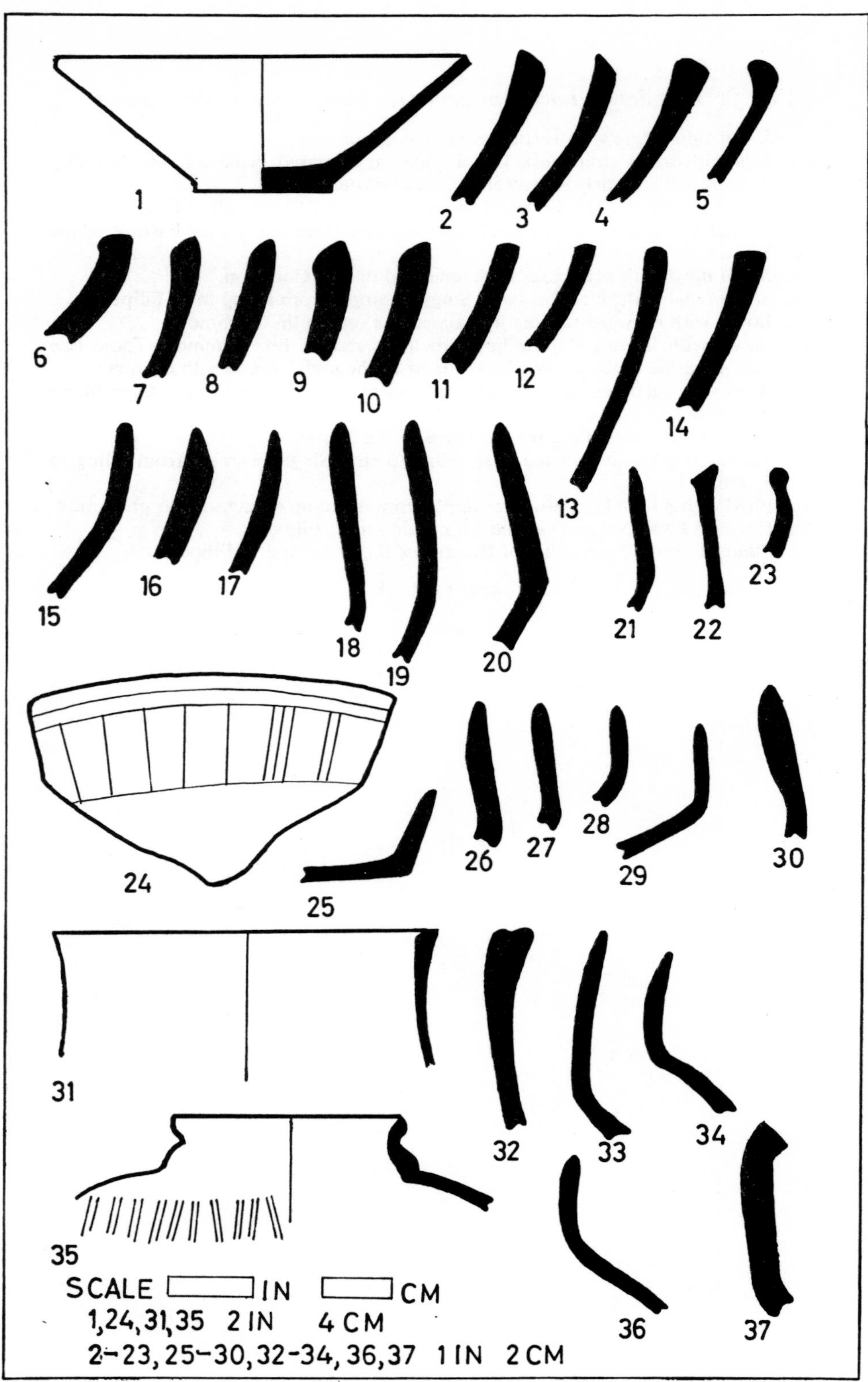
1
2
3
4
5
6
7
8
9
10
11
12
13
14
15
16
17
18
19
20
21
22
23
24
25
26
27
28
29
30
31
32
33
34
35
36
37
SCALE IN CM
1,24,31,35 2 IN 4 CM
2–23, 25–30, 32–34, 36, 37 1 IN 2 CM

FIG. 33

Fig. 33. *Fort Jesus. Local earthenware. Early seventeenth century*

1. Straight-sided bowl with chamfered lip painted and burnished on inside, from make-up of elliptical bastion. Uncommon.

2–17. Bowls similar to Fig. 32. 8–16, but painted red and burnished on inside; 6 with vertical pattern burnishing as 24 below. The characteristic bowl of the early seventeenth century.

18–21. Carinated bowls painted red and burnished on inside. Common.

22. Carinated bowl with flat top to rim and turned-out lip painted red on inside and burnished. Single example from Passage of the Steps.

23. Small shouldered bowl painted red and burnished on inside. Single example from filling of S. Filipe.

24. Pattern burnishing on 6.

25. Platter painted and burnished on inside. Single example from filling in S. Filipe.

26–30. Carinated bowls painted red and burnished above the carination on the outside. A characteristic early seventeenth-century type, commoner than the similar bowls painted on the inside.

31, 32. Jars with long neck and flat top, sometimes grooved, painted red and burnished on outside. Common.

33, 34. Jars with upright or flared neck and tapered lip. Painted red and burnished on outside. Common.

35. Jar with short neck and cordon above shoulder with vertical pattern burnishing, from filling of S. Filipe.

36. Jar with moulded neck burnished on outside. Single example from filling of S. Filipe.

37. Jar with upright neck chamfered on outside, burnished. Single example from filling of S. Filipe.

See pages 81–3, 88.

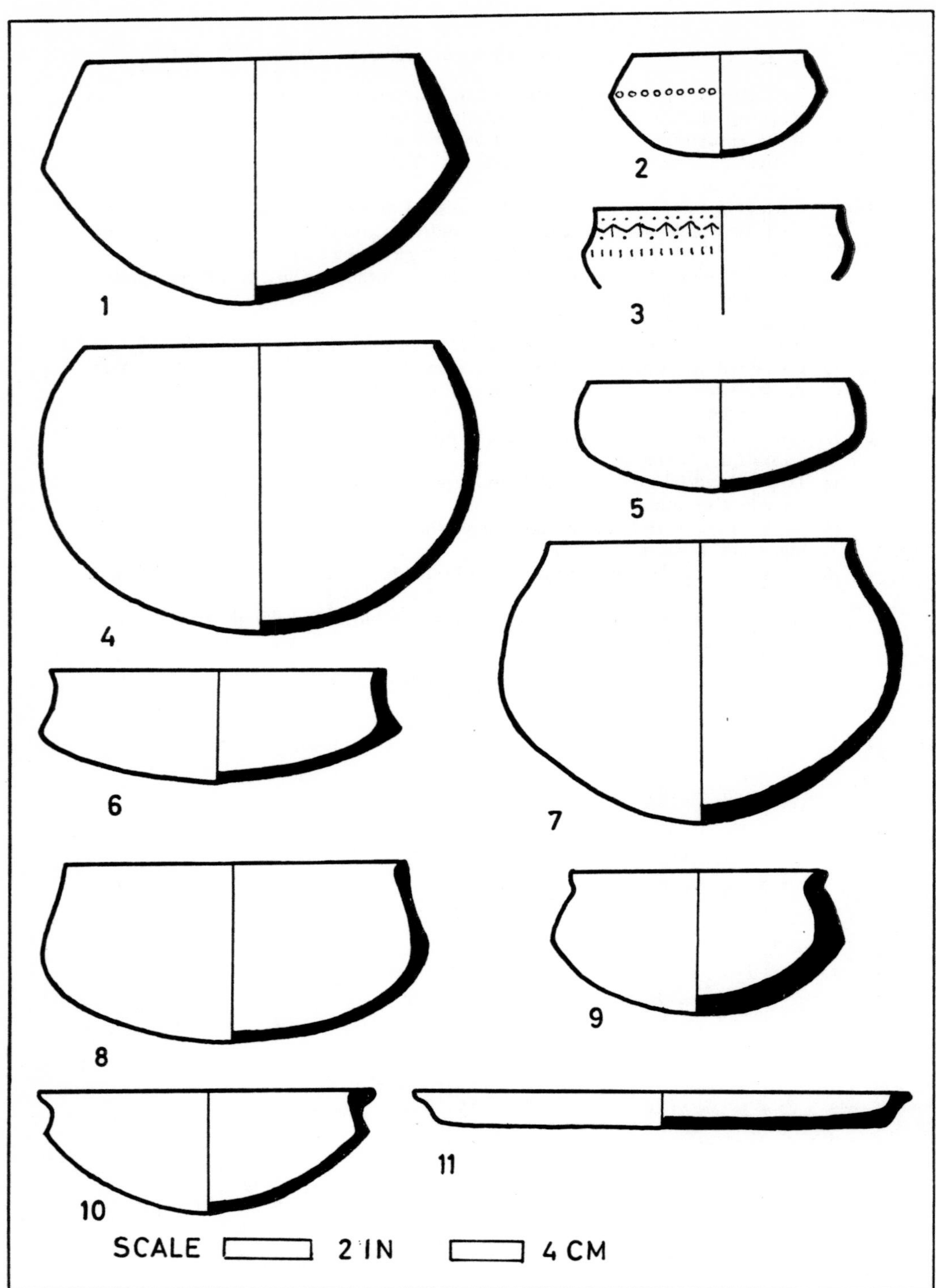

FIG. 34

Fig. 34. *Fort Jesus. Local earthenware. Late seventeenth century*

1. Deep carinated pot with convex neck, from filling of court in S. Mateus. Common.
2. Small carinated pot from gravel pit in S. Filipe. Common traditional form.
3. Small carinated pot with incised ornament 14, from disturbed level beside the well. Common traditional form.
4. Deep rounded pot with incurved lip. Common.
5. Shallow rounded pot with incurved lip. Common.
6. Shallow carinated pot with concave neck, from gravel pit in S. Filipe.
7. Deep shouldered pot with red rim. Common.
8. Shouldered pot. Common.
9. Carinated pot with thick fabric and turned-out lip, from gravel pit in S. Filipe. Uncommon.
10. Carinated pot with projecting lip and short neck, from gravel pit in S. Filipe. Uncommon.
11. Shallow pot with projecting lip, similar to Fig. 31. 1–6. Common.

See pages 81–3, 88–90.

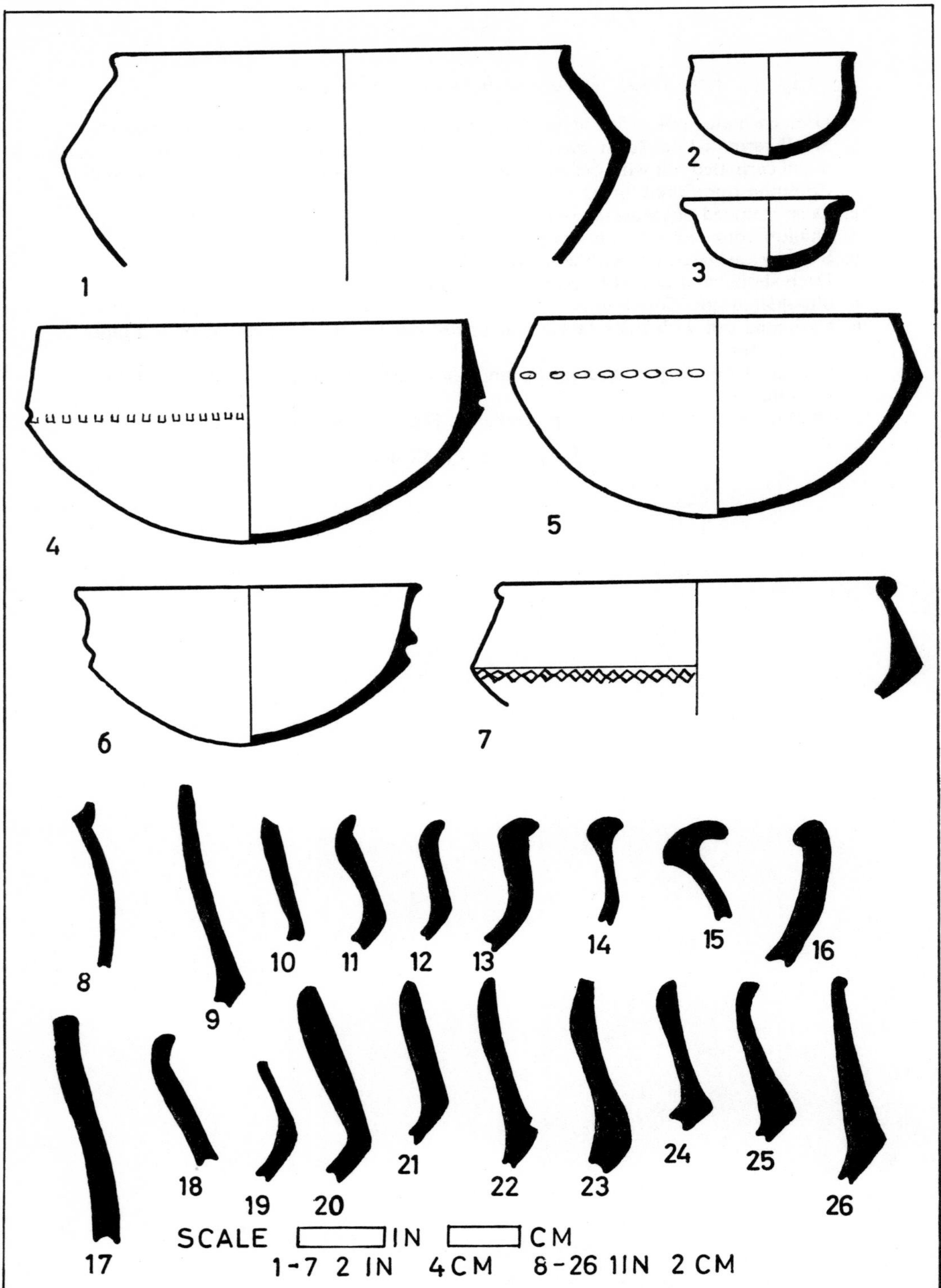
1
2
3
4
5
6
7
8
9
10
11
12
13
14
15
16
17
18
19
20
21
22
23
24
25
26
SCALE IN CM
1-7 2 IN 4 CM 8-26 1 IN 2 CM

FIG. 35

Fig. 35. *Fort Jesus. Local earthenware. Late seventeenth century*

1. Large carinated pot with undulating neck and turned-out lip, related to the pots with appliqué ornament. Common.
2. Small rounded pot with turned-out lip. Common.
3. Small rounded pot with projecting lip. Single example from level in S. Alberto.
4. Carinated pot with smooth black surface and upright neck with indentations above and ornament on carination, from filling of the court in S. Mateus.
5. Carinated pot with smooth black surface, incised line below rim and indentations on carination, from filling of room south of the room of the stands against the west parapet.
6. Pot with carved cordon ornament and smooth black surface, similar to Fig. 31. 10, from second floor of room of the stands.
7. Carinated pot with smooth black surface and rolled rim, diamond ornament on carination, from filling of court in S. Mateus. Single example of this type.
8. Thin-bodied pot similar to Fig. 30. 3, with incised ornament 3 and turned-out red lip, from pit in S. Filipe.
9. Carinated pot with long slightly concave neck, from pit in S. Filipe.
10. Carinated pot with gable-shaped rim. Single example from room of the stands.
11. Carinated pot with turned-out lip. Common.
12. Carinated pot with turned-out lip, from pit in S. Filipe. Uncommon.

13, 14. Rounded pots with projecting lip. Common.

15. Incurved pot with projecting and undercut lip. Single example from pit in S. Filipe.
16. Rounded pot with internal roll rim like Fig. 33. 6 and puckered ornament below rim, from pit in S. Filipe. Uncommon.
17. Shouldered pot from S. Filipe. Uncommon in these levels.
18. Shouldered pot from pit in S. Filipe. Uncommon in these levels.
19. Carinated pot with smooth surface, sometimes painted red above ornamented carination, from pit in S. Filipe. Uncommon.

20–2. Carinated pots, sometimes painted red above carination, from pit in S. Filipe. Common.

23. Carinated pot, painted red above carination, from room of the stands. Common.
24. Carinated pot, red above carination, from pit in S. Filipe. Uncommon.
25. Carinated pot with turned-out lip, red above carination, ornament 27 above and below carination. Single example from pit in S. Filipe.
26. Carinated pot with bead rim, smooth black surface or painted red above carination, from pit in S. Filipe. Uncommon.

See pages 81–3, 88–90.

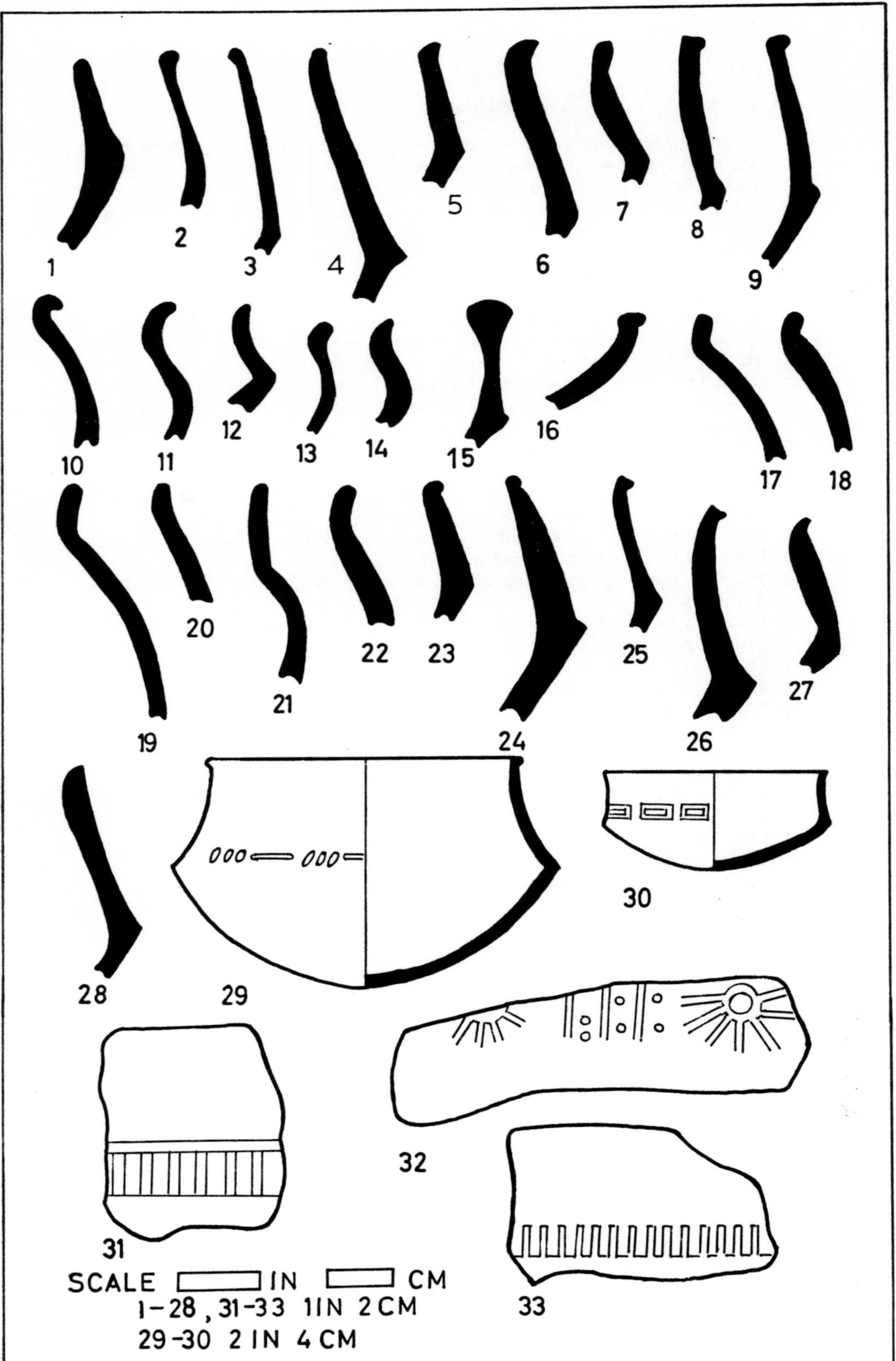
1
2
3
4
5
6
7
8
9
10
11
12
13
14
15
16
17
18
19
20
21
22
23
24
25
26
27
28
29
30
31
32
33
SCALE IN CM
1-28, 31-33 1IN 2CM
29-30 2 IN 4 CM

FIG. 36

Fig. 36. *Fort Jesus. Local earthenware. Late seventeenth century*

1. Carinated pot, ornamented on carination, from court in S. Mateus. Common.
2. Rounded pot with turned-out lip, from court in S. Mateus. Uncommon.
3. Carinated pot with inturned lip. Single example from court in S. Mateus.
4. Carinated pot with sharp carination, from court in S. Mateus. Uncommon.

5, 6. Carinated pots with turned-out lip, from filling of Captain's House. Common.

7. Carinated pot with turned-out lip, from court in S. Mateus. Common.
8. Carinated pot with flat top and projecting lip, from court in S. Mateus. Uncommon.
9. Carinated pot with bead rim, projecting carination, from court in S. Mateus. Uncommon.
10. Rounded pot with curled lip. Single example from court in S. Mateus.

11, 12. Rounded and carinated pots with deep concave or swan neck, from court in S. Mateus. Uncommon in this period.

13, 14. Small rounded pots with turned-out lip, from bottom of Passage of the Arches. Uncommon.

15. Carinated pot with thickened lip and carination resembling imported pots (Figs. 58–60), from filling of Captain's House.
16. Shallow pots, like Fig. 31. 1–6, from court in S. Mateus. Common.

17–21. Rounded and shouldered pots, sometimes painted red below rim, from court in S. Mateus. Common.

22. Shouldered pot with indented ornament, from bottom of Passage of the Arches. Uncommon.
23. Carinated pot with smooth black surface, convex neck, and bead rim, from court In S. Mateus. Uncommon.
24. Carinated pot with smooth black surface, convex neck, and bead rim, from court in S. Mateus. Uncommon.
25. Carinated pot with smooth black surface and chamfered lip, from court in S. Mateus. Uncommon.
26. Carinated pot with concave neck and chamfered rim, painted red above carination, from court in S. Mateus. Uncommon.
27. Carinated pot with turned-out lip and convex neck, red above carination, from bottom of Passage of the Arches. Uncommon.
28. Carinated pot with concave neck with red above carination, from court in S. Mateus. Common.

29, 30. Carinated pots with long neck and appliqué ornament, from pit in S. Filipe (see also Pl. 19. 1–3). Common.

31–3. Appliqué ornament of carinated pots, from pit in S. Filipe and main court.

See pages 81–3, 88–9.

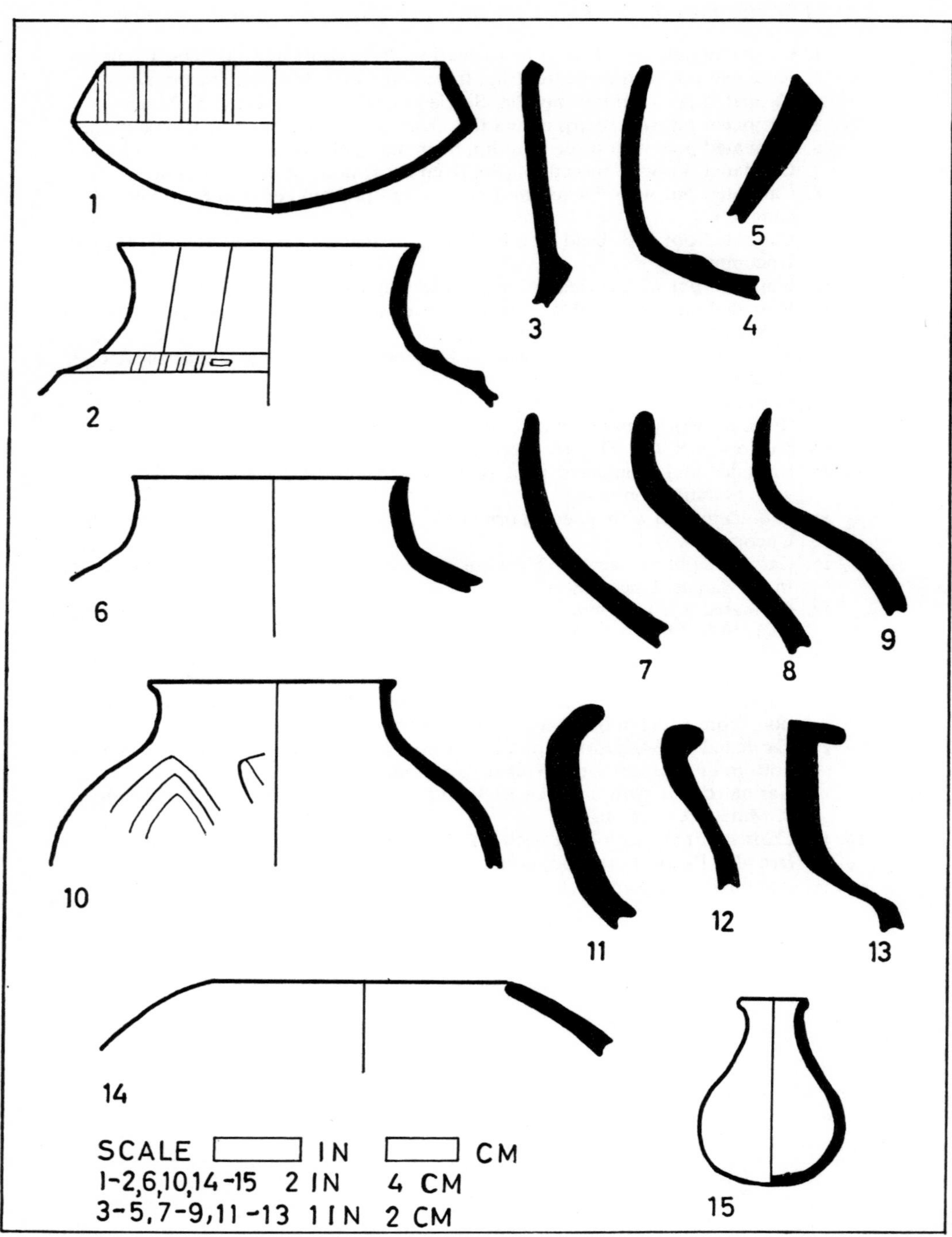

1
2
3
4
5
6
7
8
9
10
11
12
13
14
15
SCALE IN CM
1-2,6,10,14-15 2 IN 4 CM
3-5,7-9,11-13 1 IN 2 CM

FIG. 37

Fig. 37. *Fort Jesus. Local earthenware. Late seventeenth century*

1. Carinated pot with red-striped decoration, from court in S. Mateus. Uncommon.
2. Jar with long neck and striped and appliqué ornament, from court in S. Mateus. Uncommon.
3. Carinated pot with long flared neck, turned-out lip, rough surface similar to the appliqué wares, and projecting carination, from court in S. Mateus. Uncommon.
4. Jar with flared neck, similar to 2, from court in S. Mateus.
5. Bowl with outward sloping lip and striped decoration, from court in S. Mateus. Uncommon.

6, 7. Jars with flared neck, from pit in S. Filipe. Common.

8. Similar jar from court in S. Mateus. Common.
9. Jar with flared neck, thin fabric, from pit in S. Filipe. Common.
10. Jar with projecting lip, incised ornament on side, from pit in S. Filipe. Uncommon.
11. Jar with turned-out lip, from pit in S. Filipe. Common.
12. Jar with thickened lip and incised triple chevron, from pit in S. Filipe. Single specimen.
13. Jar with projecting lip, from S. Filipe.
14. Jar with wide mouth, without neck or lip, red around rim, from pit in S. Filipe. Uncommon.
15. Bottle with bag-shaped body, from area between church and cistern. Single specimen.

See pages 81–3, 87–90.

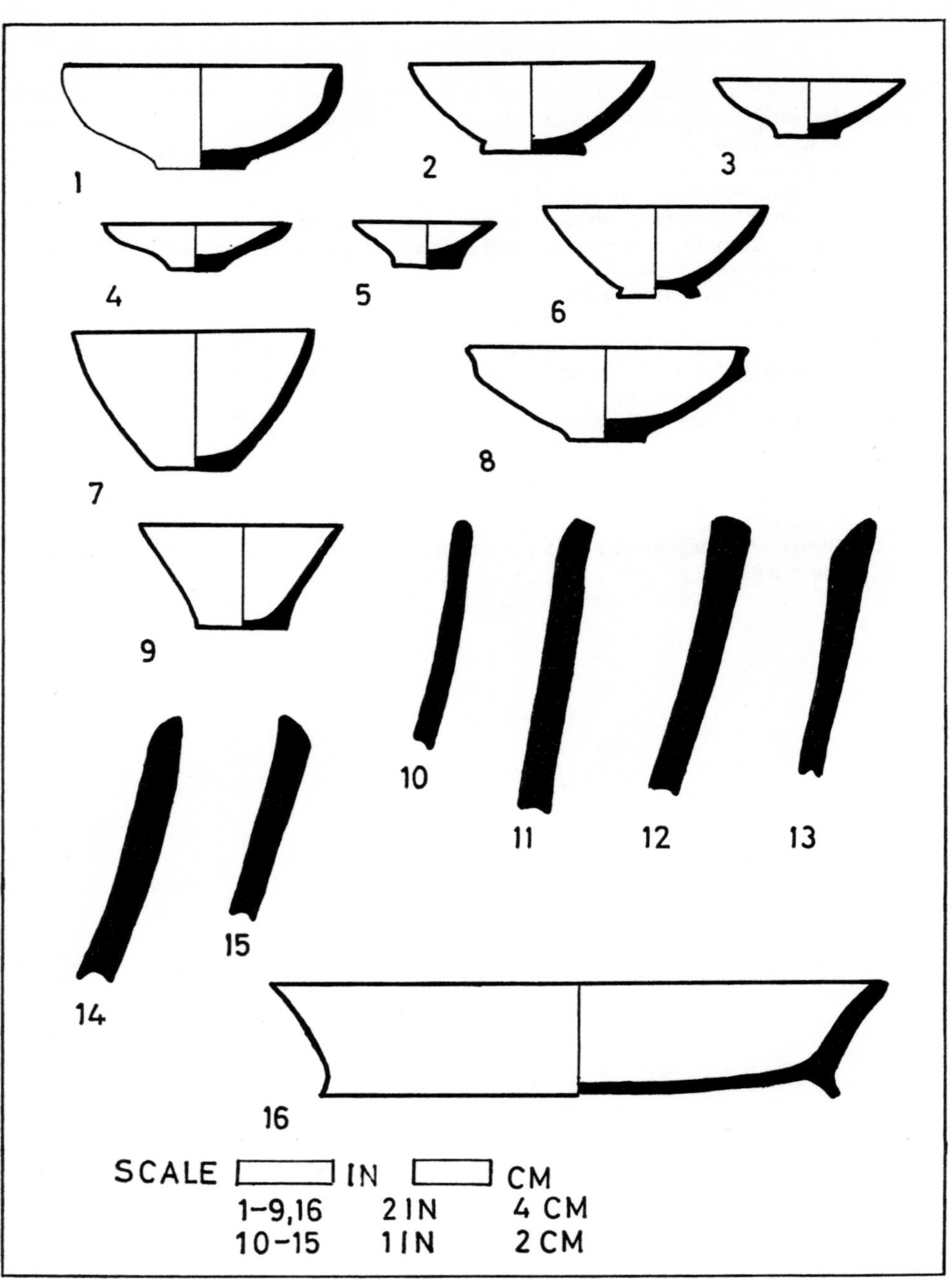
1
2
3
4
5
6
7
8
9
10
11
12
13
14
15
16
SCALE IN CM
1–9,16 2 IN 4 CM
10–15 1 IN 2 CM

FIG. 38

Fig. 38. *Fort Jesus. Local earthenware. Late seventeenth century*

1. Carinated bowl with lip of early seventeenth-century type and disk base, often burnished. Common.

2–5. Bowls with tapered lip and disk base, often burnished. Common.

6. Bowl with ring base, from main court. Common.

7. Tall bowl with flat base, from filling of court in S. Mateus. Common.

8. Carinated bowl with projecting lip similar to the shallow bowls of Fig. 31. 1–6, from room of the stands. Uncommon.

9. Tall flared bowl from filling of the court in S. Mateus. Uncommon.

10–15. Large bowls with various lips. Common.

16. Large shallow bowl with spread-ring base. Single example from pit in S. Filipe.

See pages 81–3, 88–9.

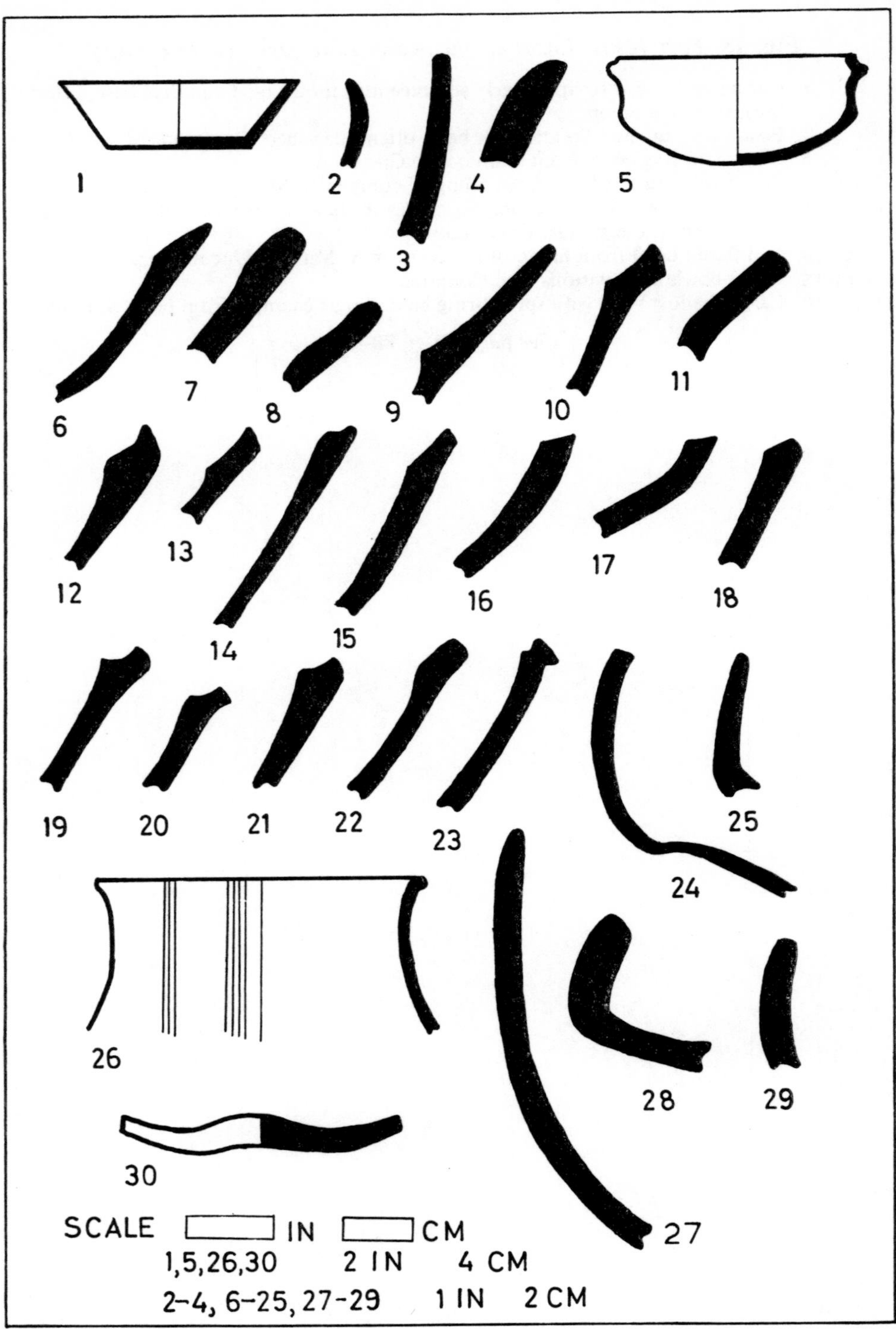
1
2
3
4
5
6
7
8
9
10
11
12
13
14
15
16
17
18
19
20
21
22
23
24
25
26
27
28
29
30
SCALE IN CM
1,5,26,30 2 IN 4 CM
2–4, 6–25, 27–29 1 IN 2 CM

FIG. 39

Fig. 39. *Fort Jesus. Local earthenware. Late seventeenth century*

1. Burnished straight-sided bowl with flat base, from filling in S. Mateus. Uncommon.
2. Small burnished bowl from S. Mateus. Uncommon.
3. Upright burnished bowl from S. Mateus. Uncommon.
4. Large burnished bowl with inward-sloping lip, from S. Mateus. Uncommon.
5. Small bowl with moulded lip and rounded base. Single example from room of the stands.

6–10. Wide-mouthed burnished bowls with flat inward-sloping lip, sometimes grooved. The characteristic burnished bowl of the late seventeenth and eighteenth century.

11–13. Similar bowls from main court. Uncommon.

14. Similar bowl from pit in S. Matias. Uncommon.

15. Similar bowl from filling of Captain's House. Common.

16–22. Similar bowls from S. Mateus. 21 and 22 single examples.

23. Bowl with red lip, from court in S. Mateus. Single example.

24, 25. Burnished jars with flared neck, from filling of court in S. Mateus. Common.

26. Jar with projecting lip and vertical pattern burnishing. Single example from pit in S. Filipe.

27. Large burnished jar with tall vertical neck. Single example from pit in S. Filipe.

28. Burnished jar with short thick neck, from filling of Captain's House. Uncommon.

29. Burnished jar with short neck, from court in S. Mateus. Uncommon.

30. Lid with turned-up rim, from S. Filipe. Uncommon.

See pages 81–3, 88–9.

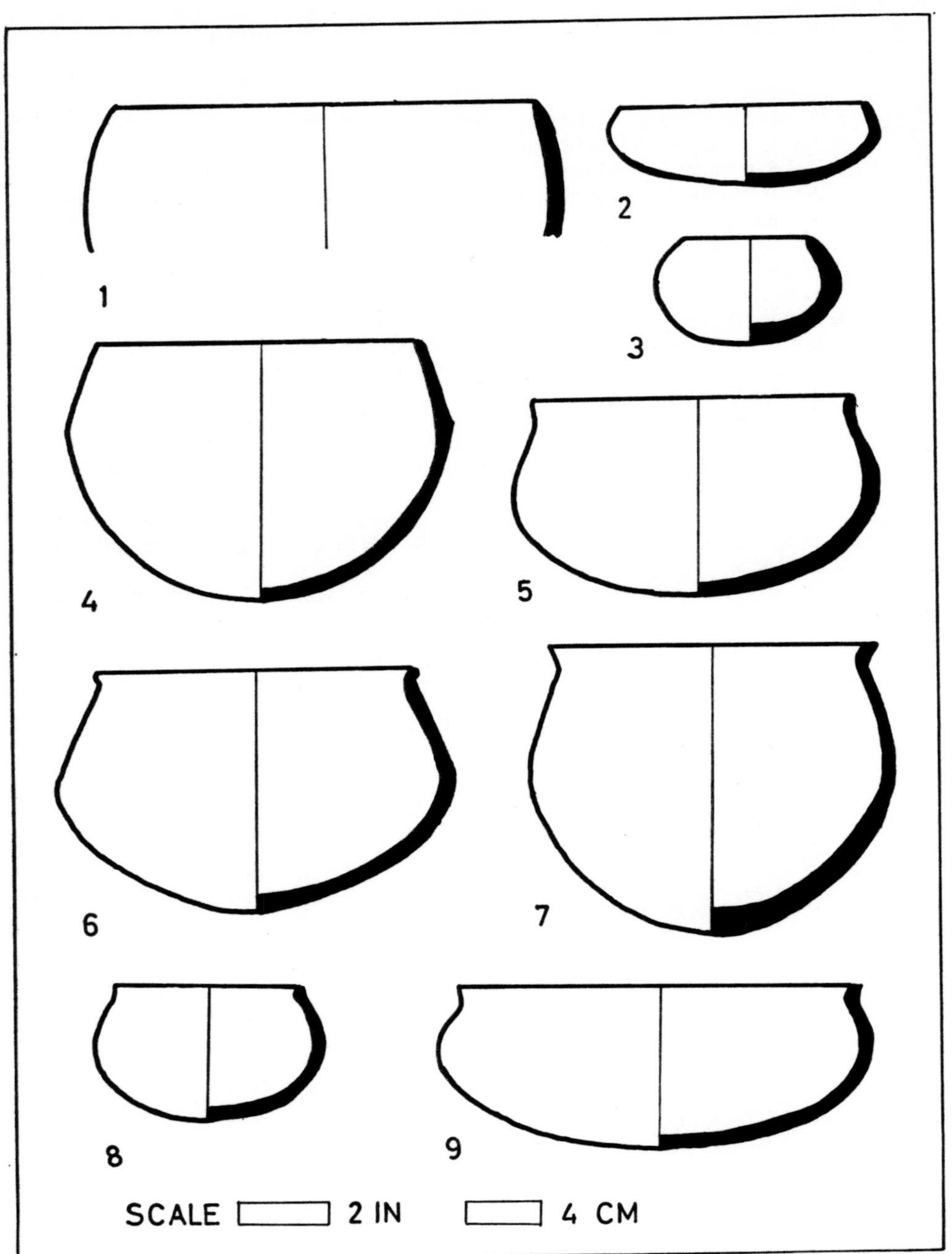

FIG. 40

Fig. 40. *Fort Jesus. Local earthenware. Eighteenth century*

1. Deep, rounded pot from main court. Common.
2. Shallow pot with incurved lip, from north court outside Captain's House. Common.
3. Small thick-sided pot with incurved lip, from north court outside Captain's House. Common.
4. Deep, rounded pot with convex neck above carination and inward chamfered lip, from S. Alberto. Uncommon.
5. Shouldered pot, often painted red on outside of lip. Common.
6. Deep, rounded pot with bead rim, from area of Captain's House. Uncommon.
7. Deep, rounded pot with turned-out lip, from area of Captain's House. Common.
8. Small rounded pot with turned-out lip, from main court. Common.
9. Shallow rounded pot with turned-out lip, from ditch in re-entrant angle of S. Filipe. Common.

See pages 81–3, 88–9.

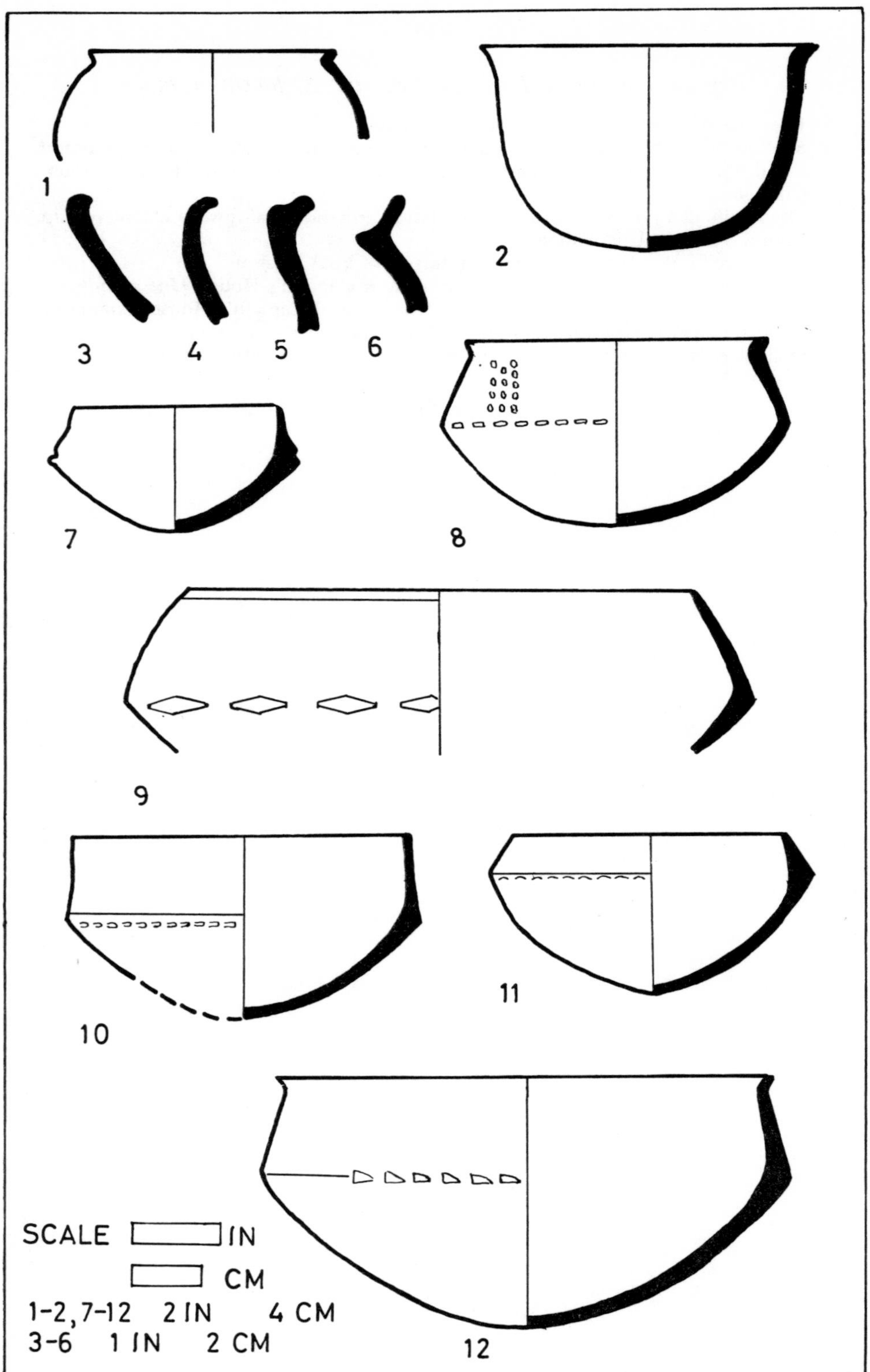

FIG. 41

Fig. 41. *Fort Jesus. Local earthenware. Eighteenth century*

1. Rounded pot with turned-out lip. Common.
2. Tulip-shaped pot from main court. Uncommon.

3, 4. Pots or jars with turned-out lip. Single examples from north court outside Captain's House.

5, 6. Pots with hollowed projecting lip. Single examples from main court and north court outside Captain's House.

7. Carinated pot with smooth black surface and carved profile, from main court. Uncommon.
8. Carinated pot with turned-out lip, neck painted red, incised ornament above carination, from main court. Common.
9. Carinated pot with black smooth surface, convex neck, and sliced ornament on carinations, from pit in west parapet walk. Common.
10. Carinated pot with smooth black surface, vertical neck, similar to Fig. 35. 4, and incised ornament, from court behind church. Uncommon.
11. Carinated pot with smooth black surface and incised ornament on carination, from court in S. Mateus. Common.
12. Carinated pot with smooth black surface and incised ornament, from same pit as 9.

See pages 81–3, 89–90.

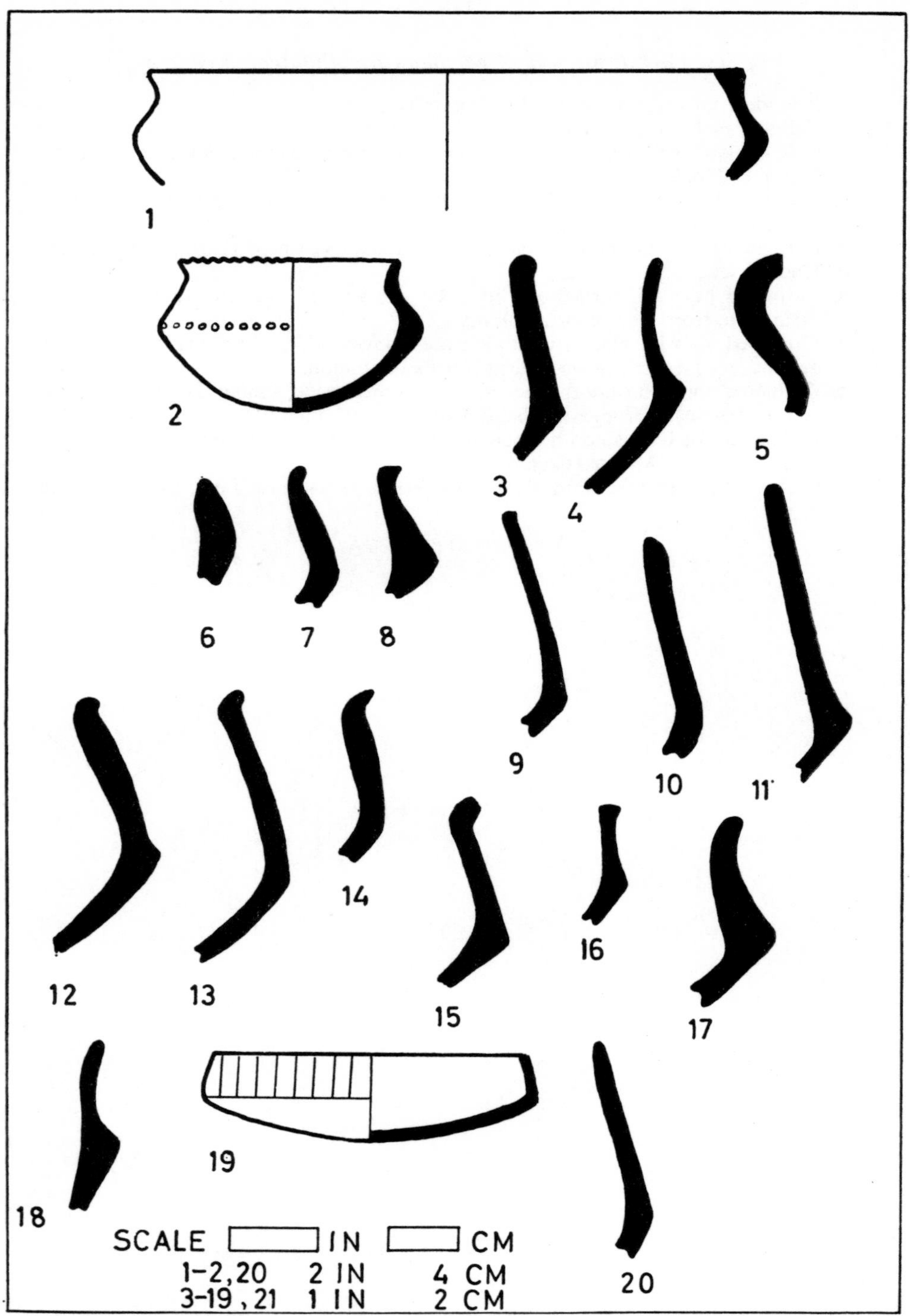
1
2
3
4
5
6
7
8
9
10
11
12
13
14
15
16
17
18
19
20
SCALE IN CM
1–2,20 2 IN 4 CM
3–19, 21 1 IN 2 CM

FIG. 42

Fig. 42. *Fort Jesus. Local earthenware. Eighteenth century*

1. Large shallow carinated pot with smooth black surface and deep concave neck. Single example from same pit as Fig. 41. 9 and 12.
2. Small carinated pot with deep concave neck and frilled edge to rim. Single example from main court.
3. Carinated pot with rolled rim. Single example from north court outside Captain's House.
4. Carinated pot with deep concave neck and frilling on carination, from pit near west parapet walk. Uncommon.
5. Carinated pot with deep concave neck and chamfered edge to lip, from court in S. Mateus. This is the earliest example of this treatment of rim. Common.
6. Carinated pot with lip of archaic type, with line incised below rim, from church. Uncommon.
7. Carinated pot with everted lip. Common.
8. Carinated pot with projecting lip and thickened carination. Single example from S. Filipe.
9. Carinated pot, smooth black surface, incised line below rim or on carination, from north court outside Captain's House. Common.
10. Carinated pot with smooth black surface with sloping outer edge to rim and sliced ornament on carination. Single example from north court behind church.
11. Large carinated pot with incised line below rim, from north court behind church. Uncommon.

12–14. Carinated pots with turned-out lip and slightly convex neck, red above carination, usually with ornament on carination. Common.

15. Carinated pot with turned-out lip, chamfered on edge, red above carination, from north court outside Captain's House. Uncommon.

16, 17. Carinated pots with turned-out lip, red above carination. Common.

18. Carinated pot with upright neck and thickened carination. Single example from main court.
19. Shallow carinated pot with red striped decoration, from north court outside Captain's House. Uncommon.
20. Long-necked carinated pot with red striped decoration, from area between church and cistern. Uncommon.

See pages 81–3, 89–90.

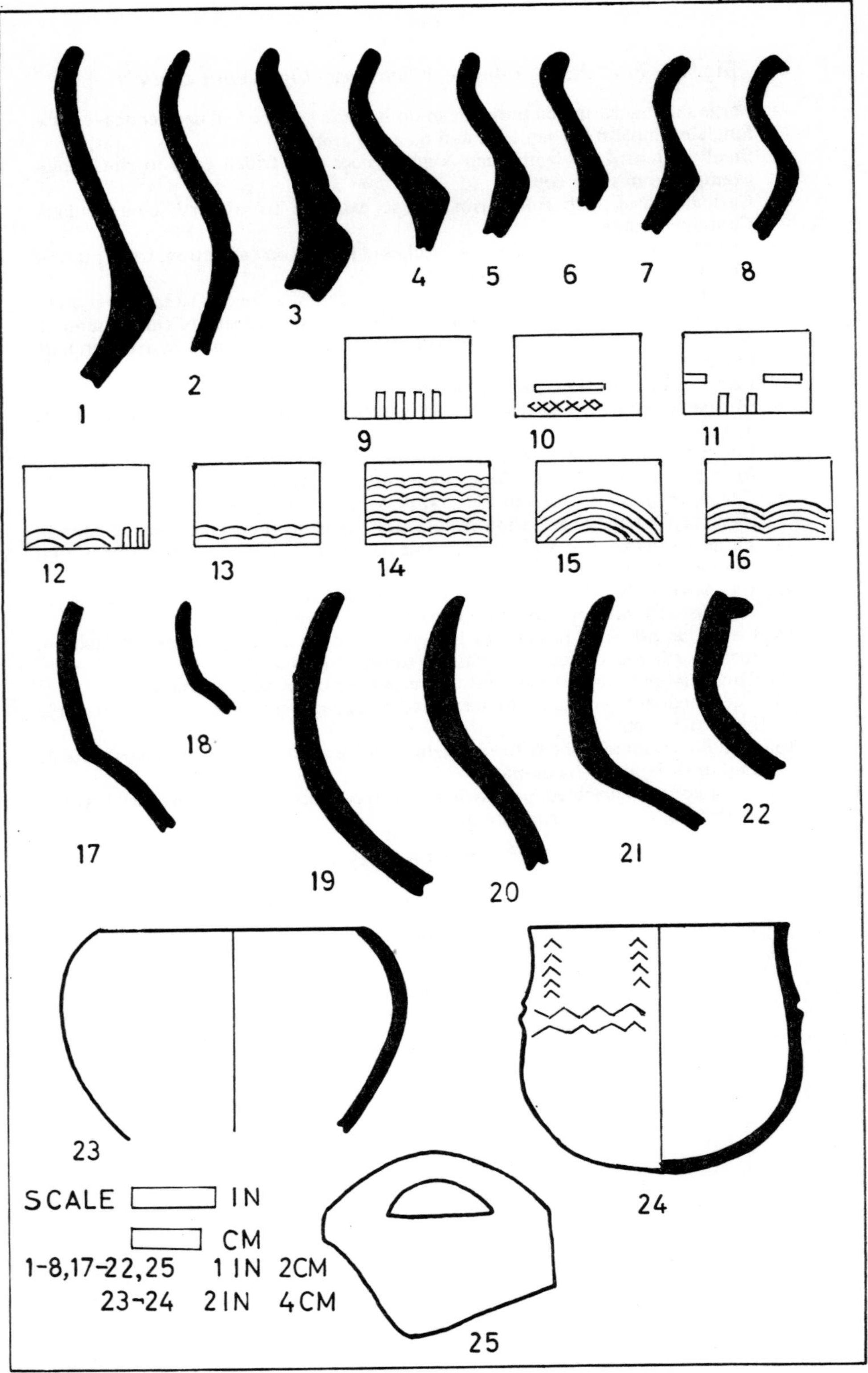
1
2
3
4
5
6
7
8
9
10
11
12
13
14
15
16
17
18
19
20
21
22
23
24
25
SCALE IN
CM
1-8,17-22,25 1 IN 2CM
23-24 2IN 4CM

FIG. 43

Fig. 43. *Fort Jesus. Local earthenware. Eighteenth century*

1. Carinated pot with long neck and appliqué ornament, from north court of Captain's House. Uncommon.
2. Carinated pot with concave neck and appliqué ornament, from barrack block. Uncommon.
3. Carinated pot with convex neck, turned-out lip and appliqué ornament, from area between church and cistern. Uncommon.
4. Carinated pot with deep concave neck and appliqué ornament, from pit near west parapet walk. Uncommon.
5. Carinated pot with convex neck and turned-out lip, from ammunition store. Common.
6. Similar pot from south barrack block. Common.
7. Carinated pot with appliqué ornament, deep concave neck, and chamfered edge to lip, from same pit as 4. Common.
8. Similar pot from the church. Common.

9–16. Appliqué patterns.

17. Thin jar with concave neck, from area of Captain's House. Common.
18. Similar jar but smaller, from church. Uncommon.
19. Jar with flaring neck, from area of west barrack block. Uncommon.
20. Jar with concave neck, from S. Mateus. Common.
21. Similar jar, from S. Matias. Common.
22. Jar with projecting and grooved lip, from S. Mateus. Uncommon.
23. Wide-mouthed jar of type of Fig. 34. 4, with incurved lip, often painted red on outside, from main court against west parapet walk. Uncommon.
24. Straight-sided cordoned vessel called a *bungu*, from area between church and cistern. Uncommon.
25. Horned bowl with hole in flange for use as a handle, from S. Matias. Uncommon.

See pages 81–5, 87, 89–90.

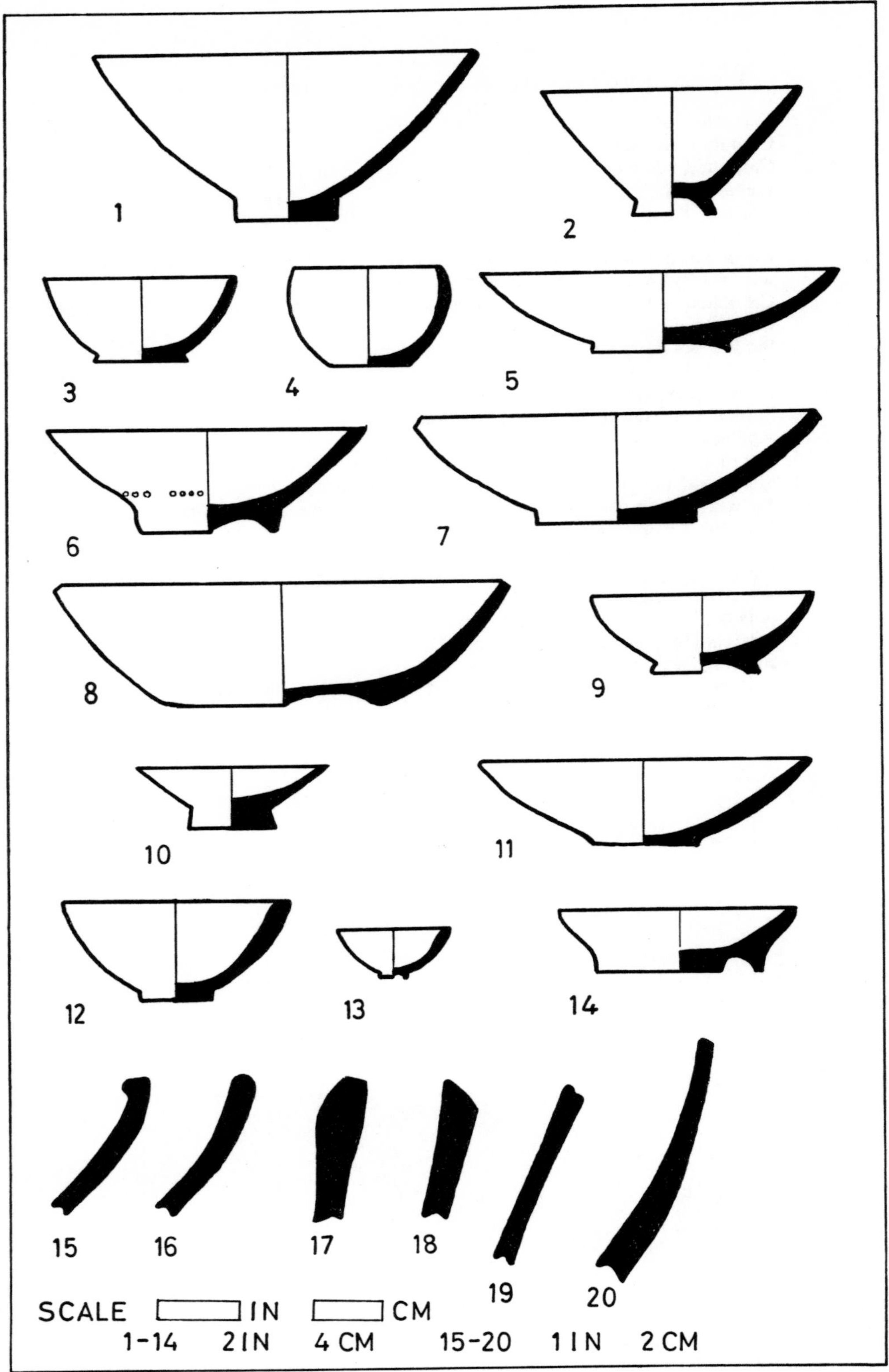
1
2
3
4
5
6
7
8
9
10
11
12
13
14
15
16
17
18
19
20
SCALE IN CM
1-14 2 IN 4 CM 15-20 1 IN 2 CM

FIG. 44

Fig. 44. *Fort Jesus. Local earthenware. Eighteenth century*

1. Large bowl with disk base. Common.
2. Bowl with ring base, from pit in west parapet walk, with Fig. 41. 9, etc. Common.
3. Small bowl with disk base and red rim. Common.
4. Small bowl with incurved lip and flat base, from court behind church. Uncommon.
5. Shallow bowl with ring base. Common.
6. Similar type of bowl with flat lip and indentation on side above ring base. Common.
7. Similar type of bowl with chamfered lip and disk base. Common.
8. Shallow bowl with chamfered lip and hollow base. Single example from church.
9. Small bowl with ring base. Common.
10. Small bowl with pedestal base. Single example from main court.
11. Bowl with thin flat red base, from S. Mateus. Uncommon.
12. Small bowl with lip like Fig. 32. 13, from area of Captain's House. Uncommon.
13. Miniature bowl with same type of lip from area of Captain's House. Uncommon.
14. Bowl with hollowed base similar to the hollow bases of K'ang Hsi type. Single example from pit near west parapet walk.
15. Shallow bowl with lip with internal roll of archaic type, from S. Mateus (cf. Figs. 33. 6 and 35. 16). Uncommon.
16. Shallow bowl with rounded lip. Common.
17. Large bowl with thickened lip, from main court. Uncommon.
18. Large bowl with outward sloping lip, from S. Mateus. Uncommon.
19. Large bowl with grooved rim. Common.
20. Large bowl hatched on rim. Single example from S. Mateus.

See pages 81–3, 88–90.

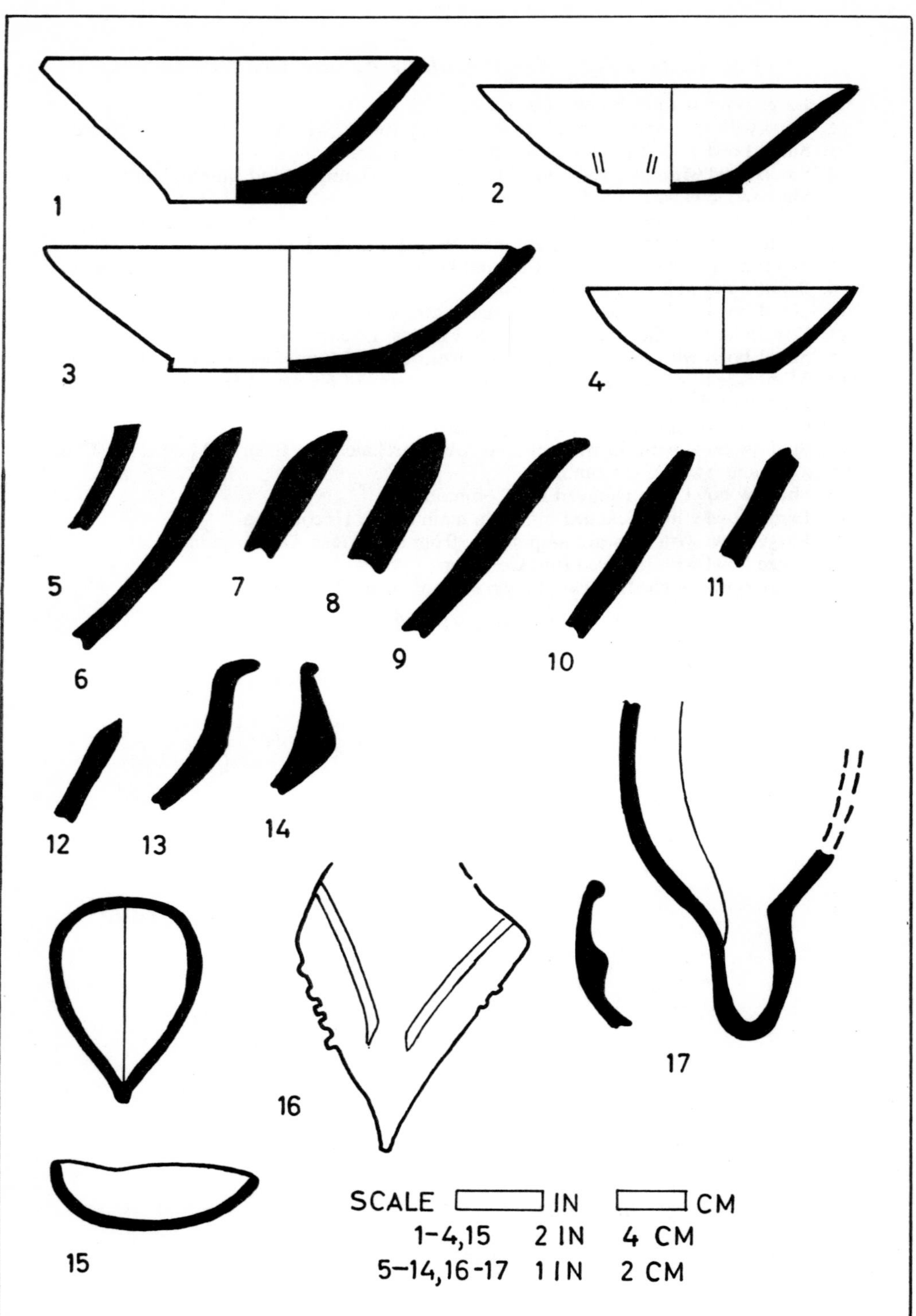
1
2
3
4
5
6
7
8
9
10
11
12
13
14
15
16
17
SCALE IN CM
1–4,15 2 IN 4 CM
5–14,16-17 1 IN 2 CM

FIG. 45

Fig. 45. *Fort Jesus. Local earthenware. Eighteenth century*

1. Large bowl with chamfered lip burnished on inside. Common.
2. Shallow bowl with tapered lip and thin disk base burnished on inside, incised lines on outside. Common.
3. Large shallow bowl with grooved lip and disk base burnished on inside. A characteristic late seventeenth-century form, continuing into the eighteenth.
4. Bowl with pointed lip and thin flat base, burnished on inside, from west barrack block. Uncommon.

5–9. Bowls, mostly shallow, with flat or inward sloping lip, burnished on inside. Common.

10. Bowl, burnished on inside, with long inner slope to lip, similar to Fig. 39. 7, from main court. Common.
11. Bowl, burnished on inside, grooved on edge of lip. Single example from church.
12. Small bowl, burnished on inside, with inner slope to lip. Single example from north court of Captain's House.
13. Bowl, burnished on inside, with projecting lip, probably with rounded bottom, from S. Mateus. Uncommon.
14. Bowl, burnished on inside and above carination on outside, carination thickened like Fig. 42. 8, bead rim. Single example from church.
15. Lamp, profile and plan. Common.
16. Large lamp with pointed lip and internal flanges, appliqué ornament on outside. Single example from pit in west parapet walk with Fig. 44. 2.
17. Large narrow lamp with interior flanges. Single example from court behind church.

See pages 81–4, 88–90.

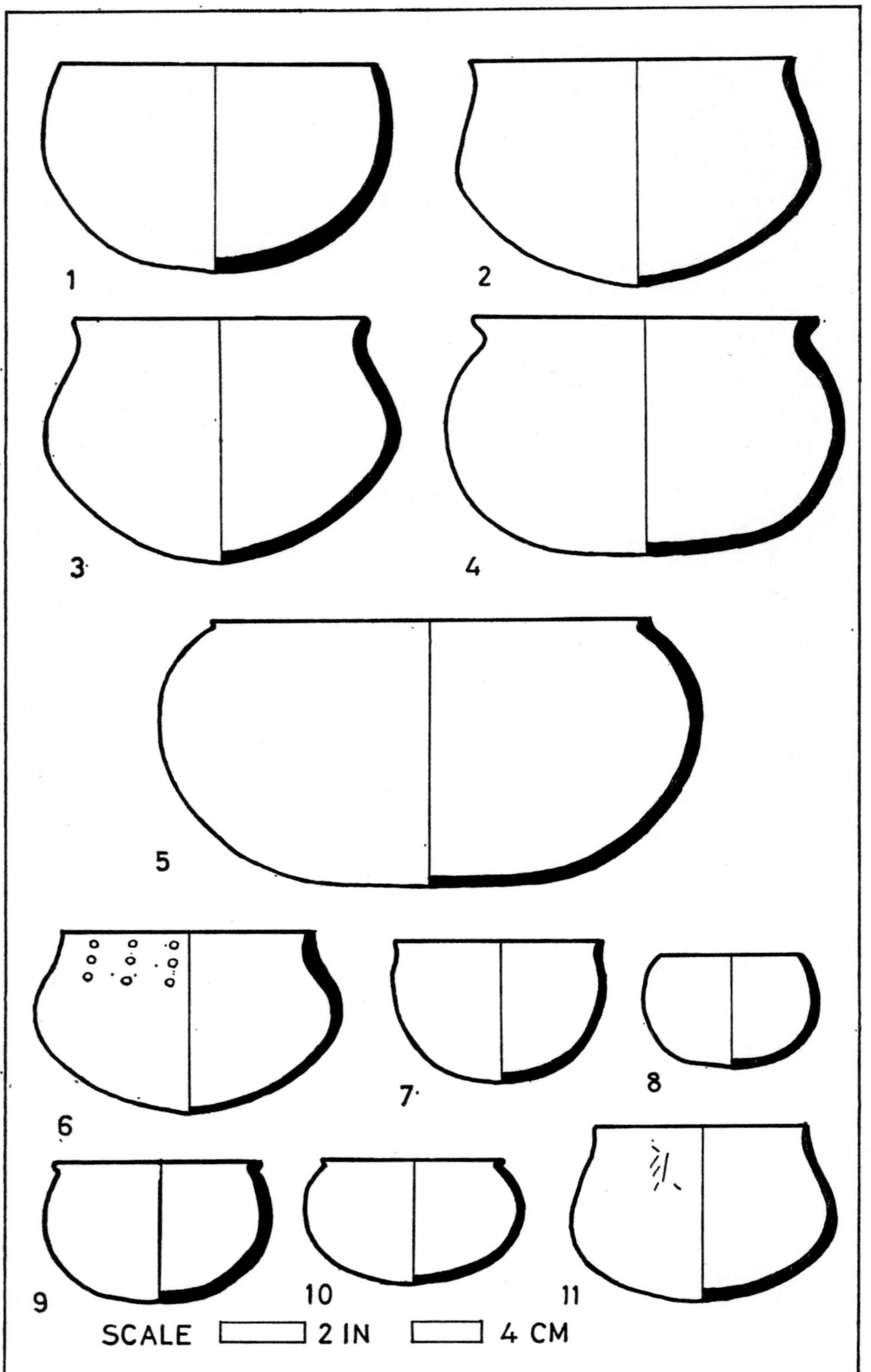

FIG. 46

Fig. 46. *Fort Jesus. Local earthenware. Nineteenth century*

1. Deep rounded pot with incurved lip. Common.
2–4. Deep rounded pots with turned-out lip. Common.
5. Rounded pot with turned-out lip. Common.
6. Shouldered pot with turned-out lip, often with incised ornament 57. Common.
7. Small shouldered pot with turned-out lip. Common.
8. Small rounded pot with incurved lip. Common.
9, 10. Small rounded pots with turned-out lip. Common.
11. Shouldered pot, often with incised ornament 49. Common.

See pages 81–3, 90–91.

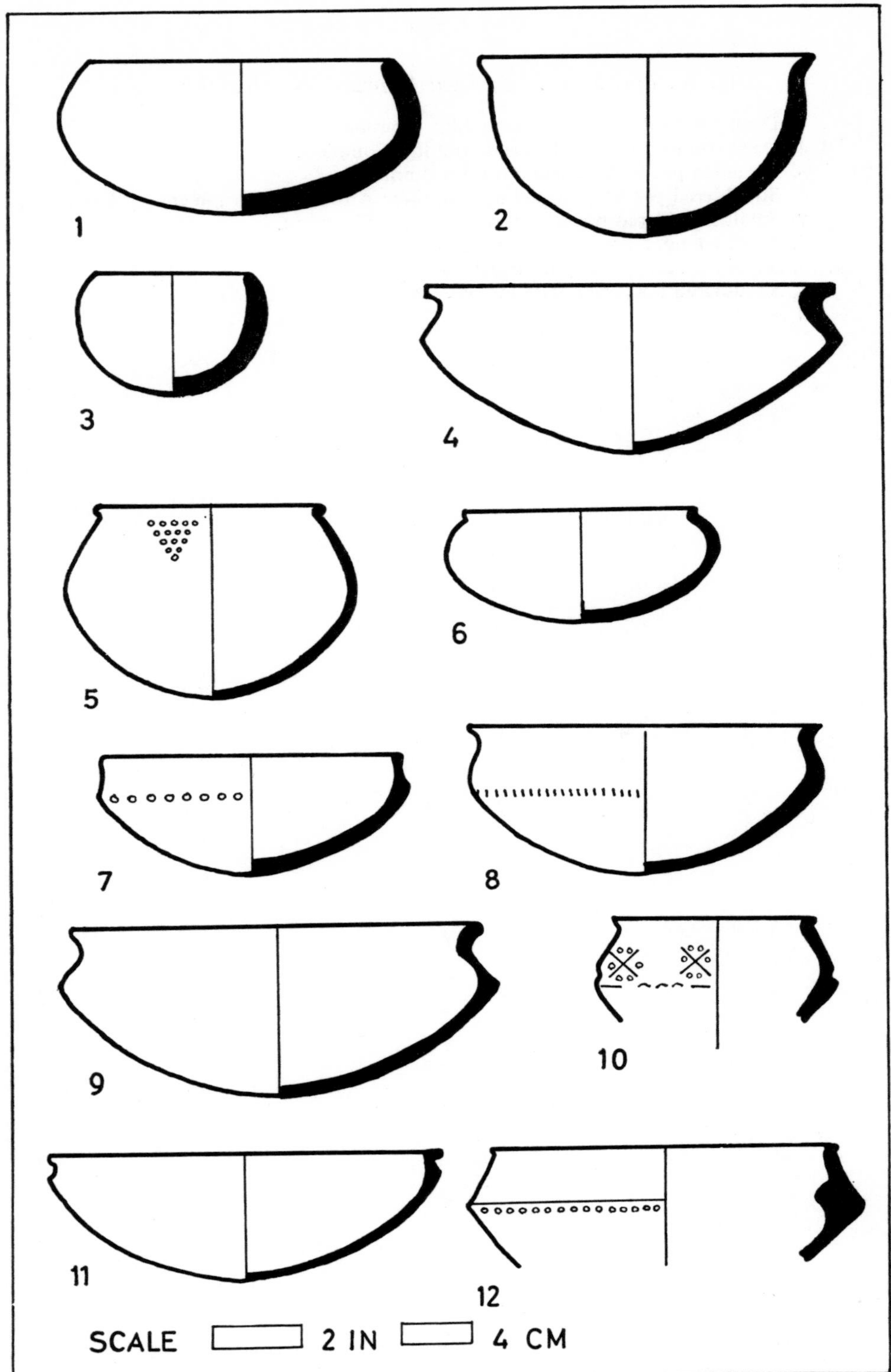

FIG. 47

Fig. 47. *Fort Jesus. Local earthenware. Nineteenth century*

1. Rounded pot, thick fabric. Common.
2. Deep rounded pot with turned-out lip, from main court. Uncommon.
3. Small rounded pot, thick fabric. Common.
4. Carinated pot with swan neck, chamfered on edge of lip. Common.
5. Rounded pot with bead rim, pudendal triangle ornament 59. Characteristic nineteenth-century type.
6. Small rounded pot with everted lip. Common.
7. Shouldered pot from south barrack block. Uncommon.
8. Carinated pot with concave neck and turned-out lip. Uncommon.
9. Carinated pot with turned-out lip. Common.
10. Small pot with turned-out lip and incised ornament in form of a saltire and roundels, 55. Single example from S. Filipe.
11. Shallow pot with turned-out lip and high carination, from main court. Uncommon.
12. Carinated pot with smooth surface, bead rim, and internal flange of unknown purpose. The flange is similar to those on the inside of the lamp, Fig. 45. 16, but the height of the bowl would be too great for a lamp. Single example from main court.

See pages 81–3, 90–1.

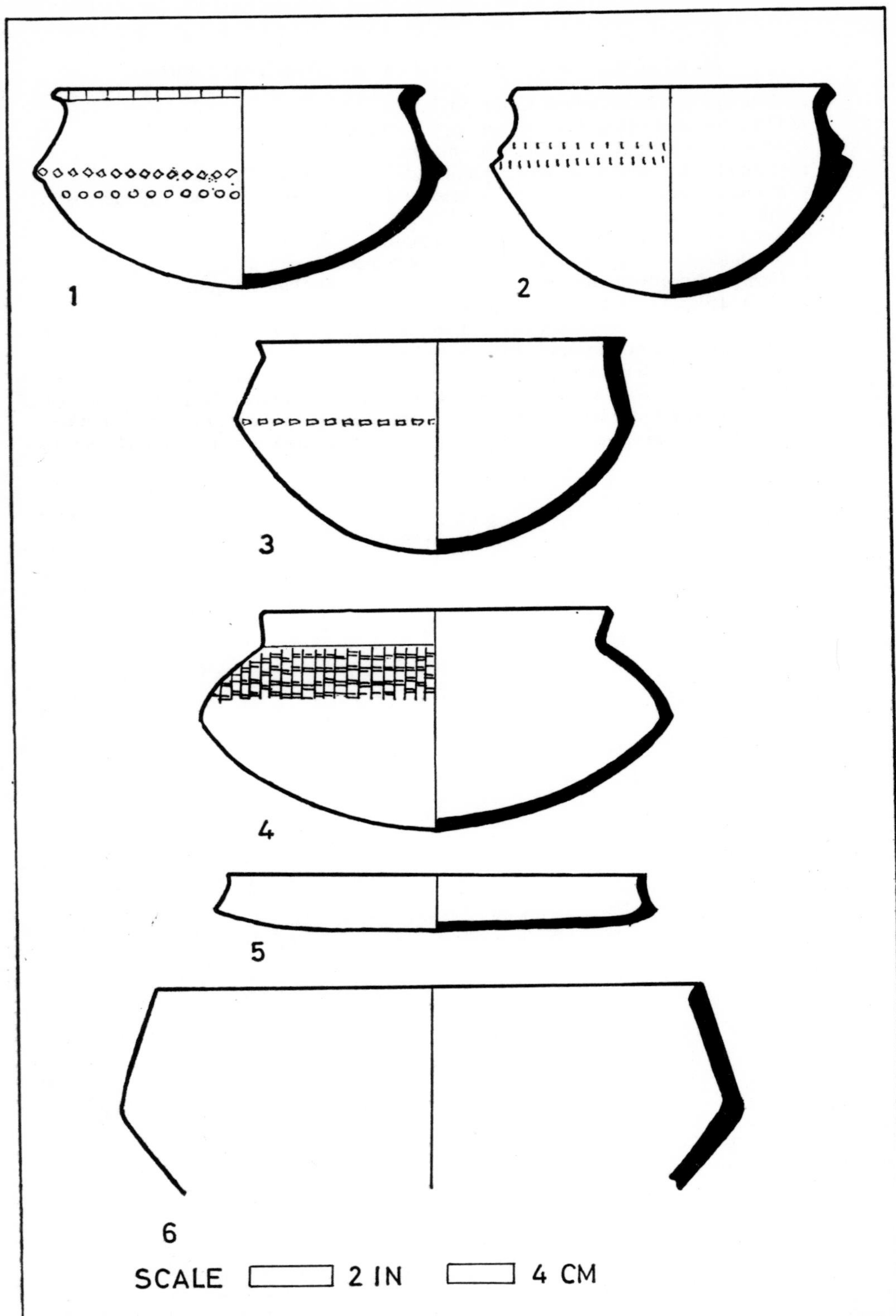

FIG. 48

Fig. 48. *Fort Jesus. Local earthenware. Nineteenth century*

1. Carinated pot with rolled and turned-out lip, notched on the edge, indented ornament above and below carination. Single example from north court behind church.
2. Similar pot with notched ornament above and below carination. Single example from south barrack block.
3. Carinated pot with projecting lip. Common.
4. Carinated pot with turned-out lip and unusual broad band of chipped ornament between vertical lines, 77. Single example from main court.
5. Shallow pot with slightly concave neck. Single example from Passage of the Arches.
6. Large carinated pot with rough surface, similar to appliqué wares, from pit in S. Matias.

See pages 81–3, 87, 90–91.

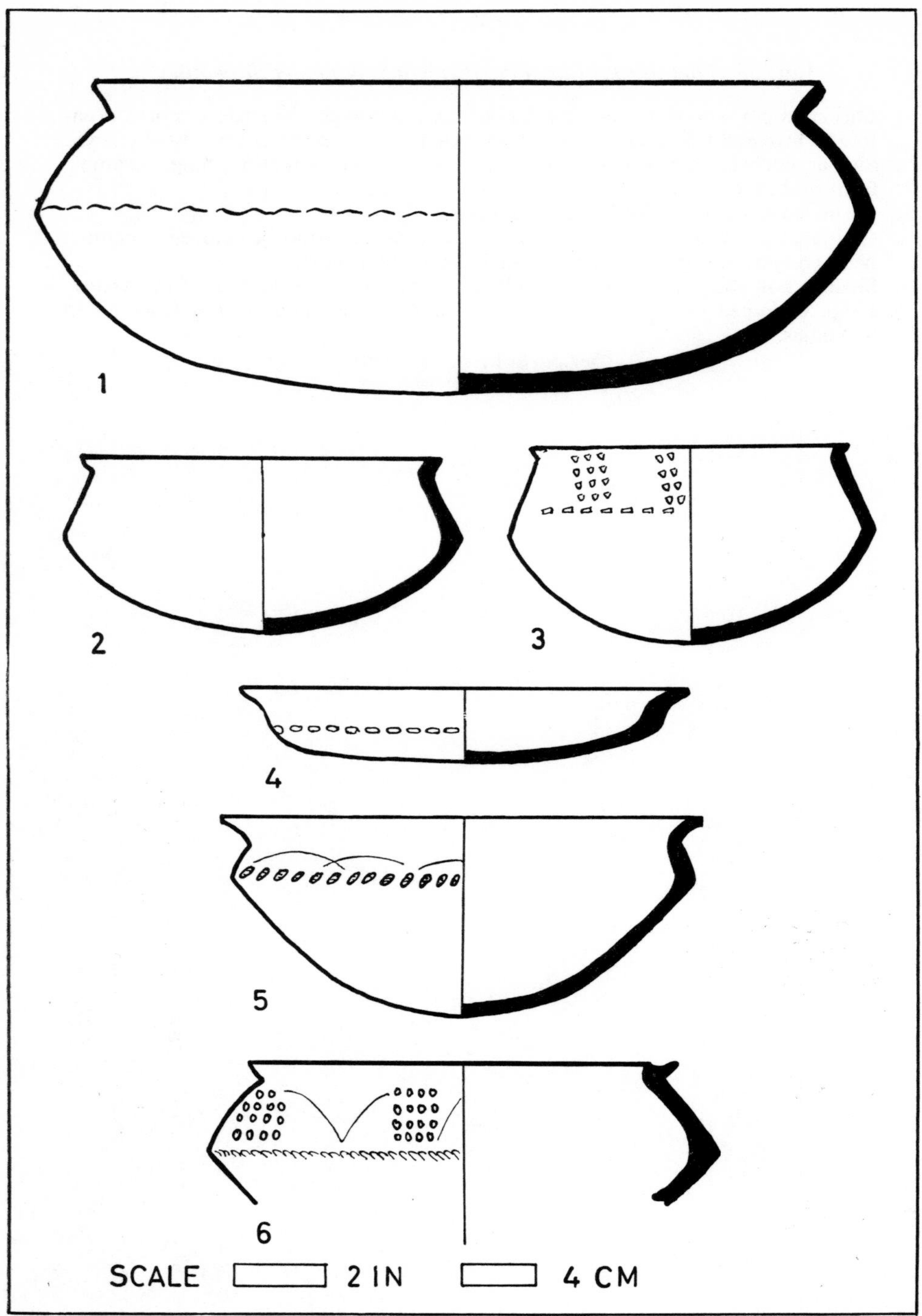

FIG. 49

Fig. 49. *Fort Jesus. Local earthenware. Nineteenth century*

1. Very large carinated pot with turned-out lip and indented ornament on carination. Single example from area of Captain's House.
2. Carinated pot with projecting lip. Common.
3. Carinated pot with slightly concave neck and projecting lip, red above carination, often with unusual ornament 62, from main court.
4. Shallow pot with projecting lip. Single example from south barrack block.
5. Carinated pot with swan neck, chamfered on edge, ornament 107 on and above carination. A characteristic nineteenth-century type.
6. Carinated pot with projecting lip, grooved on top, red above carination, with unusual ornament 66. Single example from the Passage of the Arches.

See pages 81–3, 90–1.

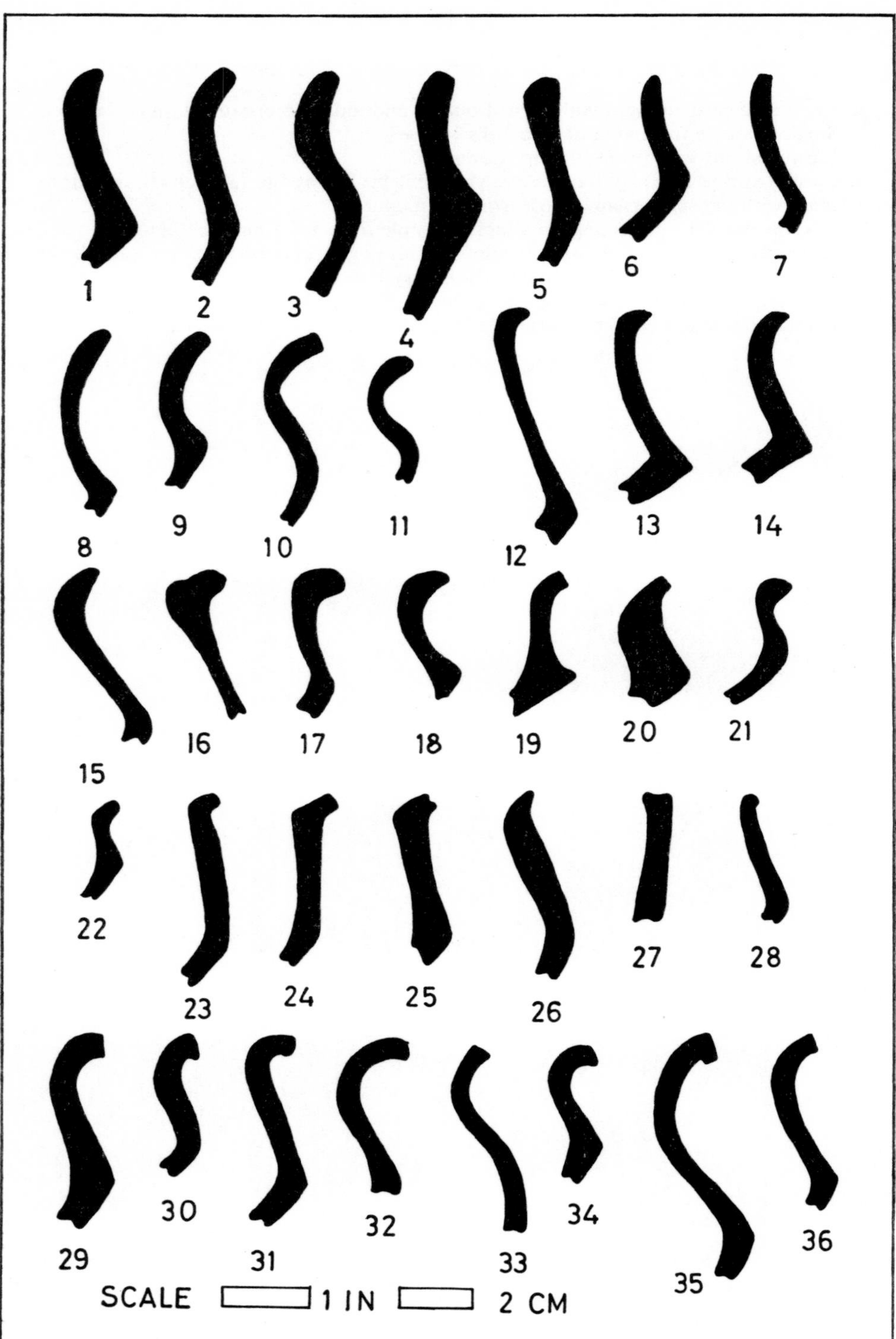
1
2
3
4
5
6
7
8
9
10
11
12
13
14
15
16
17
18
19
20
21
22
23
24
25
26
27
28
29
30
31
32
33
34
35
36
SCALE
1 IN
2 CM

FIG. 50

Fig. 50. *Fort Jesus. Local earthenware. Nineteenth century*

1–4. Carinated pots with concave neck, thick fabric. Common.
5. Carinated pot with concave neck and thickened rim. Single example from Passage of the Arches.
6. Carinated pot with concave neck. Common.
7. Carinated pot with concave neck and flat top to rim. Single example from Passage of the Arches.
8–11. Carinated pots with deep concave or swan neck, often painted red on inside of lip. Common.
12–15. Carinated pots with concave neck, from Passage of the Arches.
16. Carinated pot with projecting grooved lip and slightly convex neck, from debris of church. Uncommon.
17. Carinated pot with projecting lip, from main court. Uncommon.
18. Carinated pot with swan neck, from main court. Uncommon.
19, 20. Carinated pots with thickened carination and turned-out lip, from Passage of the Arches. Uncommon.
21, 22. Carinated pots with projecting lip, from S. Mateus and main court. Uncommon.
23, 24. Carinated pots with flat, turned-out lip, from Passage of the Arches and S. Filipe. Uncommon.
25. Carinated pot with turned-out lip, grooved on edge, from Passage of the Arches. Uncommon.
26. Carinated pot with turned-out lip, from Passage of the Arches. Uncommon.
27. Carinated pot with upright neck, grooved on top, from main court.
28. Carinated pot, thin fabric, with thickened lip, from Passage of the Arches. Uncommon.
29–36. Carinated pots with swan neck and chamfered edge to lip (Pl. 19. 4, 5). Common.

See pages 81–3, 90–91.

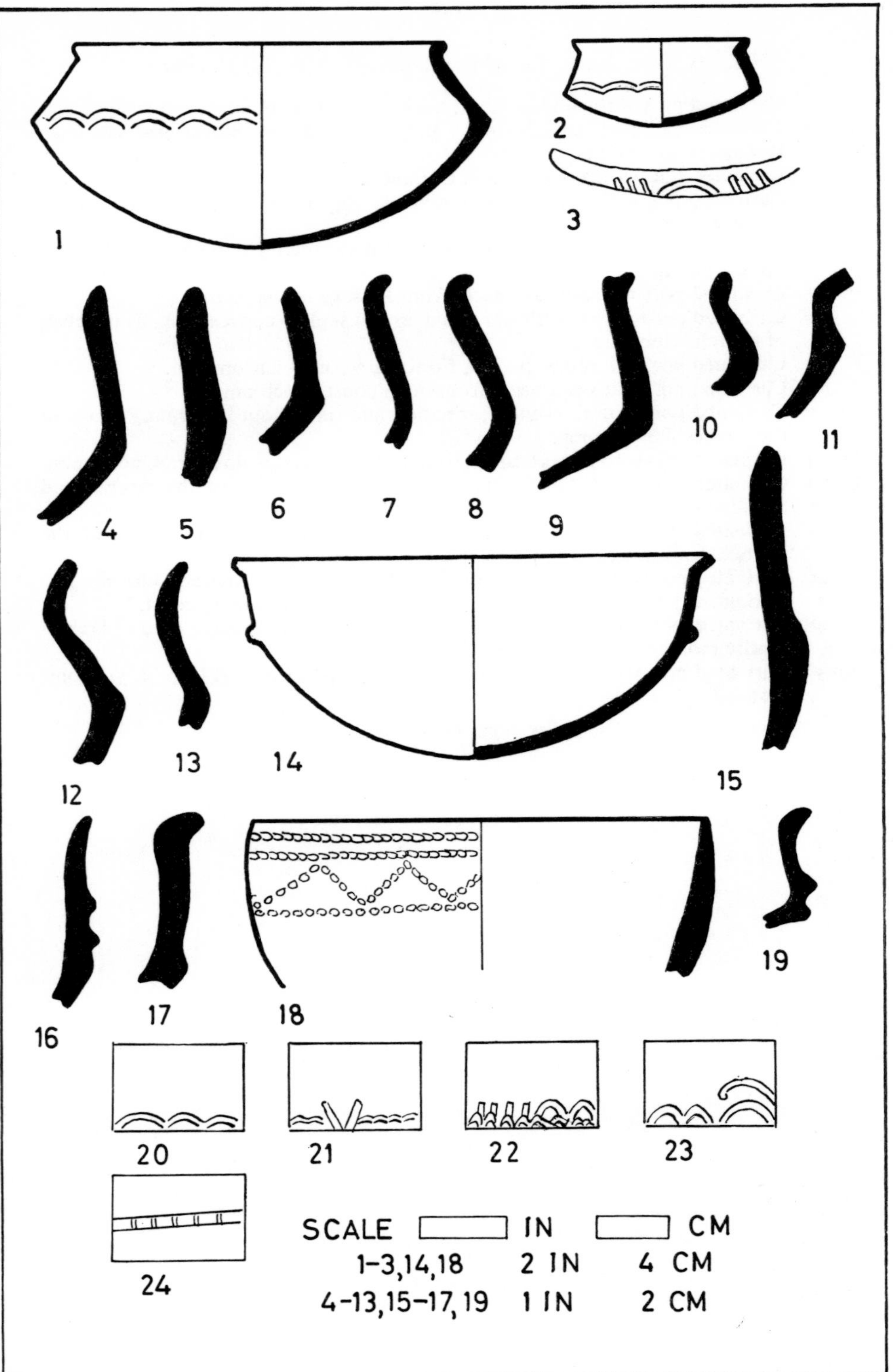
1
2
3
4
5
6
7
8
9
10
11
12
13
14
15
16
17
18
19
20
21
22
23
24
SCALE IN CM
1–3,14,18 2 IN 4 CM
4–13,15–17,19 1 IN 2 CM

FIG. 51

Fig. 51. *Fort Jesus. Local earthenware. Nineteenth century*

1. Carinated pot with turned-out lip and appliqué arcade ornament, from main court. Uncommon.
2. Small carinated pot with appliqué ornament of a wavy line, from Passage of the Arches (Pl. 19. 3). Uncommon.
3. Lamp with appliqué ornament of vertical strokes and curves, from Passage of the Arches. Uncommon.
4. Carinated pot with appliqué ornament, from S. Filipe. Uncommon.
5. Similar pot, from main court. Uncommon.
6. Similar pot with convex neck, from Passage of the Arches. Uncommon.

7–9. Similar pots with everted lip, from Passage of the Arches (Pl. 19. 2). Uncommon.

10, 11. Similar pots with concave neck, from Passage of the Arches. Uncommon.

12. Similar pot with swan neck, from south barrack block. Uncommon.
13. Similar pot with concave neck, from S. Filipe. Uncommon.
14. Pot with appliqué ornament in form of cordons, from main court. Uncommon.
15. Large carinated pot with appliqué ornament. Single example from main court.
16. Pot with ornament similar to Fig. 43. 14. Uncommon.
17. Heavy pot with turned-out lip. Single example from lamp room.
18. Rounded pot with pointed lip and chevron and cordon ornament *en barbotine*. Single example from main court.
19. Small pot with low carination and swan neck. Single example from south barrack block.

20–4. Variations of appliqué ornament, mostly on pots of eighteenth-century form: 20 on Fig. 43. 1; 21 on Fig. 43. 2; 22 on Fig. 43. 3; 23 on Fig. 43. 6; 24 on Fig. 43. 5. See also Pl. 19. 1.

See pages 81–4, 87, 90–1.

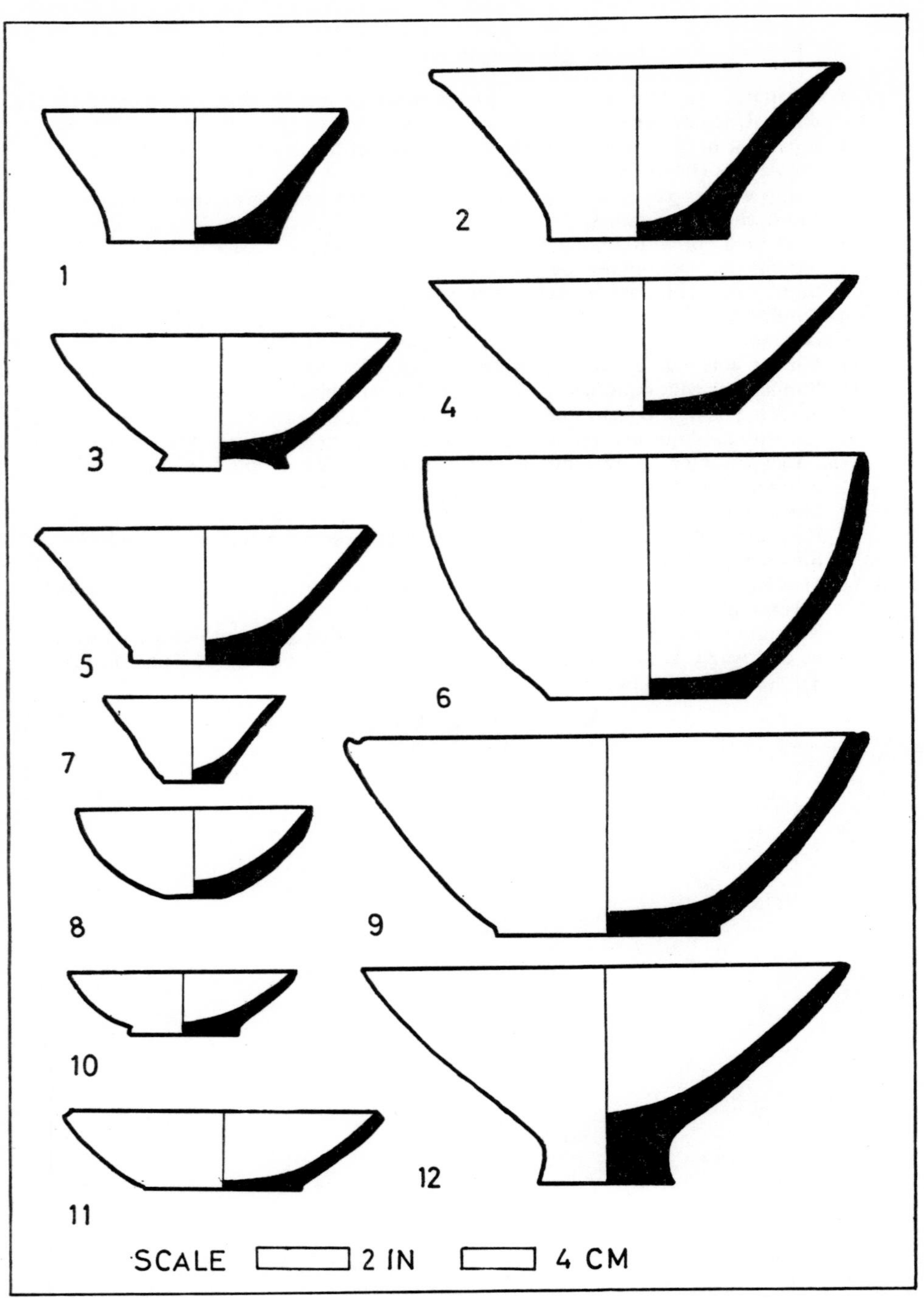

FIG. 52

Fig. 52. *Fort Jesus. Local earthenware. Nineteenth century*

1, 2. Bowls with flat base and funnel mouth. Common.
3. Bowl with spread ring base. Common.
4. Bowl with flat base and straight sides. Common.
5. Bowl with disk base and outward-sloping lip. Common.
6. Bowl with flat base and rounded sides. Common.
7. Small bowl with flat base and funnel mouth, from north court outside Captain's House. Uncommon.
8. Small bowl with flat base and rounded sides. Common.
9. Bowl with disk base and grooved lip, from Passage of the Arches. Uncommon.
10. Shallow bowl with disk base and wide mouth. Common.
11. Shallow bowl with disk base and outward-sloping lip. Common.
12. Large bowl with tall disk base from pit in S. Matias. Uncommon.

See pages 81–3, 90–91.

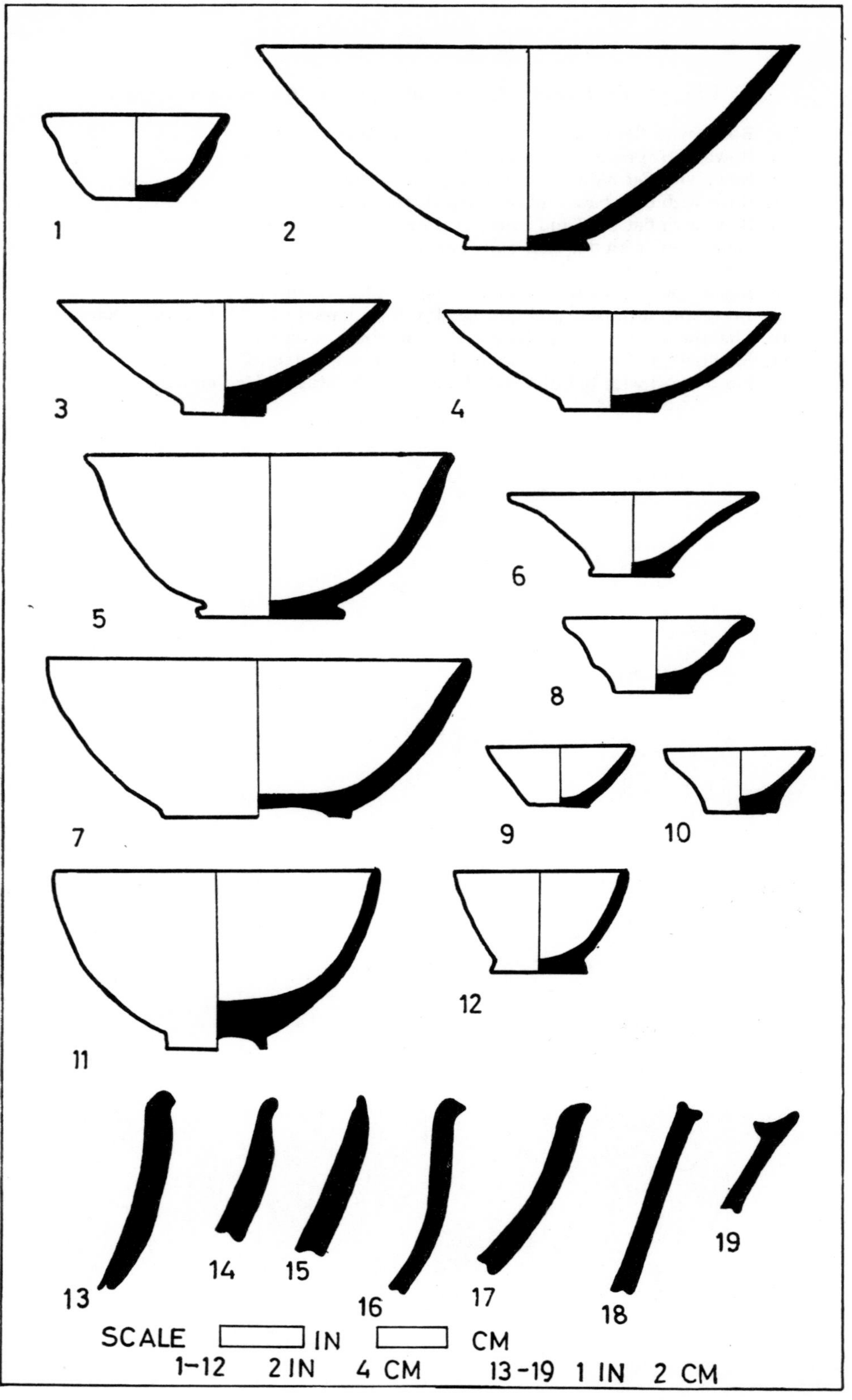
1
2
3
4
5
6
7
8
9
10
11
12
13
14
15
16
17
18
19
SCALE IN CM
1–12 2 IN 4 CM
13–19 1 IN 2 CM

FIG. 53

Fig. 53. *Fort Jesus. Local earthenware. Nineteenth century*

1. Small bowl with flat base and uneven sides, from Captain's House. Uncommon.
2. Large bowl with disk base. Common.

3, 4. Bowls with disk base. Common.

5. Bowl with disk base and rounded sides. Common.
6. Small bowl with wide mouth, from ruins of church. Uncommon.
7. Large bowl with ring base and rounded sides. Common.
8. Small bowl with uneven sides, from ruins of church. Uncommon.

9, 10. Small bowls with flat base. Common.

11. Bowl with rounded sides and ring base. Common.
12. Small bowl with rounded sides and disk base. Single example from S. Filipe.
13. Bowl, undercut below rim, from main court. Uncommon.
14. Bowl, indented outside below lip, from Passage of the Arches. Uncommon.
15. Bowl with frilling on rim and groove on inside of lip. Single example from Captain's House.
16. Bowl similar to 13 above, painted red on inside of lip, from Passage of the Arches. Uncommon.
17. Bowl similar to Fig. 41. 2, from S. Matias. Uncommon.
18. Bowl with grooving on rim, similar to Fig. 44. 19, from Passage of the Arches. Uncommon.
19. Bowl with grooving on rim painted red. Single example from Captain's House.

See pages 81–3, 90–1.

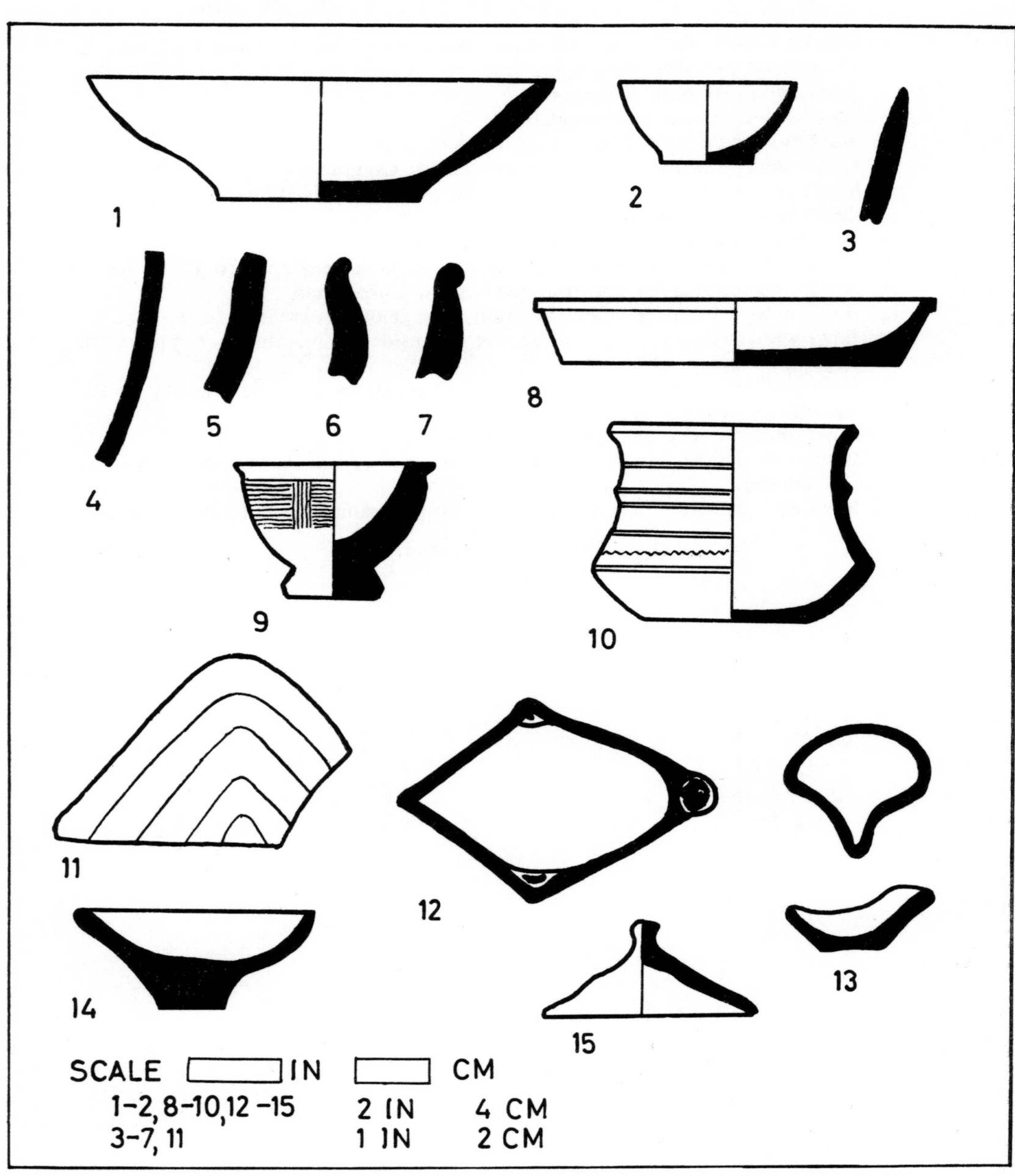
1
2
3
4
5
6
7
8
9
10
11
12
13
14
15
SCALE IN CM
1-2, 8-10, 12-15 2 IN 4 CM
3-7, 11 1 IN 2 CM

FIG. 54

Fig. 54. *Fort Jesus. Local earthenware. Nineteenth century*

1. Large bowl, burnished on inside. Common.
2. Small bowl, burnished on inside, with disk base. Common.
3. Small bowl, burnished on inside, with sharp tapered lip. Common.
4. Bowl, burnished on inside, with flat grooved lip, from Passage of the Arches. Uncommon.
5. Bowl, burnished on inside, with similar grooved lip, from Passage of the Arches. Uncommon.
6. Bowl with bead rim (cf. Fig. 31. 9), burnished outside as well as inside. Single example from Passage of the Arches.
7. Bowl, burnished on inside, with groove below lip on outside, from Passage of the Arches. Uncommon.
8. Bowl with flat base, straight sides, and projecting lip, burnished on inside, from north court of Captain's House. Uncommon.
9. Bowl on pedestal base with turned-out lip and ornamented with horizontal and vertical lines. Single example from Passage of the Arches.
10. Bowl with carved profile and flat base, a form of *bungu*. Single example from Passage of the Arches.
11. Ornamented horn of *mziga*. Single example from Passage of the Arches.
12. Lamp with three spouts, perhaps with handle at end. Single example from main court.
13. Small lamp from south barrack block. Common.
14. Lamp on pedestal base. Single example from S. Matias.
15. Lid with knob, uneven surface. Common.

See pages 81–5, 90–91.

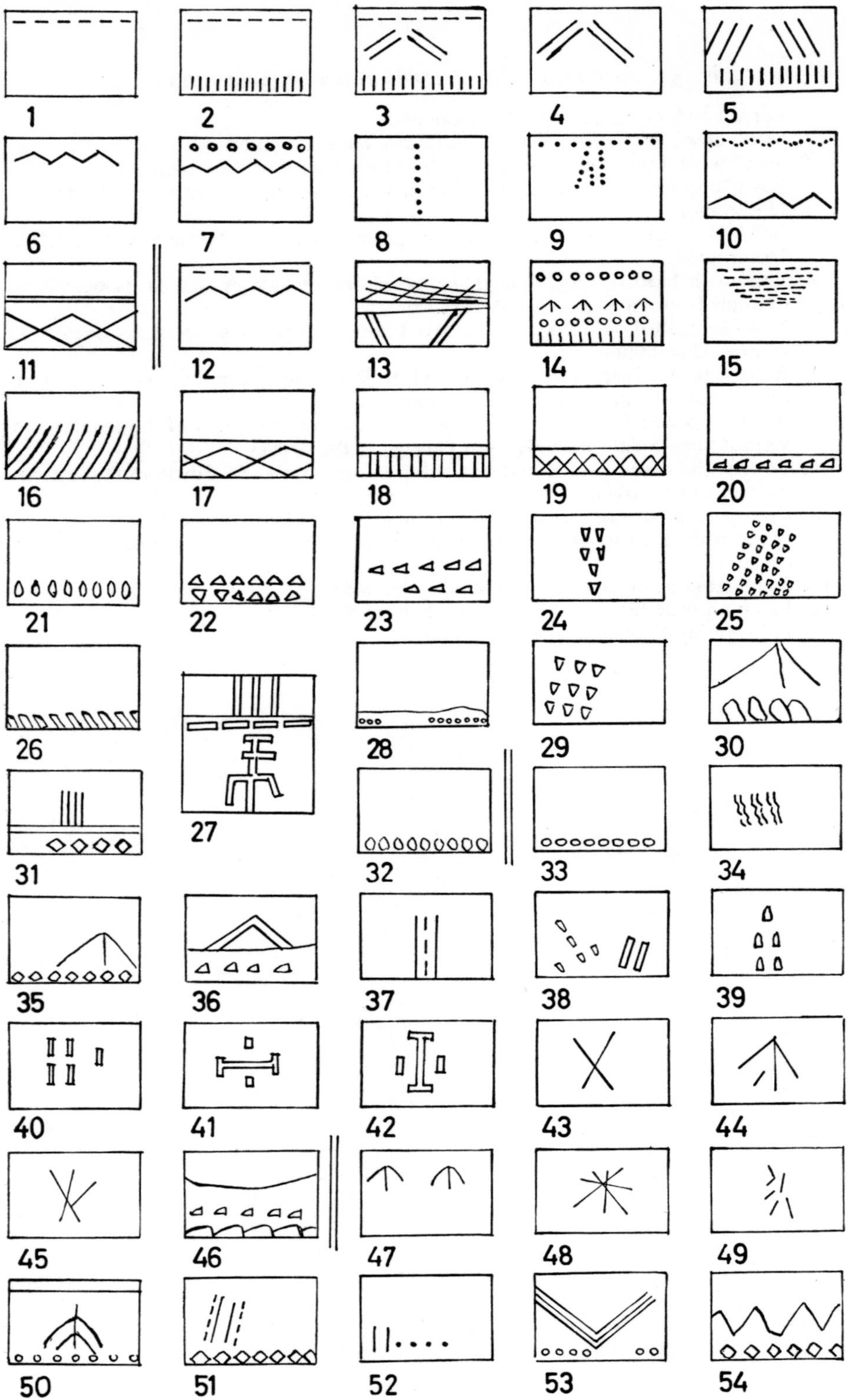
1
2
3
4
5
6
7
8
9
10
11
12
13
14
15
16
17
18
19
20
21
22
23
24
25
26
27
28
29
30
31
32
33
34
35
36
37
38
39
40
41
42
43
44
45
46
47
48
49
50
51
52
53
54

FIG. 55

Fig. 55. *Fort Jesus. Local earthenware. Patterns of incised ornament*

(11 and 17 *Carved and Sliced*)

Early seventeenth century

1. Thin-walled rounded pot, like Fig. 30. 1.
2–5. Small carinated pots, like Fig. 30. 2, 6.
6–10. Thin-walled rounded pots, like Fig. 30. 1.
11. Carved and sliced ornament on carinated pot with smooth black surface, like Fig. 31. 10.

Late seventeenth century

12. Thin-walled rounded pot, like Fig. 30. 1.
13. Thin-walled rounded pot with turned-out lip, like Fig. 30. 3.
14. Small carinated pot, Fig. 34. 3.
15. Rounded pot, like Fig. 34. 4.
16. Rounded pot with turned-out lip, like Fig. 36. 13.
17. Carved and sliced ornament on carinated pot with smooth black surface and bead rim, like Fig. 36. 24.
18–20. Carinated pots with smooth black surface, like Fig. 35. 4, 7, 26.
21. Carinated pot, like Fig. 36. 28.
22. Shouldered pot, like Fig. 36. 21 (on shoulder).
23. Rounded pot with turned-out lip, like Fig. 35. 13.
24. Rounded pot with turned-out lip, like Fig. 40. 7.
25. Carinated pot with projecting lip, like Fig. 36. 8.
26–32. Carinated pots with red neck above carination, like Figs. 34. 2; 35. 22, 23, 25; and 36. 26, 28.

Eighteenth century

33. Rounded pot, ornament on curve of pot, like Fig. 34. 4.
34, 35. Carinated pots, like Figs. 34. 2 and 35. 9.
36. Carinated pot, like Figs. 34. 1, and 35. 22.
37. Shouldered pot, like Fig. 35. 18.
38. Straight-sided bowl burnished on inside, like Fig. 44. 2.
39, 40. Shouldered pots with turned-out lip, like Fig. 40. 5.
41, 42. Rounded pots with turned-out lip, as Fig. 40. 9. Common.
43. Rounded pot with turned-out lip, like Fig. 40. 9, and wide-mouthed bowls. like Figs. 44. 7 and 45. 2.
44. Shouldered pot with turned-out lip, as Fig. 40. 5.
45. Wide-mouthed bowl, like Fig. 44. 11.
46. Carinated pot with red neck above carination, like Fig. 35. 23.

Nineteenth century

47. Small shouldered pot with turned-out lip, like Fig. 46. 7.
48. Shallow bowl, like Fig. 52. 10.
49. Shouldered pot, as Fig. 46. 11.
50. Carinated pot with straight neck, like Fig. 41. 10, and rounded pot with projecting lip and red rim, like Fig. 40. 7.
51. Carinated pot, like Fig. 36. 6.
52. Carinated pot with projecting lip, like Fig. 49. 2.
53, 54. Carinated pots, like Fig. 50. 6, 23.

See pages 85–90.

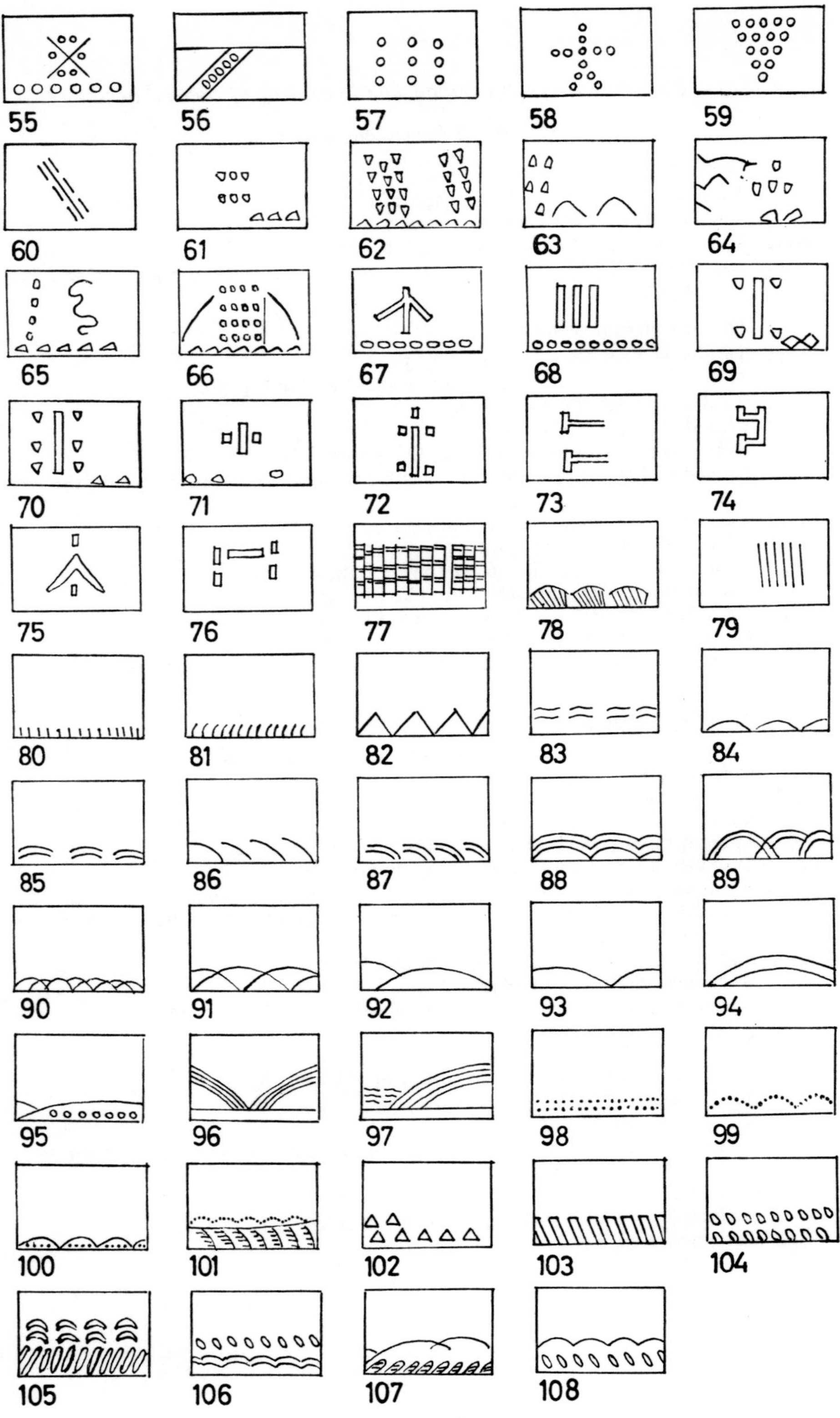

55
56
57
58
59
60
61
62
63
64
65
66
67
68
69
70
71
72
73
74
75
76
77
78
79
80
81
82
83
84
85
86
87
88
89
90
91
92
93
94
95
96
97
98
99
100
101
102
103
104
105
106
107
108

FIG. 56

Fig. 56. *Fort Jesus. Local earthenware. Patterns of incised ornament*

Nineteenth century (*continued*):

55. Carinated pot with red rim, like Fig. 42. 15, and small carinated pot, Fig. 47. 10.
56. Shouldered pot, like Fig. 40. 5.
57. Shouldered pot, as Fig. 46. 6.
58. Rounded pot with everted lip, like Fig. 36. 18.
59. Rounded pot with bead rim, as Fig. 47. 5, common, and a carinated pot, like Fig. 36. 23.

60–7. Carinated pots with red neck, like Figs. 36. 5, 28; 42. 15; 49. 6.

68–70. Carinated pots with red neck, like Fig. 50. 1.

71. Straight-sided bowl with flat base and short sides, like Fig. 39. 1.
72. Shouldered pot with red neck, like Fig. 46. 11.

73, 74. Rounded pots with turned-out lip, like Fig. 40. 7, 9.

75. Rounded pot, like Fig. 46. 1.
76. Shouldered pot with red neck, like Fig. 46. 11.
77. Carinated pot with turned-out lip, Fig. 48. 4.
78. Carinated pot, like Fig. 50. 1.

Carinated pots with concave necks and frequently chamfered edge to lip:

79. Fig. 50. 29, 35, and on bowl Fig. 53. 7.
80. Fig. 50. 30.
81. —— 29, 30.
82. —— 10, 29, 30.
83. —— 19, 30.
84. —— 9, 29.
85. —— 29.
86. —— 3, 30.
87. —— 3, 10, 29. Common.
88. —— 2, 9, 30.
89. —— 29.
90. —— 11, 30.
91. —— 19.
92. —— 30.
93. —— 19, 30.
94. —— 29.
95. —— 30.
96. —— 29, 36.
97. —— 29, 30.
98. —— 34.
99. —— 15, 19, 29, 30, 36. Common.
100. —— 30.
101. —— 32.
102. —— 35.
103. —— 30.
104. —— 30.
105. —— 19, 32.
106. —— 35.
107. Fig. 49. 5 (see also Pl. 19. 5).
108. Fig. 50. 35 (see also Pl. 19. 4).

In addition there are carinated pots with ornament similar to 1–7 on Fig. 30. 3, 4.

See pages 85–7.

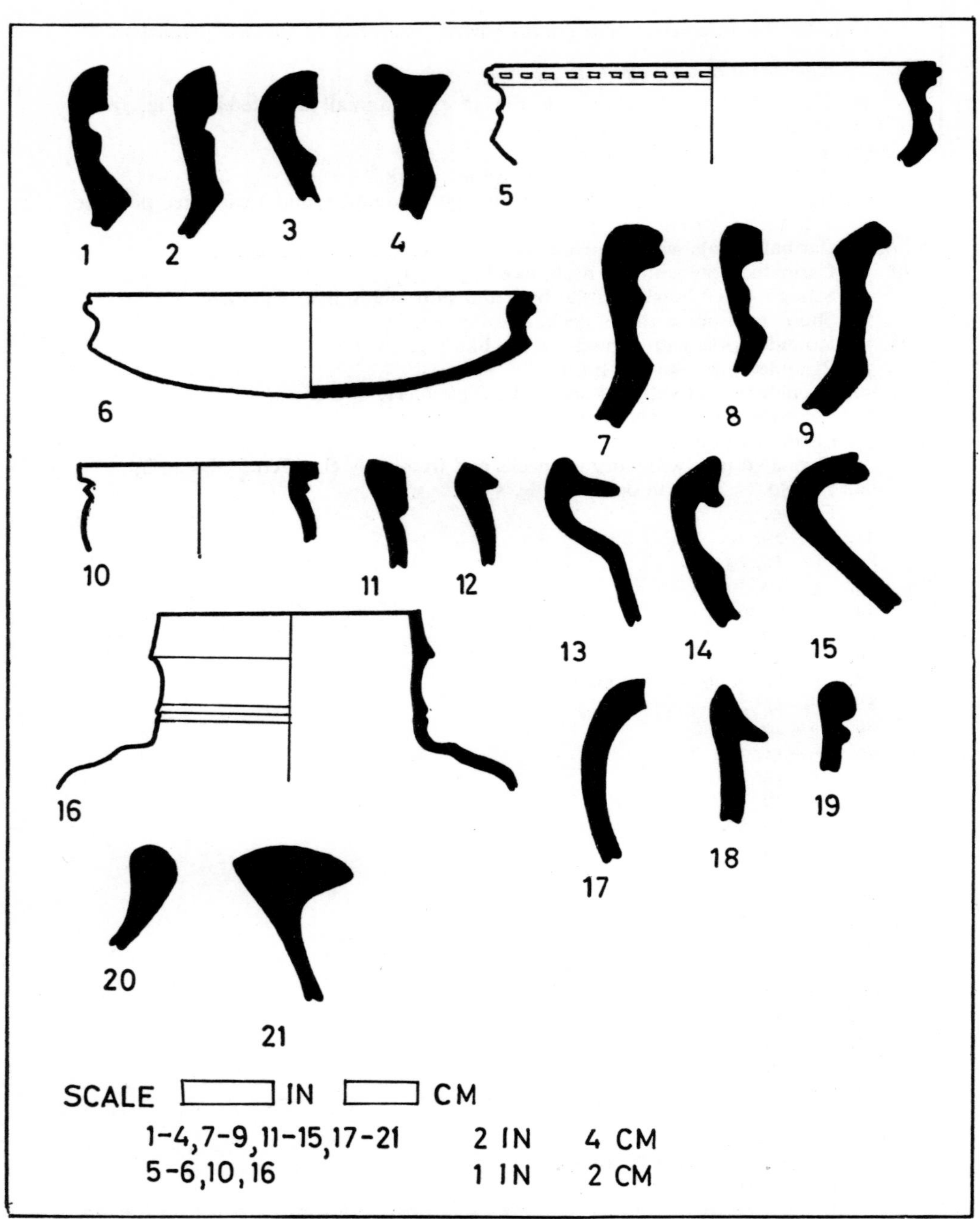
1
2
3
4
5
6
7
8
9
10
11
12
13
14
15
16
17
18
19
20
21
SCALE IN CM
1-4, 7-9, 11-15, 17-21 2 IN 4 CM
5-6, 10, 16 1 IN 2 CM

FIG. 57

Fig. 57. *Fort Jesus. Imported unglazed earthenware. Hard-baked red and soft pink wares, sometimes burnished or with mica on surface*

1, 2. Carinated pots with neck with median ridge, from filling in S. Filipe. Early seventeenth century.
3. Same, from filling in S. Mateus. Early seventeenth century.
4. Carinated pot with unusual inner lip, from filling in S. Mateus. Early seventeenth century.
5. Carinated pot with median ridge and ornamented lip, from pit in S. Filipe. Late seventeenth century. Pl. 20. 1.
6. Carinated pot without median ridge, from filling of S. Filipe. Common. Early seventeenth century.
7. Carinated pot with median ridge, from filling of Captain's House. Common. Late seventeenth century.
8, 9. Same, from between L-shaped building and outer wall of S. Matias. Late seventeenth century.
10, 11. Small jars in soft pink earthenware, from filling in S. Filipe and Passage of the Steps. Late seventeenth century.
12. Similar jar, from court in S. Mateus. Late seventeenth century.
13. Jar with projecting lip in pink slipped earthenware, from filling in S. Matias. Early seventeenth century.
14. Jar with lip and neck similar to carinated pot 3, but in pink slipped ware, from filling in S. Mateus. Early seventeenth century.
15. Jar with swan neck grooved on edge in same ware, from filling of pit in S. Filipe. Late seventeenth century.
16. Jar with long neck and broad rim in pink slipped ware, from filling of Captain's House. Late seventeenth century. Pl. 20. 3.
17. Jar with lip and grooved edge to lip on pink slipped ware, from filling of Captain's House. Late seventeenth century.
18. Jar with broad lip curled at edge in same ware, from upper filling in court in S. Mateus. Late seventeenth century.
19. Lip of jar with groove below lip, similar to Fig. 60. 9, from main court. Eighteenth century.
20. Bowl with thickened lip in same ware, from eighteenth-century level near west barrack block. Eighteenth century.
21. Flanged bowl in hard-baked red ware, mica on surface, from filling of court in S. Mateus. Late seventeenth century.

See pages 91–2.

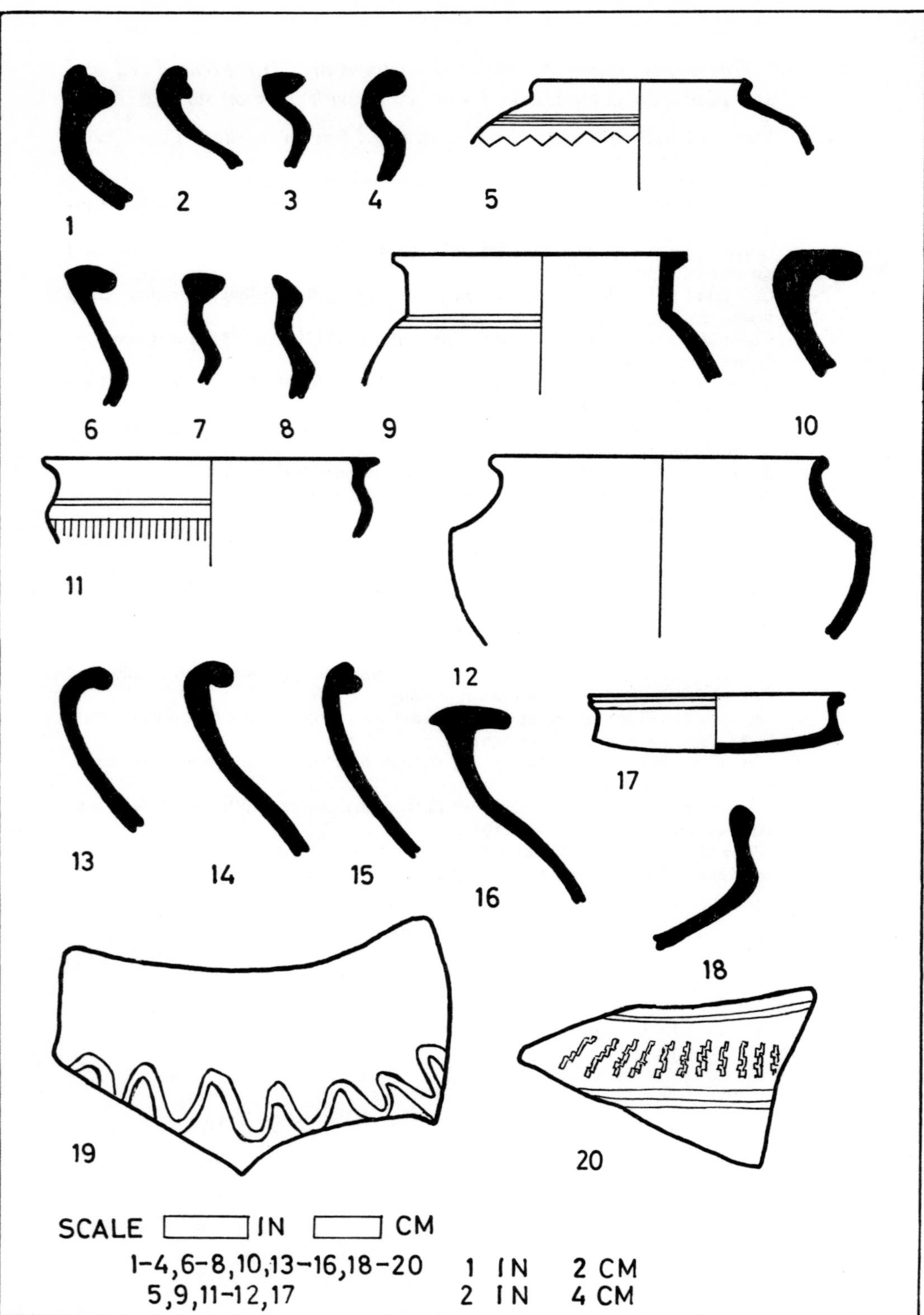
1
2
3
4
5
6
7
8
9
10
11
12
13
14
15
16
17
18
19
20
SCALE IN CM
1-4,6-8,10,13-16,18-20 1 IN 2 CM
5,9,11-12,17 2 IN 4 CM

FIG. 58

Fig. 58. *Fort Jesus. Imported unglazed earthenware. Hard-baked red and soft pink wares, sometimes burnished or with mica on surface*

1, 2. Jars with carved rims, hard-baked red body, traces of mica, from make-up of cavalier S. António. Early seventeenth century.

3. Carinated pot with projecting lip, same hard-baked body and slip, from filling of Passage of the Steps. Early seventeenth century.

4. Carinated pot with swan neck, same red body and slip, from filling of pit in S. Filipe. Late seventeenth century.

5. Small jar, thin hard-baked red body with traces of mica, from pit in S. Filipe. Late seventeenth century.

6. Similar jar, thin hard-baked red body with projecting lip and longer neck, from Passage of the Arches. Late seventeenth century.

7, 8. Similar jars, thin hard-baked red body but partially carbonized, from pit in S. Filipe. Late seventeenth century.

9. Jar with hard-baked red body with traces of mica, from pit in S. Filipe. Late seventeenth century. Pl. 20. 2.

10. Similar jar, from filling of court in S. Mateus. Late seventeenth century.

11. Small jar, similar fabric to 5, but no trace of mica, carbonized, from pit in S. Filipe. Late seventeenth century.

12. Jar in similar fabric with smoky outer surface, from pit in S. Filipe. Late seventeenth century.

13–15. Jars with rolled lip in similar hard-baked red ware but without mica on surface, from filling of pit in S. Filipe. Late seventeenth century.

16. Similar jar with projecting lip, from pit in S. Filipe. Late seventeenth century.

17. Small shallow bowl with lip grooved on edge, from south barrack block. Nineteenth century.

18. Small bowl similar to 17, from S. Filipe, Eighteenth century.

19. Wavy-line ornament on jar with burnished surface, from pit in S. Filipe. Late seventeenth century.

20. Indented ornament on jar, red body, traces of mica, from pit in S. Filipe. Late seventeenth century.

See pages 91–2.

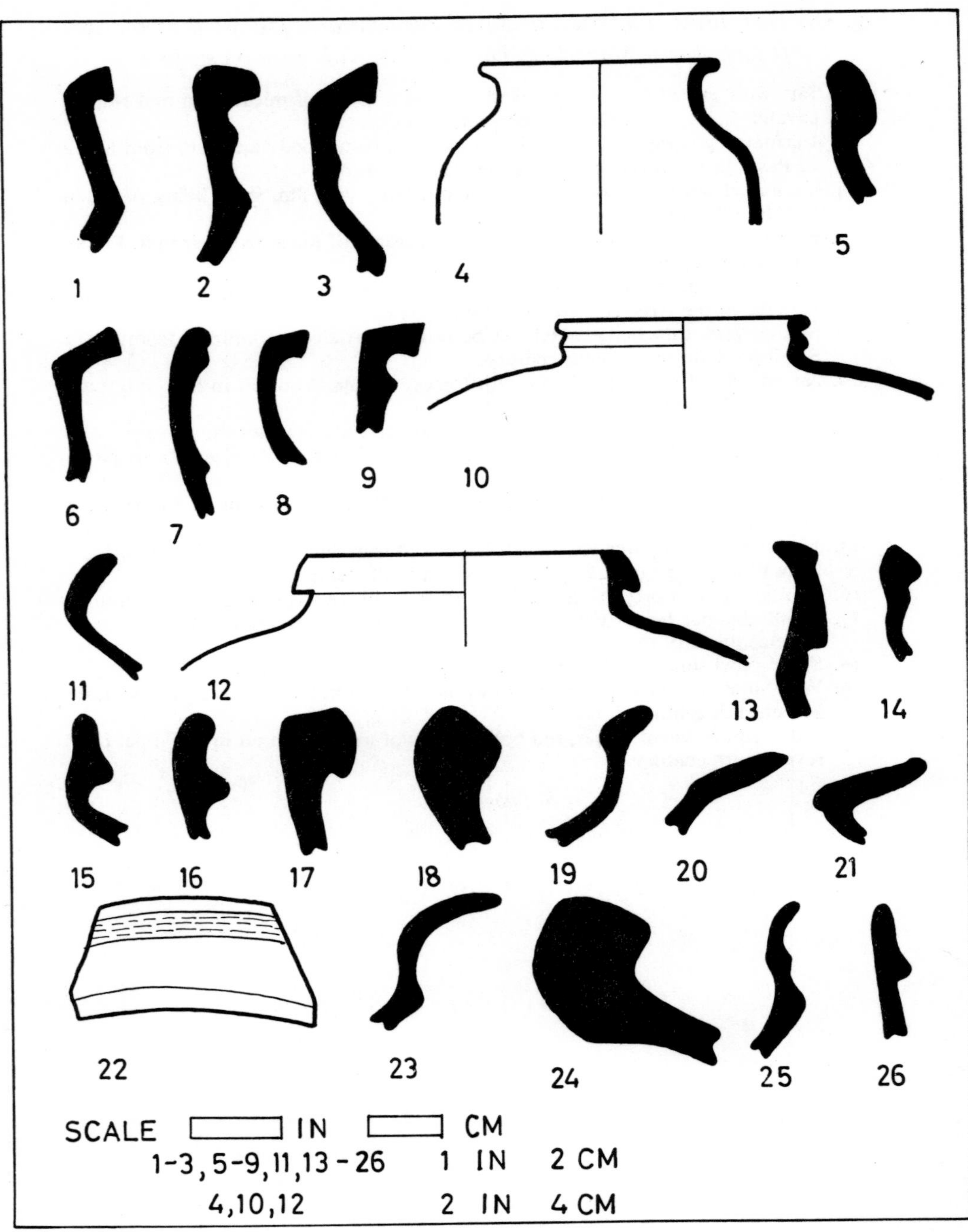
1
2
3
4
5
6
7
8
9
10
11
12
13
14
15
16
17
18
19
20
21
22
23
24
25
26
SCALE IN CM
1-3, 5-9, 11, 13-26 1 IN 2 CM
4, 10, 12 2 IN 4 CM

FIG. 59

Fig. 59. *Fort Jesus. Imported unglazed earthenware. Black ware*

1, 2. Carinated pots with hammer head, from filling of S. Mateus. Seventeenth century.
3. Similar pot, from make-up of cavalier S. António. Early seventeenth century.
4. Jar with curled lip, rough surface, from filling of S. Mateus. Common. Early seventeenth century.
5. Jar with thickened lip similar to 12, from make-up of cavalier S. António. Early seventeenth century.
6. Carinated pot with hammer head, from level between church and cistern. Late seventeenth century.
7. Carinated pot with groove on edge of lip, from area of Captain's House. Late seventeenth century.
8, 9. Carinated pots with hammer head, from filling of court in S. Mateus. Late seventeenth century.
10. Jar with groove below rolled lip, similar to Fig. 57. 19, often with white slip, from filling of Captain's House. Common. Late seventeenth century.
11. Jar like 4 with turned-out lip, from pit in S. Filipe. Late seventeenth century.
12. Jar with thickened lip, from filling over room of the stands. Late seventeenth century.
13. Similar jar, from pit in S. Filipe. Late seventeenth century.
14. Similar jar, from filling of Captain's House. Late seventeenth century.
15. Similar jar, from main court. Late seventeenth century.
16. Similar jar, from between L-shaped building and outer wall in S. Matias. Late seventeenth century.
17. Jar with heavy square lip with white slip, from filling of court in S. Mateus. Late seventeenth century.
18. Large jar with thickened lip, from filling of Captain's House. Late seventeenth century.
19. Bowl with projecting lip from west barrack block. Late seventeenth century.
20. Bowl with flat projecting lip, from main court. Late seventeenth century.
21. Similar bowl with grooved lines, from filling of Captain's House. Late seventeenth century.
22. Segment of lip of bowl 21.
23. Similar bowl, from west barrack block. Late seventeenth century.
24. Large jar with thickened lip, from area between church and cistern. Eighteenth century.
25. Carinated pot with turned-out lip and median ridge, like 2, 3, and 7, from court in S. Mateus. Eighteenth century.
26. Jar similar to 12, from S. Mateus. Eighteenth century.

See pages 91–2.

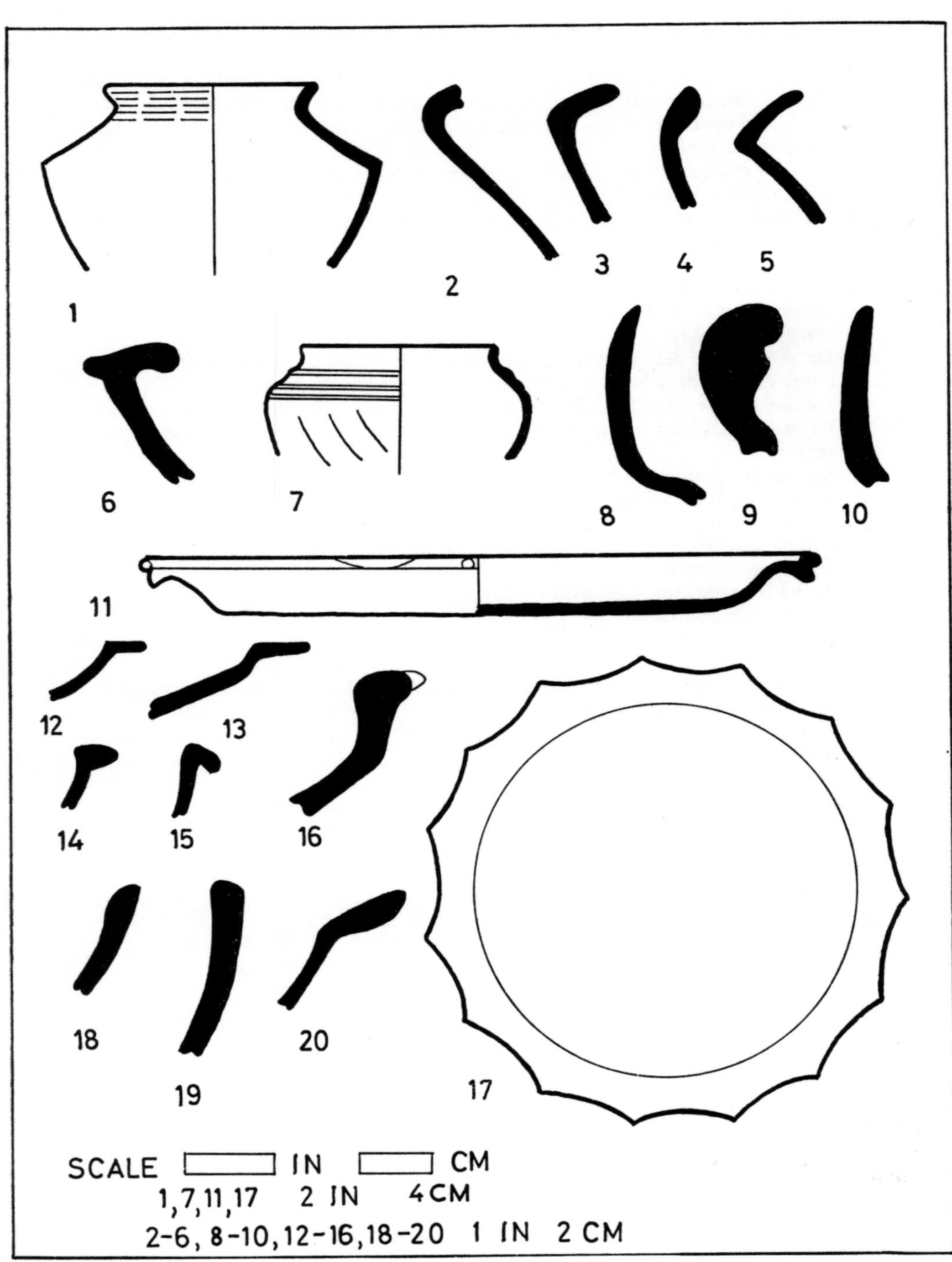
1
2
3
4
5
6
7
8
9
10
11
12
13
14
15
16
18
19
20
17
SCALE IN CM
1,7,11,17 2 IN 4CM
2-6, 8-10, 12-16, 18-20 1 IN 2 CM

FIG. 60

Fig. 60. *Fort Jesus. Imported unglazed earthenware. Black ware*

1. Carinated jar in thin, black burnished ware, from pit in S. Filipe. Late seventeenth century.

2, 3. Jars with turned-out lip grooved on edge, from pit in S. Filipe. Late seventeenth century.

4. Jar with thickened lip, from filling in S. Filipe. Late seventeenth century.

5. Jar with turned-out lip, from filling of court in S. Mateus. Late seventeenth century.

6. Jar with projecting lip, from Passage of the Arches. Late seventeenth century.

7. Small jar in thin fabric, similar to Fig. 58. 5, from south barrack block. Nineteenth century.

8. Jar with long flared neck, from court in S. Mateus. Late seventeenth century.

9. Heavy jar with undercut rim, from south barrack block. Nineteenth century.

10. Jar with upright neck burnished on both sides, from S. Mateus. Early seventeenth century.

11. Large shallow dish with stud ornament on rim, from south barrack block. Nineteenth century.

12. Small dish in thin fabric, from Passage of the Arches. Late seventeenth century.

13. Similar dish, from below Captain's House. Early seventeenth century.

14. Bowl with projecting lip, from filling of court in S. Mateus. Late seventeenth century.

15. Small bowl with turned-down lip, from filling over room of the stands. Late seventeenth century.

16, 17. Bowls with volute edge, from filling of court in S. Mateus. Late seventeenth century.

18. Bowl or platter with thickened lip, burnished on inside, from main court. Nineteenth century.

19. Bowl with lip, similar to local earthenware Fig. 33. 2, from pit in S. Filipe. Late seventeenth century.

20. Bowl with flat lip, from filling of court in S. Mateus. Late seventeenth century.

See pages 91–2.

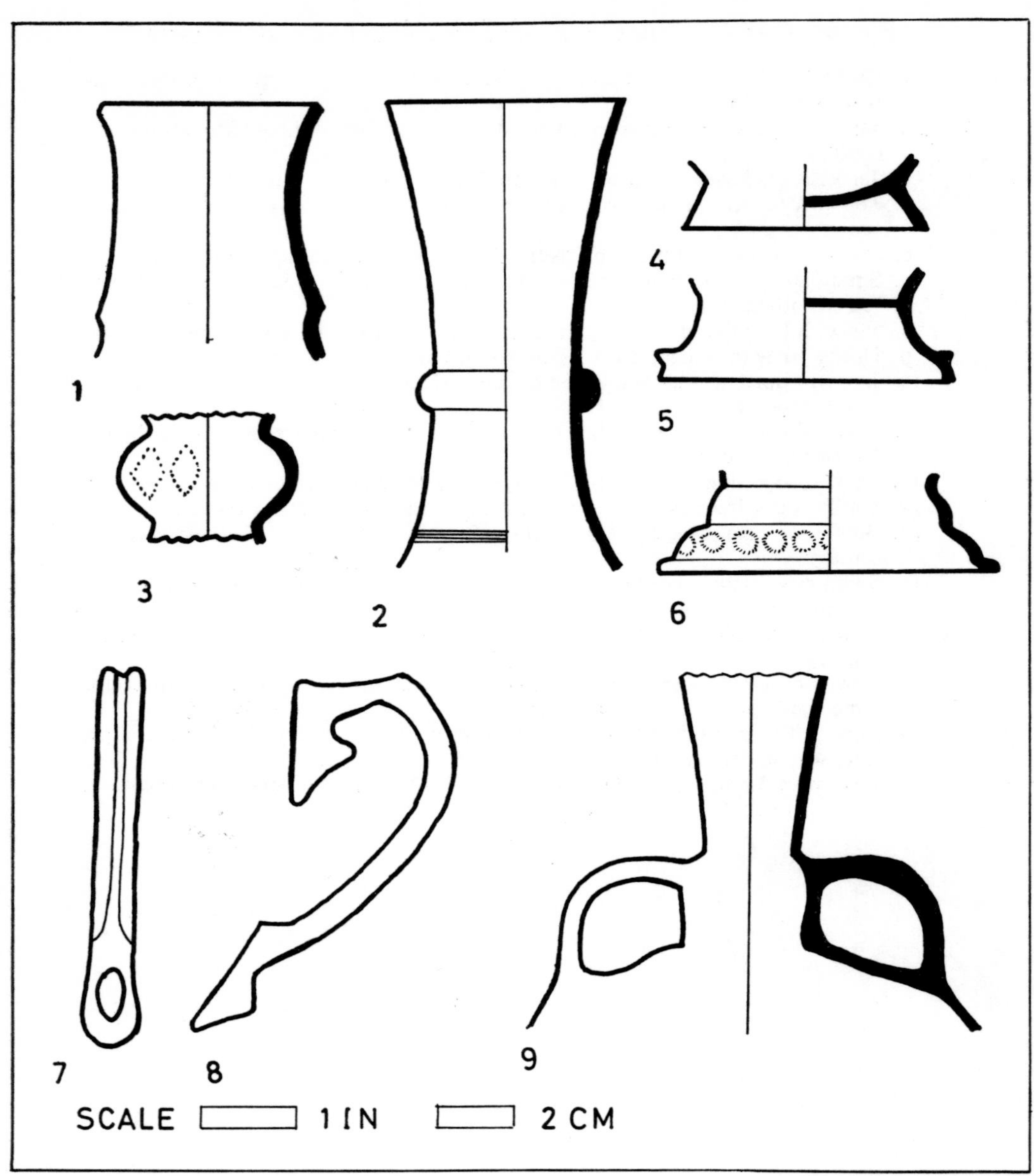

FIG. 61

Fig. 61. *Fort Jesus. Imported unglazed earthenware. Black and pink ware*

1. Bottle with flared neck, from filling of S. Mateus. Early seventeenth century.
2. Similar bottle with roll moulding on inside, from filling of Captain's House. Late seventeenth century.
3. Bulbous middle of *narghili* with incised ornament, from pit in S. Filipe. Late seventeenth century.
4. Moulded base of bottle or *narghili*, from filling of S. Filipe. Early seventeenth century.
5. Same from Passage of the Arches. Late seventeenth century.
6. Same from Captain's House. Late seventeenth century.

7, 8. Handle of jug from room of the stands. Late seventeenth century.

9. Jug with two handles attached to the neck and shoulder, in pink earthenware with a stamped pattern and metallic sheen, from filling of S. Filipe. Early seventeenth century.

See pages 91–2.

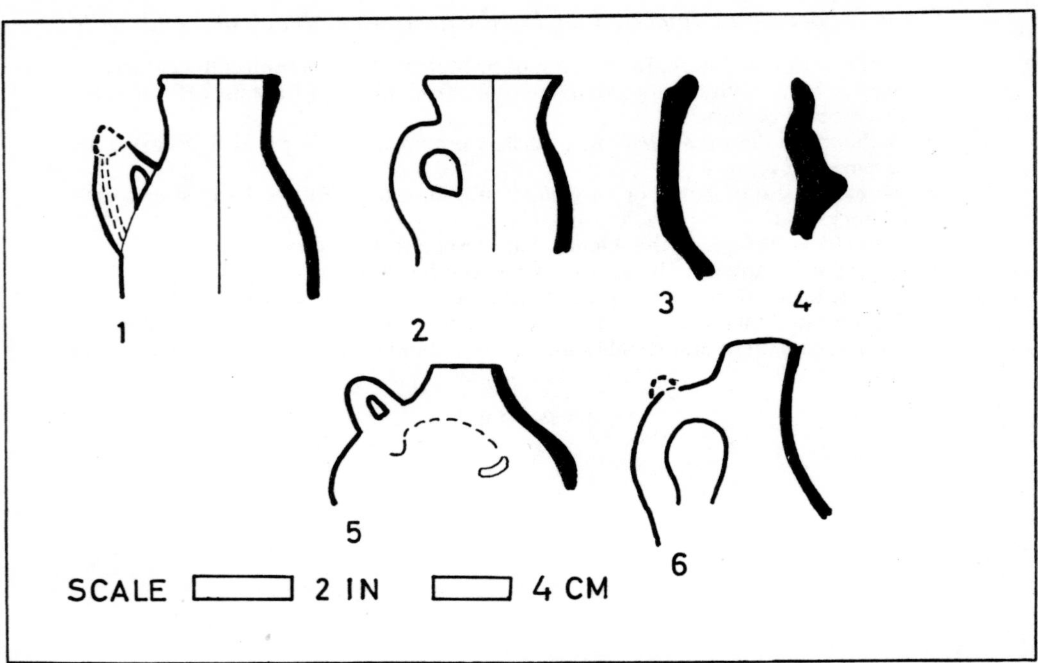

FIG. 62

Fig. 62. *Fort Jesus. Imported unglazed earthenware. Miscellaneous*

1. Tall narrow jug with vertical, pointed, and hollowed handle, brittle grey or pink body, rough surface, from upper level of court in S. Mateus. Eighteenth century.
2. Similar jug with solid rounded handle and ledge lip, same fabric, from Passage of the Arches. Nineteenth century.
3. Similar jug with pink body, from S. Mateus. Nineteenth century.
4. Similar jug with lug instead of handle, from main court. Nineteenth century.
5. Rounded flask with two or more horizontal handles, pink body, from S. Alberto. Nineteenth century.
6. Jug with vertical handle and pointed lip, greenish buff body, smooth surface, from S. Filipe. Eighteenth century.

See page 92.

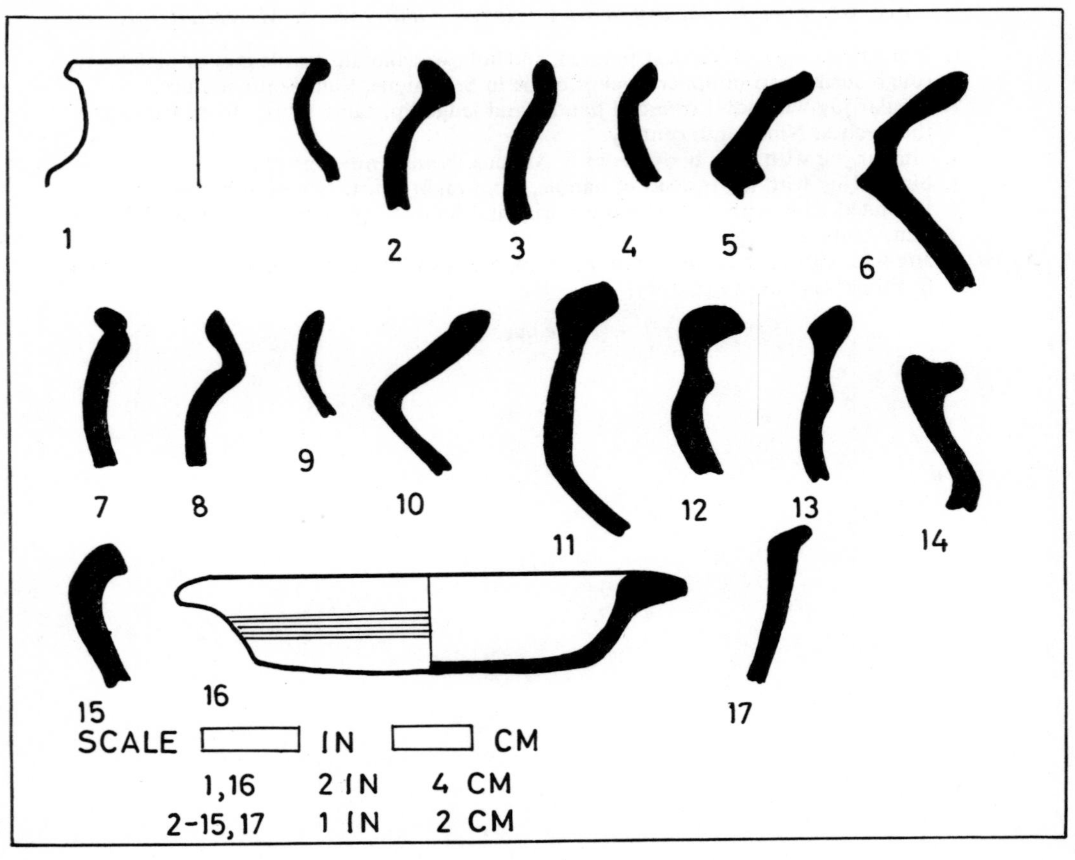
1
2
3
4
5
6
7
8
9
10
11
12
13
14
15
16
17
SCALE
IN
CM
1,16 2 IN 4 CM
2-15, 17 1 IN 2 CM

FIG. 63

Fig. 63. *Fort Jesus. Imported unglazed earthenware. Indian water pots*

1, 2. Rounded water pots, plain neck, cupped mouth, black border on outside and inside of rim, and round body on red slip, pink body, from filling of court in S. Mateus. Common. Late seventeenth century.

3. Similar pot, from below church. Common. Late seventeenth century.

4. Similar pot with plain lip, from S. Filipe. Common. Late seventeenth century.

5. Water pot with flared neck, hollowed lip, from court between church and cistern. Late seventeenth century.

6. Similar pot but hollowed at back of lip, from west barrack block. Common. Late seventeenth century.

7. Similar to 2, but with ribbing on outside of lip, from church. Uncommon. Eighteenth century.

8. Similar, from west barrack block. Uncommon. Eighteenth century.

9. Small pot with white slip, black and red bands, from court on north side of Captain's House. Eighteenth century.

10. Similar to 5 and 6, but lip thickened on top, from pit near west parapet walk. Common. Eighteenth century.

11. Similar to 1 but with projecting lip and white slip, from S. Filipe. Common. Eighteenth century.

12. Similar with projecting lip and median ridge on neck, from court behind church. Common. Eighteenth century.

13. Similar, but without projecting lip, from S. Matias. Uncommon. Eighteenth century.

14. Carinated pot with black line behind rim and on top of rim, from same pit as 10. Single specimen. Eighteenth century.

15. Unusual pot, neck straight on inside, diagonal lines on top of lip, white slip, red and black bands, from north court of Captain's House. Uncommon. Eighteenth century.

16. Dish with flat base and projecting lip, from court behind church. Common. Eighteenth century.

17. Bowl with incised sloping lip, black on top, from same pit as 10. Uncommon. Eighteenth century.

See pages 92–3.

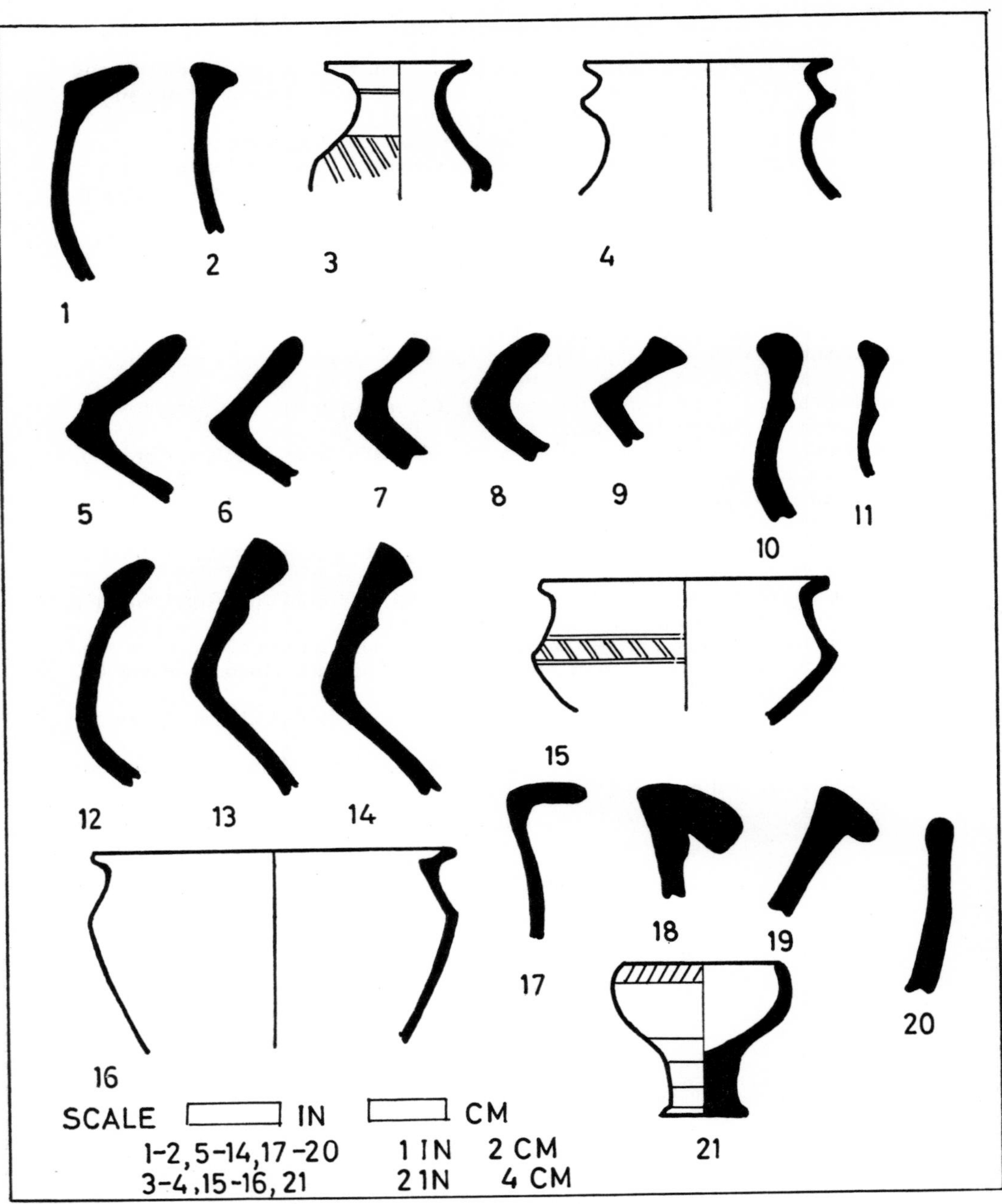
1
2
3
4
5
6
7
8
9
10
11
12
13
14
15
16
17
18
19
20
21
SCALE IN CM
1-2, 5-14, 17-20 1 IN 2 CM
3-4, 15-16, 21 2 IN 4 CM

FIG. 64

Fig. 64. *Fort Jesus. Imported unglazed earthenware. Indian water pots and other black and red painted wares*

1. Water pot with flat projecting lip, from late filling of platform over Passage of the Steps. Common. Nineteenth century.
2. Similar, from area of Captain's House. Uncommon. Nineteenth century.
3. Jar with narrow neck and projecting lip, from Passage of the Arches. Uncommon. Nineteenth century.
4. 'Concertina' neck, probably of jar, from upper filling of court in S. Mateus. Uncommon. Nineteenth century.
5. Water pot with broad projecting lip, similar to Fig. 63. 6, from Passage of the Arches. Common. Nineteenth century.
6. Similar but without hollow at back of neck. Common. Nineteenth century.
7. Water pot of usual type but without black lines, from Passage of the Arches. Uncommon. Nineteenth century.
8. Similar, from area of Captain's House. Uncommon. Nineteenth century.
9. Similar, from Passage of the Arches. Uncommon. Nineteenth century.
10. Water pot similar to Fig. 63. 12, 13, with median ridge, incurved lip, from Passage of the Arches. Uncommon. Nineteenth century.
11. Similar, from S. Alberto. Single specimen. Nineteenth century.
12. Similar with turned-out lip, from Passage of the Arches. Uncommon. Nineteenth century.
13. Water pot with flaring neck and median ridge, straight on inside of neck, from passage between L-shaped building and outer wall in S. Matias. Common. Nineteenth century.
14. Similar, from main court. Common. Nineteenth century.

15, 16. Carinated water pots with projecting lip, white slip, red and black bands on outside, from Passage of the Arches. Common. Nineteenth century.

17. Similar, from north barrack block. Nineteenth century.
18. Large bowl with projecting lip, no black lines, from Passage of the Arches. Uncommon. Nineteenth century.
19. Similar bowl, from court of Captain's House. Uncommon. Nineteenth century.
20. Upright bowl with plain lip, from main court. Single specimen. Nineteenth century.
21. Incense burner on pedestal base, white slip, black and red bands, from south barrack block. Common. Nineteenth century.

See pages 92–3.

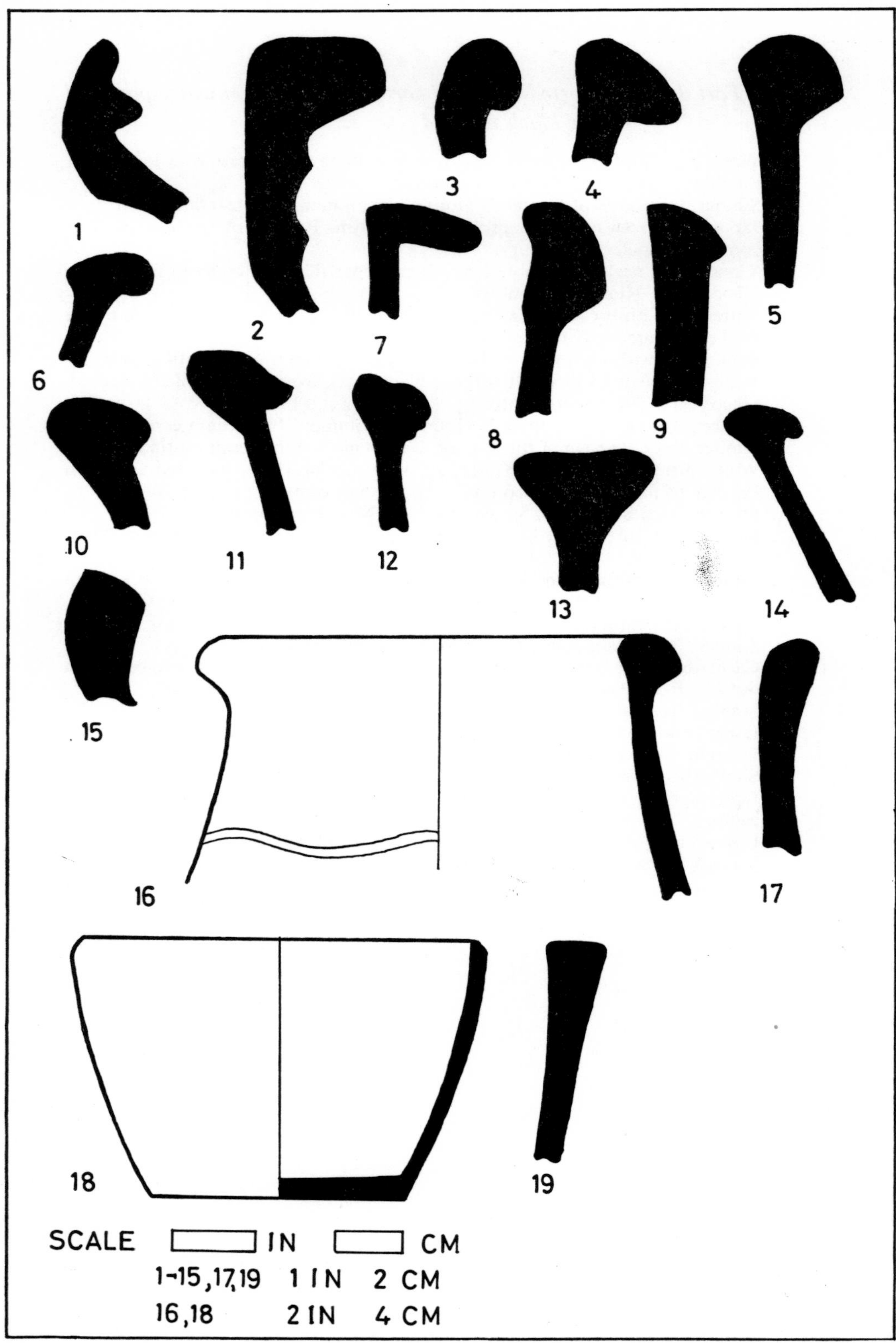
1
2
3
4
5
6
7
8
9
10
11
12
13
14
15
16
17
18
19
SCALE
IN
CM
1-15,17,19 1 IN 2 CM
16,18 2 IN 4 CM

FIG. 65

Fig. 65. *Fort Jesus. Imported unglazed earthenware. Large jars*

1. Jar with carved neck, grey body burning pink, burnished, from filling in S. Mateus. Early seventeenth century.
2. Jar with carved neck, grey body burning pink, rough outer surface, from Passage of the Steps. Nineteenth century.
3. Jar with rolled rim, hard-baked grey body burning pink, from filling of Captain's House. Late seventeenth century.
4. Heavy bowl with projecting lip, mauve-grey body, white slip on outside, from filling of Captain's House. Late seventeenth century.
5. Jar with thickened lip, mauve-grey body, white slip on outside, from filling of Captain's House. Late seventeenth century.
6. Heavy bowl with projecting lip, pink body, mauve slip on inside, from north court of Captain's House, perhaps Chinese. Eighteenth century.
7. Heavy bowl with projecting lip, pink body, traces of red slip on inside, from north court of Captain's House, perhaps Chinese. Nineteenth century.
8. Jar with thickened lip, pink body, lime coat on inside and outside, from Passage of the Steps. Nineteenth century.
9. Jar with plain lip, pink body, from main court. Nineteenth century.
10. Jar with rolled rim, pink body, from Passage of the Arches. Nineteenth century.
11. Jar with projecting lip, pink body, from Passage of the Arches. Nineteenth century.
12. Jar with projecting lip, carved underside, grey body burning pink, lime coat on outside, from main court. Nineteenth century.
13. Jar with projecting lip, pink body, from north barrack block. Nineteenth century.
14. Jar with projecting lip, pink body, from Passage of the Arches. Nineteenth century.
15. Jar with plain lip, pink body, from main court. Nineteenth century.
16. Jar with pink body, lime coat on inside, wavy line on outside, from pit in S. Filipe. Nineteenth century.
17. Jar with upright turned-out lip, wavy line on neck, from north barrack block. Late seventeenth century (?).
18. Large basin, pink body, from north court of Captain's House, perhaps Portuguese. Eighteenth century.
19. Similar vessel, pink body, from Passage of the Arches. Nineteenth century.

See pages 92–4, 117, 120.

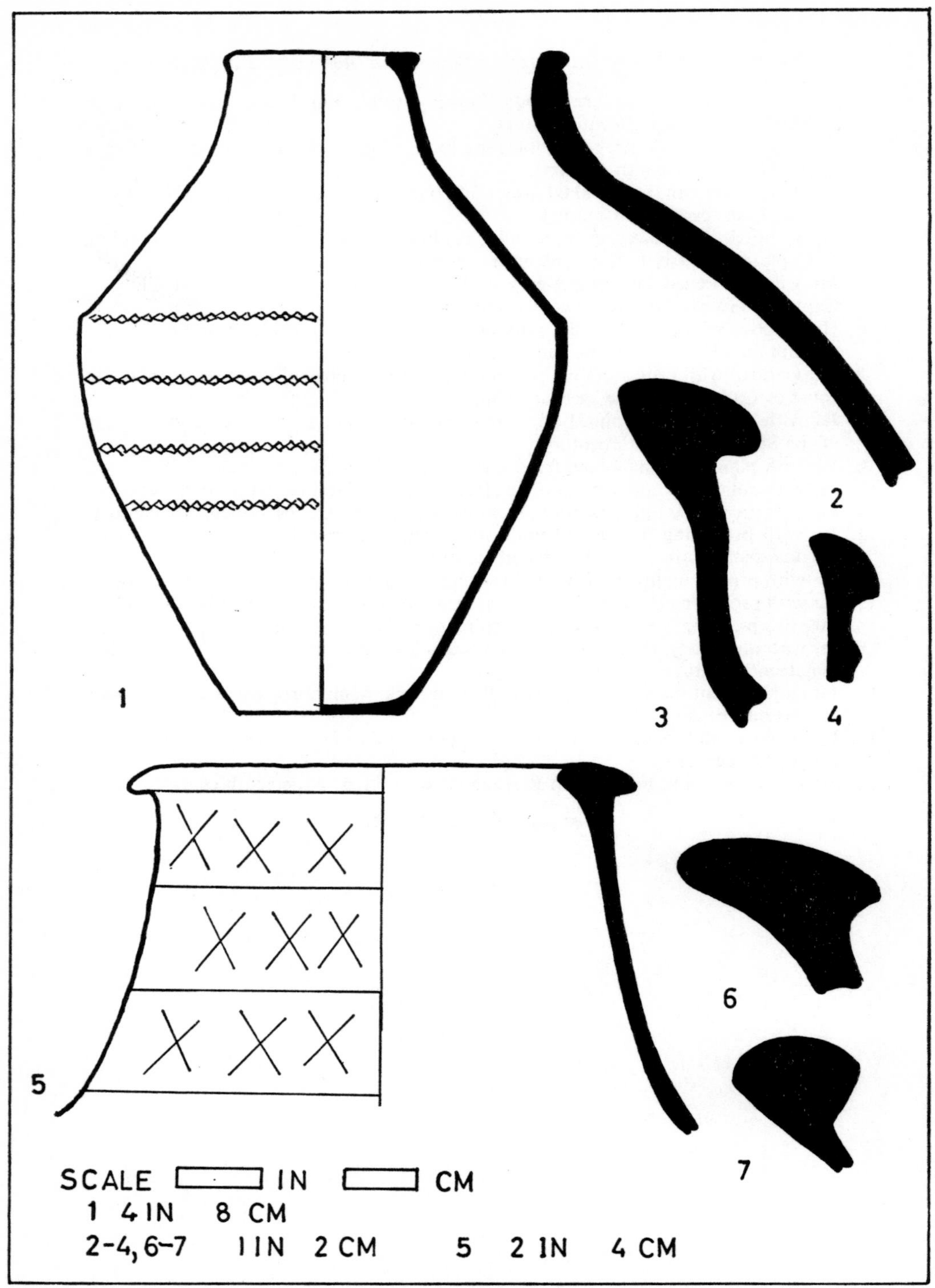

FIG. 66

Fig. 66. *Fort Jesus. Imported unglazed earthenware. Large jars*

1. Large jar with projecting lip and cordons, grey-buff body, black slip, from filling of court in S. Mateus. Common. Late seventeenth century.
2. Similar large jar but with plain lip, hard grey body and cordons. Late seventeenth century.
3. Similar jar with projecting lip, hard grey body, from pit in S. Filipe. Late seventeenth century.
4. Jar with carved neck, hard grey body, white slip, from Passage of the Arches. Nineteenth century.
5. Large jar with projecting lip, incised ornament of crosses between lines on neck, hard grey body, white slip, from north court of Captain's House. Common. Eighteenth century.
6. Similar large jar with black grits in hard grey body, from house on cavalier S. António. Nineteenth century.
7. Similar large jar with grits, from passage behind L-shaped building in S. Matias. Nineteenth century.

See pages 92–3.

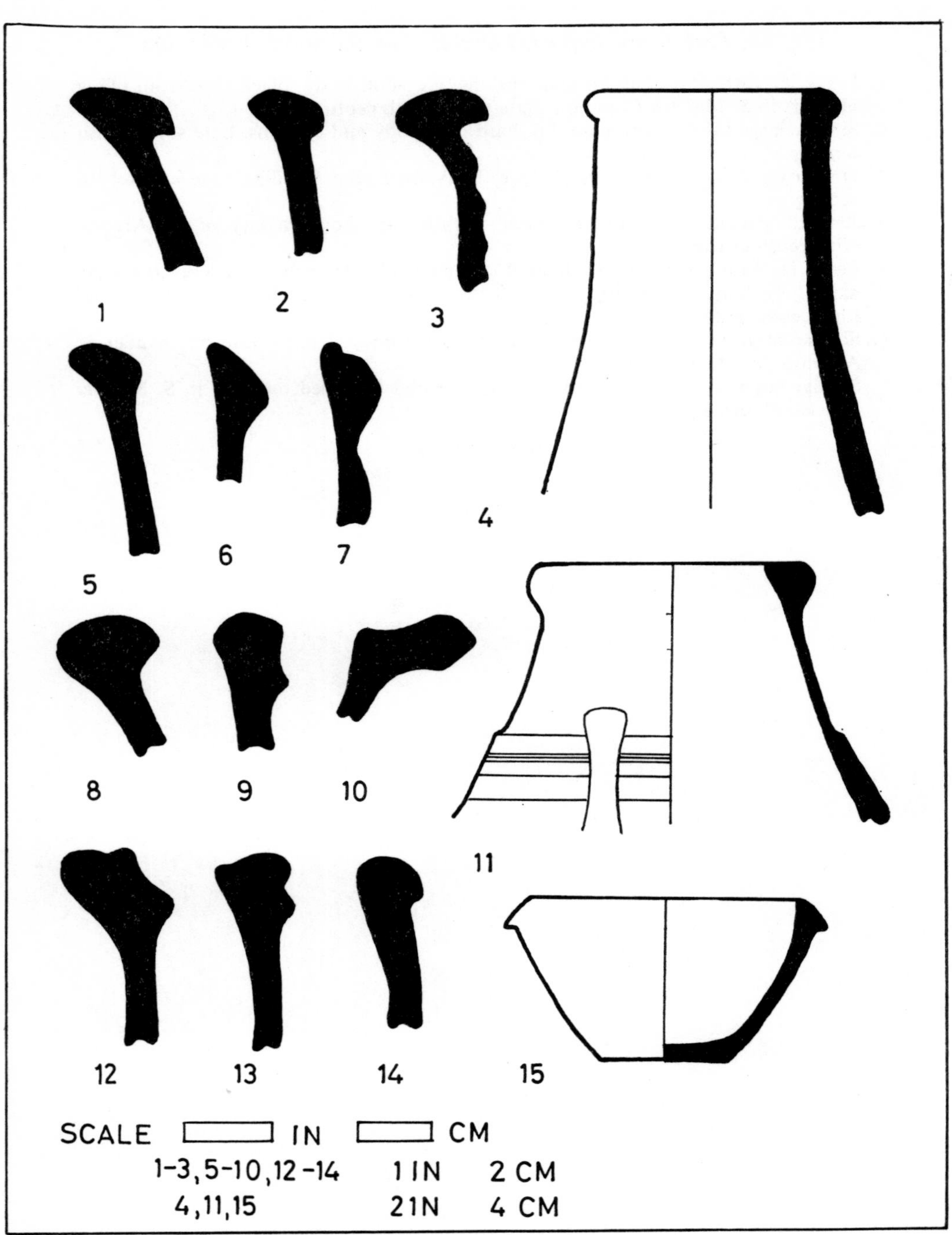
1
2
3
4
5
6
7
8
9
10
11
12
13
14
15
SCALE IN CM
1-3, 5-10, 12-14 1 IN 2 CM
4, 11, 15 2 IN 4 CM

FIG. 67

Fig. 67. *Fort Jesus. Imported unglazed earthenware. Large jars*

1. Jar with thickened lip, hard grey body, from Passage of the Arches. Nineteenth century.
2. Jar with rolled rim, hard grey body, white slip, from Passage of the Arches. Nineteenth century.
3. Jar with carved neck, hard grey body, white slip, from south barrack block. Nineteenth century.
4. Jar with rolled rim, grey body, white lime coat on outside and partly inside, from Passage of the Arches. Nineteenth century.
5. Jar with rolled rim, grey body with black grits, mauve slip on outside, from S. Filipe. Eighteenth century.
6. Jar with thickened lip, grey body with black grits, mauve slip on outside, from S. Alberto. Eighteenth century.
7. Similar jar, grey body with black grits, from Passage of the Arches. Nineteenth century.
8. Jar with rolled rim, grey body with black grits, from Passage of the Arches. Nineteenth century.
9. Jar with carved neck, grey body with black grits, white slip, from Passage of the Arches. Nineteenth century.
10. Heavy bowl with projecting concave lip, grey body with black grits, from Passage of the Arches. Nineteenth century.
11. Jar with thickened lip, cordons and vertical handles, raw buff body, black slip, from south barrack block. Nineteenth century.
12. Jar with raw buff body and black grits, black slip, from Passage of the Arches. Nineteenth century.
13. Jar with double rolled rim, buff body, black slip, from north barrack block. Nineteenth century.
14. Jar with rolled rim, buff body, black slip, from Passage of the Arches. Nineteenth century.
15. Heavy bowl, ledge rim, hard grey body. Common. Nineteenth century.

See pages 92–3, 117–18.

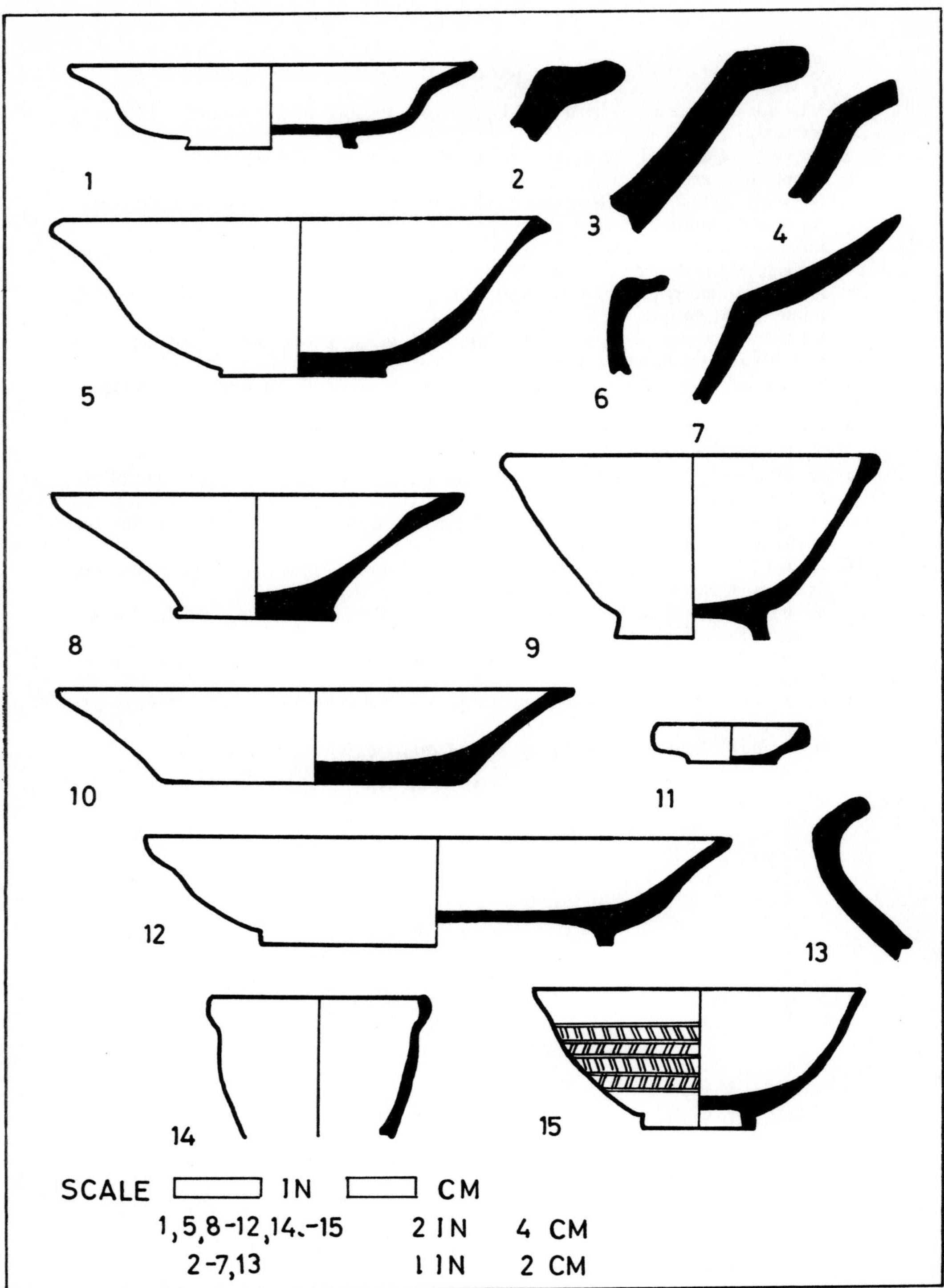
1
2
3
4
5
6
7
8
9
10
11
12
13
14
15
SCALE IN CM
1,5,8-12,14.-15 2 IN 4 CM
2-7,13 1 IN 2 CM

FIG. 68

Fig. 68. *Fort Jesus. Islamic glazed wares*

1. Plate with sloping lip, cavetto and ring base, floral design on inside in green, blue, and white, glazed also on outside over red body, from filling in S. Alberto. Cl. 1. Uncommon. Early seventeenth century. Pl. 21. 3.
2. Heavy bowl with horizontal lip, floral design in black on yellow over red body, from filling over Passage of the Steps. Cl. 2. Uncommon. Early seventeenth century.
3. Similar bowl with floral design in manganese on white over red body, from filling in S. Filipe. Cl. 1. Uncommon. Early seventeenth century.
4. Bowl with sloping lip, floral design in manganese and black on white over red body, from make-up of cavalier S. António. Cl. 1. Single specimen. Early seventeenth century.
5. Bowl with pedestal base, chevron design in black on blue over red body, from filling of S. Filipe. Cl. 4 (Pl. 21. 4). Common. Early seventeenth century.
6. Bowl or jug with concave lip, black glaze on hard grey buff body, from filling of pit in S. Filipe. Cl. 10. Single specimen. Late seventeenth century.
7. Plate with long sloping lip, black chevron pattern on turquoise glaze over red body, from filling of S. Filipe. Cl. 4. Single specimen. Early seventeenth century.
8. Bowl with sloping lip, pedestal base, branch in black on lip and star in bottom, on grey ground over hard grey body, from filling of S. Matias. Cl. 9 (Pl. 22. 2). Common. Early seventeenth century.
9. Bowl with thickened lip and ring base, grey glaze on red body, from mixed level in S. Matias. Cl. 5. Single example.
10. Plate with turned-out lip, flat base, schematized floral design in blue and turquoise on white crackled ground over red body, from south barrack block. Cl. 7 (Pl. 22. 1). Uncommon. Nineteenth century.
11. Miniature plate with thickened lip and flat base, white glaze over hard grey buff body, from filling of S. Filipe. Cl. 11. Single specimen. Early seventeenth century.
12. Plate with sloping lip and ring base, blue-and-white design of Chinese landscape on white sugary body, from filling of court in S. Mateus. Uncommon. Cl. 13 (Pl. 22. 3). Late seventeenth century.
13. Jug, turquoise glaze over red body, from filling of S. Filipe. Cl. 5. Uncommon. Early seventeenth century.
14. Bowl, blue glaze slightly iridescent on white sugary body, from filling of court in S. Mateus. Cl. 14. Single specimen. Late seventeenth century.
15. Thin bowl with ring base, incised with bands of chevron ornament under iridescent white glaze over white sugary body, in imitation of *blanc de chine*, from filling of pit in S. Filipe. Cl. 16 (Pl. 22. 4). Uncommon. Late seventeenth century.

See pages 94–8.

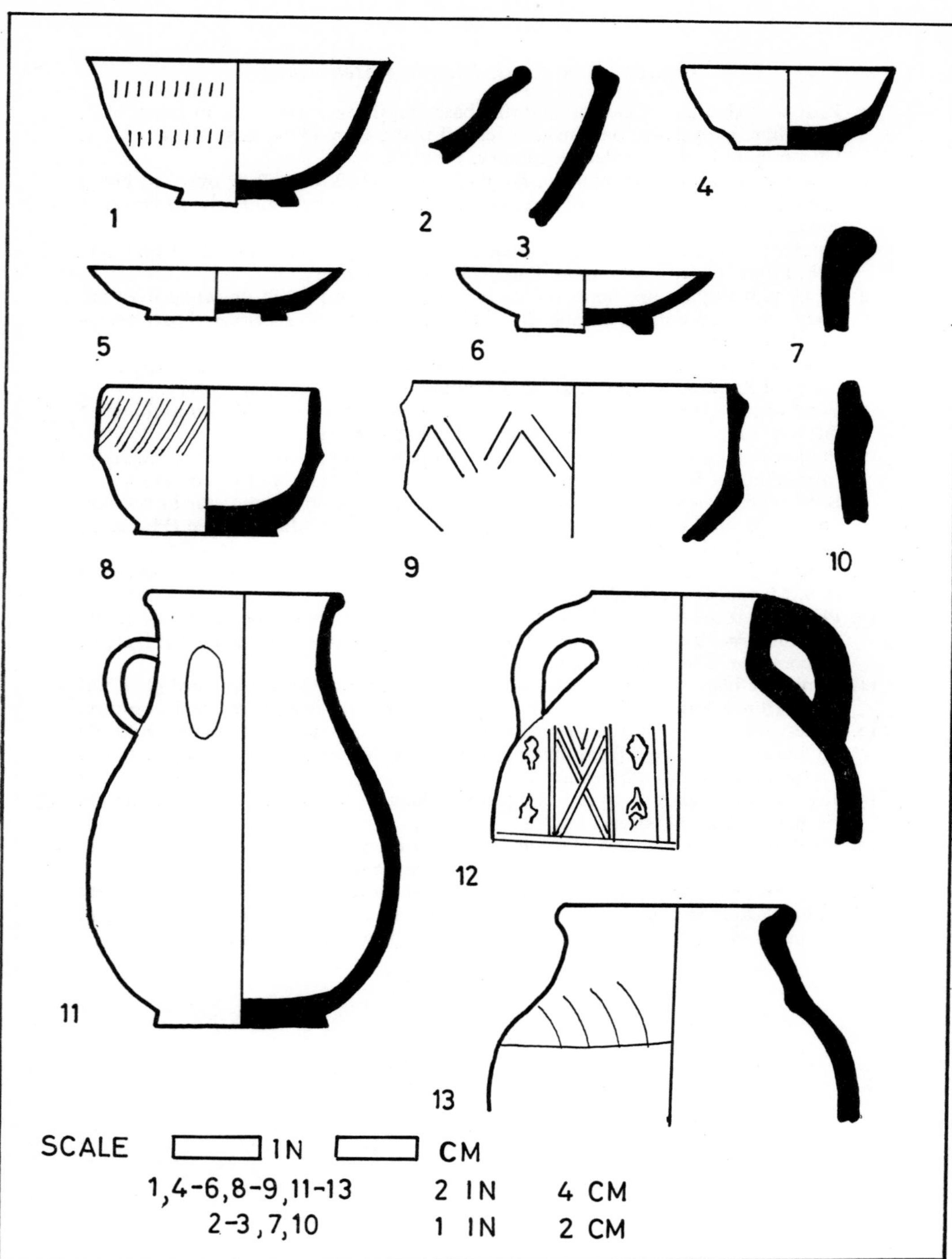
1
2
3
4
5
6
7
8
9
10
11
12
13
SCALE
IN
CM
1,4-6,8-9,11-13
2 IN
4 CM
2-3,7,10
1 IN
2 CM

FIG. 69

Fig. 69. *Fort Jesus. Islamic glazed wares*

1. Bowl with ring base, usually scored below glaze, green glaze over soft buff body, from filling of court in S. Mateus. Cl. 22 (Pl. 23. 4, 5). Late seventeenth century.
2. Bowl or small dish with concave lip, pale blue outside, yellow inside, over soft buff body, from filling of court in S. Mateus. Cl. 22. Uncommon. Late seventeenth century.
3. Bowl with incurved lip, green glaze over soft buff body, from filling of court in S. Mateus. Cl. 22. Uncommon. Late seventeenth century.
4. Bowl with pedestal base, speckled green-grey glaze over soft buff body, from filling of Passage of the Arches. Cl. 24. Uncommon. Late seventeenth century.

5, 6. Shallow plates with ring base, pale yellow-green glaze over soft buff body, from Passage of the Arches. Cl. 24. Common. Some eighteenth but most nineteenth century.

7. Jug with rolled rim, blue glaze on buff body, from filling of court in S. Mateus. Cl. 26. Late seventeenth century.

8, 9. Bowls with upright slightly concave sides, pedestal base, decorated with diagonal lines and chevrons in manganese on pale turquoise ground over soft buff body, from south barrack block. Cl. 25 (Pl. 23. 6–10). Common. Some eighteenth but most nineteenth century.

10. Similar bowl with plain yellow-brown glaze on soft buff body, from Passage of the Arches. Cl. 23. Common. Nineteenth century.
11. Jar with four handles, light grey-blue glaze on soft buff body, from main court. Cl. 24. Uncommon. Eighteenth century.
12. Jar with two handles rising to rim, parallel design of leaves and diagonal crosses in manganese and green on white, on hard buff body, from court of Captain's House. Cl. 12. Single specimen. Nineteenth century.
13. Jar or jug with rolled rim, with indentation following the curve of the body below bright blue glaze on soft buff body, from Passage of the Arches. Cl. 26. Single specimen. Nineteenth century.

See pages 94–8.

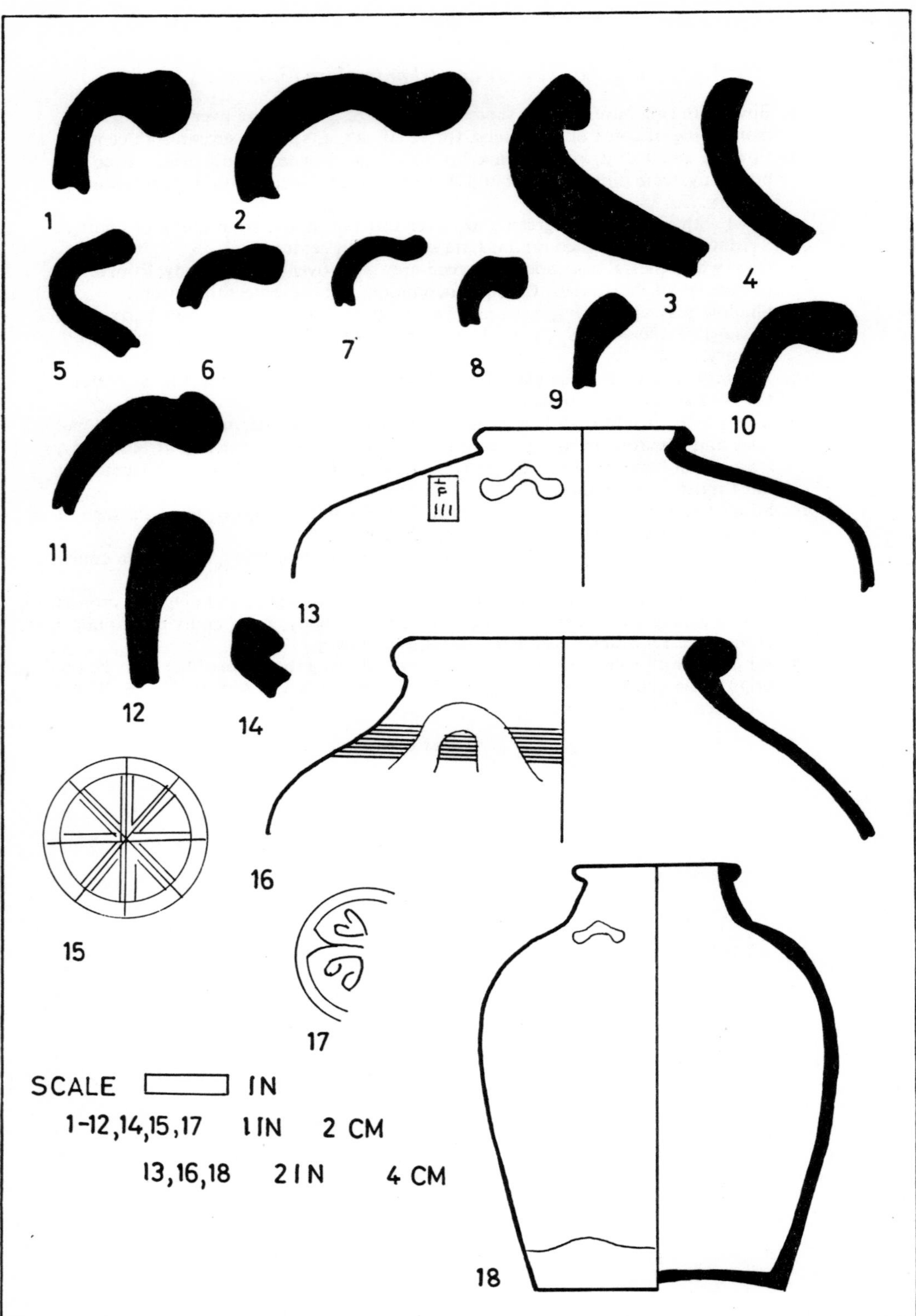
1
2
3
4
5
6
7
8
9
10
11
12
13
14
15
16
17
18
SCALE IN
1-12,14,15,17 1 IN 2 CM
13,16,18 2 IN 4 CM

FIG. 70

Fig. 70. *Fort Jesus. Chinese glazed stoneware jars*

1. Large storage jar with projecting lip grooved on top, glossy black glaze, grey body, from filling of Captain's House. Common. Late seventeenth century.
2. Similar jar from court behind church. Single specimen. Eighteenth century.
3. Similar large jar with row of studs above the shoulder, from area of Captain's House. Common. Eighteenth century.
4. Similar jar with studs but with upright neck, from main court. Single specimen. Eighteenth century.
5. Same type of jar, glaze, and body, but smaller, from filling of S. Matias. Uncommon. Early seventeenth century.

6, 7. Similar jars from filling of Captain's House. Uncommon. Late seventeenth century.

8. Similar jar from S. Alberto. Uncommon. Nineteenth century.
9. Jar with upright neck, mottled brown glaze, grey body, from room of the stands. Single specimen. Late seventeenth century.
10. Jar with projecting lip, pink body, and mauve slip, as used on the earthenware jar in Fig. 65. 6, from filling of Captain's House. Single specimen. Late seventeenth century.
11. Similar jar with projecting lip, grooved on top, similar to 1, pink body, mauve slip, from filling of S. Filipe. Single specimen. Early seventeenth century.
12. Jar with upright neck and similar body and surface, from S. Matias. Single specimen. Late seventeenth century.
13. Medium-sized jar with rolled rim, four horizontal cord handles, unreadable mark in rectangular frame on shoulder, concave base, from filling of Captain's House. Common. Late seventeenth century.
14. Similar jar from pit in S. Filipe. Uncommon. Early seventeenth century.
15. Stamp on jar with black glaze, grey-pink body, from church. Single specimen. Eighteenth century.
16. Jar with rolled rim, cordons, and horizontal handles, sienna-brown glaze over pink body. Single specimen. (Pl. 39. 1.) Late seventeenth century.
17. Stamp on jar with black glaze, buff body, from Passage of the Arches. Single specimen. Nineteenth century.
18. Small jar with four single horizontal cord handles, glossy yellow-brown glaze not reaching bottom of jar, yellow body, from filling of Captain's House. Common. Late seventeenth century.

See pages 97, 117–18.

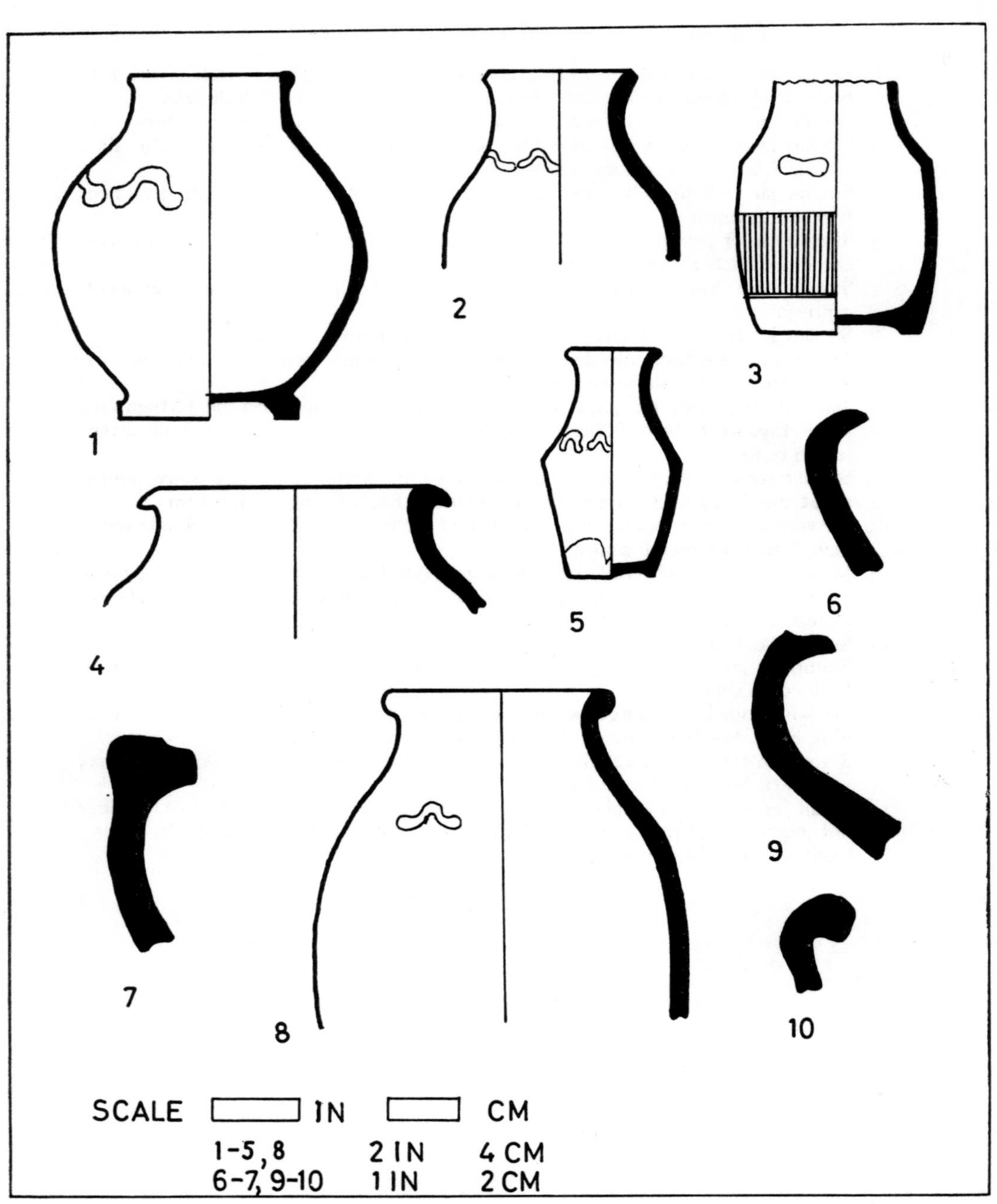

FIG. 71

Fig. 71. *Fort Jesus. Unidentified glazed wares—jars*

1, 2. Small jars with rolled rim, ring base, and two pairs of horizontal handles, brown glaze on grey body, from filling of court in S. Mateus (Pl. 39. 2). Common. Late seventeenth century.

3. Jar with two single handles, incised vertical lines on lower part of body, uncertain rim, from filling of court in S. Mateus. Single specimen. Late seventeenth century.

4. Jar with projecting lip, same glaze and body, from filling of court in S. Mateus. Common. Late seventeenth century.

5. Small narrow jar, dark-brown glaze, grey body, from court of Captain's House. Single specimen. Nineteenth century.

6. Jar with turned-out lip, dark-brown glaze, similar to 1, from upper filling of court in S. Mateus. Uncommon. Eighteenth century.

7. Large jar with projecting lip grooved on top, green-brown glaze, pink body, from S. Alberto. Single specimen. Nineteenth century.

8. Jar with rolled rim, single horizontal handles, brown glaze, buff body, varnished on inside, from Passage of the Arches. Uncommon. Nineteenth century.

9. Jar with turned-out lip, grooved on top, similar to 7, brown glaze, buff body, from Passage of the Arches. Single specimen. Nineteenth century.

10. Jar with projecting lip, poor black glaze, buff body, from Passage of the Arches. Nineteenth century.

See pages 117–19.

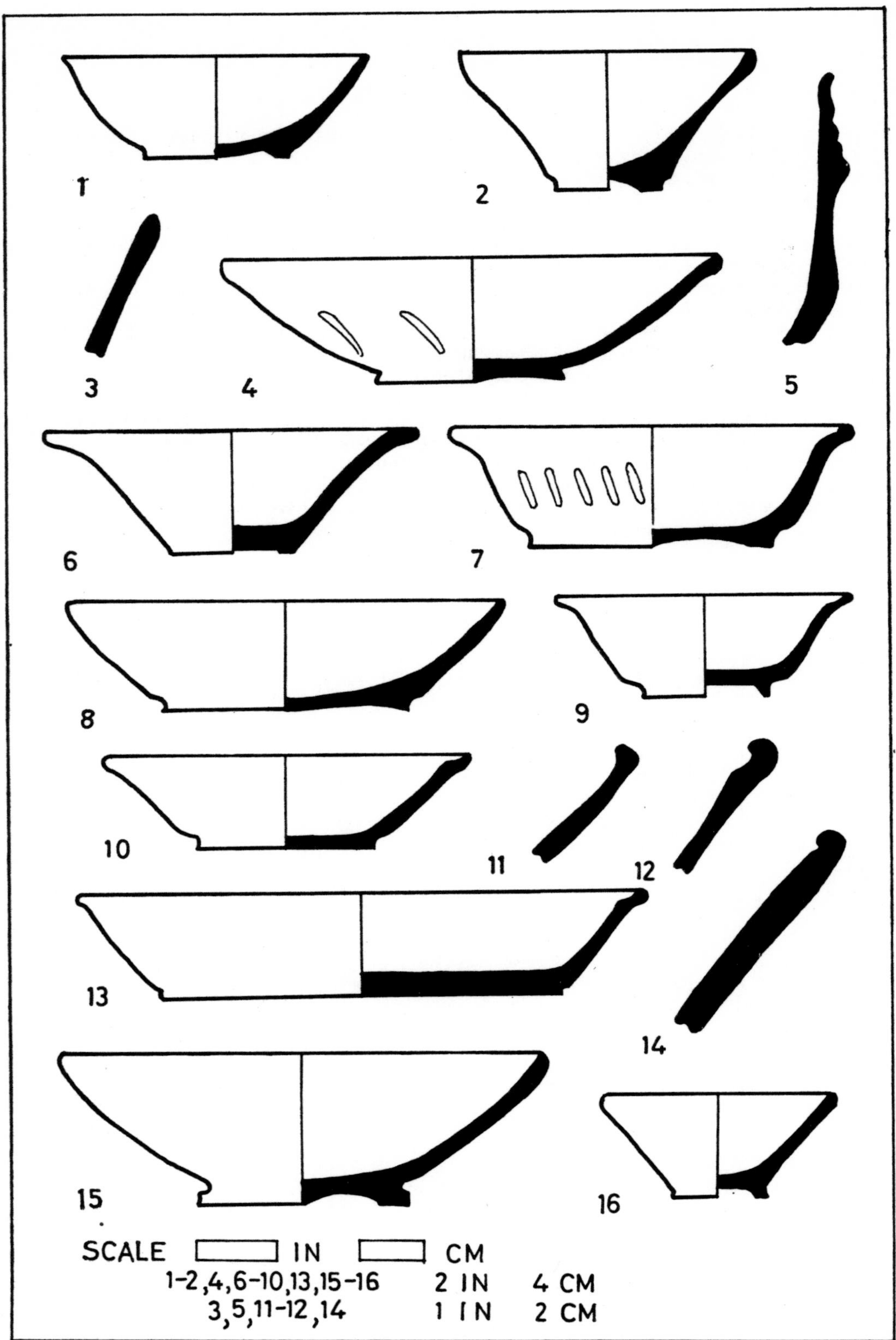
1
2
3
4
5
6
7
8
9
10
11
12
13
14
15
16
SCALE IN CM
1-2,4,6-10,13,15-16 2 IN 4 CM
3,5,11-12,14 1 IN 2 CM

FIG. 72

Fig. 72. *Fort Jesus. Unidentified glazed wares—bowls*

1. Bowl with ring base, glossy brown, grey-pink body, from main court. Common. Eighteenth century.
2. Similar bowl with incurved lip, poor grey glaze on inside only, pink body, from filling of court in S. Mateus. Common. Late seventeenth century.
3. Similar bowl to 1, green glaze, pink body, from bottom of Passage of the Arches. Common. Late seventeenth century.
4. Wide-mouthed bowl, thickened lip, pedestal base, indented ornament on sides, green glaze, grey body, from filling of court in S. Mateus. Common. Late seventeenth century.
5. Cordoned bowl or beaker, green glaze, pink body, from filling of Captain's House. Single example. Early seventeenth century.
6. Plate with rounded flanged lip, flat ring base, green glaze, one with white slip and zigzag incised ornament, grey body, from pit in S. Filipe. Common. Late seventeenth century.
7. Similar plate but with rounded edge to flange of lip, indented ornament, green glaze, grey body, from main court, same level as 1. Common. Early seventeenth century.
8. Plate with plain lip, pedestal base, brown or green glaze on grey-pink body, from filling of court in S. Mateus. Common. Late seventeenth century.
9. Plate with hollowed flanged lip, ring base, brown or green glaze, grey-pink body, from filling of court in S. Mateus. Common. Late seventeenth century.
10. Similar plate with pedestal base, green glaze, from filling of court in S. Mateus. Common. Late seventeenth century.
11. Bowl with incurved lip similar to 2, green glaze, grey body, from filling of court in S. Mateus. Common. Late seventeenth century.
12. Wide-mouthed bowl with rounded lip and groove on inside of lip, brown glaze, grey-pink body, from main court. Common. Late seventeenth century.
13. Large wide-mouthed plate with grooved flanged lip and pedestal base, similar to 10, green glaze, grey body, from filling of court in S. Mateus. Uncommon. Late seventeenth century.
14. Wide-mouthed bowl with lip similar to 12, zigzag pattern on inside, green glaze, grey body, from north barrack block. Single specimen. Late seventeenth century.

15, 16. Bowls with plain lip and ring base, brown glaze, grey-pink body, from main court. Common. Eighteenth century.

See pages 118–19.

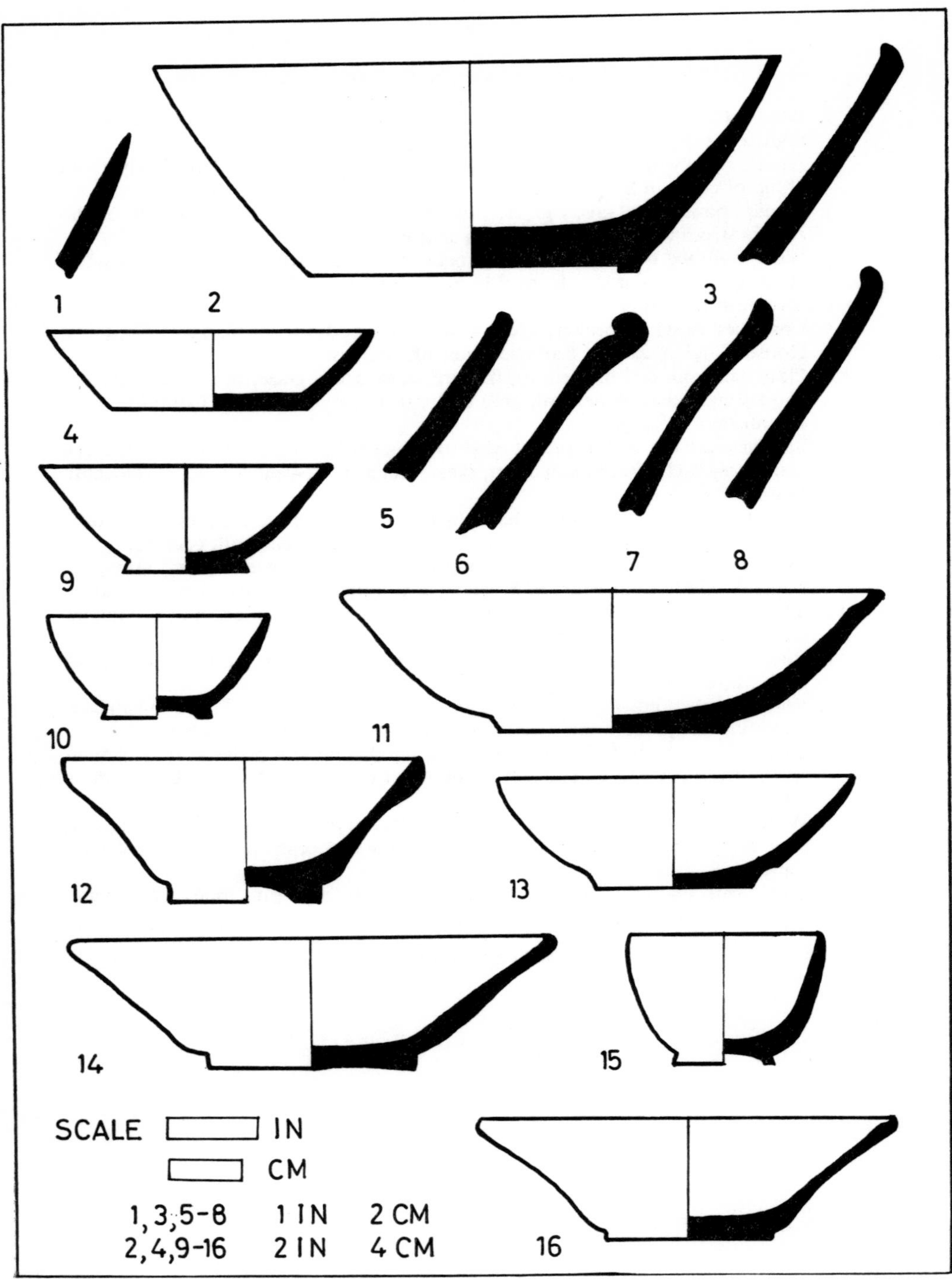
1
2
3
4
5
6
7
8
9
10
11
12
13
14
15
16
SCALE
IN
CM
1, 3, 5–8 1 IN 2 CM
2, 4, 9–16 2 IN 4 CM

FIG. 73

Fig. 73. *Fort Jesus. Unidentified glazed wares—bowls*

1. Bowl with tapered lip, brown glaze, grey body. Uncommon. Eighteenth century.
2. Large bowl, flat lip, ring base, glossy dark-brown glaze, grey body, from north court of Captain's House. Single example. Eighteenth century.
3. Similar bowl with in-turned lip, from north court of Captain's House. Common. Eighteenth century.
4. Large bowl, tapered lip, glossy brown glaze, from north court of Captain's House. Single example. Eighteenth century.
5. Bowl with ledge on inside of lip, brown glaze, grey body, from main court. Common. Eighteenth century.
6. Bowl with thickened rounded lip, groove on inside of lip, brown or light-brown glaze, pink body, from between church and cistern. Common. Eighteenth century.
7. Bowl with lip similar to Fig. 72. 2, smooth dark-brown glaze, grey body, from main court. Common. Eighteenth century.
8. Similar bowl, green glaze, grey body, from house against west wall. Uncommon. Eighteenth century.
9. Bowl with pedestal base, brown glaze, buff body, from lamp room. Common. Nineteenth century.
10. Bowl with uneven inner surface, ring base, brown glaze, pink-buff body, from main court. Common. Nineteenth century.
11. Wide-mouthed bowl with slight hollow behind lip, pedestal base, brown glaze, buff body, from Passage of the Arches. Common. Nineteenth century.
12. Bowl with thickened lip, ring base, brown glaze, buff body, from pit in S. Matias. Common. Nineteenth century.
13. Wide-mouthed bowl with plain lip, pedestal base, brown glaze, pink-buff body, from Passage of the Arches. Common. Nineteenth century.
14. Wide-mouthed bowl with rolled lip, pedestal base, brown glaze, buff body, from same pit as 12. Uncommon. Nineteenth century.
15. Bowl with plain lip, ring base, brown glaze, pink-buff body, from main court. Uncommon. Nineteenth century.
16. Wide-mouthed bowl with groove behind lip, brown glaze, buff body, south barrack block. Common. Nineteenth century. (Cf. Pl. 39. 6.)

See pages 118–19.

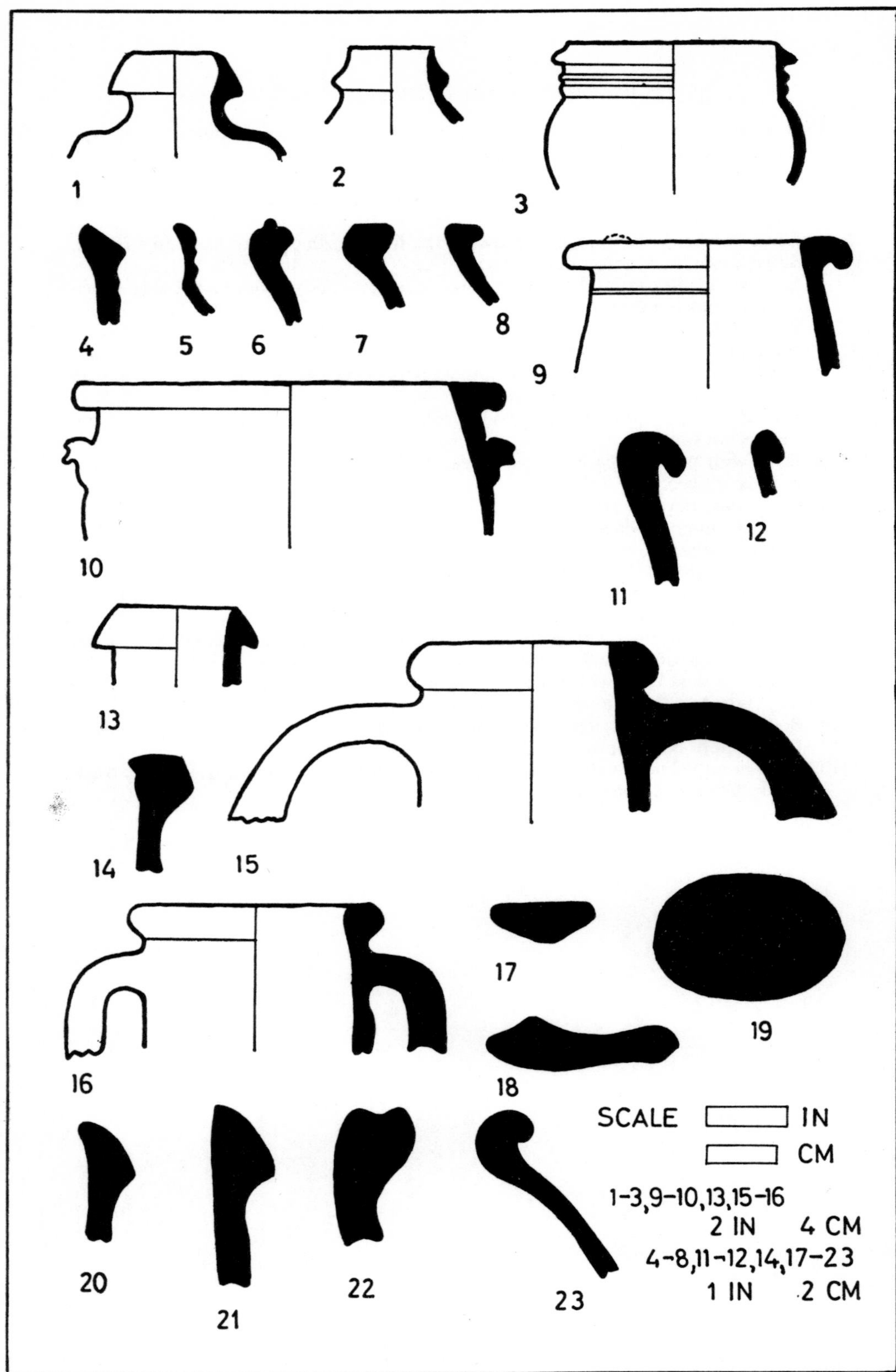
1
2
3
4
5
6
7
8
9
10
11
12
13
14
15
16
17
18
19
20
21
22
23
SCALE IN
CM
1-3,9-10,13,15-16
2 IN 4 CM
4-8,11-12,14,17-23
1 IN 2 CM

FIG. 74

Fig. 74. *Fort Jesus. Portuguese wares*

1. Demijohn, red body, brown or dark-brown glaze on inside, splashed with glaze on outside, from S. Filipe. Common. Seventeenth century. (Cf. Pl. 41. 10.)
2. Similar vessel from filling of Captain's House. Late seventeenth century.
3. Jar, red body, green glaze on outside, yellow glaze inside, from S. Alberto. Found early seventeenth, but common late seventeenth century. (Cf. Pl. 41. 11.)
4. Similar jar, from make-up of rectangular projection. Early seventeenth century.
5. Similar jar, green glaze inside and outside, from S. Alberto. Early seventeenth century.
6. Jar, dark olive outside and inside, blister on top of rim, from filling of court in S. Mateus. Late seventeenth century.
7. Similar jar, green outside, yellow inside, from filling of Captain's House. Late seventeenth century.
8. Similar jar, yellow-brown outside, dark-olive inside, from filling of Captain's House. Late seventeenth century.
9. Basin with projecting lip, red body, spotted green-yellow glaze outside, orange inside, blister on top of rim, from S. Filipe. Early seventeenth century.
10. Similar basin with vertical handles, from pit in S. Filipe. Late seventeenth century.
11. Basin with curved lip, red body, green glaze on inside, possibly not Portuguese, from S. Alberto. Early seventeenth century.
12. Similar basin but smaller, from filling of Captain's House. Late seventeenth century.
13. Demijohn, no glaze, pink ware, white slip, from S. Filipe (cf. Goggin, fig. 5*a*). Early seventeenth century.

14, 15. Two-handled olive jars, pink ware, traces of slip, from S. Mateus and S. Alberto. Early seventeenth century.

16. Similar jar, no slip, from main court. Nineteenth century.

17, 18. Sections of handles of olive jars from filling of Passage of the Steps and main court. Early seventeenth century.

19. Section of handle of olive jar, from main court. Late seventeenth century.
20. Jar with red body and grey core, from make-up of rectangular projection, probably Portuguese. Early seventeenth century.
21. Similar jar with lime coat on outside from make-up of cavalier S. António, probably Portuguese. Early seventeenth century.
22. Jar, grooved lip, red body, grey core, from Passage of the Arches, probably Portuguese. Nineteenth century.
23. Jar with rolled and undercut lip, hard pink earthenware, from Passage of the Arches, probably Portuguese. Nineteenth century.

See pages 93, 119–20.

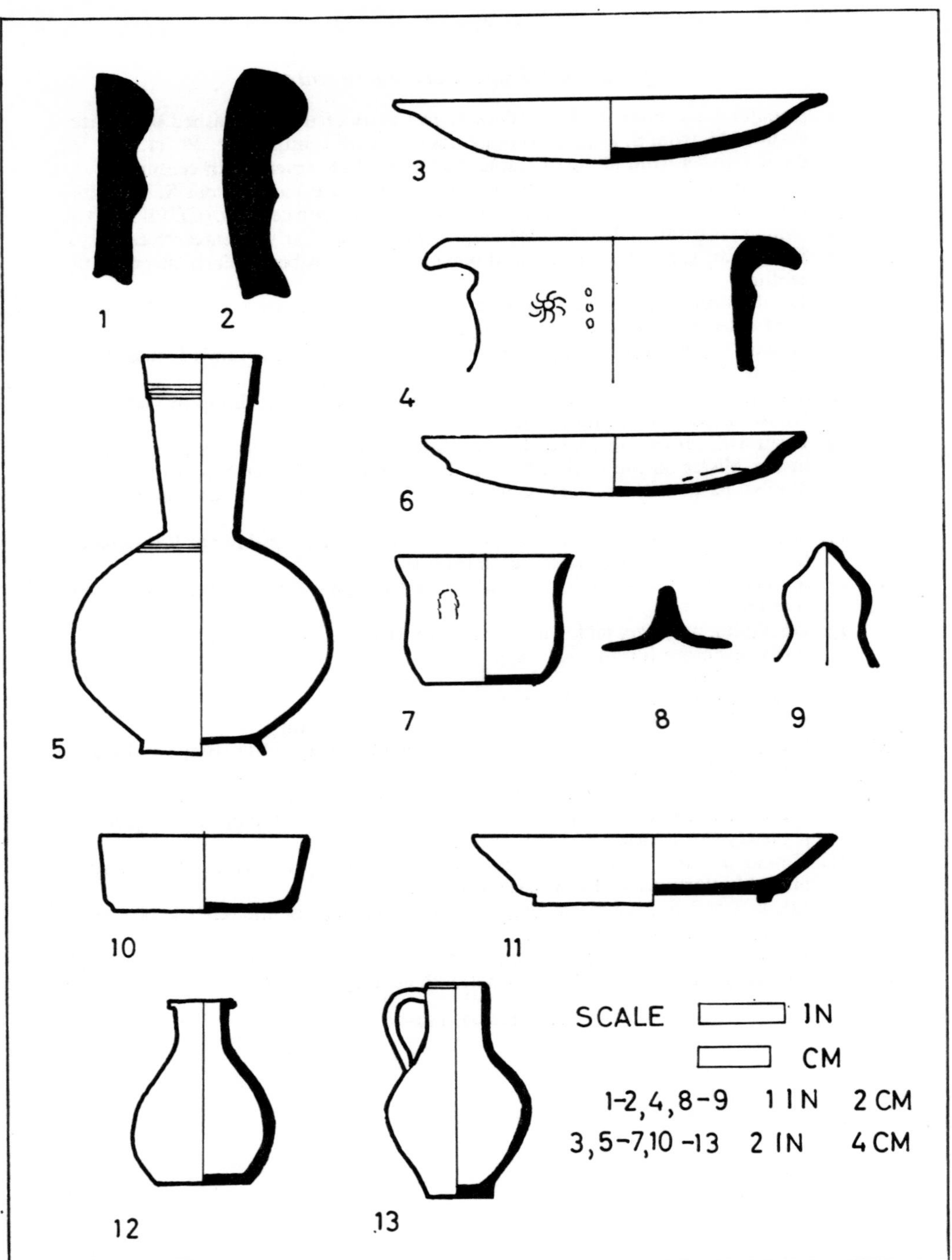
1
2
3
4
5
6
7
8
9
10
11
12
13
SCALE
IN
CM
1-2, 4, 8-9 1 IN 2 CM
3, 5-7, 10-13 2 IN 4 CM

FIG. 75

Fig. 75. *Fort Jesus. Portuguese and German wares*

1, 2. Jars with carved neck, pink body, white slip, similar to Goggin, fig. 10a, from main court. Nineteenth century.

3. Dish with pink body and dark-brown olive glaze on outside, yellow glaze on inside, from pit in S. Filipe, possibly not Portuguese. Late seventeenth century.

4. Jar with polished red surface and stamped ornament on outside, from S. Filipe. Early seventeenth century.

5. Vase in fine red polished ware, thin fabric, splayed ring base and cordon round neck and on shoulder, from pit below south barrack block. Late seventeenth century.

6. Small plate, pink surface, raised star-shaped ornament on inside, set with quartz chips, from S. Filipe. Also Pl. 40. 9. Early seventeenth century.

7. Small jar with flat base, polished red surface, thin fabric, stamped ornament on outside, from S. Filipe. Early seventeenth century.

8. Lid in red polished ware, from filling of court in S. Mateus. Late seventeenth century.

9. Similar lid, from S. Filipe. Early seventeenth century.

10, 11. Plates with blue and aubergine floral decoration on white over white paste body. Also Pl. 41. 5–8. Found in early seventeenth but common in late seventeenth century.

12. Small bottle in blue and white over white paste body, with mark HP D G in radiate cartouch (Pl. 41. 9). From pit in S. Filipe. Late seventeenth century.

13. Juglet in grey stoneware, probably German, from filling in Captain's House. Early seventeenth century.

See pages 21, 91, 119–21.

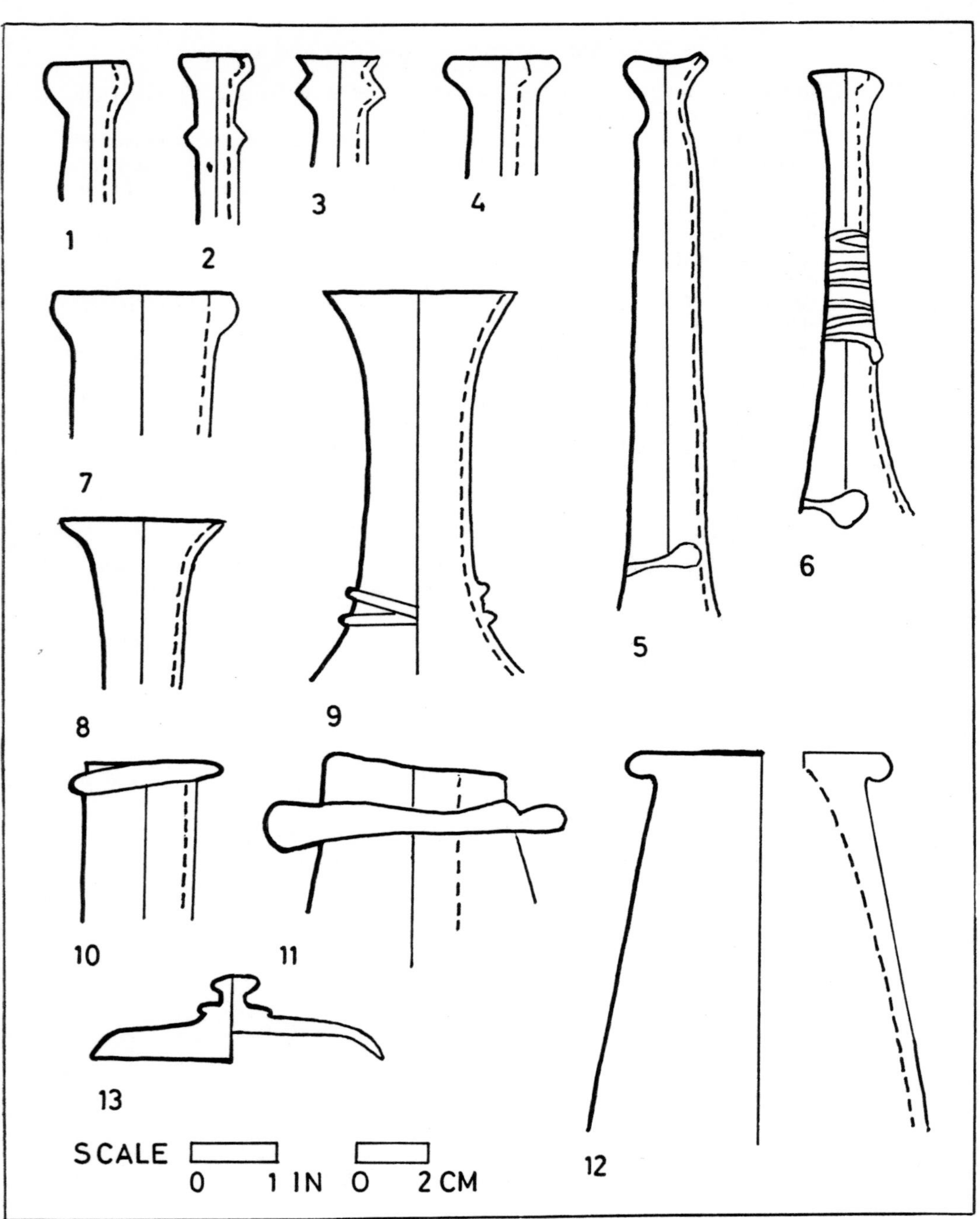

FIG. 76

Fig. 76. *Fort Jesus. Oriental and European glass*

1. Neck of *marasha* or sprinkler flask, with tucked-in lip, green glass, irregular shape. Early seventeenth century.
2. Neck of similar vessel with turned-in lip and cup mouth, smoky glass. Seventeenth century.
3. Neck of similar vessel with turned-out lip, white glass. Late seventeenth century.
4. Neck of similar but stouter vessel with turned-in lip, smoky glass. Single example. Nineteenth century.
5. Neck of similar vessel with pinched lip, green glass. Eighteenth century.
6. Neck of vessel with multiple strings, sometimes with oval base, green and smoky glass. Common. Nineteenth century.
7. Neck of jar or bottle with rolled lip, smoky and green glass. Early seventeenth century.
8. Neck of flask with turned-out lip, green glass. Eighteenth century.
9. Neck of similar vessel with strings, green glass. Nineteenth century.
10. Neck of uncertain vessel, with broad roughly made string, perhaps a lamp as 12, green glass. Single example. Eighteenth century.
11. Neck of similar vessel, single example, green glass. Eighteenth century.
12. Vessel with hole at both ends, probably a lamp glass, smoky glass, single example. Late seventeenth century?
13. Base of Venetian *tazza* in white glass, single example. Early seventeenth century.

See pages 126–7.

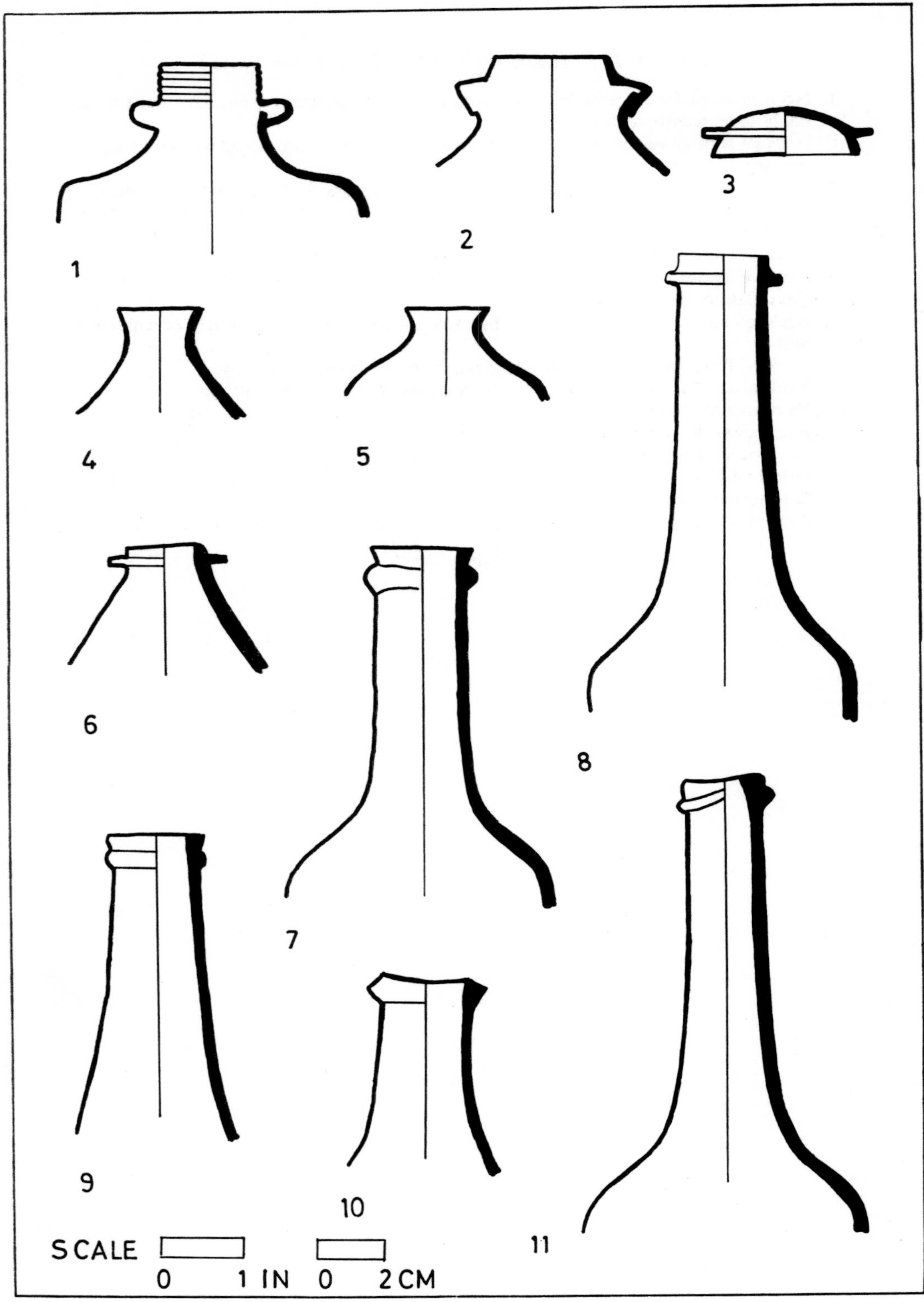

FIG. 77

Fig. 77. *Fort Jesus. European glass*

1, 2. Square case bottles with pewter cap. Dutch or English. Late seventeenth century.
3. Pewter cap of case bottle. Late seventeenth century.
4, 5. Pharmaceutical case bottles. Late seventeenth century.
6. Round bottle with short neck and string, shallow kick in bottom, cf. Hume, fig. 3 (1650–1720). Late seventeenth century.
7. Round bottle with irregular V-shaped string and turned-out lip, English, cf. Sutermeister, fig. 43. 7. Eighteenth century.
8. Round bottle with long neck and horizontal string, probably French. Late eighteenth and nineteenth century.
9. Round bottle with string and rounded lip. English. Single example. Cf. Hume, fig. 4. 17 (*c.* 1700–70) and Sutermeister, fig. 44. 3 (before 1768). Eighteenth century.
10. Round bottle with irregular V-shaped string, perhaps French. Eighteenth century.
11. Round bottle with long neck and irregular string. French, cf. Sutermeister, fig. 42. 1 (before 1758). Eighteenth and nineteenth century.

All smoky black glass.

See pages 20, 126–7.

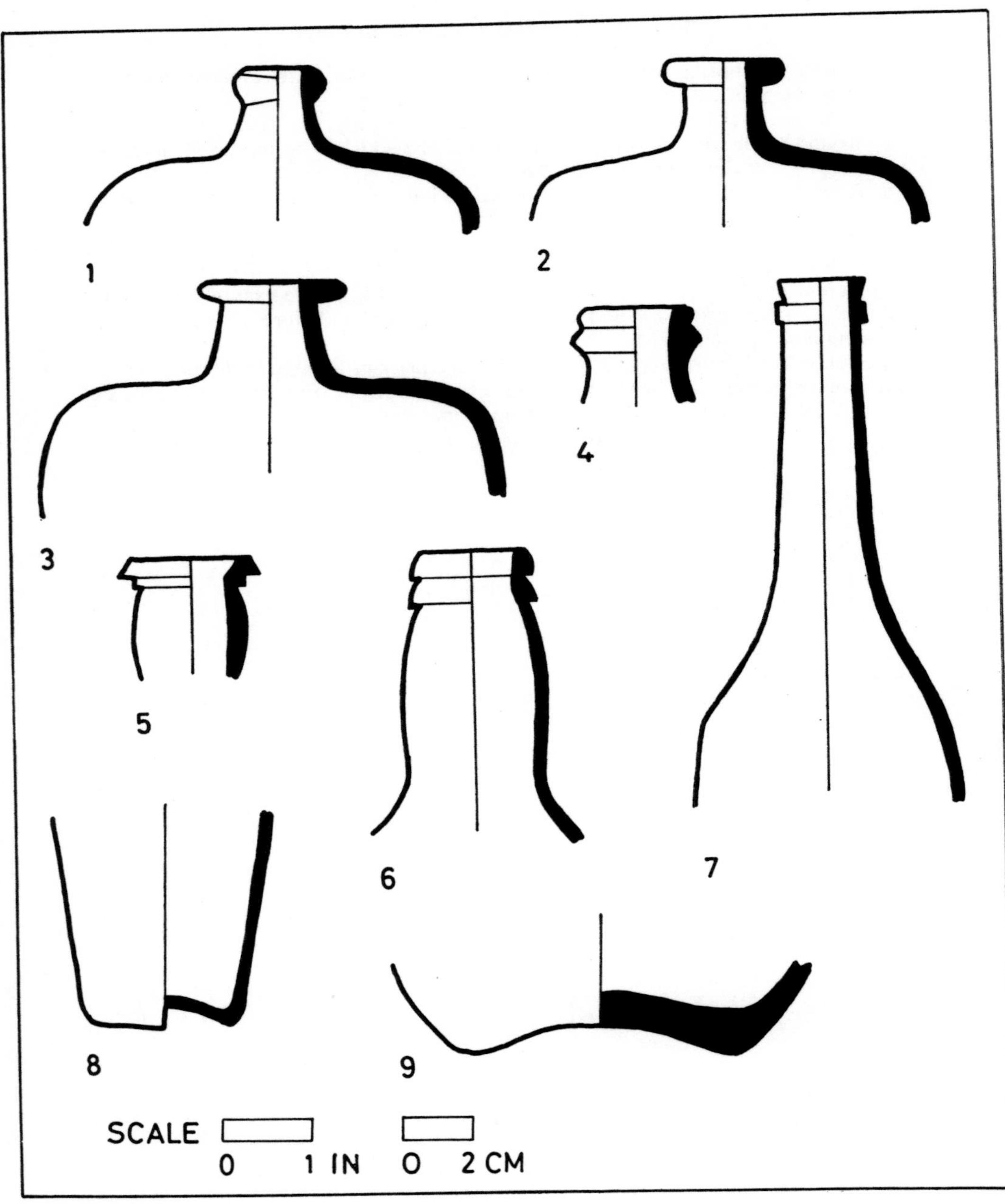

FIG. 78

Fig. 78. *Fort Jesus. European glass*

1. Case bottle with broad V-shaped string. Single example. Eighteenth century.
2. Case bottle with rounded lip. Eighteenth century.
3. Case bottle with wide lip. Eighteenth century.
4. Round bottle with rounded lip and V-shaped string. English. Single example, cf. Hume, fig. 4. 15 (1750–70). Nineteenth century.
5. Round bottle with chamfered lip and string and convex neck, cf. Hume, fig. 5. 26 (1750–80). Nineteenth century.
6. Round bottle with turned-out lip and string. English. Cf. Hume, fig. 5. 22 (1790–1820). Nineteenth century.
7. Round bottle with turned-out lip and raised band. French. Eighteenth and nineteenth centuries.
8. Base of small case bottle, neck probably as Fig. 77. 4 and 5. Late seventeenth century.
9. Base of bottle with shallow kick. Late seventeenth century.

All smoky black glass.

See pages 126–7.

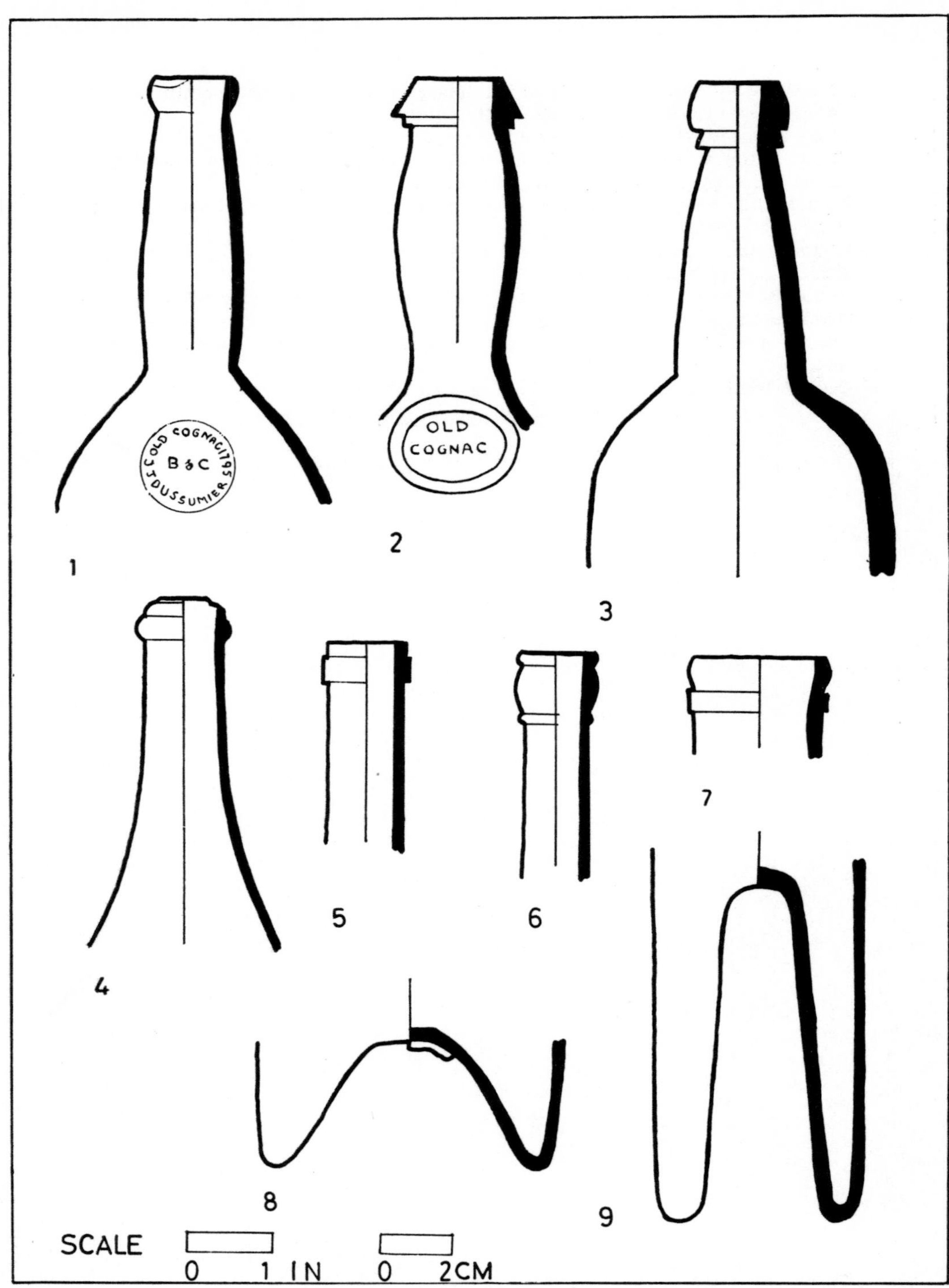
OLD COGNAC 1795
B & C
J. DUSSUMIER
OLD
COGNAC
1
2
3
4
5
6
7
8
9
SCALE
0 1 IN
0 2CM

FIG. 79

Fig. 79. *Fort Jesus. European glass*

1. Round bottle with broad string of archaic type, convex neck, with mark 'B & C Old Cognac 1795—J. J. Dussumier'. Nineteenth century.
2. Round bottle with chamfered neck and square string, mark 'Old Cognac', cf. Hume, fig. 5. 16 (1750–80). Single example. Nineteenth century.
3. Round bottle with broad rounded lip and string, pale-green metal. Nineteenth century.
4. Round bottle with rounded neck and broad rounded string, pale-green metal. Burgundy or Champagne bottle. Nineteenth century.
5. Round bottle with raised band. French. Single example. Nineteenth century.
6. Round bottle with rounded lip, convex band and rounded string below it, pale-green metal. Single example. Nineteenth century.
7. Round bottle or jar and raised band, pale-green metal. Single example. Nineteenth century.
8. Base of bottle with kick. French post-1760, perhaps from 4. Late eighteenth century.
9. Base of bottle with high kick. French, nineteenth century, perhaps from 5.

Smoky black glass, unless otherwise stated.

See pages 126–7.

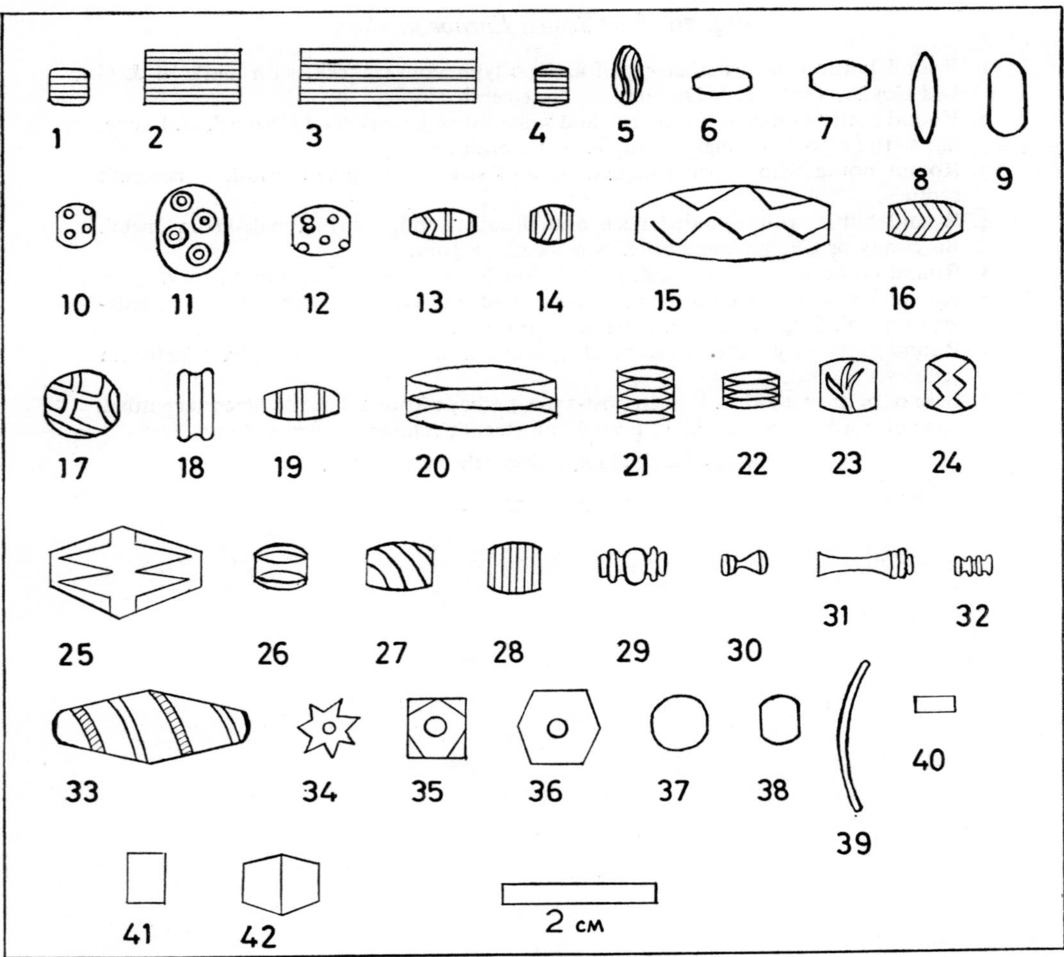
1
2
3
4
5
6
7
8
9
10
11
12
13
14
15
16
17
18
19
20
21
22
23
24
25
26
27
28
29
30
31
32
33
34
35
36
37
38
39
40
41
42
2 cm

FIG. 80

Fig. 80. *Fort Jesus. Beads*

Drawn glass

1. Small white on black striped. (Cl. C. 1.) Eighteenth and nineteenth centuries.
2. Dark blue with white pin stripe. (Cl. C. 4.) Nineteenth century.
3. Long cylinder with red stripe bordered with gold on white ground. (Cl. C. 6.) Nineteenth century.
4. Small beads striped red, blue, and green on white ground. (Cl. C. 2,3, 5, 7–9.) Eighteenth and nineteenth centuries.

Wound glass

5. Black with white strand. (Cl. D. 3.) Nineteenth century.

6, 7. Elliptical beads, white, black, pink, yellow, bright blue, dark blue, and transparent green. (Cl. E. 1–7.) Late seventeenth but commonest in nineteenth century.

8, 9. Ring beads, yellow, blue, green, aubergine, black, transparent. (Cl. F. 1–6.) Late seventeenth but commonest in nineteenth century.

10. Black with white eyes. (Cl. G. 1*a*.) Late seventeenth century.
11. Large eye bead with white eyes on blue ground. (Cl. G. 1*b*.) Late seventeenth century.
12. Eye bead with multiple eyes in red, white, and blue. (Cl. G. 1*c*.) Nineteenth century.

13, 14. Chevron beads with white lines on black (Cl. G. 2*a*.) Late seventeenth century.

15. Large black on white chevron bead (Cl. G. 2*b*.) Nineteenth century.
16. Chevron bead with white lines on pink. (Cl. G. 2*c*.)
17. Trellis design with white lines on black. (Cl. G. 3.) Late seventeenth century.
18. Bead with sunken band, white on black. (Cl. G. 4.) Late seventeenth century.
19. Transparent red with white lines. (Cl. G. 5.) Nineteenth century.
20. Rosetta bead, green on white. (Cl. G. 6*a*.) Early seventeenth century.
21. Rosetta bead, dark blue and white. (Cl. G. 6*b*.) Late seventeenth century.
22. Rosetta bead, red, white, and pale blue. (Cl. G. 6*c*.) Eighteenth century.
23. Beads with white sprays on pink, green, and deep-blue ground. (Cl. G. 7*a*–*c*.) Late seventeenth to nineteenth century.
24. Faceted, light blue on white. (Cl. I. 3.) Nineteenth century.
25. Large camel or donkey bead of rosetta type, in blue and white heptagonal section. (Cl. H. 2.) Late seventeenth century.
26. Dark-blue melon bead. (Cl. I. 8*b*.) Nineteenth century.
27. Yellow cable bead. (Cl. I. 9.) Eighteenth century.

Ivory

28. Chanelled cordoned bead. Nineteenth century.

29–31. Baluster beads. Late seventeenth century.

32. Similar. Early seventeenth century.
33. Large bead inlaid with bands of pink glaze and black diagonal lines. Nineteenth century.

Jet

34. Star. Late seventeenth-century level.
35. Faceted standard cylinder. Eighteenth century.

Pewter

36. Standard cylinder, hexagonal in section. Eighteenth century.

Resin

37. Sphere. Late seventeenth century.

Clay

38. Oblate. Late seventeenth century.

Shell

39. Achatina disk. Early seventeenth to nineteenth century.

40, 41. Marine shell cylinders. Early seventeenth to late nineteenth century.

42. Marine shell cylindrical bicone. Late seventeenth to nineteenth century.

See pages 128–33, 139–47.

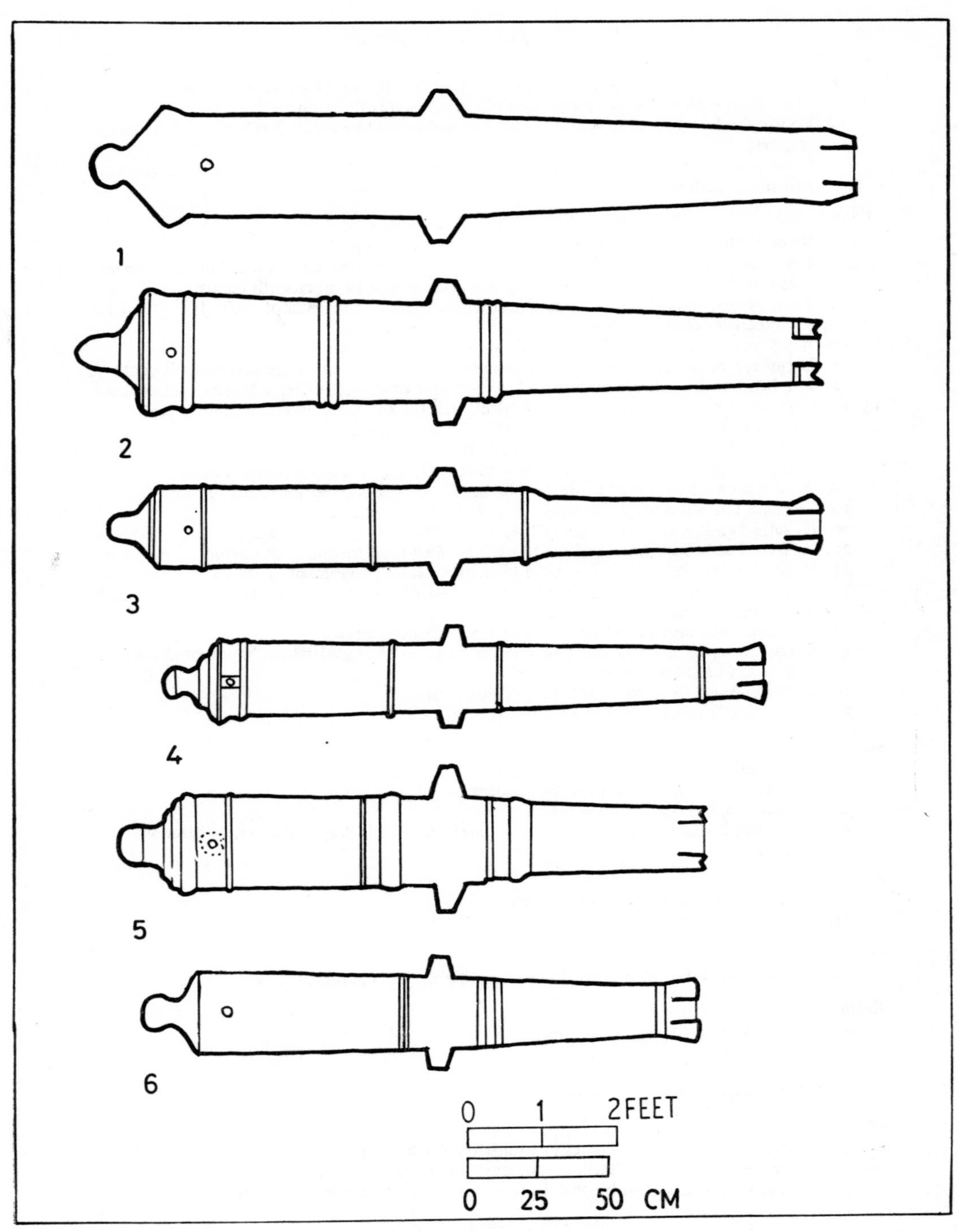

FIG. 81

Fig. 81. *Fort Jesus. Cannon*

1. Cannon, bore 5 in., length 7 ft. 7 in., rounded cascable. Iron flaking in longitudinal strips. English, perhaps early seventeenth century.
2. Cannon, bore 6½ in., length 7 ft. 9 in., conical cascable. Venetian, made in Bergamo *c.* 1684.
3. Cannon, bore 4¼ in., length 7 ft. 7 in., flattened cascable. English demi-culverin *c.* 1696.
4. Cannon, bore 4¼ in., length 6 ft. 8 in., nail-headed cascable. English minion *c.* 1706.
5. Cannon, 18-pounder, bore 5 in., broken, rounded cascable. English, eighteenth
6. century.
   Cannon, bore 4 in., length 5 ft. 5 in., rounded cascible. Iron flaking in longitudinal strips. English, perhaps seventeenth century.

See pages 30, 47, 52, 150–4.

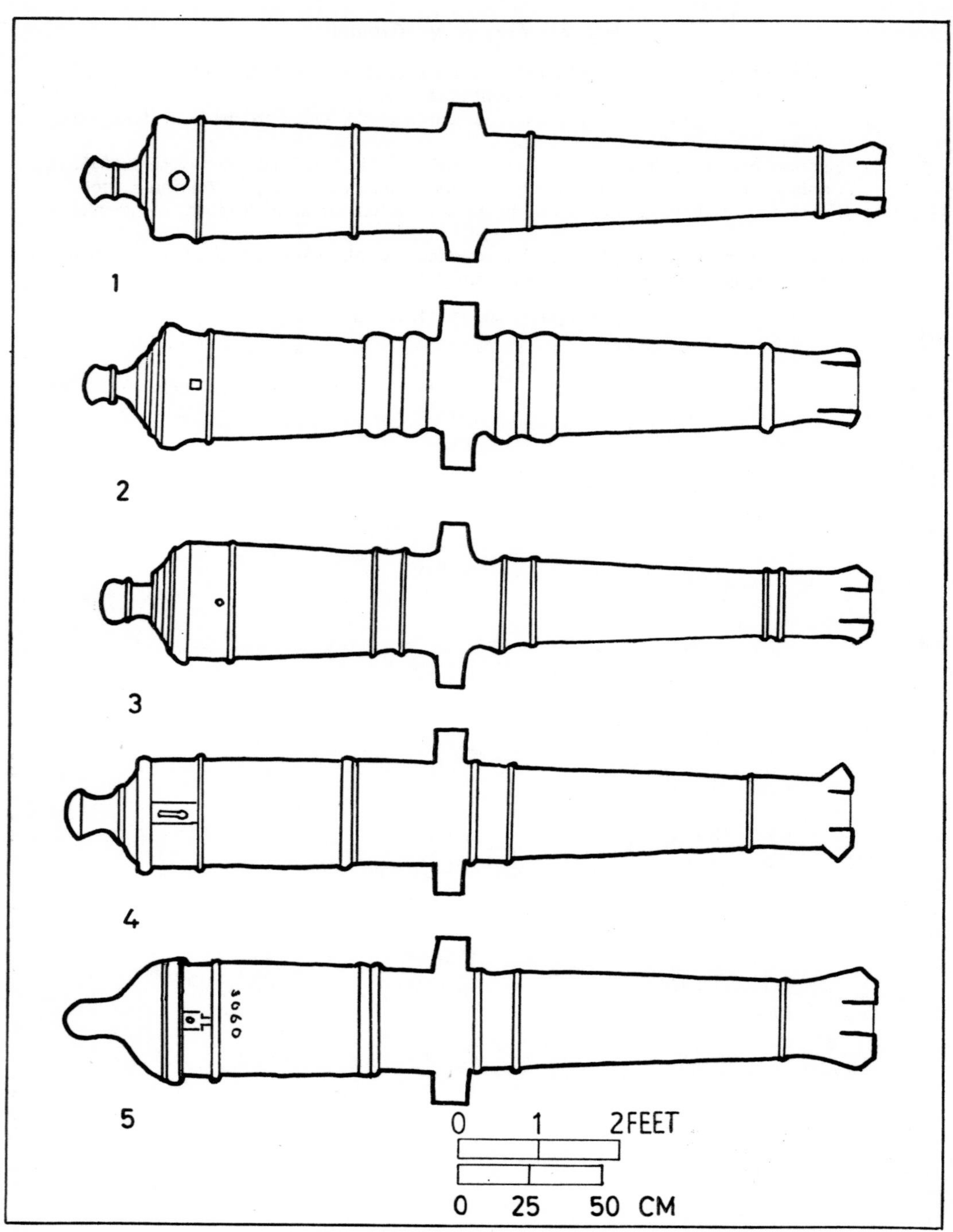

FIG. 82

Fig. 82. *Fort Jesus. Cannon*

1. Cannon, bore 5½ in., length 8 ft. 2 in., oval cascable. French 24-pounder of 1794.
2. Cannon, bore 7 in., length 8 ft., rounded cascable. English 56-pounder. Eighteenth century.
3. Cannon, bore 5¾ in., length 7 ft. 8 in., rounded cascable. English 24-pounder 1760–80.
4. Cannon, bore 5½ in., length 8 ft., rounded cascable. English heavy 24-pounder 1742–63.
5. Cannon, bore 5 in., length 8 ft., Swedish 18-pounder of 1752.

See pages 150–4.

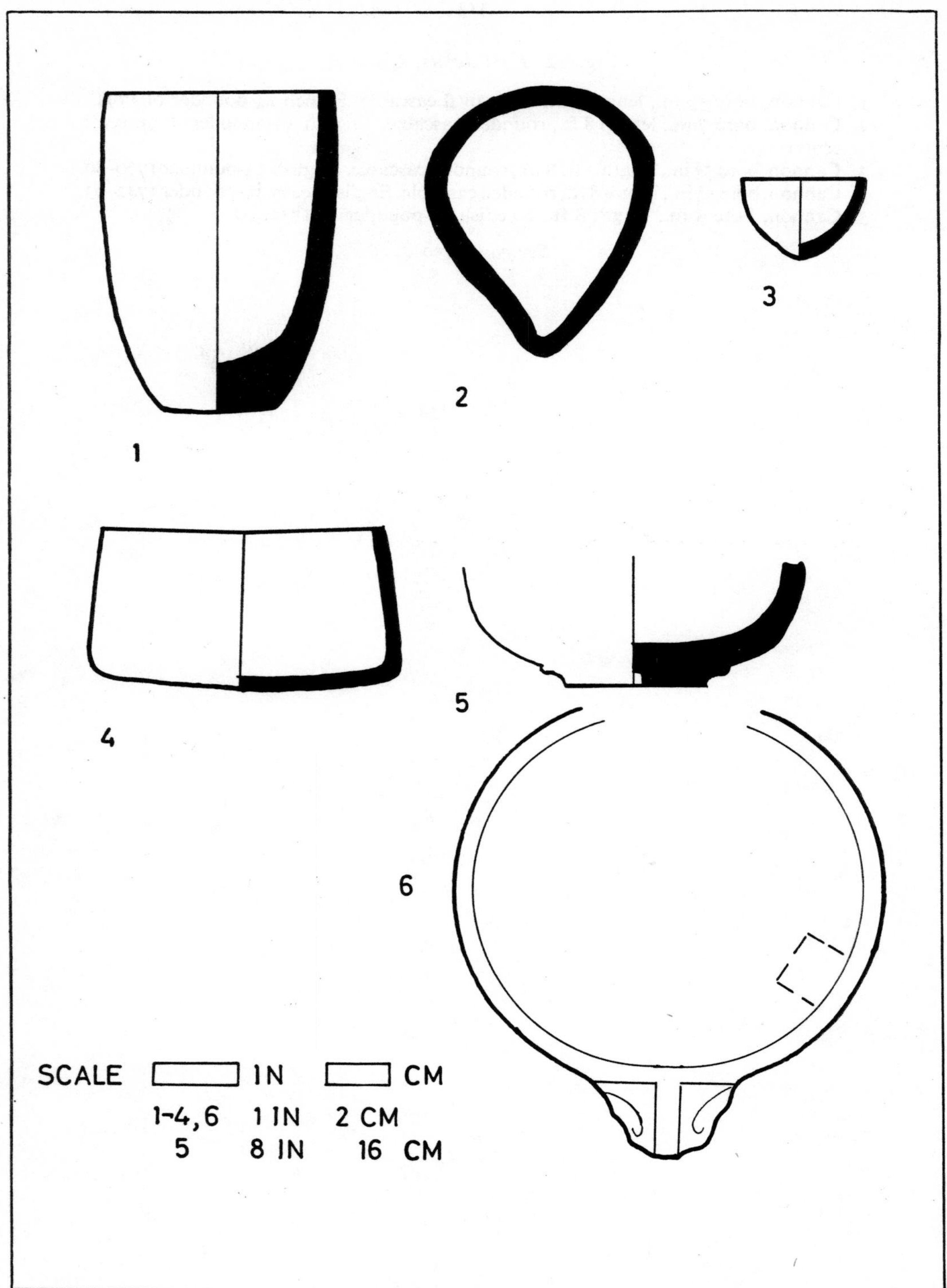

FIG. 83

Fig. 83. *Fort Jesus. Crucibles and stone vessels*

1, 2. Crucible, 10 cm deep and 7 cm wide, from upper filling of court in S. Mateus. Eighteenth century. Local.

3. Small crucible, 3·5 cm wide, from pit in S. Filipe. Local, late seventeenth century.

4. Small oblong box with short sides inclined inwards, in grey soapstone, from filling of court in S. Mateus, perhaps locally made. Late seventeenth century.

5. Bottom of large carved and plastered bowl in white stone, base 33·04 cm, internal diameter 45·7 cm. In the base, a socket 5·08 cm deep for fixing on a stand. Probably Portuguese, although it was found in the north court of the Captain's House.

6. Carved marble or alabaster bowl, probably European, from disturbed level in S. Alberto.

See pages 60, 157.

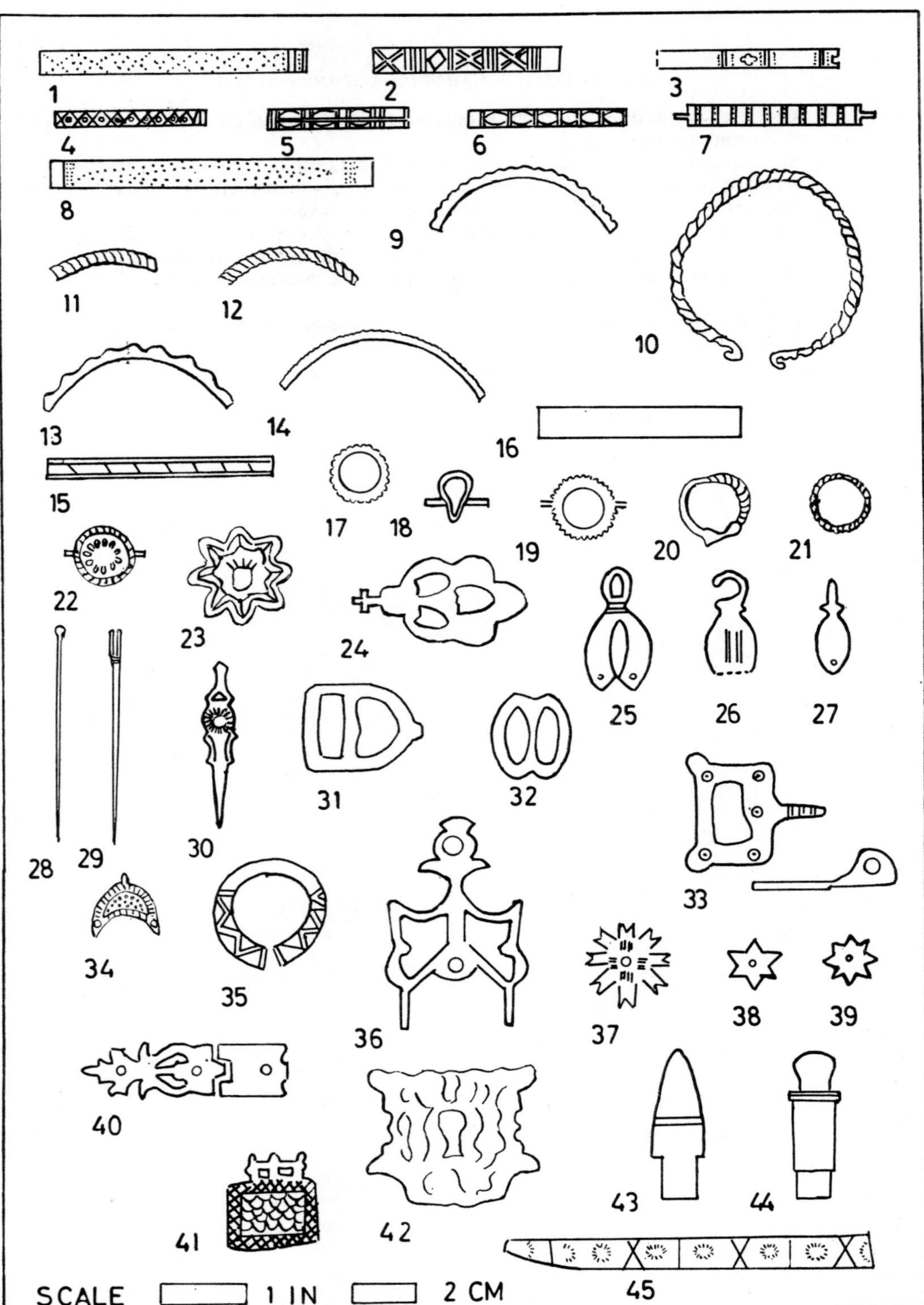
1
2
3
4
5
6
7
8
9
10
11
12
13
14
15
16
17
18
19
20
21
22
23
24
25
26
27
28
29
30
31
32
33
34
35
36
37
38
39
40
41
42
43
44
45
SCALE
1 IN
2 CM

FIG. 84

Fig. 84. *Fort Jesus. Ornaments and fittings*

1. Brass strip bracelet with incised ornament. Arab, late seventeenth century.
2, 3. Similar. Arab, early eighteenth century.
4. Similar. Arab, eighteenth century.
5. Similar. Perhaps European, eighteenth century.
6, 7. Similar. Perhaps European, nineteenth century.
8. Similar. Arab, nineteenth century.
9. Copper bracelet, serrated outside, smooth inside. Arab nineteenth century.
10. Copper bracelet in form of cable, with turned-back ends. Arab, nineteenth century.
11. Glass bangle in form of cable, cream colour. Indian, early eighteenth century.
12. Similar, but green. Indian, early seventeenth century.
13. Similar, with irregular projections on outside, black. Indian, late seventeenth century.
14. Similar, with interrupted serrated edge, black. Indian, late seventeenth century.
15. Similar, with yellow and red diagonal stripes on black ground. Indian, late seventeenth century.
16. Similar, with broad rounded section, black. Indian, eighteenth century.
17. Brass ring with volute edge, from filling of S. Alberto. Arab, early seventeenth century.
18. Silver ring with double cockle shell, from filling of S. Alberto. Portuguese, early seventeenth century.
19. Brass ring with serrated edge and socket for bezel, from filling in S. Alberto.
20. Brass-bound brass ring with two knobs. Local, eighteenth century.
21. Thin brass cable ring. Arab, eighteenth century.
22. Base silver ring with round plate in form of a marigold with embossed petals. Arab, eighteenth century.
23. Bronze badge in the form of an eight-pointed star with a device like a conventional grenade in centre and tang at back, from filling in S. Alberto. Early seventeenth century.
24. Belt end in brass with studs, from the filling of court in S. Mateus. Probably Portuguese, eighteenth century.
25. Brass locket in form of a two-lobed bean, flat plate on back missing, from filling in S. Filipe. Portuguese, early seventeenth century.
26. Brass locket, oval with four vertical lines in middle of flat plate on back, from filling of S. Matias. Portuguese, early seventeenth century.
27. Plain brass locket from filling of court in S. Mateus. Portuguese, late seventeenth century.
28. Brass pin with round head, from filling of S. Filipe. Portuguese, early seventeenth century.
29. Two-looped brass pin. Arab, eighteenth century.
30. Brass pendant. Arab, nineteenth century.
31. Brass buckle. Portuguese, late seventeenth century.
32. Brass buckle from filling of Captain's House. Portuguese, late seventeenth century.
33. Bronze buckle with pierced end. Probably Arab, nineteenth century.
34. Silver crescent. Nineteenth century.
35. Pair of bronze crescents. Nineteenth century.
36. End of buckle, from filling of court in S. Mateus. Portuguese, late seventeenth century.
37. Brass eight-pointed star, points with fishtail ends, four pairs of raised lozenges around the centre. From filling of S. Matias, perhaps Portuguese, early seventeenth century.
38–9. Six- and eight-pointed brass stars with central hole. Arab, late seventeenth century.
40. Brass ornament on hinge with tang at back of ornament, from filling of court in S. Mateus. Portuguese, late seventeenth century.
41. Lead pendant with reticulated and trellis ornament. Arab, nineteenth century.
42. Brass pierced ornamental key plate, from Captain's House. Portuguese, late seventeenth century.
43. Ivory finial. Arab, eighteenth century.
44. Similar. Arab, nineteenth century.
45. Copper strap for hinge of box. Arab, nineteenth century.

See pages 157–9, 161.

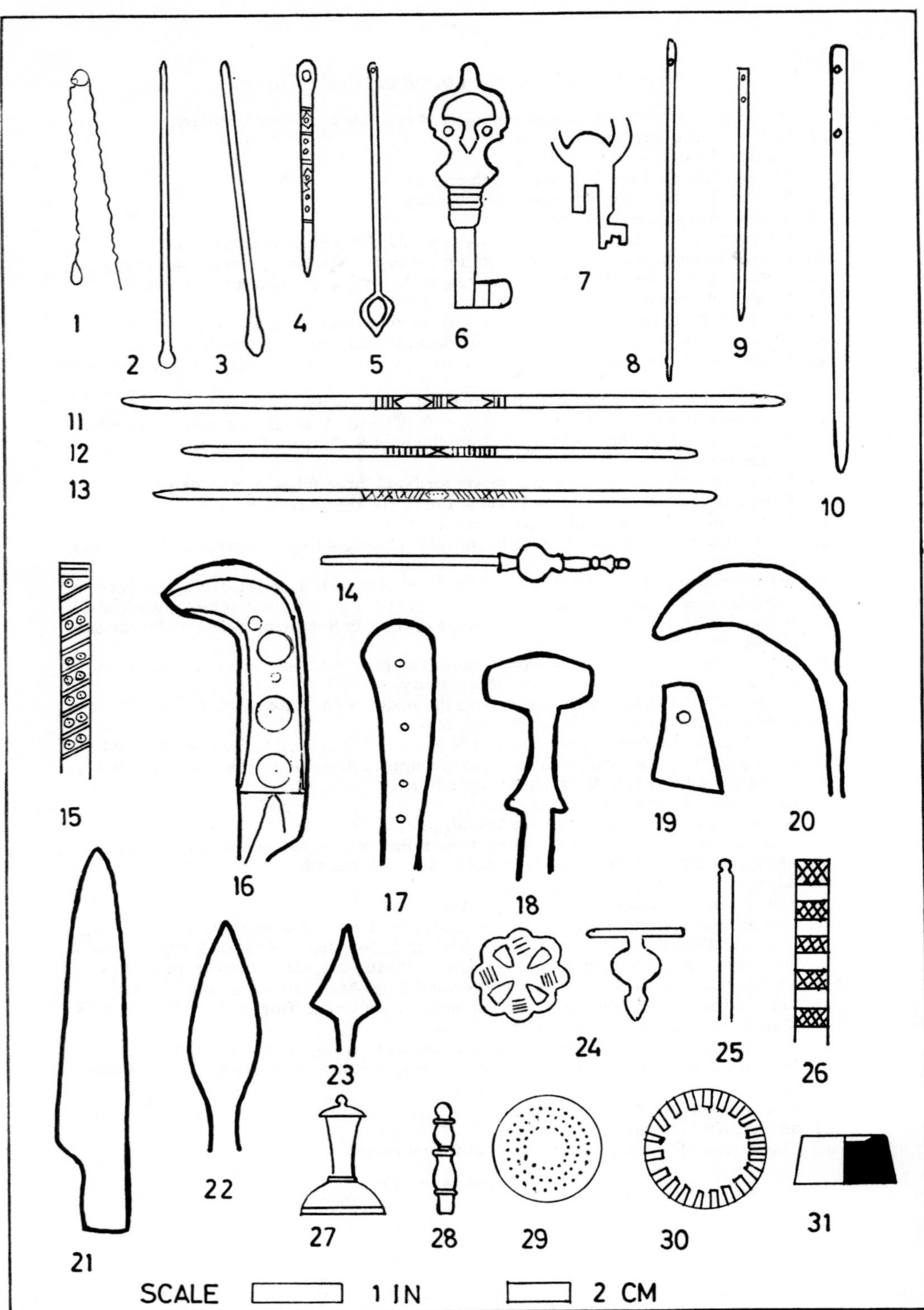
1
2
3
4
5
6
7
8
9
10
11
12
13
14
15
16
17
18
19
20
21
22
23
24
25
26
27
28
29
30
31
SCALE 1 IN 2 CM

FIG. 85

Fig. 85. *Fort Jesus. Implements*

1. Copper ear picks and spoon on ring with twisted shaft, from filling of S. Mateus. Arab, early seventeenth century.
2. Copper ear spoon with pointed shaft, from filling of pit in S. Filipe. Probably Arab, late seventeenth century.
3. Similar instrument from north corner of Captain's House. Arab, eighteenth century.
4. Copper toothpick. Arab, eighteenth or nineteenth century.
5. Instrument of uncertain use, consisting of a ring, 7 mm diameter, at the end of a rod. Arab, eighteenth century.
6. Copper key from pit in S. Filipe. Portuguese, late seventeenth century.
7. Thin copper key or latch, 2 mm thick, from disturbed level, perhaps Portuguese.
8. Copper needle with one eye, from filling of court in S. Mateus. Probably Arab, late seventeenth century.

9, 10. Similar, with two eyes. Common. Arab, nineteenth century.

11. Copper eye pencil, with hatched and diamond ornament. Common. Arab, late seventeenth and eighteenth century.
12. Copper eye pencil with cross and hatched ornament. Arab, eighteenth century.
13. Copper eye pencil with trellis and dot ornament. Arab, eighteenth century.
14. Copper kohl stick with moulded handle. Arab, eighteenth century.
15. Ivory knife handle, perhaps European, late seventeenth century.
16. Ivory knife handle, once ornamented with gold or silver roundels, from the Passage of the Arches. Arab, eighteenth century.
17. Plain ivory knife handle. Arab, eighteenth century.
18. Wooden handle (? for knife). Arab, eighteenth century.
19. Ivory knife handle with hole for suspension and socket for tang. Arab-African, nineteenth century.
20. Curved iron knife or razor. Arab-African, eighteenth century.
21. Iron knife, possibly European, late seventeenth century.

22, 23. Iron arrow heads. Arab-African, eighteenth century.

24. Copper eight-lobed stamp, pierced in four places, from Captain's House. Probably Portuguese, late seventeenth century.
25. Ivory peg, from filling of S. Filipe. Portuguese, early seventeenth century.
26. Ornamented ivory tube, perhaps a flute, from filling of S. Alberto. Probably Arab-African, late seventeenth century.
27. Ivory pawn, from filling of S. Filipe. Portuguese, early seventeenth century.
28. Ivory bobbin from filling of S. Mateus. Portuguese, late seventeenth century.
29. Clay disk, perhaps piece in a game. Arab-African, eighteenth century.

30, 31. Similar, nineteenth century.

See pages 159–61.

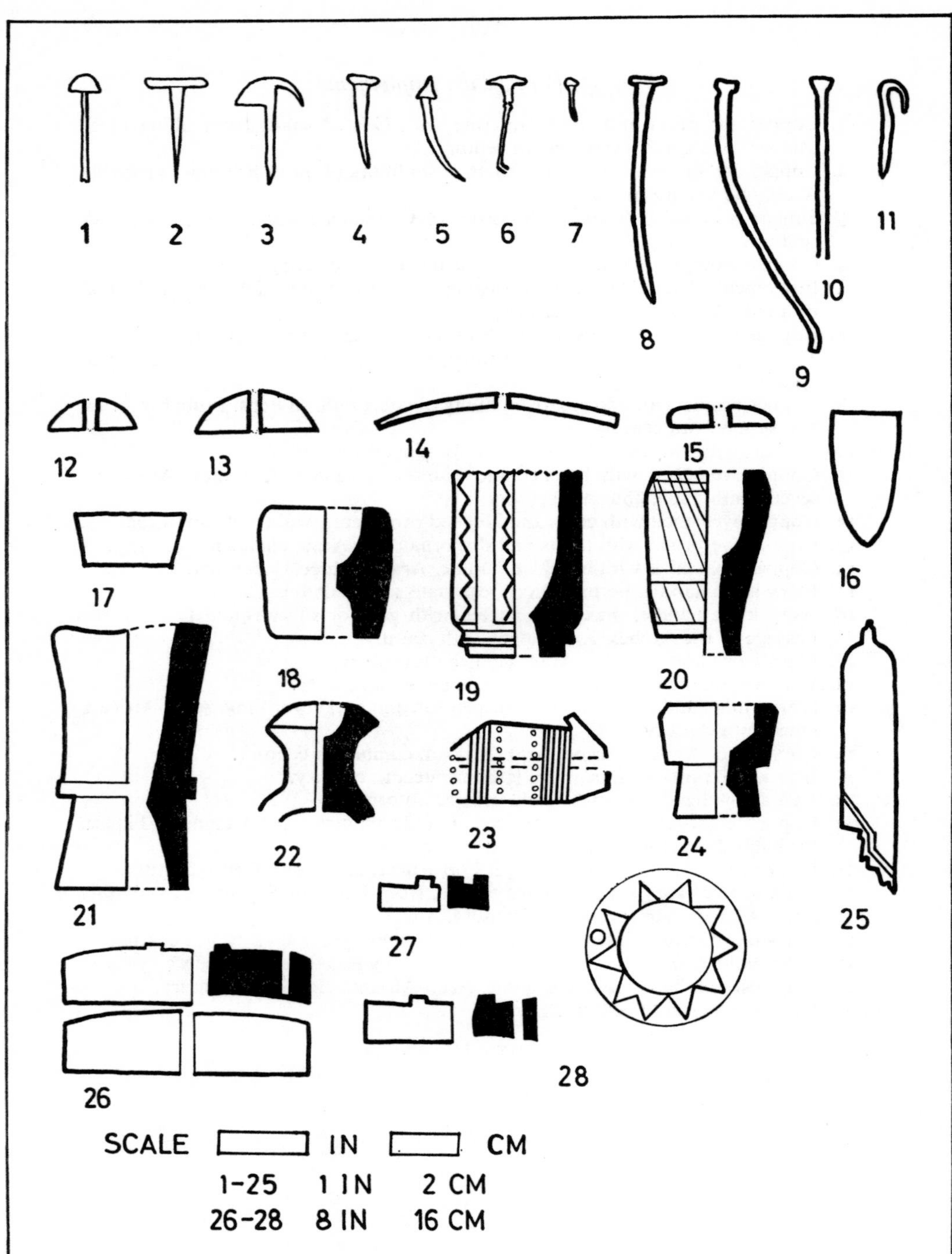

1
2
3
4
5
6
7
8
9
10
11
12
13
14
15
16
17
18
19
20
21
22
23
24
25
26
27
28
SCALE IN CM
1–25 1 IN 2 CM
26–28 8 IN 16 CM

FIG. 86

Fig. 86. *Fort Jesus. Fittings*

1. Copper nail with round head, from filling of S. Matias. Early seventeenth century.
2. Similar, with broad flat head, from filling of S. Matias. Early seventeenth century.
3. Similar, with large round dished head, from filling of court in S. Mateus. Late seventeenth century.
4. Small copper nail, from Captain's House. Late seventeenth century.
5. Copper nail with pointed head, from Captain's House. Late seventeenth century.
6. Copper nail with head and shaft made separately, from pit in S. Filipe. Late seventeenth century.
7. Small copper tack, from pit in S. Filipe. Late seventeenth century.
8. Long copper nail. Late seventeenth century.
9. Long copper nail with small head, from pit in S. Filipe. Late seventeenth century.
10. Long copper nail with small head. Eighteenth century.
11. Small copper hook. Late seventeenth century.

All above probably Portuguese.

12. Pierced clay disk, 2·5 cm diam., probably a loom weight. Arab-African, early seventeenth century.

13–15. Similar disks, 3·25 cm, 6·75 cm, and 2·75 cm diam. Arab-African, late seventeenth century.

16, 17. Clay stoppers. Arab-African, nineteenth century.

18. Clay pipe bowl for *narghili*, from below floor of Captain's House. Arab-African, early seventeenth century.

19. Similar pipe bowl with alternate panels of red and black chevrons on white ground, from filling of S. Filipe. Arab, early seventeenth century.

20–2. Pipe bowls from filling of court in S. Mateus. Arab-African, late seventeenth century.

23. Pipe stem holder from pit in S. Filipe. Arab-African, late seventeenth century.

24. Pipe bowl, Arab-African, eighteenth century.

25. Brass primer for cannon. European, nineteenth century.

26. Large gritstone rotary quern, 57 cm diam., from ammunition store. Arab-African, early eighteenth century.

27. Normal coral rotary quern, 25·4 cm diam. Arab-African, nineteenth century.

28. Basalt rotary quern, 40·6 cm diam. Perhaps from Comoros, nineteenth century.

See pages 30, 160–1.

Plates

1. Air photograph: Fort Jesus from the west (1969)

2. Air photograph: Fort Jesus from the south-east (1969)

3 A. Fort Jesus from Mombasa harbour, *c*. 1824. Sketch in Owen, *Narrative of Voyages to explore the shores of Africa*

3 B. Fort Jesus from Mombasa harbour, *c*. 1846. Sketch in Krapf, *Travels, Researches and Missionary Labours in East Africa*

4 A. Fort Jesus from the north, *c.* 1846. Sketch in Guillan, *Documents sur l'histoire, la géographie et le commerce de l'Afrique orientale*

4 B. Fort Jesus from the south-east, 1861. Sketch in von der Decken, *Reisen in Ost-Afrika*

5 A. West wall showing re-entrant angles, *c.* 1870. Photograph in Mbarak Ali Hinawy, *Al Akida and Fort Jesus*

5 B. Sea front, 1894. Photograph in the National Maritime Museum, Greenwich

6 A. Sea front from north-east, 1969

6 B. Sea front from east

7 A. Sea front from south-east

7 B. Outer gate

8 A. West parapet walk

8 B. West parapet walk, steps, and room of the stands

9 A. Remains of the church

9 B. The gatehouse

10 A. Passage of the Arches

10 B. Passage of the Steps

11 A. Inner face of Arab gun-platform

11 B. Doorway and attached pillar of portico to Captain's House

12 A. Painted dado in portico

12 B. Turret in S. Alberto bastion

13 A. Projection of S. Filipe bastion

13 B. Cavalier S. António

14 A. Door with sunken panels and palm-leaf decoration

14 B. Arms of Archduke Albert of Hapsburg

14 C. Arms of King Philip II of Spain

14 D. Arms of Mateus Mendes de Vasconcelos

15. Paintings from the face of the platform in S. Mateus bastion. Photographs by J. Jewell

16. Paintings from the face of the platform in S. Mateus bastion. Photographs by J. Jewell

17 A. Platform before removal of the paintings

17 B. Inscription on the paintings

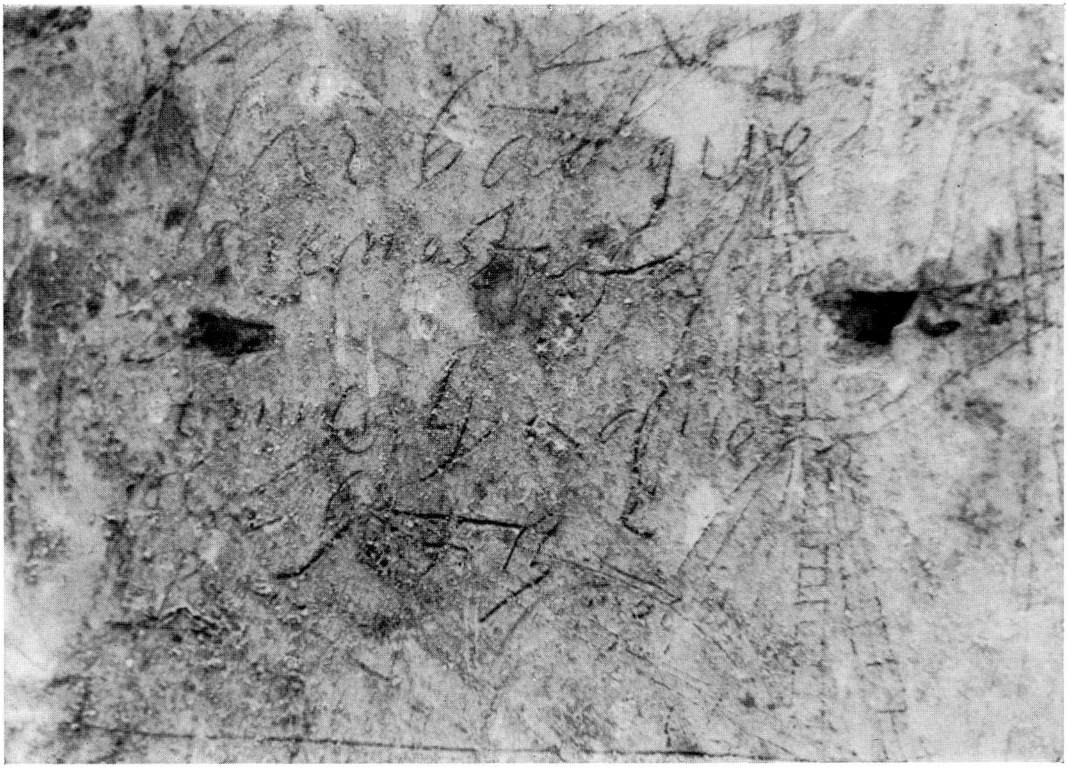

18 A–C. Details of paintings

19. UNGLAZED EARTHENWARE

ineteenth-century carinated cooking-pots with appliqué ornament, from Passage of the Arches. 1. Fig. 51. 22 on Fig. 43. 3 (eighteenth-century form). 2. Fig. 43. 15 (eighteenth-century ornament) on Fig. 51. 7. 3. Fig. 51. 2.

ineteenth-century carinated cooking-pots with incised ornament and chamfered lip, from Passage of the Arches. 4. Ornament 108 on Fig. 50. 35. 5. Ornament 107 on Fig. 49. 5.

agments of bowls with egg-shaped receptacles, nineteenth century. 6. From Passage of the Arches. 7. From main court. 8. From north court of the Captain's House.

(Scale about $\frac{1}{3}$ natural)

See pages 82–7, 90

20. IMPORTED UNGLAZED EARTHENWARE

1. Hard-baked, red-bodied carinated pot made on the wheel, probably Indian. Fig. 57. 5, from pit in S. Filipe, late seventeenth century. 2. Jar in a thin, hard-baked, red earthenware with metallic sheen, probably mica. Fig. 58. 9, from pit in S. Filipe, late seventeenth century. 3. Jar with pink slip, probably Indian. Fig. 57. 16, from filling of Captain's House, late seventeenth century. 4–6. Jars in a thin, black, polished ware with stamped ornament, late seventeenth century: (4) from pit in S. Filipe, (5) from filling of the Captain's House; (6) from pit in S. Filipe. 7–13. Carved bosses and fragments of flasks in a pink-bodied ware with metallic sheen, similar to 2: (7, 8) from pit in S. Filipe, late seventeenth century; (9) from filling of S. Filipe, early seventeenth century; (10) from main court, late seventeenth century; (11) from main court, early seventeenth century; (12) from north court of Captain's House, eighteenth century; (13) from filling of S. Filipe, early seventeenth century.

(Scale about $\frac{1}{3}$ natural)

See pages 91–2

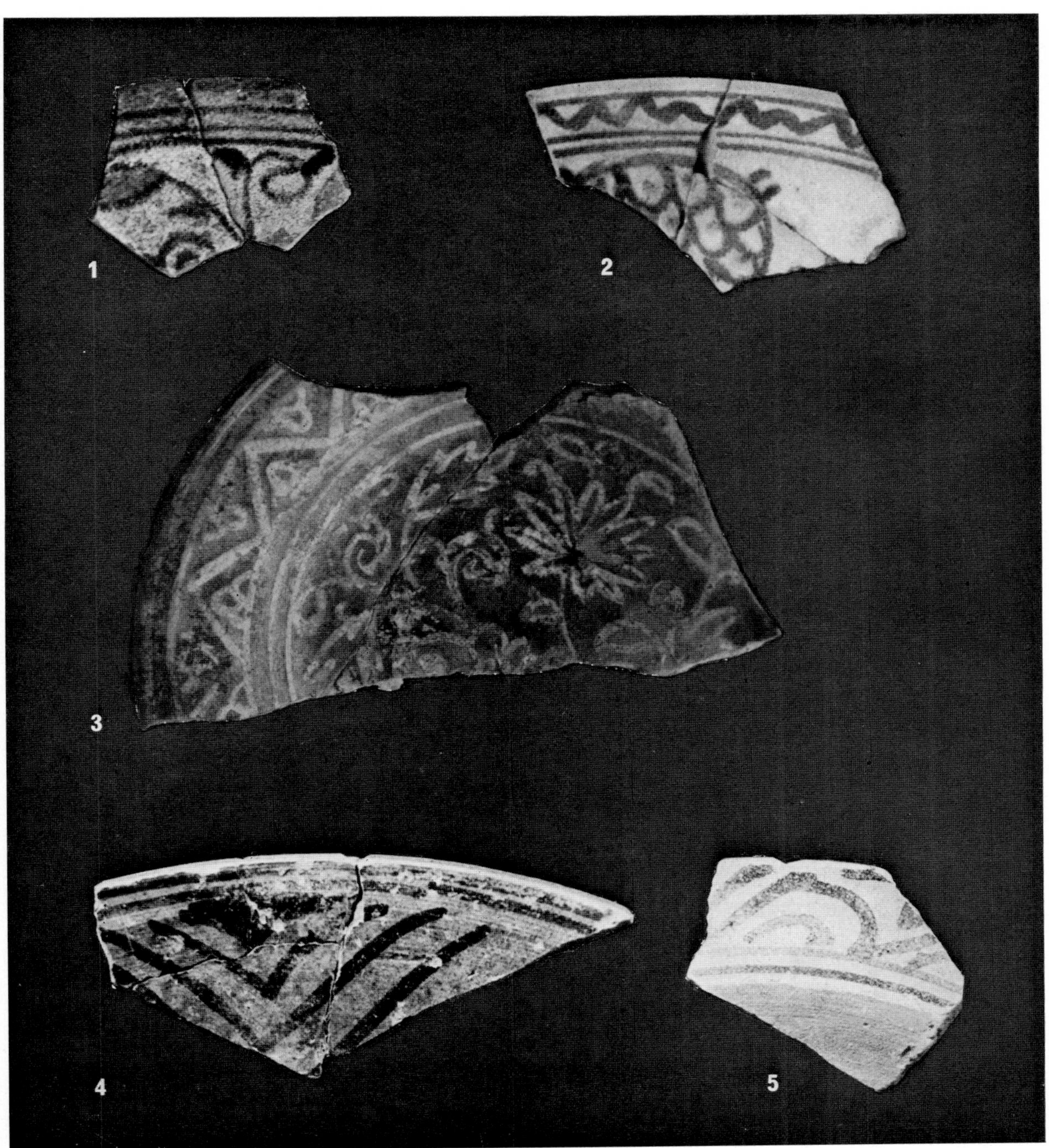

21. ISLAMIC GLAZED WARE

1. Plate with floral decoration in blue and green on white over a red body (Cl. 1), from filling of S. Filipe, early seventeenth century. 2. Similar plate with zigzag border and formalized floral motif in bottom, in black and turquoise on decayed yellow ground (Cl. 1), from filling of S. Alberto, early seventeenth century. 3. Plate with floral design and zigzag border in green, aubergine, and white, transparent glaze on back (Cl. 3), diam. 26 cm. Fig. 68. 1, from filling in S. Alberto, early seventeenth century. 4. Bowl with short lip and chevron motif on inside in black on blue ground (Cl. 4), from filling of S. Filipe, early seventeenth century. 5. Plate with similar design in black on grey ground over a grey-buff body (Cl. 9), from same.

(Scale 1 and 2, and 4 and 5, about $\frac{1}{3}$ natural)

See pages 94–6

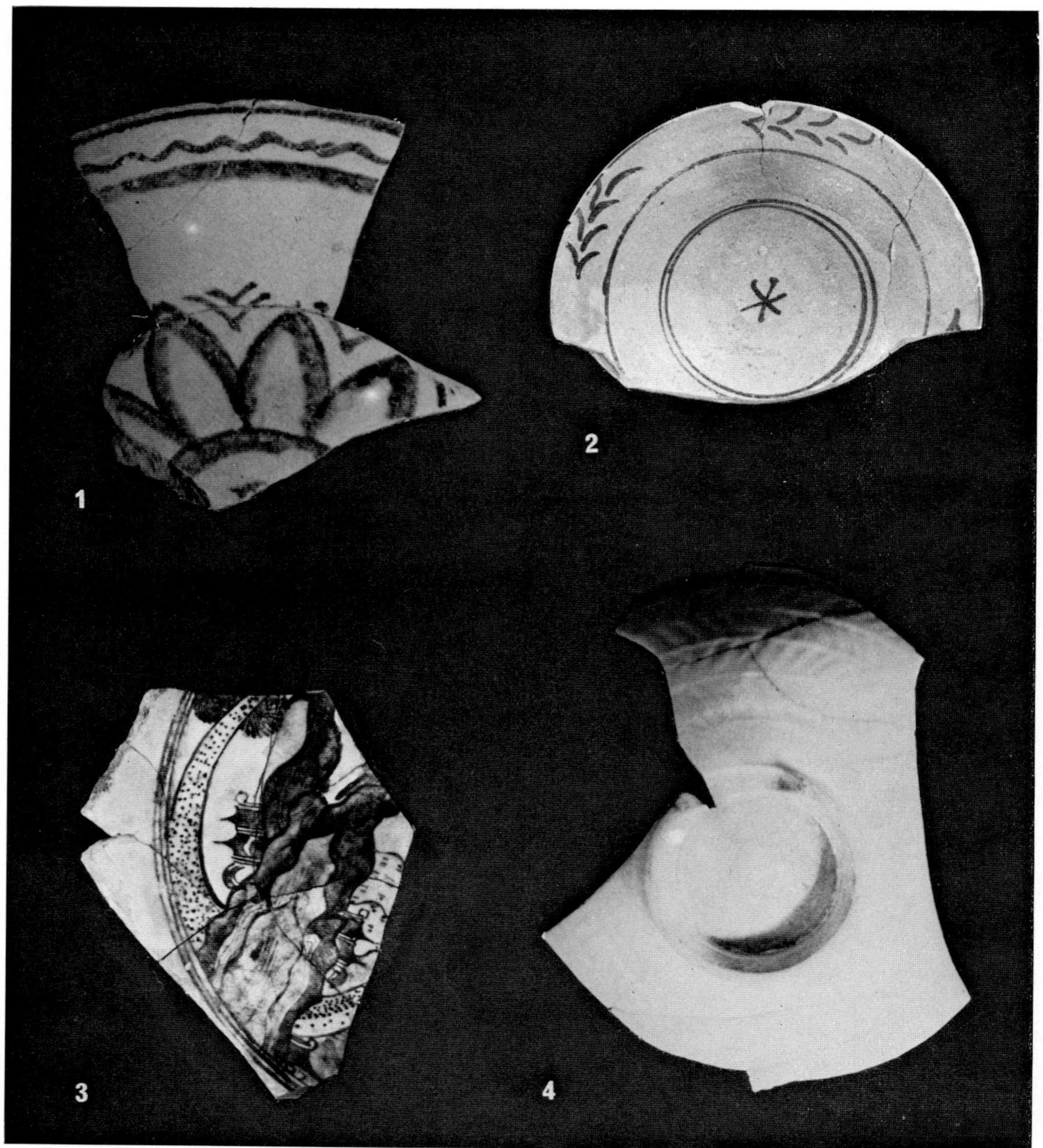

22. ISLAMIC GLAZED WARE

1. Plate with flat base and decoration in blue and turquoise on white, in same style as Cl. 1, under a crackled white glaze (Cl. 7), Fig. 68. 10, from south barrack block, nineteenth century. 2. Plate with design similar to Cl. 4, black on grey over a grey-buff body (Cl. 9), diam. 25 cm from filling of S. Matias, early seventeenth century. 3. Plate with landscape design in blue on white, in imitation of Wan Li wares on white sugary body (Cl. 13), from bottom of Passage of the Arches, late seventeenth century. 4. Bowl with bands of chevron ornament on outside, incised under a white glaze with muslin-like surface, due to decay of glaze (Cl. 16), Fig. 68. 15, from pit in S. Filipe, late seventeenth century.

(Scale, except 2, about $\frac{1}{3}$ natural)

See pages 94–7

23. ISLAMIC GLAZED WARE

1, 2. Plates with willowy floral design in turquoise green on white, sometimes stained by green (Cl. 17), from court in S. Mateus, late seventeenth century. 3. Plate with schematized floral design in chocolate on cream (Cl. 19), from court S. Mateus, late seventeenth century. 4, 5. Thin bowls with green glaze and vertical scoring on outside below glaze on soft buff body (Cl. 22), from court in S. Mateus, late seventeenth century. 6–10. Bowls with schematized floral designs or geometrical motifs in black on pale-blue ground (Cl. 25), nineteenth century: (6) from Passage of the Arches; (7) from court in S. Mateus; (8–10) from Passage of the Arches.

(Scale about $\frac{1}{4}$ natural)

See pages 94–8

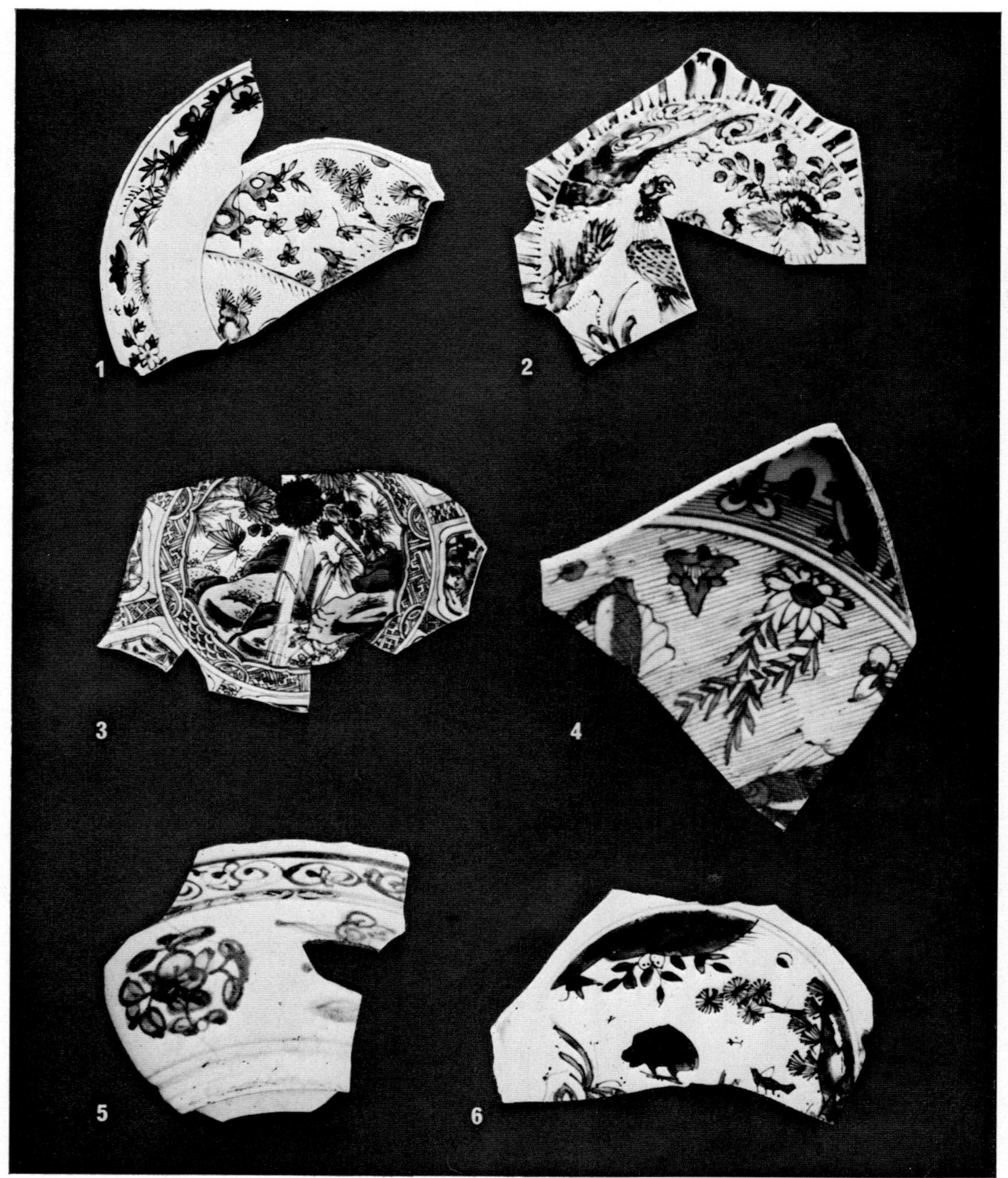

24. CHINESE PORCELAIN—MING

Blue-and-white. 1. Small plate with landscape (Cl. 1*a*), from filling of S. Filipe, early seventeenth century. 2. Plate with bird and painted gadroons on rim, extending over cavetto (Cl. 1*b*), from same. 3. Plate with elaborate panelled border (Cl. 2), from filling of S. Mateus, early seventeenth century. 4. Plate with aquatic scene on a hatched ground (Cl. 1*c*), from filling of court in S. Mateus, late seventeenth-century level. 5. Heavy bowl with lotus blossom and classical scroll border (Cl. 3), from pit in S. Filipe, late seventeenth-century level. 6. Large bowl with aquatic scene (Cl. 5*a*), from filling of S. Filipe, early seventeenth century.

(Scale about $\frac{1}{3}$ natural)

See pages 98–102

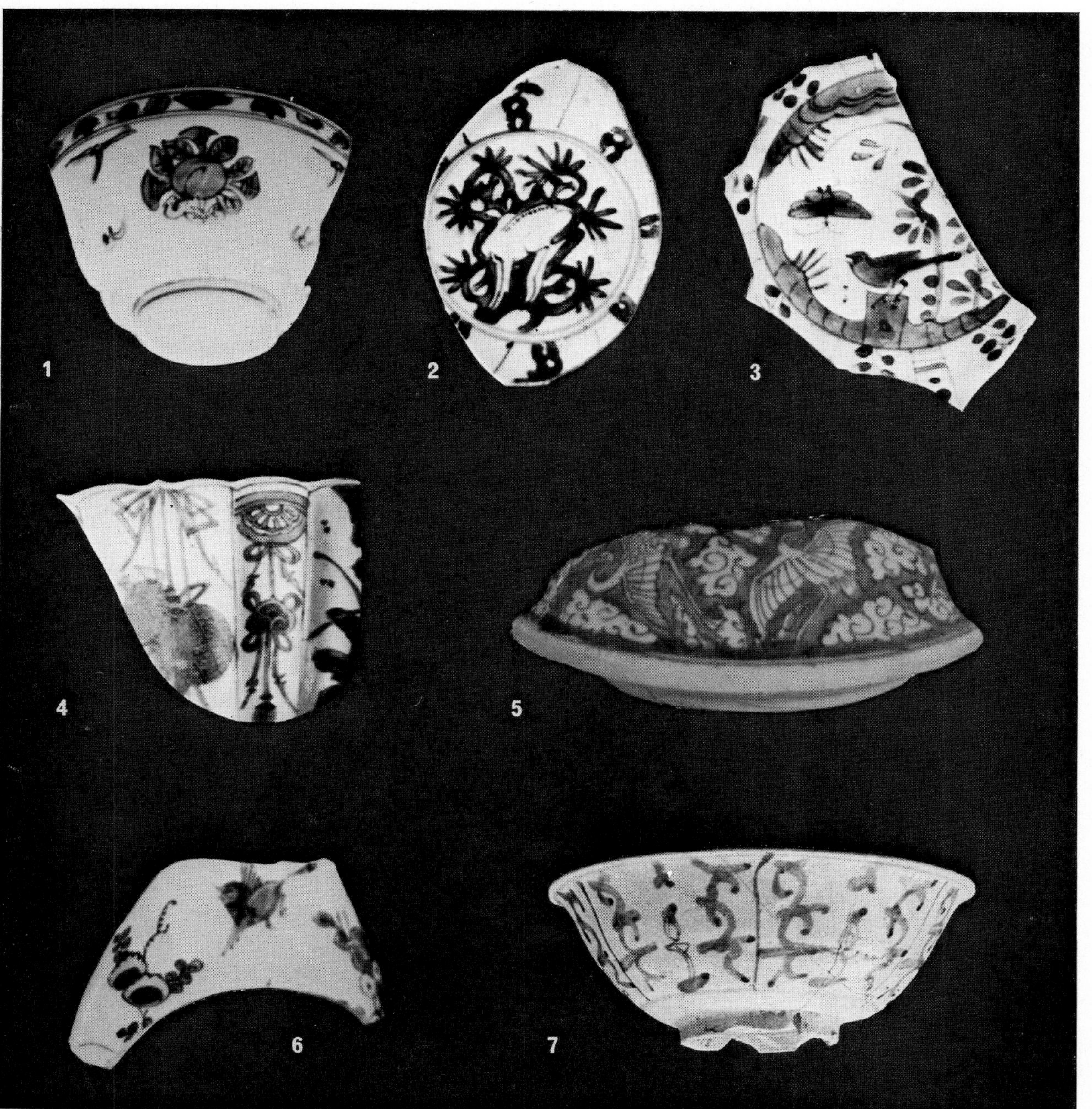

25. CHINESE PORCELAIN—MING

Blue-and-white. 1. Bowl with open lotus blossom (Cl. 6*a*), from filling of S. Filipe, early seventeenth century. 2. Bowl with doe in bottom, thin fabric (Cl. 9*a*), from same. 3. Bowl with birds and butterflies, thin fabric (Cl. 9*c*), from nineteenth-century level. 4. Bowl with precious things in fluted panels (Cl. 10), from S. Filipe, early seventeenth century. 5. Lid with phoenix in white on a blue ground (Cl. 11*a*), diam. 18 cm, from below Captain's House, early seventeenth century. 6. Vase with birds in two shades of blue (Cl. 13*b*), from filling of S. Filipe, early seventeenth century. 7. Bowl with tendril design on a cream ground, bare ring in bottom (Cl. 16), diam. 18 cm, from filling of S. Alberto, early seventeenth century.

(Scale, except 5 and 7, about $\frac{1}{3}$ natural)

See pages 98–102

26. CHINESE PORCELAIN—MING

White. 1. Lid with incised floral design (Cl. 20), diam. 20 cm, from below platform in S. Mateus, early seventeenth century.

Swatow ware. 2. Plate with floral design in red and green on a white body (Cl. 22), diam. 26 cm, from filling of S. Alberto, early seventeenth century.

K'ANG HSI

Polychrome (iron-red, green, yellow, and aubergine). 3, 4. Bowl with mark Hua-yü-T'ang ch'ing ya chih (Cl. 1*a*), diam. 15·5 cm, from pit in S. Filipe, late seventeenth century. 5. Similar bowl, mark unread, from filling of court in S. Mateus, late seventeenth century. 6. Large plate with flowers on a red trellis ground, grooved ring base (Cl. 1*c*), from pit in S. Filipe, late seventeenth century.

(Scale $\frac{1}{4}$ natural)

See pages 98–103, 116

27. CHINESE PORCELAIN—K'ANG HSI

olychrome (iron-red, green, yellow, and aubergine). 1. Jar with small handles on shoulders, with under-glaze blue as well as other olours (Cl. 1*e*), diam. of mouth 12·5 cm, from pit in S. Filipe, late seventeenth century. 2. Small bowl with rosette border, yellow n green ground on outside (Cl. 2), from same. 3. Cup with mottled green and yellow (egg-and-spinach) decoration (Cl. 3), with blue-and-white design in bottom (Cl. 23), diam. 3·6 cm, from same.

lue-and-white. 4. Small bottle with floral decoration in dark and light blue (Cl. 5*a*), from same. 5, 6. Bowl and cup with similar ecoration in two tints of blue (Cl. 5*a*), from court in S. Mateus, late seventeenth century. 7. Fine bowl with figures in garden and broad fluted panels in two tints of blue (Cl. 5*d*), from Captain's House, late seventeenth century.

(Scale 4–7 about ½ natural)

See pages 98–101, 103, 106

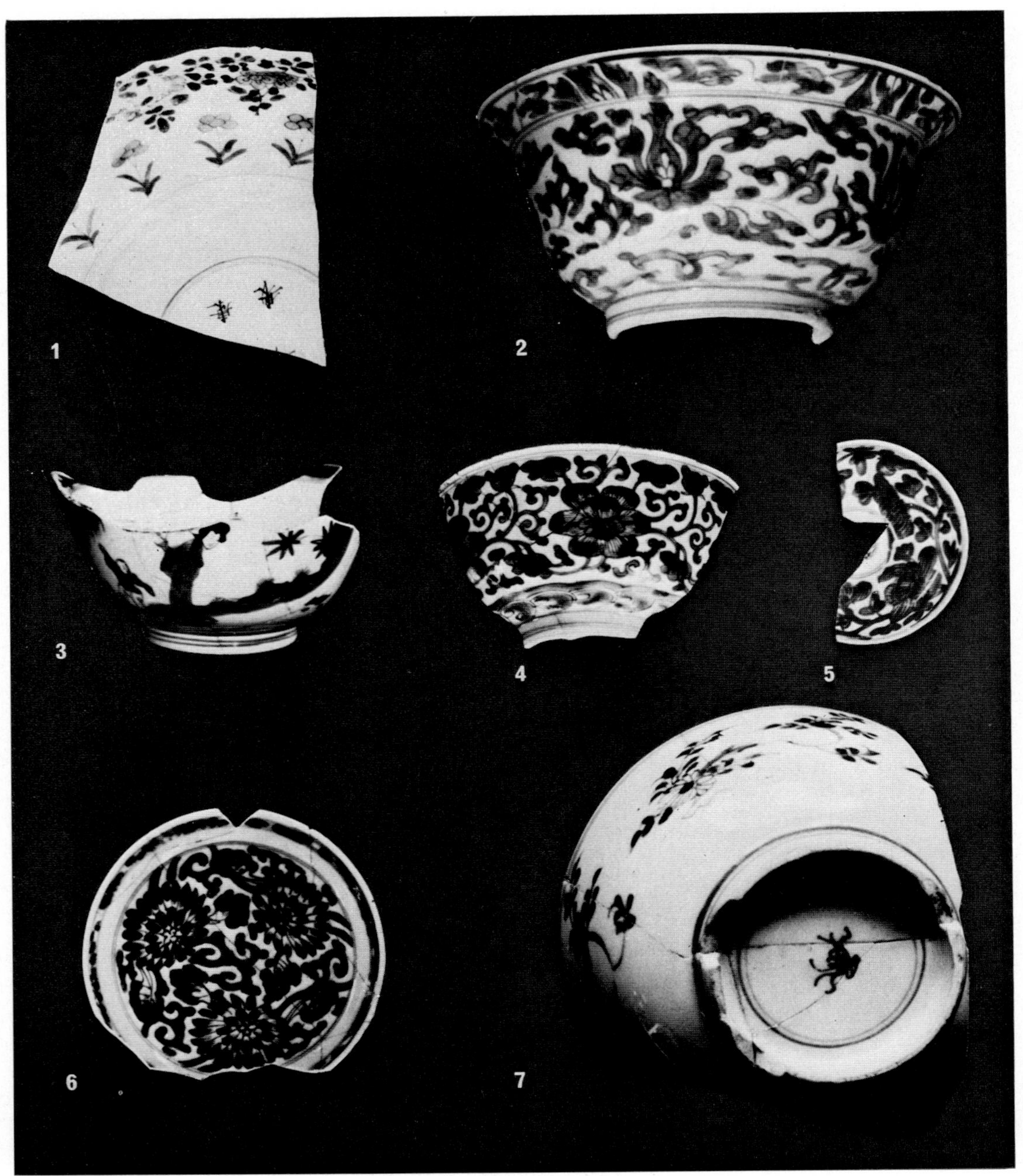

28. CHINESE PORCELAIN—K'ANG HSI

Blue-and-white. 1. Plate with series of sprays above the base in two tints of blue, K'ang Hsi mark (Cl. 5*c*), diam. 18 cm, from pit in S. Filipe, late seventeenth century. 2. Bowl with turned-out lip and lotus tendrils on outside, K'ang Hsi mark (Cl. 6*a*), diam. 16 cm, from Captain's House, late seventeenth century. 3. Similar bowl, with figures in a garden, K'ang Hsi mark (Cl. 6*c*), diam. 16 cm, from pit in S. Filipe, late seventeenth century. 4–6. Bowl (diam. 11 cm), lid (diam. 9 cm), and saucer (diam. 14 cm), with peony design (Cl. 6*d*), from same. 7. Bowl with floral design in outline and solid blue, mark two fishes (Cl. 8) diam. 13 cm, from same.

See pages 98–101, 104

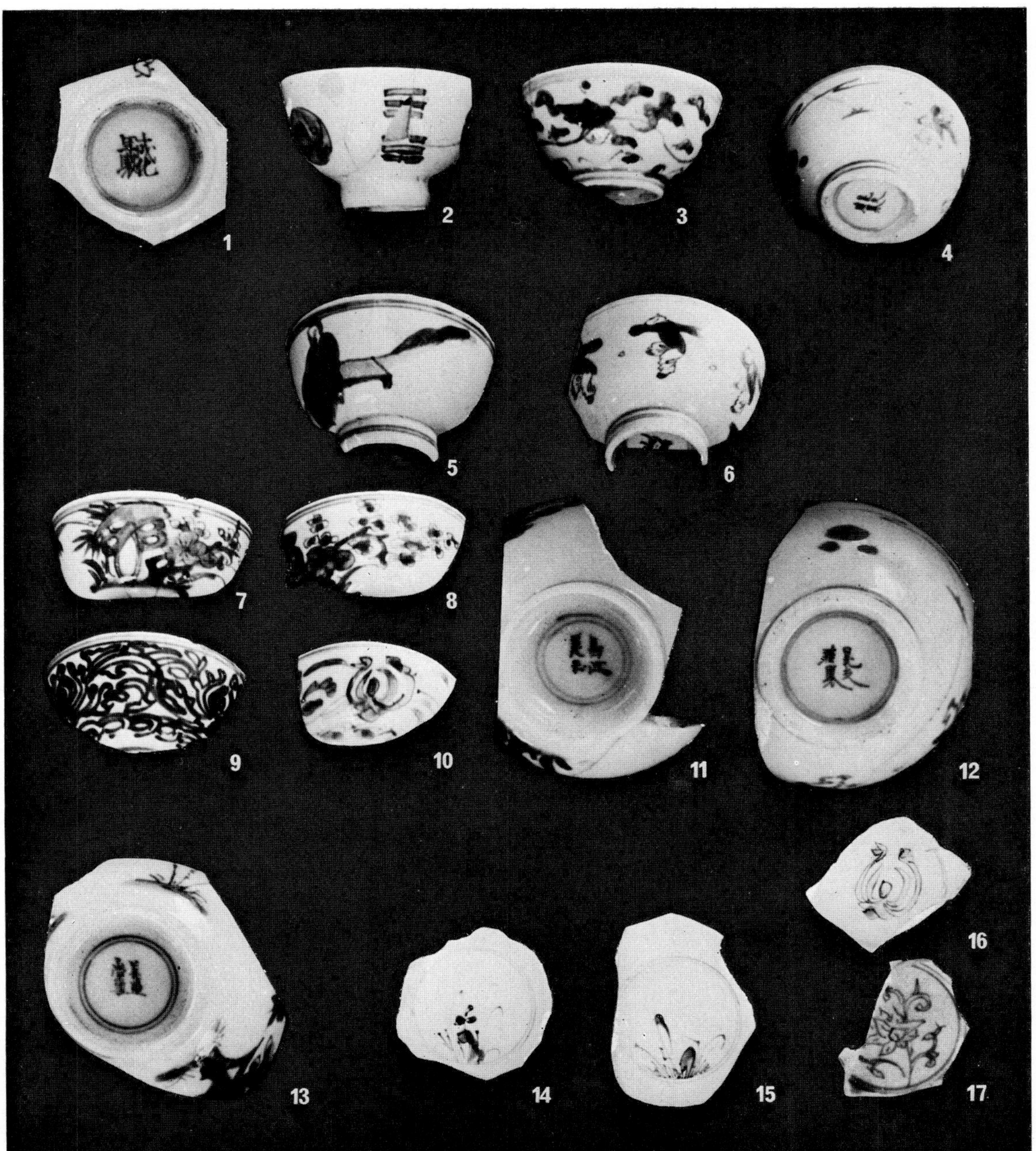

29. CHINESE PORCELAIN—K'ANG HSI

Blue-and-white. 1. Base of cup with Ch'êng-Hua mark (Cl. 10*b*), diam. 3 cm, from pit in S. Filipe, late seventeenth century. 2. Bowl with yin yang and pa-kua motifs, diam. 8 cm, marks k'un shan mei yu ya chih (Cl. 11*a*), from same. 3. Similar bowl with sprays and tendrils (Cl. 11*b*), from same. 4. Similar bowl with dancing boys, mark K'un yu ya chih (Cl. 11*c*), from same. 5. Similar bowl with immortal and landscape (Cl. 11*d*), from same. 6. Same as No. 4. 7, 8. Similar bowl with design of trees, 'the three friends' (Cl. 11*f*), from same. 9. Similar bowl with schematized lotus design (Cl. 11*g*), from same. 10. Similar bowl with lotus blossoms (Cl. 11*h*), from same. 11. Mark k'un shan mei yü on base of bowl (Cl. 11*f*), from same. 12. Mark k'un yu ya chih on base of bowl (Cl. 11*c*), from same. 13. Mark Jui-yün t'ang chih on base of bowl (Cl. 11*c*), diam. 12 cm, from same. 14, 15. Design in bottom of bowl (Cl. 11*f*), from same. 16. Design in bottom of bowl (Cl. 11*g*), from same. 17. Floral design in outline in bottom of small bowl, mark Ch'êng-Hua in square (Cl. 12), from steps to west wall, late seventeenth century.

See pages 98–101, 105, 116

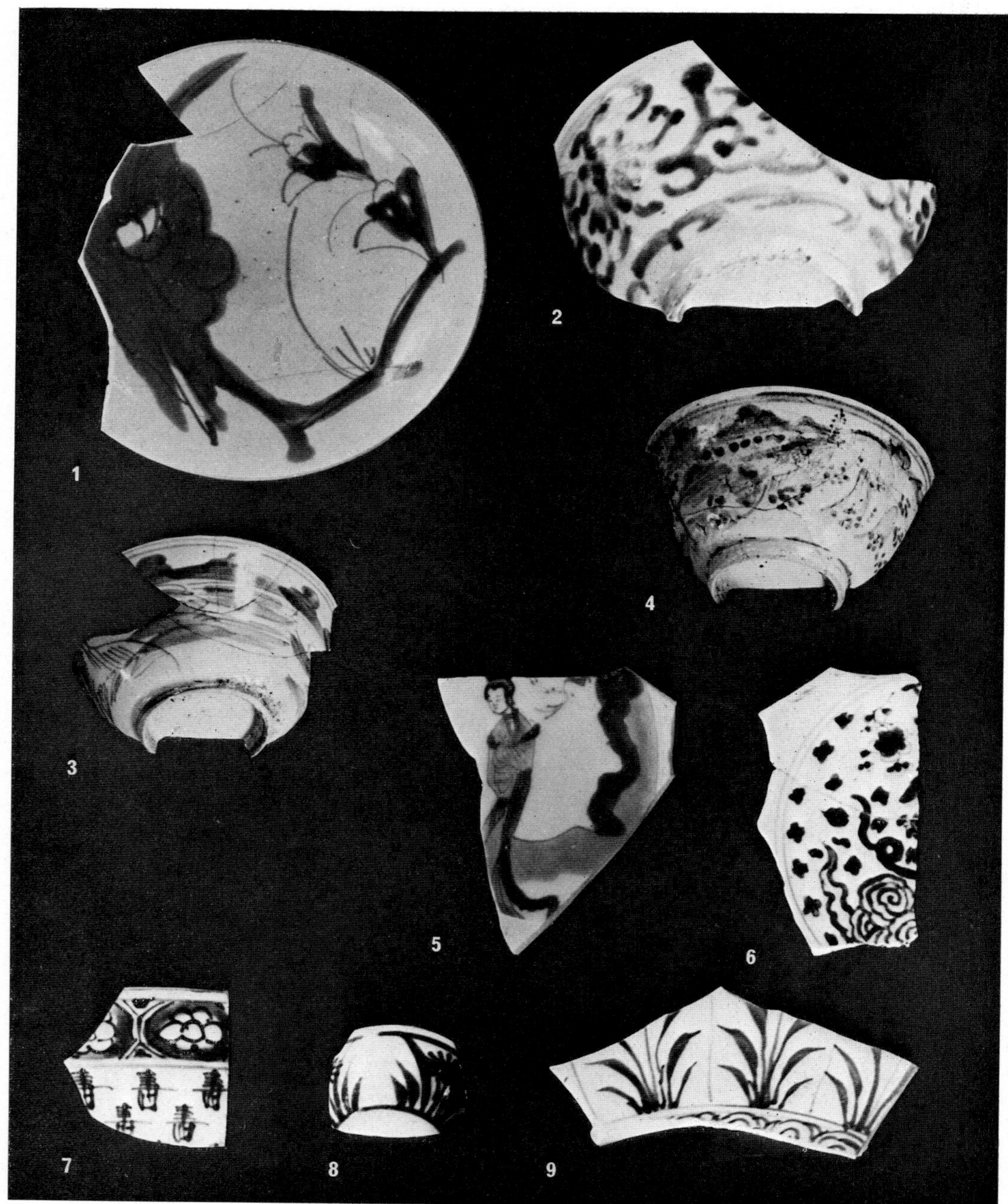

30. CHINESE PORCELAIN—K'ANG HSI

Blue-and-white. 1. Shallow plate with artemesia leaf and branch with buds (Cl. 13), diam. 19 cm, from Captain's House, late seventeenth century. 2. Bowl with roughly drawn flower, perhaps an aster (Cl. 14), diam. 14 cm, from pit in S. Filipe, late seventeenth century. 3, 4. Similar bowls with landscape designs in similar rough style (Cl. 15), diam. 16 cm and 14 cm, from same. 5. Plate with pavilion scene in deep blue, mark K'ang Hsi (Cl. 17*a*), from Captain's House, late seventeenth century. 6. Bowl with design of symbols on a dead-white ground (Cl. 19*a*), from main court, eighteenth century. 7. Large bowl with medallions on ground of characters, border of rosettes (Cl. 16*b*), from court of S. Mateus, late seventeenth century. 8, 9. Stem cup and small plate with water-weed design in solid blue (Cl. 18), from court in S. Mateus, late seventeenth century.

(Scale 5–8 about ½ natural)

See pages 98–101, 105

31. CHINESE PORCELAIN—K'ANG HSI

Coffee outside, blue-and-white inside. 1. Bowl with tendril and blossoms (Cl. 20*a*), diam. 16 cm, from pit in S. Filipe, late seventeenth century. 2. Bowl with phoenix with long tail (Cl. 20*b*), from same. 3. Small cup with landscape in bottom (Cl. 20*g*), diam. 8 cm, from same. 4. Saucer with brazier and incense burner (Cl. 20*j*), diam. 10 cm, from same.

Café-au-lait *outside, blue-and-white inside.* 5. Bowl with floral spray, mark Ch'êng-Hua (Cl. 21*a*), from Captain's House, late seventeenth century. 6. Plate with floral sprays, mark Ch'êng-Hua (Cl. 21*a*), diam. 22 cm, from same. 7. Plate with schematized lotus design, mark Chia Ching (Cl. 21*b*), from pit in S. Filipe, late seventeenth century. 8. Bowls and plates with various borders (Cl. 21*c*), from same.

Powder blue outside, blue-and-white inside. 9. Plate with sprays in white on blue ground outside, similar floral design to Cl. 21 inside (Cl. 24), from same.

(Scale 2 and 5 about $\frac{2}{3}$, and 7 and 9 $\frac{1}{2}$ natural)

See pages 98–101, 105–6

32. CHINESE PORCELAIN—K'ANG HSI

Blanc de chine. 1, 2. Cups with carved tendril ornament (Cl. 30*a*), diam. 7 cm and 6·5 cm, from pit in S. Filipe, late seventeenth century. 3. Fragments of figurines of dog of Fao and birds (Cl. 30*c*), from Captain's House, late seventeenth century. 4. Lid of box, 9 cm long, with carved phoenix and tendril ornament (Cl. 30*d*), from same. 5. Bowl with incised floral design in panels (Cl. 30*f*), from same.

Celadon. 6. Plate with incised ornament of cloud scrolls under a glassy glaze (Cl. 31*a*), diam. 30 cm, from pit in S. Filipe, late seventeenth century.

(Scale 3 and 5 about ⅓ natural)

See pages 98–101, 106–7

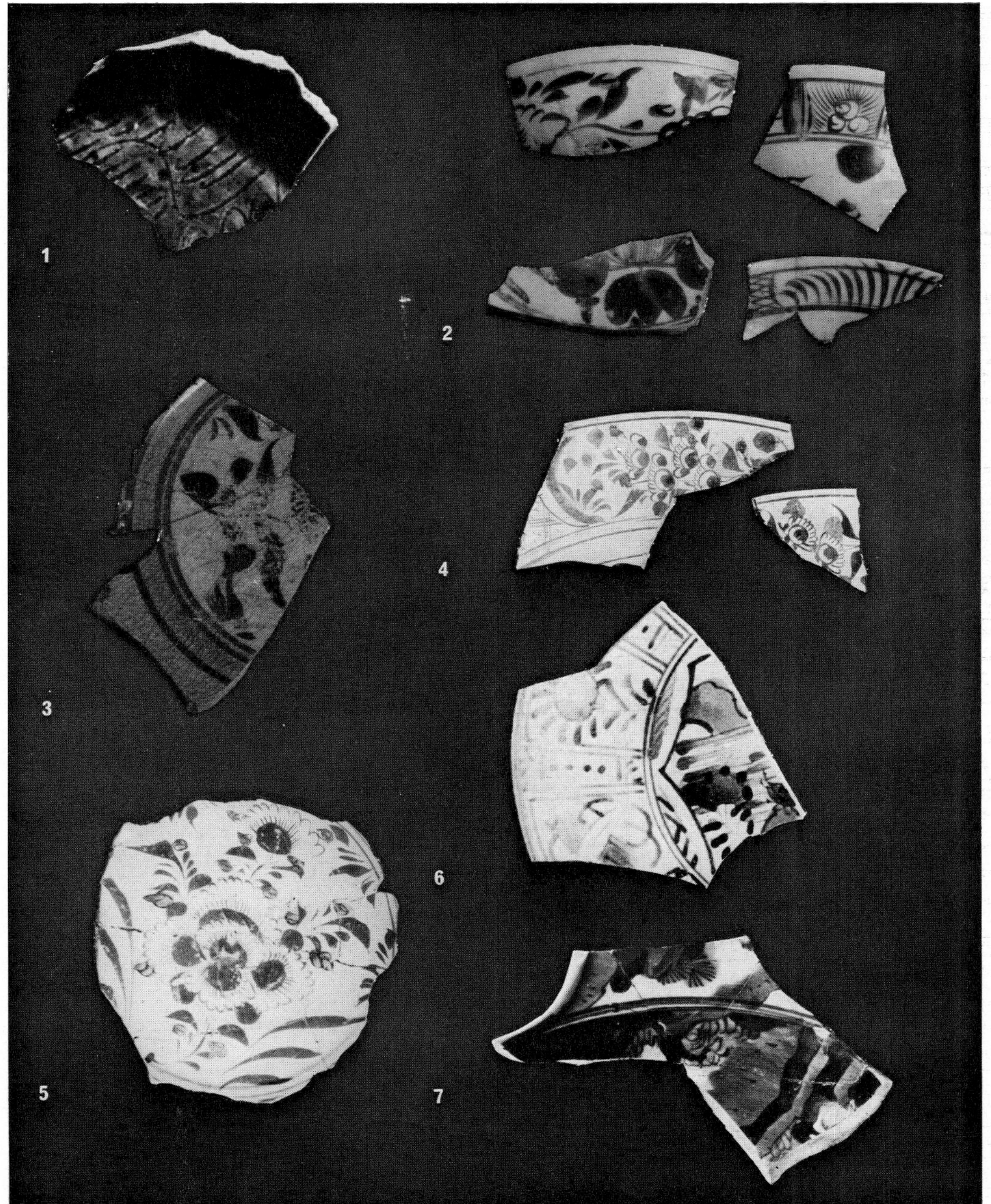

33. CHINESE PORCELAIN—K'ANG HSI

Dark blue. 1. Plate with incised ornament on coarse buff body (Cl. 32), from pit in S. Filipe, late seventeenth century.

Swatow wares. 2. Bowls and plates with floral decoration in solid red and green on a white or grey-white ground (Cl. 33), from same. 3. Similar decoration on a transparent crackled celadon body (Cl. 33), from same.

Matt surface. 4. Plate with similar decoration on a matt buff ground on a buff body (Cl. 34*a*), from same. 5. Similar with a large flower in bottom, on the same matt ground and body (Cl. 34*b*), diam. 18 cm, from Captain's House, late seventeenth century.

Japanese blue-and-white. 6. Plate with flat rim decorated with panels in Wan Li style (Cl. 35), from same. 7. Basin with prominent volutes around rim, landscape design in rich blue (Cl. 36), from court in S. Mateus, late seventeenth century.

(Scale about $\frac{1}{4}$ natural)

See pages 98–101, 107

34. CHINESE PORCELAIN—EIGHTEENTH AND NINETEENTH CENTURY

Polychrome (iron-red, rose-pink, green, yellow, and gold leaf). 1. Plate with 'three friends' design in iron-red, green, and gold leaf (Cl. 1*a*), from S. Alberto, eighteenth century. 2. Bowl with floral decoration in rose-pink and green (Cl. 3), diam. 9 cm, from Captain's House, eighteenth century. 3. Plate with landscape design in underglaze blue with border in green, red, and gold leaf (Cl. 1*b*), from main court, eighteenth century. 4. Plate with floral design in red, green, and underglaze blue (Cl. 2), diam. 12 cm, from Passage of the Arches, eighteenth century. 5. Cups and plates with floral decoration in rose-pink, green, and red, often in panels or trellis (Cl. 4*a*), from main court, eighteenth century.

(Scale 1, 3, and 5 about $\frac{1}{2}$ natural)

See pages 100–1, 107–8

35. CHINESE PORCELAIN—EIGHTEENTH AND NINETEENTH CENTURY

Polychrome. 1. Plates and bowls with floral decoration, often with broad borders in red, green, aubergine, and blue (Cl. 4*b*), from main court, eighteenth century. Scale about $\frac{1}{2}$ natural. 2. Bowl with green trellised medallions outlined in red, red floral sprays (Cl. 7*a*), diam. 15 cm, from same. 3. Bowl with broad red border of water-weeds and close trellis in red, often with red chrysanthemum on base (Cl. 7*b*), diam. 11·5 cm, from same. 4. Plate with floral design in green, yellow, and pink with incised outlines on a grey-white ground (Cl. 8), from Captain's House, eighteenth century. Scale about $\frac{1}{2}$ natural. 5. Bowl with yellow ground and sprays in rose-pink, green, and overglaze blue in quatrefoil panels, square mark on base (Cl. 10), diam. 14 cm, from Passage of the Arches, nineteenth century.

Blue-and-white. 6. Bowl with rosette band (Cl. 12*a*), diam. 10 cm, from main court, eighteenth century. 7. Bowl with trellis and spray bordeı (Cl. 12*b*), from north court of Captain's House, eighteenth century. Diam. 10 cm. 8. Bowl with floral design (Cl. 13*a*), diam. 16 cm, from south barrack block, nineteenth century. 9. Plate with design of horses drawn without outlines (Cl. 13*a*), diam. 30 cm, from Passage of the Arches, nineteenth century.

See pages 100–1, 108–9

36. CHINESE PORCELAIN—EIGHTEENTH AND NINETEENTH CENTURY

Blue-and-white. 1. Bowl with floral design in style similar to Pl. 35. 8 (Cl. 13*b*), diam. 14 cm, from north barrack block, nineteenth century. 2. Bowlwith floral design (Cl. 13*a*), diam. 12 cm, from Passage of the Arches, nineteenth century. 3. Bowl with motif similar to K'ang Hsi (Cl. 14), Pl. 30. 2, double circle on base (Cl. 13*a*), diam. 12 cm, from main court, eighteenth century. 4. Plate with landscape design and elaborate border on rim (Cl. 14), diam. 24 cm, from main court, nineteenth century. 5. Bowl with trellis and spray on outside, square mark on base (Cl. 15), diam. 12 cm, from south barrack block, nineteenth century. 6. Similar bowl (Cl. 15), from south barrack block. 7. Bowl with chrysanthemum and tendril design (Cl. 16*a*), diam. 13 cm, double circle on base, from south barrack block, nineteenth century. 8. Similar design but different treatment (Cl. 16*a*), diam. 18 cm, from Captain's House eighteenth century.

See pages 100–1, 109

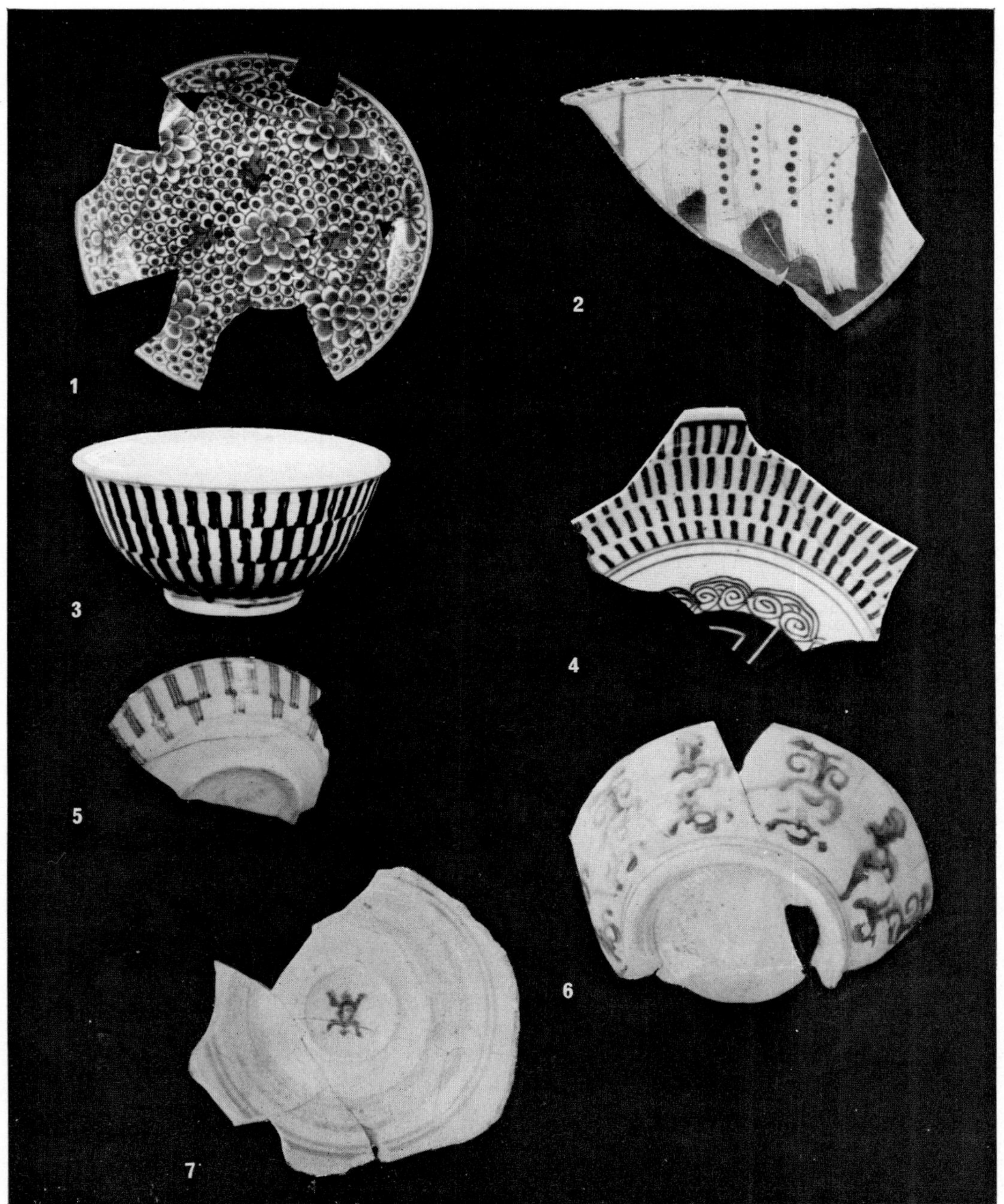

37. CHINESE PORCELAIN—EIGHTEENTH AND NINETEENTH CENTURY

Blue-and-white. 1. Plate with over-all design of blossoms and buds (Cl. 17), diam. 22 cm, from south barrack block, nineteenth century. 2. Basin with landscape design (Cl. 18*c*), from Passage of the Arches, nineteenth century. Scale about ¼ natural. 3. Bowl with character or comb over-all design (Cl. 19*a*), diam. 11 cm, from S. Filipe, eighteenth century. 4. Plate with similar design (Cl. 19*b*), diam. 19 cm, from S. Filipe, nineteenth century. 5. Small bowl with degenerate design of same motif (Cl. 19*c*), diam. 12 cm, from Passage of the Arches, nineteenth century. 6, 7. Bowl with shou character in panels on outside, bare ring with shou character in bottom (Cl. 21), diam. 13 cm, from same.

See pages 100–1, 109

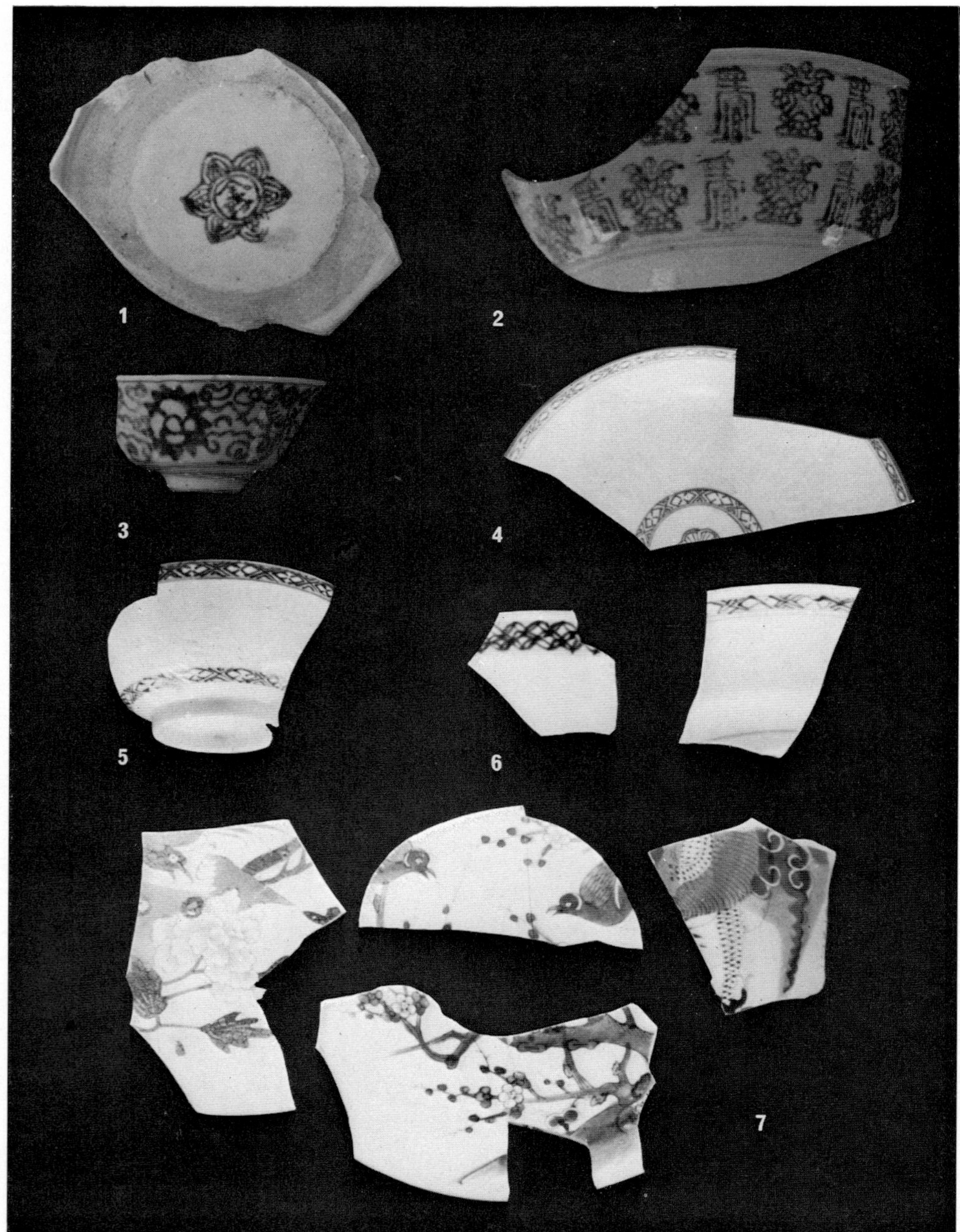

38. CHINESE PORCELAIN—EIGHTEENTH AND NINETEENTH CENTURY

Blue-and-white. 1, 2. Large bowl with two rows of differing versions of shou character in sepia on a grey-buff ground, bare ring with ch'uan in petal-shaped mark in bottom (Cl. 22), diam. 24 cm, from the Passage of the Arches, nineteenth century. 3. Bowl with tendril design in sepia on grey ground (Cl. 24*b*), diam. 13 cm, from Captain's House, nineteenth century. 4. Plate with incised floral ornament and blue border with diamond pattern (Cl. 27*b*), diam. 20 cm from main court, nineteenth century. 5. Bowl with similar pattern (Cl. 27*a*), diam. 14 cm, from north barrack block, nineteenth century. 6. Plates with similar blue borders but without incised ornament (Cl. 27*c*), from S. Mateus and main court, nineteenth century. Scale about $\frac{1}{3}$ natural.

Blue-and-white and aubergine. 7. Plate with tall base and design of birds in blue and aubergine (Cl. 28), from main court, nineteenth century. Scale about $\frac{1}{3}$ natural.

See pages 100–1, 109–10

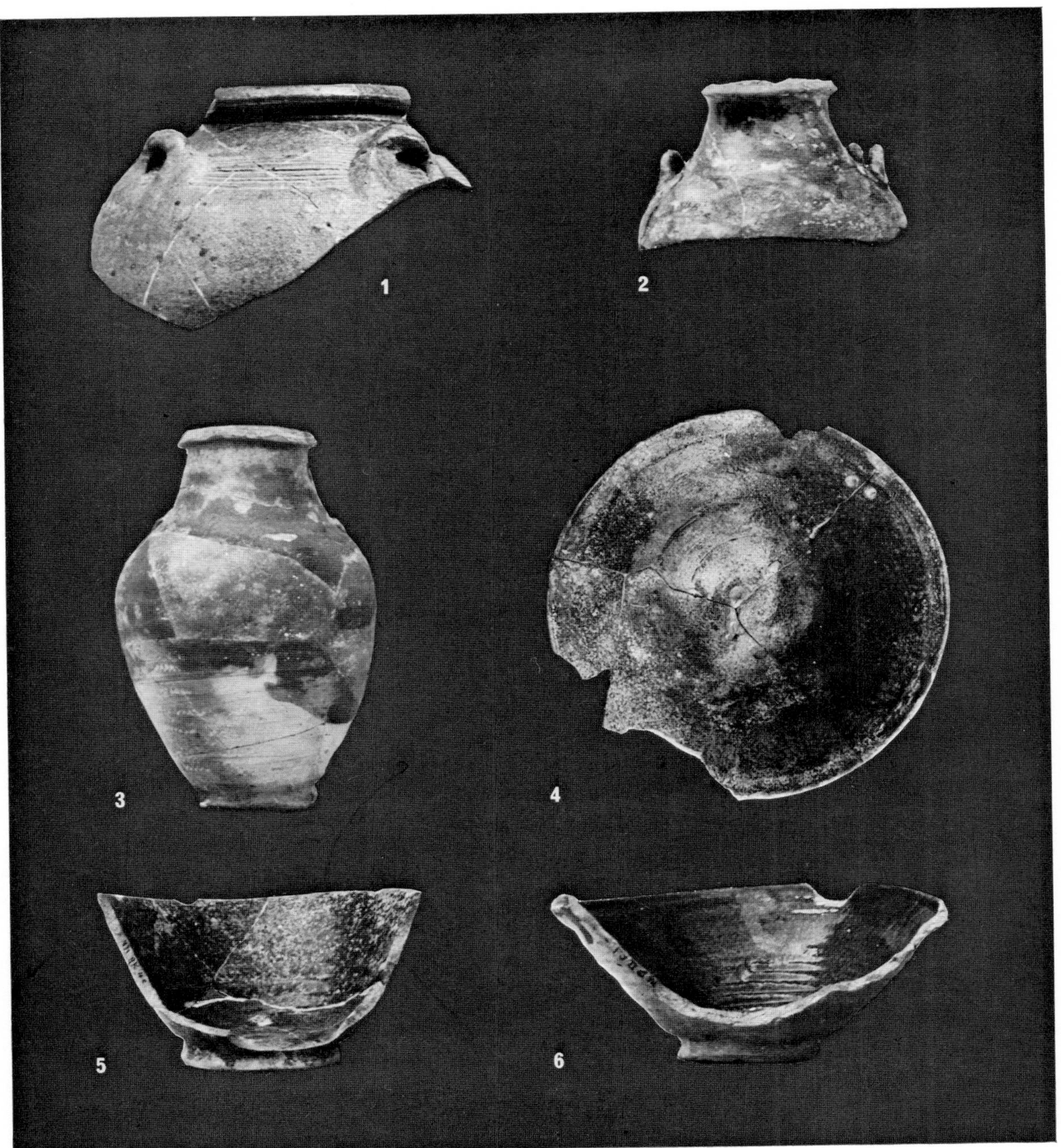

39. MISCELLANEOUS GLAZED WARES

1. Jar with brown glaze on grey body, burning purple, probably Kalong ware (Fig. 70. 16), diam. of mouth 15 cm, from Captain's House, late seventeenth century. 2. Small jar, smooth blotchy olive-brown glaze on grey body, burning pink, two pairs of horizontal handles, diam. of mouth 7 cm (Fig. 71. 2) from court in S. Mateus, late seventeenth century. 3. Similar jar, rough brown-grey glaze on buff body, burning pink, height 30 cm, from north barrack block, eighteenth century. 4. Plate with slightly concave bare disk base, blotchy olive-green glaze on grey body, burning pink, diam. 29·5 cm, from court in S. Mateus, late seventeenth century. 5. Bowl with bare ring base, smooth brown glaze on pink body, diam. 24 cm, from north court of Captain's House, eighteenth century. 6. Bowl with ring base, smooth brown glaze on pink body, diam. 23 cm, from pit in S. Alberto, eighteenth century.

See pages 117–19

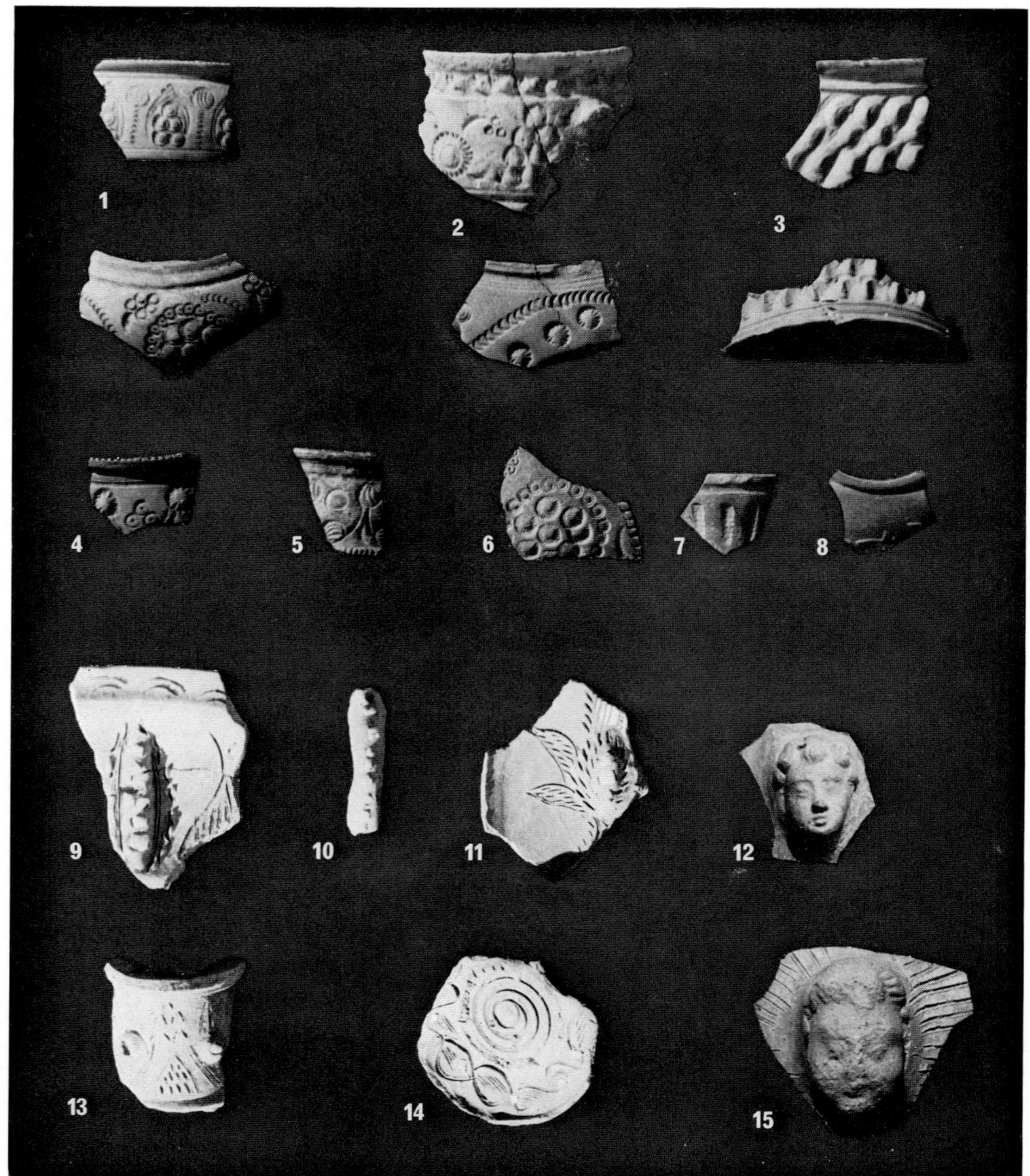

40. PORTUGUESE WARES

1–8. Bowls and small pots with moulded and stamped ornament in red polished ware, early seventeenth century: (1) from filling of S. Matias; (2–7) from filling of S. Filipe; (8) from filling of S. Alberto. 9–11, 13, 14. Thin pink ware studded with quartz chips, early seventeenth century: (9) small plate from filling of S. Filipe (Fig. 75. 6); (10) handle of jug from same; (11) small plate from same; (13) neck of bottle from filling of S. Alberto; (14) inside of lid from filling of S. Matias. (12, 15) Moulded angel heads in red polished ware from pit in S. Filipe, late seventeenth century.

(Scale $\frac{1}{2}$ natural)

See page 120

41. PORTUGUESE WARES

1–6. Plates with floral designs in blue outlined in aubergine (Fig. 75. 11), from pit in S. Filipe, late seventeenth century. 7, 8. Plates with vertical side with similar decoration on outside and a form of tassel mark on the bottom (Fig. 75. 10), diam. 15 cm, from Captain's House, late seventeenth century. 9. Small bottle in blue and white with mark HPDG (Fig. 75. 12), height 10 cm, from pit in S. Filipe, late seventeenth century. 10. Neck of demijohn with splashed brown glaze mostly inside, from filling of S. Alberto, early seventeenth century. 11. Neck of jar, green glaze outside, olive inside, from same. (Fig. 74. 3).

(Scale, 1–6 and 10 and 11, $\frac{1}{3}$ natural)

See pages 119–21

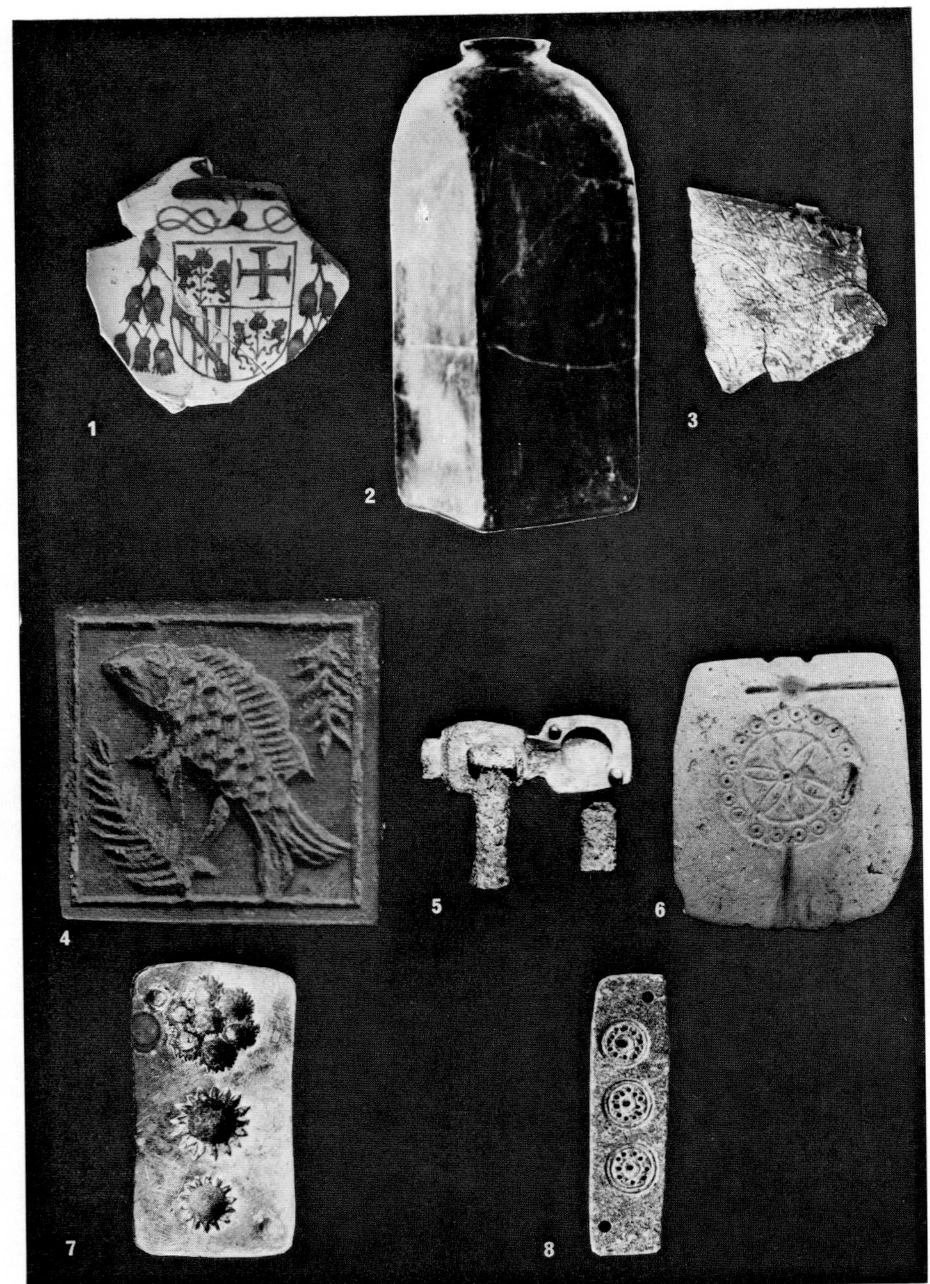

42. MISCELLANEOUS OBJECTS

1. Base of plate in blue outlined in aubergine (as Pl. 41. 1–6) with arms of Cardoso quartering Teixeira and perhaps de Matos, from bottom of the Passage of the Arches, late seventeenth century. 2. Glass case bottle, 27·9 cm by 10·8 cm, from late seventeenth-century level in main court. 3. Engraved copper plate, 8·9 cm at widest, from nineteenth-century level in S. Alberto. 4. Copper mould with fish and palms, 2·9 cm square, from Captain's House, late seventeenth century. 5. Copper mould for making 13-mm shot, from Captain's House, late seventeenth century. 6. Mould for ornament, diam. 5·7 cm, made from a sherd of green-glazed pink-bodied earthenware (Islamic Cl. 5), from filling of court in S. Mateus, late seventeenth century. 7. Copper mould for ornaments, length 3·8 cm, from S. Mateus, nineteenth-century level. 8. Grey stone mould for ornament, length 7·6 cm, from Passage of the Arches, nineteenth century.

See pages 120, 126, 160

43. RELIGIOUS MEDALLIONS

1, 2. Oval bronze medallion once gilt, height 3·18 cm, width 2·54 cm. On one side the Virgin in glory with clasped hands, around VIRGO SINE PECATO OP CONC (the representation of the Virgin in the cult of the Immaculate Conception). On the other side a chalice with rays and kneeling angels, around SLIL SA in exergue ROMA. From eighteenth-century level in S. Alberto. 3, 4. Octagonal gilt-bronze medallion with ring, height 2·54 cm, width 1·91 cm. On one side bust of Christ with halo in high relief, around SALVATOR MUNDI. On other side veiled bust of Virgin with halo in high relief, around MATER SALVATOR. From nineteenth-century level in S. Alberto. 5, 6. Octagonal bronze medallion with ring, perhaps once gilt, height 1·91 cm, width 1·27 cm. On one side Virgin in glory, the representation of the cult of the Immaculate Conception. On the other side a cloaked male bust holding chalice to left, above R. PASCUAL. From disturbed level in S. Alberto. 7, 8. Oval bronze medallion, height 1·27 cm, width 1·9 cm, with projections in centre of all four arcs. On one side the Virgin and Joseph adoring Christ in cradle; on the other, the flight into Egypt. From early seventeenth-century level in S. Filipe. 9. Small bronze figure, height 3·18 cm, of man in robes holding infant Christ in one arm and an orb with a cross in other hand. At back prong with horizontal hole for attachment. From surface level in S. Alberto.

See page 159

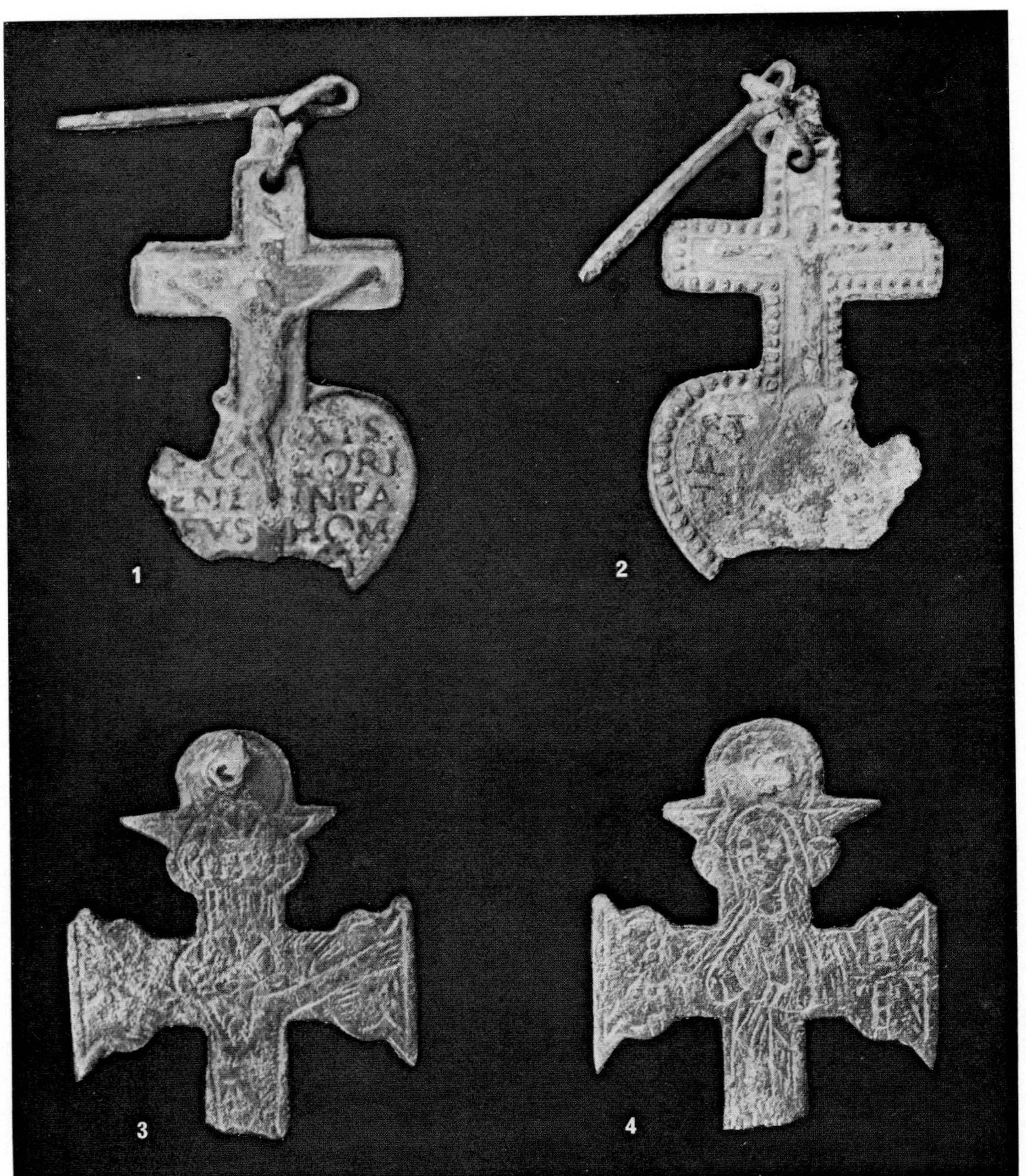

44. RELIGIOUS MEDALLIONS

1, 2. Thin bronze cross rising from a heart, with ring and pin (height 4 cm, width 2·5 cm). On one side of the cross a crucifixion and on the heart letters:

XIS
P CC CORT
ENI NPA
EVS HOM

On the other side of the cross another crucifixion; on the heart a veiled figure with a small cross at the side. From disturbed level outside S. Alberto. 3, 4. Bronze cross with cyma moulding at ends, hole for pin on top (width 2·5 cm). On one side engraved figure of Christ on the Cross with letters T NR P; on tne other the Virgin. From Captain's House, late seventeenth-century level.

See page 159

Index